A POLITICAL AND ECONOMIC DICTIONARY OF WESTERN EUROPE

A POLITICAL AND ECONOMIC DICTIONARY OF WESTERN EUROPE

Claire Annesley

FIRST EDITION

Routledge
Taylor & Francis Group

LONDON AND NEW YORK

First Edition 2005
Routledge
Haines House, 21 John Street, London WC1N 2BP, United Kingdom
(A member of the Taylor & Francis Group)

ISBN 1 85743 214 2

Development Editor: Cathy Hartley
Copy Editor and Proof-reader: Simon Chapman

Typeset in Times New Roman 10/12

Typeset by AJS Solutions, Huddersfield – Dundee
Printed and bound by MPG Books, Ltd, Bodmin, Cornwall

In memory of
Colin Annesley
1942–2004

FOREWORD

This **POLITICAL AND ECONOMIC DICTIONARY OF WESTERN EUROPE** aims to give a comprehensive overview of the political and economic situation in contemporary Western Europe. In an ever-changing world, there is no ideal time to record the political and economic state of the region. Yet, in our era of transient internet knowledge, it seems essential that at some point such facts are consigned to print. This Dictionary may be regarded as a first point of reference for research on the region.

The longest entries in the Dictionary are those for the individual states of Western Europe—from Iceland to Greece and from Portugal to Finland. Each entry provides a general account of political and economic conditions since the Second World War or democratic revolutions through a historical survey and up-to-date data. These overviews are supplemented by individual entries for main political parties, institutions and economic organizations, such as employers' organizations and trade unions. They are—with the exception of national legislatures and central banks—listed under their English names followed by that name in the national language. Entries for current elected heads of state, heads of government and ministers of finance provide a snapshot of political actors at the time of writing. Where appropriate, indications are given of when terms of office expire so that the reader will be able to gauge when information might become outdated. The Dictionary also includes entries for important international institutions and organizations; on key terms and concepts relevant to the region; and for some of those countries outside of the region that exercise a key influence on it, whether, for example, through trade, political alliance or as a source of controversy within it. There is extensive cross-referencing between entries, indicated by the use of **bold type**. However, in order to avoid a surfeit of bold type, references to the main states of Western Europe themselves, and to the USA, appear for the most part in light face.

Manchester, February 2005

THE AUTHOR

Claire Annesley has been Lecturer in European Politics at the University of Manchester since 2000. Prior to that, she was researcher in the Political Economy Research Centre (PERC) at the University of Sheffield. Her main areas of research are in the fields of comparative politics, political economy and welfare states. Recent publications include *Postindustrial Germany: Services, Technological Transformation and Knowledge in Unified Germany* (Manchester University Press, 2004); articles in *Comparative European Politics*, *British Journal of Politics and International Relations* and *German Politics*, and book chapters on United Kingdom welfare policy under New Labour.

Entries by Annika Bergman of the University of Edinburgh, Sascha Feuchert of Justus-Liebig-Universität Giessen, Jocelyn Mawdsley of the University of Manchester, Nick Stevenson of the University of Nottingham and Peter Wells of Sheffield Hallam University are also included in the Dictionary. Where an entry has been written by a contributor other than Claire Annesley, the contributor's name appears at the end of the relevant entry.

ACKNOWLEDGEMENTS

The author wishes to acknowledge the following as invaluable sources of information for the present volume: *West European Politics*, *Government and Opposition*, *The Economist* and The World Bank's *World Development Indicators 2003*, as well as official websites and offices of government departments and the BBC.

The following people must be thanked for checking draft entries: Gudmundur Árnason, Annika Bergman, Yoram Gorlizki, Georg Grote, Doug Jaenicke, Jill Lovecy, Jocelyn Mawdsley, Dimitris Papadimitriou, Elisa Roller and Rorden Wilkinson. Special thanks are due to Geoff Roberts, whose careful comments on the Dictionary were greatly appreciated, and to Sascha Feuchert for continual encouragement and excellent advice. Responsibility for the final product lies, as ever, with the author.

ABBREVIATIONS

Av.	Avda (Portuguese, avenue)	HM	Her/His Majesty
		Km	Kilometre
Ave	Avenue	No.	Number/numéro
Bldg	Building	NY	New York
Blvd	Boulevard	PO(B)	Post Office (Box)
CEO	Chief Executive Officer	PPP	Purchasing-power parity
Chair.	Chairman/woman	Pres.	President
DC	District of Columbia	R.	Rua (Portuguese, road)
Dir	Director	Rd	Road
Dr	Doctor	s/n	sin número (Spanish, without number)
Edif.	Edificio (Spanish, Portuguese, building)	Sec.	Secretary
GDP	Gross Domestic Product	Sq	Square
Gen.	General	St	Saint
GNP	Gross National Product	St/Str	Street
Gov.	Governor	Tel	Telephone

INTERNATIONAL TELEPHONE CODES

The code and relevant telephone number must be preceded by the International Dialling Code of the country from which you are calling.

Other international telephone codes relevant to this book:

A

Accession

Accession, in the context of European politics, means joining the **European Union (EU)**. Since 1993 the accession process has had four elements. Negotiations, co-ordinated by the **European Commission**, are conducted between the applicant states and the EU. Then accession partnerships are drawn up. These are designed to help applicant states meet the **Copenhagen criteria**. The applicant states meet with the EU at the annual European Conference which, since 1998, has provided a forum for dialogue between member and applicant states. When the EU is satisfied that applicant states have fulfilled the Copenhagen criteria, an accession treaty is agreed. Approval in the form of an absolute majority is required from the **European Parliament**. This has to be ratified by the parliaments of all of the existing member states and—usually through a referendum—by the applicant country.

Most recently (on 31 March 1998) EU accession negotiations have been launched with Cyprus, the Czech Republic, Estonia, Hungary, Poland and Slovenia; and (on 15 February 2000) with Bulgaria, Latvia, Lithuania, Malta, Romania and Slovakia. Accession negotiations were successfully concluded with all but two (Bulgaria and Romania) of these applicant states in December 2002 in Copenhagen, Denmark, and accession treaties were signed in April 2003 in Athens, Greece.

Referendums to ratify the accession treaty were held in all of the accession states (except Cyprus) in 2003, and all were in favour of EU membership. The results (date; yes vote; turn-out) were: Malta (8 March; 53.6%; 91%); Slovenia (23 March; 89.61%; 66%); Hungary (12 April; 83.8%; 46%); Slovakia (16–17 May; 92.5%; 52.2%); Lithuania (10–11 May; 91%; 64%); Poland (8 June; 77%; 59%); Czech Republic (15–16 June; 77.3%; 55.2%); Estonia (14 September; 66.9%; 63%); Latvia (20 September; 67%; 72.53%). Ten states became members of the EU on 1 May 2004. Bulgaria and Romania hope to complete accession negotiations by 2007. The European Commission has recommended opening accession negotiations with Croatia in April 2004 and with **Turkey** in October 2005.

Acquis communautaire

The *acquis communautaire* is the entire body of **European Union (EU)** law. It is a composite of founding treaties, treaty amendments, regulations and directives made

1

by the European institutions, and judgments pronounced by the **European Court of Justice**. States applying to join the EU are required to fully adopt and enforce the *acquis communautaire* through their national law in order to meet the **Copenhagen criteria**.

Action Committee for Democracy and Pension Rights

The Action Committee for Democracy and Pension Rights, or Aktiounskomitee fir Demokratie a Rentegerechtegkeet, is a populist party in Luxembourg. Established in 1987, it campaigns predominantly for a reform of the pension system. It advocates the harmonization of the pensions contributions and entitlements for employees in the private sector with those for privileged public-sector workers. The party claims to have influenced the agenda of pension reforms during the 1990s. More generally the party campaigns for sustainable use of Luxembourg's social and environmental resources and seeks to prevent non-national firms and individuals benefiting from national resources. It raises concerns about Luxembourg's loss of national sovereignty through the process of European integration. In the most recent general election, held on 13 June 2004, the party won 9.9% of the vote and seven seats in the 60-seat **Chambre des Députés**.

> *Chair. of the Parliamentary Group:* Gast Gibéryen
> *Address:* 9 rue de la Loge, 1945 Luxembourg
> *Tel:* (0)46-37-42
> *Fax:* (0)46-37-45
> *E-mail:* adr@chd.lu
> *Internet:* www.adr.lu

Agriculture

Agriculture has been one of the most important economic sectors in the context of Western European and **European Union (EU)** politics. In the early years of the post-Second World War and **Cold War** eras, Western Europe's priority was to achieve self-sufficiency in food and policy was directed at raising productivity. In more recent years concerns have shifted in the direction of the environment, sustainability, food quality and safety.

The **Treaty of Rome** (1957) established the Common Agricultural Policy (CAP). The CAP aimed to increase agricultural production, stabilize markets, assure supplies at reasonable prices, and ensure a fair standard of living for those working in agriculture in the **European Economic Community (EEC)**. To meet these goals, the CAP promoted the principles of market unity, community preference and financial solidarity. These meant that there was a single market in agriculture, tariff barriers were established to protect the internal market, and a fund—the European Agricultural Guidance and Guarantee Fund—was established to redistribute agricultural expenditure in the EEC. A key feature of the CAP was that the EEC paid guaranteed prices to producers for agricultural products (cereals, wheat, barley, sugar and bovine meat). These prices were set centrally by agriculture ministers in the **Council of the European Union** and the EEC was committed to buying up surpluses if prices fell. The CAP accounts for around 50% of the total budget of the **European Community**.

By the 1970s the guaranteed price system had stimulated agricultural productivity to such an extent that surpluses were being produced. However, there existed strong resistance from member states to reform of the system of fixed prices. Reform of the CAP proved difficult as all of the member states had a vested interest in retaining the policy, decisions in the Council have to be made unanimously, and many member states were influenced by strong farmers' lobbies. Reform was eventually successful in the early 1990s following pressure from the international community in the General Agreement on Tariffs and Trade Uruguay Round in 1986 to liberalize agricultural trade, and from the environmental lobby to stop over-farming. By 1992 a CAP reform had been agreed which reduced guaranteed prices and compensated farmers' loss of incomes through an alternative method of individual direct payments to farmers. Further reform was required to prepare the EU for the accession of new member states from the predominantly rural **Central and Eastern European Countries (CEECs)**. Concerns were raised that transferring the existing level of support to CEECs would increase the CAP budget and place a burden on the net contributor states (e.g. Germany).

The **European Commission**'s Agenda 2000 programme sought to prepare the CAP for future EU enlargement. Agenda 2000 also sought to broaden agriculture to include social, cultural and environmental aims as well as the traditional concerns of productivity. The 2002 mid-term review of Agenda 2000 proposed a number of reforms to the CAP. The main elements of this reform were: to 'decouple' direct payments to farms from production; linking direct payments to goals such as environment, food safety and animal welfare standards; promoting rural development; and cutting intervention prices for some products. A compromise reform was passed on 26 June 2003 in response to strong opposition by France which is a net beneficiary of CAP. The compromise retained some cases of direct payments linked to production. The Commission claimed that the reform marked the 'beginning of a new era'. It offered more transparency and value for money to consumers and tax payers. It also claimed that the reform removed significant distortions in international trade which harmed developing countries. However, farmers' lobbies and international organizations representing developing countries strongly criticized the reform.

Ahern, Bertie

Bertie Ahern has been Taoiseach (Prime Minister) of the Republic of Ireland since June 1997 and was reappointed for his second term of office in June 2002. The government that he heads is a coalition between **Fianna Fáil (FF)**, which he has led since 1994, and the **Progressive Democrats (PD)**. Ahern's first FF-PD coalition lasted for a full five-year parliamentary term, making it the longest serving government in the history of the Republic. The success of FF-PD coalitions has been attributed to their management of the economy, including Ireland's entry into the final stages of **Economic and Monetary Union**, as well as the successful negotiations of the **Good Friday Agreement** on **Northern Ireland** with the United Kingdom in 1998.

Born on 12 September 1951 in Dublin, Ahern was educated at University College Dublin and worked as an accountant before entering politics. Ahern was a member of Dublin City Council in 1978–88 and Lord Mayor of the city in 1986–87. First elected to the **Dáil Éireann** in 1977 for Dublin-Finglas constituency, he has represented Dublin Central since 1981. In the Dáil Ahern was an assistant government whip in 1980–81 and opposition chief whip in 1982–84. He has held a number of ministerial posts, including those of Minister of Labour in 1987–91 and Minister of Finance in 1991–94. Bertie Ahern is separated from his wife, Miriam, and from his long-term partner, Celia Larkin.

Address: Department of the Taoiseach, Government Bldgs, Upper Merrion St,
Dublin 2, Ireland
Tel: (0)1 6194020/4021/4043
Fax: (0)1 6764048
E-mail: taoiseach@taoiseach.gov.ie
Internet: www.taoiseach.gov.ie

Air transport

Air transport is a large industry that has grown rapidly over the past few decades on account of the globalization of production and distribution, and of the increased significance of foreign tourism. Since 1960 European passenger traffic has risen by 9% annually; and cargo traffic by 11%. It has been a highly regulated sector from its origins: states were granted sovereignty over their air space, and flights were arranged as a series of bilateral agreements. European states each supported their own national flag carrier (e.g. Lufthansa, Air France, Aer Lingus).

Since the 1980s air transport in Europe has undergone a gradual process of deregulation and liberalization. The **Treaty of Rome** (1957) aimed for full freedom of movement for goods, services, people and capital between member states. Air transport was, however, excluded from this provision because of the special nature of the industry: it had public service obligations, and there are security concerns. From the late 1970s pressure to deregulate air transport grew. The **European Commission**, consumers and airlines, and the right-wing governments in the United Kingdom and the Netherlands all sought deregulation.

In the late 1980s two events accelerated the process of liberalization. In 1987 the **European Court of Justice** ruled in the Nouvelles Frontières case that Community competition policy applied to air transport. In the same year the **Single European**

Act, intended to support the completion of the **Single European Market**, came into force and the **Council of the European Union** was obliged to liberalize the sector. This was achieved in three packages of measures, implemented in December 1987, June 1990 and July 1992, which liberalized tariffs, capacity (the number of passengers and number of flights), and entry to market, and banned anti-competitive behaviour. They also introduced the freedom to provide multi-designation (more than two carriers can operate on one route) and cabotage (the right of an airline of a member state to operate a route in another member state).

Air transport was fully liberalized by 1 April 1997. The evidence is that the dominant position of national flag carriers in domestic markets has been eroded, a number of new carriers have been introduced to the industry (there was a total of 139 in 2000, compared with 77 in 1992), the number of air routes has increased and tariffs have been reduced, especially by low-cost airlines such as **Ryanair**. The European Commission introduced further guide-lines on state aid for national flag carriers in 1994: it is now only permitted if it meets the 'market economy investment principle'. That is, public aid is deemed legitimate if the Commission considers that a private investor would have invested in the same way. Many airlines were given state aid during the period of restructuring in the early 1990s, but the Commission now considers state aid to be no longer necessary. Following the **11 September** terrorist attacks in 2001, air transport suffered a severe fall in passenger numbers, which affected a number of European airlines. In October 2001 the Commission allowed Belgium to issue an emergency bridging loan worth €125m. to the debt-ridden national airline Sabena, but it objected to the state offering any additional funds. Sabena was formally declared bankrupt in November 2001.

The next stage in the liberalization of air transport would entail the reform of air traffic control. Air space is currently controlled by 73 different air traffic control centres. Consequently Europe cannot cope with the growth in air traffic, and the difficulty of co-ordinating such a multitude of control centres leads to one flight in four being delayed. The Commission launched proposals for a Single Sky policy in 2001, with the aim of creating a single air space and of achieving better co-ordination between air traffic control centres.

Akademikernes Centralorganisation – *see* Danish Confederation of Professional Associations

AKAVA – *see* Confederation of Unions for Academic Professionals, Finland

Aktiounskomitee fir Demokratie a Rentegerechtegkeet – *see* Action Committee for Democracy and Pension Rights, Luxembourg

Åland Islands

The Åland Islands is an archipelago of 6,500 islands located in the Baltic Sea between Sweden and Finland. Part of Sweden until 1809, the Åland Islands then became part of the Grand Duchy of Finland in the Russian Empire. The islands sought reunification with Sweden in 1917 when Finland gained independence from **Russia**, but Finland refused this. The issue was referred to the League of Nations which in 1921 proposed that Finland would be granted sovereignty but that the Åland Islands would be guaranteed cultural autonomy, be given a system of self-government and be a demilitarized, neutral region of Finland. The Åland Islands is today an autonomous region of Finland which retains Swedish as its official language.

Åland Islands self-government is guaranteed by the parliament, the Lagtinet, which is made up of 30 members, elected for a four-year term. The Lagtinet is entitled to pass laws in the areas of education, culture, health, environment, transport, industry, local government, policing, postal communications and broadcasting. The Finnish government governs in the areas of foreign affairs, law, customs and taxation.

The population of the Åland Islands is 26,200 (2004) and the largest island, Åland, which accounts for 70% of the area, hosts 90% of the total population. The capital is Mariehamn. The economy is based on shipping, trade and tourism. Unemployment is low at 1.8% (2004) but income levels on the Åland Islands are lower than on mainland Finland.

Algemeeen Christelijk Vakverbond – *see* Federation of Christian Unions, Belgium

Alleanza Nazionale – *see* National Alliance, Italy

Alliance 90/The Greens

Alliance 90/The Greens, or Bündnis 90/Die Grünen, is the green party in Germany. It is considered to be the most successful green party in Western Europe. The party is the outcome of a series of mergers between the West German Green Party (Die Grünen) and its post-1989 counterparts from the **German Democratic Republic (GDR)**. These were the East German Green Party, with which the West German Green Party merged one day after the first all-German elections in December 1990, and Alliance 90, which joined the all-German Green Party in 1993.

The West German Green Party began as a grass roots movement in the 1970s and established itself as a formal party in 1980. The party, originally divided between the 'Realos', who sought political office, and the 'Fundis', who thought that political power would undermine the party's grass roots democratic principles, campaigned for environmentally responsible politics, disarmament and the phasing out of nuclear energy. The Green Party's first electoral successes were in local and regional (*Land*)-level politics. It entered the **Bundestag** in 1983 when it first overcame the 5% hurdle, winning 5.6% of the vote and 27 seats. The party entered into its first *Land*-level coalition government in Hesse in 1985 with the **Social Democratic Party of Germany (SPD)**, and **Joschka Fischer** became the environment minister. This coalition was short-lived, but the party subsequently governed in a number of successful SPD-Green coalitions at *Land* level.

The East German Green Party was founded in November 1989, shortly after the fall of the **Berlin Wall**. Its origins date back to 1986 when a small environmental movement in the GDR developed. Bündnis 90 was originally an alliance of three peace and civil rights movements—Initiative für Frieden und Menschenrechte (founded in 1986), Demokratie Jetzt and Neues Forum (both established in September 1989)—which campaigned for democratic reform in the GDR and eventually joined together as a formal party in 1991. In the only democratic elections in the GDR, held in March 1990, the Green Party won just 2% of the vote and Alliance 90 won 2.9%. In the first all-German elections, held in December 1990, the 5% hurdle was applied separately to the East and the West. In the East the two parties formed an electoral alliance and won 6% of the vote and eight seats in the Bundestag. The West German Green Party failed to reach the 5% threshold. In the following Bundestag election in 1994 the merged Alliance 90/The Greens won 7.3% of the vote and 49 seats.

Alliance 90/The Greens entered into a coalition government at national level with the SPD following the Bundestag elections in September 1998. The party had three ministers, including Joschka Fischer as foreign minister. Despite some difficulties, this coalition formed a second government following the September 2002 elections when the SPD narrowly managed to retain its status as largest party. In fact the re-election of the SPD-Green coalition had much to do with the popularity of the Greens and their foreign minister Fischer in particular. The 2002 election campaign focused strongly on Fischer and the party made significant electoral gains: a record 8.6% of the vote and 55 seats, including its first directly elected constituency seat. Today the party is more successful in western than in eastern Germany.

The Red-Green coalition has committed itself to phase out nuclear energy, it has introduced an environmental tax, reformed citizenship laws and passed legislation to allow homosexual marriages. The two parties have been divided on the deployment of German *Bundeswehr* troops abroad. They agreed to send troops on peace-keeping missions in **Kosovo** in 1999 and in Macedonia in 2001, but Chancellor **Gerhard Schröder** had to attach a vote of confidence to a Bundestag decision on sending troops to Afghanistan in 2001 as Alliance 90/The Greens were strongly opposed. Both parties opposed the deployment of troops in the war in **Iraq** in 2003.

Party Leaders: Reinhard Bütikofer and Claudia Roth
Address: Platz vor dem Neuen Tor, 10115 Berlin or POB 040609, 10063 Berlin, Germany
Tel: (0)30 284420
Fax: (0)30 28442210
E-mail: info@gruene.de
Internet: www.gruene.de

Alliance Party

The Alliance Party, or Samfylkinginflokkurinn, is the main social democratic party in Iceland. It is the result of a merger in 1999 of the People's Alliance, the Social Democratic Party, the Women's List and the National Movement. The party promotes the principles of freedom and democracy, **women**'s liberation, equal rights and social responsibility. In the May 1999 elections the party won 17 seats in the 63-seat **Althingi** and increased its representation to 20 seats in the most recent election on 10 May 2003. It narrowly failed to gain the status of the largest party in that election.

Party Leader: Össur Skarphédinsson
Address: Hallveigarstíg 1, 101 Reykjavík, Iceland
Tel: (0)5511660
Fax: (0)5629155
E-mail: samfylking@samfylking.is
Internet: www.samfylkingin.is

Alogoskoufis, Georgios

Georgios Alogoskoufis has been Minister of Finance of Greece since March 2004 when **New Democracy (ND)** came to power. Alogoskoufis was elected as a member of parliament for ND in 1996 and again in 2000 and 2004. Born on 17 October 1955 in Athens, Alogoskoufis studied economics at the University of Athens and the London School of Economics (LSE) in the United Kingdom. He worked as an academic at the University of London and the LSE in the 1980s and more recently was a professor at the Economic University of Athens. He has acted as adviser to the **European Commission** and the **World Bank**. Georgios Alogoskoufis is married to Dika Agapitidou and has a son and two daughters.

Address: 5–7 Nikis St, Syntagma Sq., Athens, Greece
Tel: (0)210 3332000
Fax: (0)210 3612503
E-mail: ypetho@mnec.gr
Internet: www.ypetho.gr

Althingi

Parliament

The Althingi is the unicameral parliament of Iceland. It is made up of 63 members who are directly elected by a system of proportional representation for a four-year term. Following the most recent elections, held on 10 May 2003, candidates of five political parties were returned (number of seats in brackets): **Progressive Party** (12), **Liberal Party** (4), **Alliance Party** (20), **Independence Party** (22) and **Left-Green Alliance** (5). At present 19 members (30.2%) of the Althingi are **women**. The Althingi shares legislative power with the President—**Ólafur Ragnar Grímsson** since 1996.

> *Address:* 150 Reykjavík, Iceland
> *Tel:* (0)5630500
> *Fax:* (0)5630550
> *Internet:* www.althingi.is

Althydusamband Íslands – *see* Icelandic Confederation of Labour

Amsterdam Treaty – *see* Treaty of Amsterdam

An Chúirt Uachtarach – *see* Supreme Court, Ireland

Andorra

Andorra is a tiny principality on the Pyrenean border between France and Spain, covering just 468 sq km. Its capital is Andorra la Vella. Andorra has been jointly ruled for 700 years by the co-princes. These are the Spanish Bishop of Urgel (currently Joan Enric Vives i Sicilia) and the French President (currently **Jacques Chirac**).

Political and administrative reforms in the second half of the 20th century led to Andorra's first written constitution in 1993. This transformed the principality into an independent state. The co-princes remain Andorra's heads of state but the roles are largely symbolic. Legislative power lies with the Consell General which is made up of between 28 and 42 representatives who are elected for a four-year term. One-half of the general councillors are elected by Andorra's seven parishes and the other half are elected by a national ballot. The government of Andorra directs the principality's national and international politics. The current Prime Minister, Marc Forné Molné of the economic liberal Partit Liberal d'Andorra, has held this office since 1994.

The population of Andorra is 64,000 (2003) and the main languages are Catalan, Spanish and French. The economy is largely based on tourism: an estimated

9m. visitors arrive annually. Andorra also has a strong banking industry and status as a tax haven.

Anotati Diiskisis Enoseon Dimosion Ypallion – *see* Confederation of Public Servants, Greece

Arbeiderpartiet – *see* Labour Party, Norway

Ásgrímsson, Halldór

Halldór Ásgrímsson has been Prime Minister of Iceland since September 2004. The government he heads is a coalition between his **Progressive Party (FSF)** and the **Independence Party**. Ásgrímsson took over as Prime Minister from David Oddsson of the Independence Party as part of a post-election deal. Oddsson took the post of foreign minister, which Ásgrímsson had formerly held. Ásgrímsson served as a member of the **Althingi** in 1974–78, and again from 1979. He was vice-chairman of the FSF in 1980–94 and since 1994 he has been the party's chairman. He was Minister of Fisheries in 1983–91, Minister of Justice in 1988–89, Minister for Nordic Co-operation in 1985–87 and Minister for Foreign Affairs and External Trade in 1995–2004.

Born on 8 September 1947, Ásgrímsson studied at the Co-operative College of Iceland and the Bergen and Copenhagen Universities of Commerce. In 1973–75 he worked as a lecturer in economics and business administration at the University of Iceland.

Address: Prime Minister of Iceland, Stjórnarrádshúsinu vid Lækjartorg, 150 Reykjavík, Iceland
Tel: (0)4548400
Fax: (0)5624014
E-mail: postur@for.stjr.is
Internet: www.forsaetisraduneyti.is

Assemblée Nationale

National Assembly

The Assemblée Nationale (National Assembly) is the lower house of the bicameral parliament in France. It is made up of 577 members: 555 for mainland France and 22 for the country's overseas territories. The Assemblée Nationale is responsible for passing laws and supervising the government. It shares legislative power with the **Sénat**, though in most instances final authority lies with the Assemblée Nationale.

Members are elected to the Assemblée Nationale by a two-ballot simple majority system. To be elected on the first ballot candidates must obtain an overall majority of votes (more than one-half of the votes). If this is not achieved, a second ballot is held one week later. Candidates must have obtained votes equal to those of 12.5% of the total electorate (not votes cast) to be allowed to proceed to the second round. The winner of the second round is the candidate who obtains the most votes, regardless of whether there is an absolute majority. Members are elected for a term of five years. The Assemblée Nationale can, however, be dissolved early by the President.

Following the most recent election to the Assemblée Nationale, held on 9 June (first ballot) and 16 June (second ballot) 2002, five main political groups were formed (number of seats in brackets). The **Popular Movement** (357), the **Socialist Party** (140), **Union for French Democracy** (29), the group of the **Communist Party** (21) and the **Greens** (3). In the 2002 Assemblée Nationale 70 (12.2%) of the 577 members are **women**.

Address: 126 rue de l'Université, 75355 Paris 07 SP, France
Tel: (0)1-40-63-60-00
Fax: (0)1-45-55-75-23
E-mail: infos@assemblee-nationale.fr
Internet: www.assemblee-nat.fr

Assembléia da República

Assembly of the Republic

The Assembléia da República (Assembly of the Republic) is the unicameral parliament of Portugal. It is composed of 230 members who are elected by a system of proportional representation for a four-year term. The most recent elections were held on 20 February 2005. In the current parliament six parties are represented. These are (number of seats in brackets) the **Socialist Party** (120), the **Social Democratic Party** (72), the **Communist Party of Portugal** (12), the **Popular Party** (12), the **Left Bloc** (8) and the **Green Party** (2). Of the current members of parliament 44 (19.5%) are **women**.

The powers of the Assembléia da República have extended since the Constitution was first written in 1976. It has gained extensive legislative powers and exclusive right to legislate in the areas of electoral law and the education system. It also has a wide range of powers to hold the government to account. Since 1976 these powers have been increasingly exercised in committees rather than plenary sessions.

Address: Palácio de S. Bento, 1249-068 Lisbon, Portugal
Tel: (0)21 3919000
Fax: (0)21 3917440
E-mail: Correio.Geral@ar.parlamento.pt
Internet: www.parlamento.pt

Associação Industrial Portuguesa – *see* Portuguese Industrial Association

Austria

Austria is a Federal Republic in the east of Western Europe. The current Second Republic was established in 1945 at the end of the Second World War and seven years' *Anschluss* (annexation) to Nazi Germany.

Area: 84,000 sq km; *capital:* Vienna (Wien); *population:* 8m. (2001).

The Constitution of 1945 established the Second Republic as a federal state in which sovereignty is shared between nine provinces, or *Länder*, and the federal government. Legislative power is vested in the bicameral parliament composed of the lower **Nationalrat** which is directly elected by a system of proportional representation; and the upper **Bundesrat**, which represents the interests of the provinces. Executive power lies with the Chancellor—since 2000 **Wolfgang Schüssel**. The non-executive head of state is the President of the Republic, who is directly elected in a two-round ballot for a six-year term. The current President is **Heinz Fischer**, elected in April 2004.

Austria was part of the Austro-Hungarian Empire in 1869–1918 and had a multinational composition: in 1910 just 48% of the inhabitants of Vienna had been born in the city; around 25% were of Czech or Moravian descent and 8.6% were Jewish. In the post-Second World War period a strong, more homogeneous national Austrian identity developed. However, on account of its geographical position, Austria still regarded itself as a bridge between eastern and western Europe. Post-war Austria adopted a firm position of neutrality during the **Cold War** when allied troops left in 1955, and did not become a member of the **North Atlantic Treaty Organization**. It also remained outside of the **European Community (EC)** until after the fall of the **Berlin Wall**.

Austria applied for membership of the EC in 1989 and a referendum was held on the issue of membership on 12 June 1994 following parliamentary endorsement. The referendum produced a vote which overwhelmingly favoured membership (yes 66.6%; turn-out 82%). Austria joined the **European Union (EU)** on 1 January 1995. By joining the EU, Austria had to give up its traditional role as intermediary between eastern and western Europe, and close its borders to immigrants, refugees and asylum seekers from eastern and south-eastern Europe. **Immigration** has in recent years become an important political issue in Austria.

The Austrian Second Republic has traditionally been characterized by its moderate style of politics and social consensus. It was governed in 1947–66 and in 1987–2000 by a Grand Coalition of the **Social Democratic Party of Austria (SPÖ)** and the conservative **Austrian People's Party (ÖVP)**. The SPÖ provided the Chancellor for coalition governments continuously in 1970–99. With this system of consensus, a system of *Proporz* developed whereby state sector jobs were allocated among members of these two main parties, leading to patronage, inefficiency and corruption. Attempts have been made since the 1980s to challenge the tradition of consensus and dismantle the system of *Proporz*, but with little success. By the late 1990s the consensus of national politics had been disturbed. A key factor is the shift to the right of the liberal **Austrian Freedom Party (FPÖ)** in 1986 when **Jörg Haider** became leader. Under his leadership, the party moved to the extreme right of the political spectrum and sought to influence government policy on immigration, proposing a constitutional amendment stating that Austria was not a country of immigration, requiring non-Austrians to carry identity cards, strengthening military border controls, and adding further restrictions to opportunities for non-Austrians to gain full **citizenship** status. Since the early 1990s immigration policy has become more restrictive.

In the October 1999 Nationalrat elections the social consensus was upset again when the FPÖ made significant electoral gains and eventually entered into coalition government with the ÖVP. In the polls the SPÖ lost votes and seats but nevertheless retained the status of largest party. The FPÖ made substantial gains through a campaign that opposed immigration and criticized corruption and sleaze among the political class of the two dominant parties. It even overtook the ÖVP—by 415 votes—to gain the status of second largest party in the Nationalrat. The ÖVP had stated that it would go into opposition if it slipped into third place. However, it eventually reneged on this pledge as forming a coalition with the SPÖ, FPÖ and ÖVP in first, second and third place respectively proved difficult. The SPÖ refused to enter into coalition with the FPÖ but entered into coalition negotiations with the ÖVP; these came close to successful completion, but failed after three months' talks. The SPÖ then tried to form a minority government, which also failed. Eventually, after just five days' negotiations, the conservative ÖVP leader, Wolfgang Schüssel, announced that his party would form a coalition with the FPÖ. The ÖVP-FPÖ coalition marked the end of consensual, centrist politics in Austria and the inclusion of a far-right party in national government caused outrage in Austria and the international community. The 14 other member states of the EU imposed diplomatic sanctions on Austria. These sanctions had few practical consequences and were lifted when an EU report found that the coalition did not undermine European values. However, FPÖ leader **Jörg Haider** did resign as party chairman.

The ÖVP-FPÖ government proved to be a volatile coalition. Internal disputes within the FPÖ on government taxation policy led to the resignation of four key FPÖ ministers (including the Vice-Chancellor, Susanne Riess-Passer, and finance minister **Karl-Heinz Grasser**). Nevertheless, the coalition was controversially reformed following the November 2002 Nationalrat elections. Then the ÖVP gained the status as largest party for the first time since 1966. The SPÖ came second and the FPÖ, its worst ever electoral performance notwithstanding, third. The **Green Party** achieved its best ever result. The ÖVP entered coalition negotiations first with the Greens, and then with the SPÖ. It then decided to form a second coalition government with the FPÖ after negotiations which lasted just four days.

The two controversial ÖVP-FPÖ coalitions headed by Chancellor Wolfgang Schüssel have implemented a number of ambitious reforms. They have begun to weaken the system of *Proporz* and to reform the old-fashioned public administration system. They have implemented economic reforms to reduce the budget deficit and reform the welfare state; and they have raised the retirement age, reformed dismissal legislation and introduced university tuition fees.

Post-war Austria has struggled with the issue of whether Austria was a willing ally or victim of the Nazi regime. These issues were widely discussed in 1988 on the occasion of the 50th anniversary of the *Anschluss* of Austria by Nazi Germany (which had been endorsed by referendum among the Austrian population). It was revealed in 1988 that the then Austrian President, Kurt Waldheim, had lied about his role, during the Second World War, as an officer in a military unit which is known to have committed atrocities in the Balkans. The ÖVP strove to resolve the long-standing issue of compensation for **Holocaust** victims and slave labourers and, in October 2000, Austria signed an agreement with the USA and six **Central and Eastern European Countries**.

Economy: The Austrian economy has enjoyed fast growth, low inflation and low **unemployment** for much of the post-war period. It is based on its main exports—machinery, metals, paper, textiles, food, livestock—and a strong tourist industry. Austria nationalized much of state industry and banks in the post-war period in order to defend national sovereignty and resist Soviet claims for reparations. Key nationalized sectors played an important role in the post-war reconstruction: they provided basic materials, infrastructure and services to private manufacturing industry. State-owned firms were also used as tools of social and economic policy.

GNP: US \$194,700m. (2001); *GNP per caput:* \$23,940 (2001); *GNP at PPP:* \$215,000m. (2001); *GNP per caput at PPP:* \$26,380 (2001); *GDP:* \$188,546m. (2001); *exports:* \$99,795m. (2001); *imports:* \$99,762m. (2001); *currency:* euro; *unemployment:* 4.0% (2002).

The characteristics of the post-war Austrian economy have been those of a strong corporatist political economy. Economic decision-making has been conducted by four key peak associations representing labour and capital which have close links with the two parallel parties, the **Social Democratic Party of Austria (SPÖ)** and the conservative **Austrian People's Party (ÖVP)**, in parliament. Typically, economic and social policy-making in Austria has been conducted through negotiations between the relevant ministries and the social partners; only once a deal has been reached is this presented to parliament. The strong emphasis on consensus among social partners has ensured continuity and stability in economic policy.

Despite the dominance of the SPÖ in the post-war period, this corporatist tradition has meant that the Austrian **welfare state** is more conservative than social democratic in orientation. A large proportion of welfare spending is on transfer payments, which remain closely linked to occupation status, the welfare state is funded by individual social insurance contributions rather than general taxation, and there is a comparatively low rate of female participation in the labour market. Social consensus led to full employment and agreement between social partners ensured that wage demands during recessions were modest and that little time was lost annually to strikes.

The corporatist, consensual tradition provided for stable and predictable economic management in the 1950s, 1960s and 1970s, but it has struggled to adapt to provide rapid economic solutions in the globalized era. The oil crises of the 1970s revealed weaknesses in nationalized firms and Austria fell into recession. However, it managed to secure economic growth through bigger budget and trade deficits—an approach which has been referred to as Austro-Keynesianism. It also pursued a hard currency policy, locking the Schilling to the German Deutsche Mark and following the monetary policy of the German **Bundesbank**.

There has been wide speculation that globalization will lead to a 'deaustrification' of the corporatist political economy. Privatization policies since the mid-1980s have weakened the role of labour in key areas of the economy, but on the whole economic adjustment has been conducted within the framework of corporatism and social partnership. A growth in electoral support in the 1980s and 1990s for anti-corporatist political parties—the **Green Party** and the **Austrian Freedom Party (FPÖ)**—and the inclusion of the FPÖ in government were perceived as developments likely to weaken the corporatist framework. However, social partners have redefined themselves as the 'brokers' of modernization and as the symbol of stability in the period of upheaval and rapid change. They were also at the forefront of the campaign to support Austria's **accession** to the **European Union (EU)**.

A founder member of the **European Free Trade Association** in 1960, Austria joined the EU in 1995. It later qualified for participation in the final stages of **Economic and Monetary Union (EMU)**. Prior to the 1995 election, Austria had a budget deficit equivalent to almost 5% of its gross domestic product and this threatened to jeopardize its chances of meeting the **convergence criteria** for EMU, which stipulated a maximum deficit of 3%. The SPÖ-ÖPV grand coalition in 1995–99 implemented a package of austerity measures to reduce the budget deficit. This entailed cuts to the public sector and social spending. Macroeconomic performance improved considerably, with average economic growth of 2.5%, an inflation rate of 0.6%, the highest ever numbers in employment and falling unemployment rates. Fiscal reforms also left the Austrian tax-payer with more disposable income.

The right-wing coalition ÖVP-FPÖ implemented a further programme of budget consolidation, with the finance minister **Karl-Heinz Grasser** aiming to reduce the budget deficit to zero. This consolidation was attempted not by cutting public spending but by increasing revenue. State assets were privatized, existing charges (e.g. road tolls) were raised and new charges were introduced for some health and education services. The tax burden increased to its highest ever level and planned tax cuts were postponed following severe flooding in the summer of 2002. During the government's second term it began to reform the welfare state, introducing a universal child allowance (*Kinderscheck*) for all parents, regardless of employment status, tackling the sensitive issue of pension reform and raising the age of retirement. Austria had used early retirement schemes to remove people from the labour market and in the mid-1990s only 8.8% of 60–64 year-olds were in active employment. Overall, in the second term, economic growth was slow and unemployment increased rapidly.

Austrian Freedom Party

The Austrian Freedom Party, or Freiheitliche Partei Österreichs (FPÖ), is located on the extreme right wing of the Austrian political spectrum. Founded in 1955, the FPÖ was originally a party with both liberal and nationalistic wings. The nationalistic wing of the party came to dominate when **Jörg Haider** became leader in 1986. Since then the party has become known for its anti-**immigration** and anti-asylum policies, and for Haider's controversial remarks on Nazi Germany.

Under Haider's leadership the party made significant electoral gains. In the March 1989 provincial elections in Carinthia, FPÖ gained the status of second largest party and Haider was elected as governor. He was the first governor not to come from the **Austrian People's Party (ÖVP)** or the **Social Democratic Party of Austria**. Haider was defeated in a vote of confidence in 1991, but was re-elected in 1999.

The FPÖ made significant gains in the 2000 general elections, winning 27% of the vote in the Nationalrat, and the party entered into a national coalition with the ÖVP under the leadership of ÖVP Chancellor **Wolfgang Schüssel**. The coalition eventually collapsed because Haider led a revolt in the party against FPÖ ministers, forcing them to resign. Wolfgang Schüssel called new elections in November 2002 instead of negotiating new appointments, and promised to retain the most popular FPÖ ministers, such as finance minister **Karl-Heinz Grasser**, if the ÖVP were re-elected. In the 2002 election the FPÖ lost 10% of the vote but still won 18 seats in the 183-seat Nationalrat. After brief negotiations the FPÖ entered into a second coalition with the ÖVP.

Party Leader: Ursula Haubner
Address: Theobaldgasse 19, 1060 Vienna, Austria
Tel: (0)1 512-35-35-0
Fax: (0)1 512-35-35-9
E-mail: bgst@fpoe.at
Internet: www.fpoe.at

Austrian People's Party

The Austrian People's Party, or Österreichische Volkspartei (ÖVP), is the large Christian democratic party in Austria. Founded in 1945, the party traditionally represents the interests of farmers, entrepreneurs and public servants. The party promotes Christian values in politics and stands for a sustainable social market economy. It advocated a reform of Austria's **welfare state** and a more flexible labour market. The party has favoured and campaigned for Austria's membership of the **European Union (EU)** and promotes the eastern **enlargement** of the EU.

The ÖVP has governed for much of the post-war era. It formed a government on its own in 1966–70 and governed in a Grand Coalition with the **Social Democratic Party of Austria (SPÖ)** in 1945–66 and in 1986–2000. Since 2000 the ÖVP has led a coalition with the extreme right-wing **Austrian Freedom Party (FPÖ)** under the leadership of Chancellor **Wolfgang Schüssel**. Following the November 2002 general elections the party won 79 seats in the 183-seat **Nationalrat**, its best ever performance. Controversially it decided to form a second coalition with a weaker FPÖ, rather than negotiate a coalition with the SPÖ or the **Green Party**.

Party Leader: Wolfgang Schüssel
Address: Lichtenfelsgasse 7, 1010 Vienna, Austria
Tel: (0)1 40-126-0
Fax: (0)1 40-126-109
E-mail: E-mail@oevp.at
Internet: www.oevp.at

Austrian Trade Union Federation

The Austrian Trade Union Federation, or Österreichischer Gewerkschaftsbund (OeGB), is the main trade union organization in Austria. Founded in 1945, today it represents around 1.4m. employees in 13 individual trade unions. The OeGB represents the interests of its members to employers, the state and to all political parties; it is a non-partisan organization.

The OeGB's political objectives are to improve the voice of labour in the economy and society, to defend social security, to improve working conditions, the democratization of the workplace and to campaign for full employment.

Gen. Sec.: Fritz Verzetnitsch
Address: Hohenstaufengasse 10–12, 1010 Vienna, Austria
Tel: (0)1 53-444-0
E-mail: friedrich.verzetnitsch@oegb.at
Internet: www.oegb.at

B

Balkenende, Jan Peter

Jan Peter Balkenende has been the Christian democrat Prime Minister and Minister of General Affairs of the Netherlands since 22 July 2002. His first government, a coalition between the **Christian Democratic Appeal (CDA)**, the **People's Party for Freedom and Democracy (VVD)** and the **List Pim Fortuyn (LPF)**, lasted only 87 days, making it the shortest-lived Dutch government since 1945. It collapsed because of conflicts between ministers from the LPF. Since 27 May 2003 Balkenende has been head of his second government which is a coalition between the CDA, the VVD and **Democrats 66**.

Balkenende was a member of the **Eerste Kamer** of the Dutch parliament for just one term, in 1998–2002, and leader of the CDA parliamentary party from 1 October 2001. Though young and relatively inexperienced in national politics, Balkenende has been credited for reversing the fortunes of the CDA. The massive swing towards the CDA in the 2002 elections was the expression of the electorate's dissatisfaction with the centre-left coalition. This had been particularly incited by the right-wing politician **Pim Fortuyn**, who was murdered nine days before the elections. In the campaign for the May 2002 general election, Balkenende promised to tighten **immigration** policies and to oblige foreigners to integrate more into Dutch society. He has also expressed his opposition to euthanasia, gay marriage and the use of marijuana.

Born on 7 May 1956 in Kapelle, Balkenende graduated in history and law at the Free University of Amsterdam. In 1992 he obtained a doctorate in law with a thesis on government regulation and civil-society organizations. He was legal affairs policy officer at the Netherlands Universities Council in 1982–84 and then worked for the policy institute of the CDA until 1998 and part-time, in 1993–2002, as professor of Christian social thought at the Free University. Balkenende was a member of Amstelveen municipal council in 1982–98 and leader of its CDA group from 1994. Jan Peter Balkenende is married and has one daughter.

Address: Ministry of General Affairs, Binnenhof 19, POB 20001, 2500 EA The Hague, Netherlands
Tel: (0)70 3564100

Fax: (0)70 3564683
E-mail: via www.minaz.nl/english/general/e-mail/index.html
Internet: www.minaz.nl/english/prime_minister/index.html

Banca d'Italia

The Banca d'Italia, the central bank of Italy, was founded in 1893. It became the sole institution authorized to issue banknotes in 1926 and a public-law institution in 1936. The autonomy of the bank increased in the 1980s and 1990s. It is now independent of the Treasury and has the autonomy to set interest rates. Since the start of stage three of **Economic and Monetary Union**, on 1 January 1999, the Banca d'Italia has been a member of the **European System of Central Banks** and the **Eurosystem** and it implements the decisions of the **European Central Bank** in Italy.

Gov.: Antonio Fazio
Address: Via Nazionale 97, 00184 Rome, Italy
Tel: (0)06 47921
Fax: (0)06 47922253
E-mail: stampabi@bancaditalia.it
Internet: www.bancaditalia.it

Banco de España

The Banco de España, the central bank of Spain, dates back to 1782 as the Banco Nacional de San Carlos. During the Franco dictatorship in 1939–75 the Banco de España was an arm of the Ministry of Finance, but from 1959 the regime became slightly less interventionist. After 1975 the Banco de España was transformed into a central bank with full responsibility for the regulation and supervision of the financial system. The 1994 Ley de Autonomía (Law of Autonomy) awarded the bank significant freedom.

A member of the **European Union** since 1986, Spain fulfilled the **convergence criteria** for membership of **Economic and Monetary Union (EMU)** in 1998 and the Banco de España subsequently became a member of the **European System of Central Banks**, the **Eurosystem** and the **European Central Bank (ECB)**. At the start of stage three of the EMU, on 1 January 1999, the Banco de España transferred responsibility for monetary and exchange rate policy to the ECB. Following two amendments to the Ley de Autonomía, in 1997 and 1998, the Banco de España now implements ECB policy regulations.

Gov.: Jaime Caruana
Address: Alcalá 48, 28014 Madrid, Spain
Tel: (0)913 385000
E-mail: comunicacion@bde.es
Internet: www.bde.es

Banco de Portugal

The Banco de Portugal, the central bank of Portugal, was founded in 1846 and has been the sole issuer of Portuguese banknotes since 1891. Originally a private company, the bank was nationalized in 1974. Following Portugal's **accession** to the **European Community** in 1986 the bank took on more responsibility, and an Organic Law in 1990 gave the Banco de Portugal's board of directors greater independence. The bank's autonomy was further strengthened following amendments to the Organic Law in 1995 and 1998.

Since the start of stage three of **Economic and Monetary Union**, on 1 January 1999, the Banco de Portugal has been a member of the **European System of Central Banks** and the **Eurosystem**, and it implements the decisions of the **European Central Bank** in Portugal.

Gov.: Vítor Constâncio
Address: R. do Ouro 27, 1100-150 Lisbon, Portugal
Tel: (0)21 3213200
Fax: (0)21 3464843
E-mail: info@bportugal.pt
Internet: www.bportugal.pt

Bandalag Starfsmanna Ríkis og Bæja – *see* Confederation of State and Municipal Employees, Iceland

Bank of England

The Bank of England is the central bank of the United Kingdom. Founded in 1694, it was nationalized in 1946, but was later granted operational independence by the **Labour Party** government in 1997. Now the Bank's Monetary Policy Committee has responsibility for setting interest rates to meet the government's inflation targets.

The Bank of England has been the sole issuer of banknotes in England and Wales since the mid-19th century. It is also responsible for maintaining the stability of the financial system and, since the mid-1990s, it has been reviewing the implications of a possible introduction of the **euro** to the United Kingdom, which opted out of the single currency.

The Bank of England is a member of the **European System of Central Banks**, which comprises the central banks of all **European Union** member states plus the **European Central Bank**.

Gov.: Mervyn King
Address: Threadneedle St, London EC2R 8AH, United Kingdom
Tel: (0)20 7601 4444
Fax: (0)20 7601 5460
E-mail: enquiries@bankofengland.co.uk
Internet: www.bankofengland.co.uk

Bank of Greece

The Bank of Greece has been that country's central bank since 1927. The Statute of the Bank of Greece was amended in 1998 and 2000 to prepare the institution for membership of the **euro area**. The amendments safeguard the independence of the bank and make price stability its primary objective.

Greece qualified for membership of **Economic and Monetary Union** in 2000 and since 1 January 2001 the Bank of Greece has formed part of the **European System of Central Banks** and of the **Eurosystem**. The Bank is responsible for implementing the monetary and exchange rate policy of the **European Central Bank** in Greece.

Gov.: Nicholas C. Garganas
Address: 21 E. Venizelos Ave, 102 50 Athens, Greece
Tel: (0)210 3201111
Fax: (0)210 3232239
E-mail: secretariat@bankofgreece.gr
Internet: www.bankofgreece.gr

Banque Centrale du Luxembourg

The Banque Centrale du Luxembourg is that country's central bank. Founded in 1998, it was established so that Luxembourg would meet the criteria for participation in **Economic and Monetary Union (EMU)**. These required all participating states to have an independent central bank which implements the policy of the **European Central Bank (ECB)** at national level. The Banque Centrale du Luxembourg replaced the Institut Monétaire Luxembourgeois which had been founded in 1983.

Since the start of stage three of EMU on 1 January 1999 the Banque Centrale du Luxembourg has been a member of the **European System of Central Banks** and the **Eurosystem**, and it implements the decisions of the ECB.

Gov.: Yves Mersch
Address: 2, blvd Royal, 2983 Luxembourg
Tel: (0)47-74-1
Fax: (0)47-74-49-10
E-mail: info@bcl.lu
Internet: www.bcl.lu

Banque de France

The Banque de France, the central bank of France, was founded in 1900. Originally a private company, the bank was nationalized in 1945. It became independent in 1993 in order to ensure stability in monetary policy and to prepare the country for membership of **Economic and Monetary Union (EMU)**.

Since the start of stage three of EMU on 1 January 1999 the Banque de France has been a member of the **European System of Central Banks** and the **Eurosystem** and it implements the decisions of the **European Central Bank** in France.

Gov.: Christian Noyer
Address: 31 rue Croix-des-Petits-Champs, 75001 Paris, or POB 140-01, 75049 Paris Cedex 01, France
Tel: (0)1-42-92-42-92
Fax: (0)1-42-92-39-40
E-mail: service-de-presse@banque-france.fr
Internet: www.banque-france.fr

Banque Nationale de Belgique

The Banque Nationale de Belgique, or Nationale Bank van België, the central bank of Belgium, was founded in 1850. As well as issuing banknotes, it provides services to the public, companies, the state and the financial world.

Since the start of stage three of **Economic and Monetary Union** on 1 January 1999 the Banque Nationale de Belgique has been a member of the **European System of Central Banks** and the **Eurosystem** and it implements the decisions of the **European Central Bank** in Belgium.

Gov.: Guy Quaden
Address: blvd de Berlaimont 14, 1000 Brussels, Belgium
Tel: (0)2 221-21-11
Fax: (0)2 221-31-00
E-mail: secretariat@nbb.be
Internet: www.bnb.be

Barroso, José Manuel Durão

José Manuel Durão Barroso is President of the **European Commission** for the term 2004–08. Barroso struggled in November 2004 to obtain approval from the **European Parliament** for his proposed cabinet of commissioners. After initially defending the controversial Italian nominee, Rocco Buttiglione, Barroso later accepted the Italian's resignation and proposed a new team of commissioners.

Prior to being nominated for the post of Commission President Barroso was Prime Minister of Portugal for the centre-right **Social Democratic Party (SDP)**. A member of the SDP since 1980, Barroso was first elected as a member of parliament in 1985 and was elected a further six times. In the **Assembléia da República** he served as chairman of the Foreign Affairs Committee in 1995–96. Barroso served as State Secretary and Minister for Foreign Affairs and Prime Minister in 2002–04.

Born on 23 March 1956 in Lisbon, Barroso studied law at the University of Lisbon and European studies and political science at the University of Geneva. He was visiting professor at Georgetown University, Washington, DC, in 1996–98 and head of the International Relations Department, Lusíada University, in 1995–99. José Manuel Durão Barroso is married to Margarida Sousa Uva and has three children.

Address: Berlaymont, 1048 Brussels, Belgium
Tel: (0)2 298-81-52
Fax: (0)2 292-14-94
E-mail: jose-manuel.barroso@cec.eu.int
Internet: www.eu.int/comm/commission_barroso/president/index_en.htm

Basque Country

The Basque Country is situated predominantly in the north of Spain, but also extends into the south-west of France. In Spain the Basque Country and its language were oppressed by the Franco dictatorship in 1939–75. Following Spain's successful transition to democracy the region became one of the country's 17 autonomous communities and its Statute of Autonomy granted it the highest possible degree of devolution. The Basque parliament and government, located in the regional capital Vitoria, has control over economic policy (including tax-raising powers), security and education.

There exists in the Basque Country a strong nationalistic movement which demands a referendum on independence or 'the right to self-determination' for the Basque Country. Politically the claim to independence is voiced by two main nationalist parties: the **Basque Nationalist Party (PNV)** and Batasuna (Unity). PNV campaigns for Basque independence through negotiation with national government. It has governed in the Basque Country since the first regional elections were held in 1980. In the most recent regional elections, held in 2001, the party increased its share of the vote to 43%. It has also entered into national alliances (though not coalitions) with the **Popular Party (PP)**. In 2002 the PNV Premier of the Basque Country, Juan José Ibarretxe, drew up a proposal for an independent state which envisaged the Basque Country as a free state that maintains some associations with Spain.

Batasuna—previously known as Herri Batasuna and Euskal Herritarok—campaigns for independence through violence: it is the political wing of the terrorist organization ETA (Euskadi ta Askatasuna—Basque Homeland and Liberty). Since ETA was established in 1968 in Franco's Spain it has killed more than 800 politicians, judges, journalists, businessmen and members of the armed forces. In 1995 José María Aznar, then leader of the PP, and Prime Minister of Spain in 1996–2004, narrowly escaped assassination. The entire leadership of Herri Batasuna was arrested in 1997 and in 1998, under a new leadership and renamed Euskal Herritarok, the party declared a cease-fire, which lasted for 14 months. During this time it worked with PNV in a joint effort to negotiate more autonomy. The party was relaunched as Batasuna following the end of the cease-fire in 1999. Prime Minister Aznar, whose government had granted the region more autonomy during his first term in 1996–2000, no longer relied on the support of the nationalists in his second term in 2000–04. He clamped down on the Basque terrorists and supported a ban of the Batasuna party which was implemented in 2002. Aznar later blamed the 11 March 2004 Madrid terrorist bombings on ETA; the PP lost the general election held three days after the bombings as it emerged that al-Qa'ida had been responsible for the attacks.

The Basque Country has a population of 2.1m. It is one of the few industrialized regions of Spain with an economy traditionally oriented towards steel, shipbuilding, machine tools and aerospace. The region, reliant on heavy industry, experienced a significant industrial and economic decline following the oil crises of the 1970s. Despite periods of economic growth from the late 1980s, the region suffers an above average rate of **unemployment** and below average standard of living. The central government has invested in the region to reshape its heavy industry and the Basque government has sought to strengthen the small and medium-sized enterprise sector.

Basque Nationalist Party

The Basque Nationalist Party, or Euzko Alderdi Jeltzalea-Partido Nacionalista Vasco (EAJ-PNV), is a moderate nationalist political party in Spain. Founded in 1895, it existed as an underground organization during the Franco dictatorship. Today EAJ-PNV campaigns, through negotiation, for an independent state in the **Basque Country** and promotes the rights, culture and language of the Basque people.

EAJ-PNV has governed in the Basque Country since the first regional elections were held in 1980. In the most recent regional elections, held in 2001, the party increased its share of the vote to 43%. It has also entered into alliances (though not coalitions) at national level with the **Popular Party**. The EAJ-PNV has seven seats in the current national parliament, the **Congreso de los Diputados**, which was elected on 14 March 2004.

Pres.: Josu Jon Imaz
Address: Ibáñez de Bilbao 16, 48001 Bilbao, Spain
Tel: (0)94 4039400
Fax: (0)94 4039415
E-mail: internet@eaj-pnv.com
Internet: www.eaj-pnv.com

Basque Workers' Solidarity

Basque Workers' Solidarity, or Eusko Langileen Alkartasuna (ELA), is the trade union confederation that operates solely in the **Basque Country** in Spain. Originally founded in 1911, ELA worked underground and in exile during the years of the Franco dictatorship. It became active again in the region in 1976 and won legal recognition in 1977. Today, ELA represents around 102,000 members organized in four affiliated trade union federations. It is itself affiliated to **ETUC**.

Sec.-Gen.: José Elorrieta
Address: Barrainkua 13, 48009 Bilbao, Spain
Tel: (0)94 4037700
Fax: (0)94 4037777
E-mail: internac.ela@euskalnet.net
Internet: www.ela-sindikatua.org

Belgium

Belgium is a small state in the north of Western Europe, traditionally divided into two culturally, linguistically and politically distinct regions. Flanders in the north is Flemish-speaking and Walloon in the south is French-speaking. Separate political and economic organizations exist in each region. Traditionally French-speakers have dominated the Belgian state, despite the fact that they were outnumbered by the Flemish-speaking population. From the late 1960s resentment of this imbalance of power was expressed in riots and in the growth of Flemish nationalism.

Area: 31,000 sq km; *capital:* Brussels; *population:* 10m. (2001).

Founded as a constitutional monarchy in 1830, the head of state since 1993 has been King Albert II. Originally a unitary state, power in Belgium was divided between the two houses of parliament: the **Kamer** and the **Sénat**. It was a system of symmetrical bicameralism, and the Sénat could block legislation deriving from the lower house. The Belgian state underwent a series of institutional reforms in 1970, 1980 and 1988 to better accommodate regional demands and diffuse regional conflict. These reforms established the administrative regions of Flanders, Walloon and (bilingual) Brussels with members of the national parliament sitting in regional authorities. Powers over policy areas such as public works, the environment, employment, health and transport were devolved to the regions. In addition, authorities representing three linguistic communities—French, Flemish and German—were established to manage education and cultural policy.

Belgium was transformed into a full federal state composed of communities and regions with a constitutional amendment agreed in the 'Saint Michael's Accord' in September 1992 and voted into law in July 1993. The bicameral parliament was reduced in size; the Kamer from 212 seats to 150, and the Sénat from 184 seats to 71. Also, the Sénat can no longer block federal legislation; it now exists to mediate conflicts between the constituent institutions of the federal state. On 21 May 1995 the Belgian electorate voted for the first time for both the national and the regional parliaments, the 118-seat Vlaamse Raad (Flemish Parliament), the 75-seat Conseil Wallon (Walloon Parliament), the 75-seat Conseil Régional Bruxellois (Brussels Regional Parliament) and the 25-seat Rat der Deutschsprachigen Gemeinschaft (Council for the German-speaking Community). In addition, the 75 members of the Walloon Council plus 19 members of the Brussels Regional Council form the

Conseil de la communauté française (the Council of the French Community); and six members of the Brussels Regional Council also serve as delegates in the Flemish Council. Federal and regional elections are all held on one day, on ballot papers the size of newspapers. Voting in Belgian elections is compulsory.

The formalization of a federal state has not been wholly successful in reducing nationalist sentiment. During the 1990s support for the extreme right-wing **Vlaams Blok**, the party representing the Flemish nationalists, increased steadily. In the 1995 elections the party increased its level of support in the national parliament to 6.6% and in the Flemish Parliament to 12.3%. It also won 27.2% of votes in Belgium's second city, Antwerp. Its support continued to increase in the 1999 and 2003 elections, but it has been excluded from power by a 'cordon sanitaire' imposed by all mainstream parties. The party was formally banned by the Belgian courts in 2004, but its leaders plan to form a new party.

Belgian politics has been dominated in the post-Second World War era by the Christian People's Party, now the **Flemish Christian Democrats**, and the Christian People's Party, now the **Humanist Democratic Centre**, on the right; and by the French- and Flemish-speaking Socialist Parties on the left. In elections held on 13 June 1999 support for the conservative-socialist coalition of Jean-Luc Dehaene, which had introduced constitutional reform and prepared the Belgian economy for membership of the final stage of **Economic and Monetary Union**, collapsed. A number of scandals—ranging from the justice system's handling of the paedophile Marc Dutroux to hormone and dioxin scandals in **agriculture** and political and financial corruption among socialist politicians in the Augusta helicopter affair—eroded confidence in the parties which had dominated the post-war political scene. After decades dedicated to managing regional conflict and institutional and constitutional reform, the focus of politics shifted to ethical issues, democracy and transparency.

In 1999 Belgian politics were transformed again when the **Flemish Liberal and Democrat Party (VLD)**, the liberal parties which formed the **Reformist Movement**, the green parties (AGALEV and **Confederated Ecologists for the Organization of Original Struggles**) and the Vlaams Blok made substantial electoral gains. The leader of VLD, **Guy Verhofstadt**, became Prime Minister, heading a coalition between his party and five other liberal, socialist and—for the first time in Belgian politics—green parties. Verhofstadt was the first liberal Prime Minister in Belgium for 61 years, and his 1999 government was the first without Christian Democrat participation in 41 years. He formed a second coalition with both socialist parties, but without the greens, following the 18 May 2003 elections.

Economy: Belgium was the first nation in continental Western Europe to industrialize. A founder member of the **European Coal and Steel Community**, its economy specialized until the 1960s in the production of raw materials, coal and steel, and industrial products. Since the decline of heavy industry, Belgium's main exports have been machinery and electrical equipment, chemicals, vehicles, metals and diamonds. It also has a growing service economy with Belgium's capital,

Brussels, hosting a number of international organizations, including the **European Union (EU)** and the **North Atlantic Treaty Organization**.

GNP: US $245,300m. (2001); *GNP per caput:* $23,850 (2001); *GNP at PPP:* $269,000m. (2001); *GNP per caput at PPP:* $26,150 (2001); *GDP:* $229,610m. (2001); *exports:* $213,811m. (2001 including Luxembourg); *imports:* $203,106m. (2001 including Luxembourg); *currency:* euro; *unemployment:* 7.5% (2002).

Belgium's post-war economy can be classified as a model of negotiated capitalism with a high degree of corporatism. Representatives of labour and capital were awarded a high degree of autonomy to agree wage, labour and welfare policy. Social partnership became institutionalized in 1952 in the Conseil National de Travail (CNN—the National Labour Council). Until the recession of the 1970s social partners generally followed the guide-lines set by the Social Pact in 1944 and the Productivity Agreement in 1952. The Belgian **welfare state** is organized along the lines of the corporatist or conservative model and most social spending is concentrated on transfer payments to mitigate occupational risks such as **unemployment** or ill health, and to provide levels of benefit that preserve the status of the male breadwinner. Social security benefits are funded by employee and employer contributions and insurance schemes are managed by social partners.

The Belgium economy has suffered from a series of recurring problems since the 1970s. The 1970s recession led to a rapid rise in rates of unemployment which doubled in the two years 1974–76, and by 1981 Belgium had the highest level of public-sector debt in the **Organisation for Economic Co-operation and Development**. The impact of the recession was greater in the French-speaking region of Walloon, which has the older industrial tradition, than in the traditionally rural, Flemish-speaking region of Flanders, which had successfully attracted more modern investment. Since the 1970s Flanders has outperformed Wallonia and there has been a redistribution of national wealth to the poorer region. The traditional institutions of social partnership struggled to provide solutions to Belgium's economic problems and the state became increasingly involved in corporatist decision-making from the mid-1970s, transforming the bipartite system to a tripartite form of social partnership.

In Belgium, increases in wages and welfare benefits are traditionally indexed to price increases. Labour organizations were reluctant to accept a policy of wage restraint to accelerate economic and employment growth. Instead, labour market policies concentrated on public subsidies and demand-led measures. Policies also sought to reduce the labour supply by banning the recruitment of foreign workers, offering early retirement schemes and extending the duration of education. In the 1980s schemes to redistribute work through cuts in working hours were also attempted. The state also tried to cut welfare spending by restricting the entitlement of all workers except the male breadwinner to benefit. In the 1980s there was no employment expansion in Belgium and at the start of the 1990s unemployment remained high and productivity and employment growth was slow.

In the 1990s Belgium struggled to meet the criteria for membership of the final phase of **Economic and Monetary Union** on account of its public debt to gross

domestic product ratio—the highest in the EU. The conservative-socialist government reduced the budget for 1996/97 in order to successfully meet the **convergence
criteria**. The two liberal-led coalitions in 1999–2003 and from 2003 onwards have
since managed to balance the national budget and have started to cut national debt.
However, unemployment remains high and regional inequalities persist. In some
areas of Wallonia (Liège and Charleroi) unemployment rates are as high as 35%.

Berlin Wall

The Berlin Wall, 155 km in length, physically divided the east and west parts of the
city of Berlin, Germany, for 28 years. In fact, the whole border between the
German Democratic Republic (GDR) and the Federal Republic of Germany
was guarded. A barrier between socialist east and capitalist west, the Berlin Wall
became a metaphor for political and military division in Europe during the
Cold War.

Construction of the Berlin Wall by the GDR began overnight on 13 August 1961.
According to GDR propaganda, the purpose of the Berlin Wall was to protect East
Germans from the 'fascist' west: it was an 'Antifaschistischer Schutzwall'. In reality
it was a measure to stem the mass migration of GDR citizens and thus human capital
to the west. A number of GDR citizens did manage to overcome the barrier and flee
to the west through tunnels, hidden in cars, or in boats. But more than 80 were killed
by border guards while attempting to escape. **Willy Brandt**, mayor of Berlin in
1963, negotiated with the GDR that West Berliners be allowed to pass to the East to
visit relatives over the Christmas period. From 1972 the Fundamental Treaty
between the two Germanys allowed for more movement and journalists and
pensioners in the GDR were allowed to pass to the west. In 1989 civil rights
movements across the GDR protested for democratic reforms and more freedom
to travel.

On 9 November 1989 the GDR regime agreed to introduce new travel regulations
and this policy was announced at a press conference by the East German politician
Günter Schabowski. When asked by an Italian journalist when the regulations for
'permanent emigration' come into force, Schabowski hesitated and, finding no
answer in his brief, replied spontaneously that they did so immediately. The press
conference was reported on West German news 'Tagesthemen' to which East
German citizens had access. On hearing that the borders were open, GDR citizens
descended *en masse* to the border checkpoints which were then opened by guards.
That night East and West Berliners celebrated together and began to dismantle the
concrete construction.

The fall of the Berlin Wall on 9 November 1989 is also used to symbolize the
collapse of socialist Eastern Europe, and the end of the Cold War. Today, only small
parts of the Berlin Wall remain standing. However, many Germans refer to a 'wall in
the heads' that still divides the unified state.

Berlusconi, Silvio

Silvio Berlusconi is the controversial Prime Minister of Italy. He was appointed to that office in 2001 when his party **Forza Italia** and their electoral allies, the **Northern League** and the **National Alliance**, gained a majority in the **Camera dei Deputati** as the House of Freedoms coalition. A businessman predominantly in the area of **media**, Berlusconi's fortune has been estimated at US $14,000m. and he is Italy's richest citizen. Born on 29 September 1936 in Milan, Berlusconi graduated in law from Milan University in 1961. He set up a construction company and built Milano 2, a garden suburb on the outskirts of the northern city. From this his business interests expanded into media (Mediaset), financial services and entertainments. He entered politics in 1993, establishing Forza Italia as a new party to fill the gap left by the collapse of the Christian Democrats (DC) in the *mani pulite* (clean hands) corruption scandals and investigations of 1992. Berlusconi sought to present himself as the new face of Italian politics and as a leader who would deliver a less corrupt and more efficient state.

Berlusconi first became Prime Minister following the 27 March 1994 election and headed a coalition with the Lega Nord and the National Alliance. The government resigned on 22 December 1994 following conflicts with his two coalition partners and because he had become subject to legal investigations relating to money-laundering, complicity in murder, connections with the Mafia, tax evasion and the bribing of politicians, judges and the tax police. Berlusconi became Prime Minister for the second time following the general election held on 13 May 2001; the campaign for the House of Freedoms coalition had been focused predominantly on him. A more stable premiership than the first, it has nevertheless generated numerous controversies in both domestic and international politics.

In Italy Berlusconi has been criticized for passing laws to promote and protect his own business interests. For example, he introduced a new communications bill which would lead to the privatization of the state television network in such a way that it does not infringe on private television interests and would permit him to extend his newspaper empire. He has also passed laws to make Italy's Prime Minister and four other leading officials immune from prosecution during their term of office. He argued that the incumbent Prime Minister should not be expected to experience the 'indignity' of standing trial. However, the Italian President, **Carlo Ciampi**, refused on 15 December 2003 to sign the communications bill that had been passed by both houses of parliament on the grounds that it reversed a ruling of Italy's **Constitutional Court**. Berlusconi refused to acknowledge the points made by the President's report and proposed to pass an emergency decree instead. The Constitutional Court ruled on 13 January 2004 that Berlusconi's immunity law violated two articles of the Constitution: that all citizens are equal before the law; and that citizens have the right to defend their interests in court.

Internationally, Berlusconi has made a number of controversial statements which have been widely condemned. Shortly after the **11 September** 2001 terrorist attacks he commented on the 'superiority' of western civilization in contrast to Islamic countries which show less respect for 'religious and political rights'. Also, at the start of Italy's presidency of the **European Union** in 2003 Berlusconi appeared before the **European Parliament (EP)**. In response to critical comments made by the German social democrat member of the EP Martin Schulz, Berlusconi likened him to a Nazi concentration camp guard and refused to withdraw the remark.

Address: Palazzo Chigi, Piazza Colonna 370, 11186 Rome, Italy
Tel: (0)06 677191
Fax: (0)06 67793169
E-mail: urpdie@governo.it or BERLUSCONI_S@camera.it
Internet: www.palazzochigi.it/Presidente

Blair, Tony

Tony Blair is Prime Minister of the United Kingdom. He took office for the first time in May 1997 when the **Labour Party** won a landslide victory in the **House of Commons** (418 of 659 seats). He commenced a second term of office in June 2001 after elections in which the Labour Party won another large majority, losing just six seats in parliament. Blair announced on 30 September 2004 that he would stand for one more term of office in 2005, but would not seek re-election for a fourth term.

A member of the Labour Party since 1975, he was first elected to the House of Commons for the Sedgefield constituency in 1983. While the Labour Party was in opposition, Blair served as opposition Spokesman for Energy in 1988, for Employment in 1989 and Home Affairs in 1992. Elected as leader of the Labour Party in 1994 following the death of John Smith, Blair campaigned for reform of Clause 4 of the Labour Party's constitution, which committed the party to the goal of collective ownership. The proposal was accepted in 1995 and it shifted the party towards the political centre, securing Blair's reputation as a modernizer and as the architect of 'New Labour' and the so-called 'Third Way'.

As Prime Minister, Blair has successfully led the Labour Party's programme of social and constitutional reform, including devolution for **Wales**, **Scotland** and **Northern Ireland**. However, he has shown frustration at the slow pace of change and his hands are tied by Chancellor **Gordon Brown**'s tight control over government spending. Blair has developed a strong profile in European and international politics. He is committed to the project of European integration and has close links with many European leaders on both the left and right of the political spectrum. Blair has also fostered close relationships with US Presidents Bill Clinton and George W. Bush. A particularly close ally of Bush, Blair strongly supported, and committed UK troops to, the US-led war in **Iraq** in 2003, despite the absence of a **United Nations** mandate. Until the war in Iraq Blair enjoyed unprecedented approval ratings for a Labour Prime Minister serving a second term of office. He has, however, regularly been criticized for, on the one hand, being overly concerned with media image and 'spin' and, on the other hand, his presidential style of leadership.

Blair was born on 6 May 1953 in Edinburgh, Scotland. He studied law at Oxford University and trained as a barrister. He is married to Cherie Booth and they have four children.

Address: 10 Downing St, London SW1A 2AA, United Kingdom
Fax: (0)20 7925 0918
E-mail: www.number-10.gov.uk/output/Page821.asp
Internet: www.number-10.gov.uk

Bloco de Esquerda – *see* Left Bloc, Portugal

Bondevik, Kjell Magne

Kjell Magne Bondevik has been Prime Minister of Norway since October 2001. A member of the **Christian People's Party (KrF)**, he currently heads a minority government together with the **Conservative Party** and the **Liberals**. The parties won voter favour in 2001 by promising improvements in public services; they have also reduced taxes, using income from Norwegian oil wealth instead. In addition, Bondevik agreed not to raise the issue of whether Norway should submit a new application for membership of the **European Union**.

Bondevik was first elected to the Norwegian **Storting** in 1973 and served as leader of the KrF in 1983–95. He was state secretary in the Office of the Prime Minister in 1972–73, Minister for Church and Education in 1983–86, Deputy Prime Minister in 1985–86 and Minister for Foreign Affairs in 1989–90. Bondevik first served as Prime Minister in 1997–2000 until an environmental dispute brought down his centrist minority coalition.

Born on 3 September 1947 in Molde, Bondevik is a graduate in theology from Norway's Free Faculty of Theology. In 1979 he was ordained as a priest in the Lutheran Church of Norway. He is married and has three children.

Address: The Office of the Prime Minister, Akersgt 42 or POB 8001 Dep, 0030
Oslo, Norway
Tel: (0)22-24-90-90
Fax: (0)22-24-95-00
E-mail: postmottak@smk.dep.no
Internet: odin.dep.no/smk/engelsk/index-b-n-a.html

Brandt, Willy

Willy Brandt was a social democratic politician and statesman in the Federal Republic of Germany (FRG). He was mayor of West Berlin (in 1957–66) when the **German Democratic Republic (GDR)** built the **Berlin Wall** (on 13 August

1961) and was the first social democratic Chancellor of the FRG, in 1969–74. During the **Cold War** Brandt's *Ostpolitik* promoted *détente* and co-operation between the two German states and other **Central and Eastern European Countries**. His *Ostpolitik* was central to the process which culminated in the fall of the Berlin Wall, the end of the Cold War and the unification of Germany. When the Berlin Wall fell, Brandt—who was not otherwise a religious man—thanked God that he had been given the opportunity to witness the event. He addressed a crowd of East and West Berliners in front of the Berlin mayor's office on 10 November 1989 and opened the first all-German parliamentary session in December 1990. He also led the **Bundestag** vote in 1991 in favour of moving the seat of parliament from Bonn to Berlin.

Brandt was born Herbert Ernst Karl Frahm on 18 December 1913 in Lübeck. Brandt, who never met his father, was brought up in a working-class, social democratic family by his grandfather. He was the only working-class boy at the prestigious Johanneum Gymnasium (grammar school) from which he obtained his *Abitur* in 1932. After school he worked briefly as a trainee in a shipping firm. Brandt joined the Socialist Worker Youth Movement (Sozialistische Arbeiterjugend) in 1929 and one year later he was encouraged to join the **Social Democratic Party of Germany (SPD)** by his mentor, the SPD politician Julius Leber. He left the SPD in favour of the left-wing Socialist Worker Party (SAP—Sozialistische Arbeiterpartei) in 1931 and became the chairman of its youth movement. As a prominent socialist activist in Lübeck, Brandt was forced into exile in 1933 when the National Socialists came to power. Shortly after the collapse of the Weimar Republic, he fled to Norway via Denmark and assumed the name Willy Brandt for the first time. In Norway he studied history, worked as a journalist and was politically active in the exiled SAP. Brandt travelled to Berlin in 1936 to co-ordinate the SAP underground organization, and to Spain in 1937 as a journalist to report on the Spanish civil war. Brandt was stripped of his German citizenship in 1938. When Norway was occupied by German forces in 1940 Brandt was taken prisoner of war until he escaped to Sweden. There he worked as a journalist and was awarded Norwegian citizenship by the Norwegian government-in-exile. Brandt became active in the European social democratic movement in 1942 and rejoined the SPD. At the end of the war he returned to Germany, first to report on the Nuremberg war trials in 1945–46, and then as a press attaché for the Norwegian government in Berlin. He regained his German citizenship, but retained his exile name.

Brandt's political career in the SPD took off slowly: as a returned exile he was treated with suspicion by some elements of the party. In his home town, Lübeck, there was support for him to become mayor but this move was blocked by the party headquarters in Hanover. Brandt's attempts to become chairman of the Berlin party were blocked twice, as were his attempts to be elected onto the executive committee of the federal SPD. Brandt was a member of the Bundestag in 1949–57 and eventually became mayor of Berlin in 1957, following the death Ernst Reuter in 1953 and then that of his successor as mayor, Otto Suhr, in 1957. As mayor, Brandt became a popular and prominent politician both in Germany and—following the construction of the Berlin Wall—internationally. During his years as mayor of the divided city he drew up with SPD colleague Egon Bahr the first phases of his *Ostpolitik*. He developed a programme called *'Wandel durch Annäherung'* (change through *rapprochement*) and agreed a deal in 1963 with the GDR allowing West Berliners to travel to the East over the Christmas period.

Brandt was the SPD's Chancellor candidate against Konrad Adenauer in 1961 and against Ludwig Erhard in 1965. In both elections the SPD's vote increased, although not sufficiently to grant it the status of largest party in the Bundestag. The SPD entered into a Grand Coalition with the **Christian Democratic Union (CDU)** and the **Christian Social Union (CSU)** in 1966 under Kurt Georg Kiesinger and, as Vice-Chancellor and foreign minister, Brandt worked to improve the FRG's relations with Eastern European states. From 1964 he was leader of the SPD.

In 1969 Brandt became the first social democratic Chancellor of the FRG following the formation of a coalition between the SPD and the liberal **Free Democratic Party (FDP)**. During his five years in office, Brandt significantly developed his *Ostpolitik*. He visited Erfurt in the GDR and received a visit from the GDR's Prime Minister, Willi Stoph, in 1970. In August 1970 he signed the Treaty of Moscow and in December the Treaty of Warsaw. These aimed to improve relations between the FRG, the Soviet Union and Poland; the states agreed to respect the existing national borders and to seek peaceful solutions to conflict. In Poland in December 1970, at the site of the Warsaw Ghetto, Brandt made a gesture which made a lasting impression in the international community: he fell to his knees, expressing an apology for the crimes of Nazi Germany. Brandt was awarded the Nobel Peace Prize in 1971 for his *Ostpolitik* and policy of *détente*. As Chancellor, Brandt worked domestically to strengthen democracy in Germany: his campaign slogan had been *'Mehr Demokratie Wagen'* (Dare more democracy). His government passed a series of reforms to legalize divorce, improve the rights of **women**, reduce discrimination against homosexuals, and reduce the age of voting. It also expanded democratic rights in the workplace through institutions of co-determination.

Brandt's politics were considered controversial among the opposition CDU/CSU. The right wing in Germany considered him a traitor for having left Germany during the war and for accepting the sovereignty of the GDR and thus the division of Germany in his *Ostpolitik*. The opposition sought to defeat Brandt's government in 1972 through a constructive vote of no confidence. This attempt narrowly failed: the CDU/CSU needed 249 votes but won just 247. Allegedly Brandt was saved by the GDR 'buying' two votes in the Bundestag to keep him in power. Brandt's status in Germany grew and the SPD's campaign slogan for the 1972 election was simply *'Wählt Willy Brandt'* (Vote for Willy Brandt). The SPD managed to gain the status of the largest party in the Bundestag and formed another coalition with the liberal FDP. In 1973 Brandt travelled to Israel and was the first German Chancellor to address the **United Nations** in New York.

By 1974 Brandt's politics had been overtaken by a series of health problems and personal scandals. Brandt was prone to depression and would withdraw from the political scene, leaving others to deal with the detail of politics. He was hospitalized for an operation on his throat and the tabloid press also made big news of Brandt's love affairs. However, his downfall came when it was revealed that his personal assistant, Günter Guillaume, was a spy for the GDR. Brandt resigned as Chancellor on 6 May 1974 and was replaced by SPD politician Helmut Schmidt. Following his resignation Brandt (re)turned to the international political scene. He was president of the Socialist International in 1976–92 and campaigned on issues of international development and peace. He was a member of the **European Parliament** in 1979–83. He remained leader of the SPD until 1987 and a member of the Bundestag until 1992. Willy Brandt died on 8 October 1992 in Unkel. He had been married three times and had four children, one from his first marriage and three from his second.

Breton, Thierry

Thierry Breton has been Minister of Finance in France since February 2005 following the resignation of Hervé Gaymard on account of a property scandal. Breton was, prior to this, chief executive of France Telecom and is credited with steering the company out of a debt crisis in 2002. As Minister of Finance Breton has the task of stabilizing the economy and the ministry—Breton is the fourth finance minister since the government of **Jean-Pierre Raffarin** came to office in 2002.

Born on 15 January 1955 in Paris, Breton studied at the Ecole supérieure d'électricité. His professional career was based in major French companies such as Bull, Thomson and France Telecom. Thierry Breton is married and has three children.

> *Address:* Ministry for Economics, Finance and Industry, 139 rue de Bercy, Télédoc 536, 75572 Paris CEDEX 12, France
> *Tel:* (0)1-40-04-04-04
> *Fax:* (0)1-53-18-36-40
> *E-mail:* dircom-cnt@dircom.finances.gouv.fr
> *Internet:* www.finances.gouv.fr

Brown, Gordon

Gordon Brown is Chancellor of the Exchequer (Minister of Finance) in the United Kingdom. He was appointed to this post in 1997 when the **Labour Party** was elected to government. Brown gained the reputation of 'Iron Chancellor' in the early years for his prudent management of the economy and control of public spending. He has, however, significantly improved the stability of the British economy and increased public spending on health and education. On becoming Chancellor, Brown immediately gave operational independence to the **Bank of England** and he stated in October 1997 that he would rule out Britain's entry into the **euro** for the lifetime of the first Labour government and has, in addition to the formal **convergence criteria** of the **European Union**, set his own criteria to test the British economy's suitability for membership of the single currency.

Born on 20 February 1951 in Glasgow, Brown studied at Edinburgh University and worked as a lecturer at Edinburgh and Caledonian University in 1976–80 and in Scottish television in 1980–83. Brown's political interests started as a student when he was chairman of the Labour Club and elected rector of the University's student court in 1972–75. He was elected onto the executive of Scottish Labour in 1977 and has been Member of Parliament for the constituency of Dunfermline East since 1983. Brown was opposition Chancellor in 1992–97 and he reluctantly agreed in 1994 not to oppose **Tony Blair** in the Labour Party leadership contest that followed John Smith's death.

Address: HM Treasury, 1 Horse Guards Rd, London SW1A 2HQ, United Kingdom
Tel: (0)20 7270 4558
Fax: (0)20 7270 4861
E-mail: public.enquiries@hm-treasury.gov.uk
Internet: www.hm-treasury.gov.uk

Bundesbank

The Bundesbank, the central bank in Germany, was founded in 1957. An independent institution free from political interference, the Bundesbank pursued a policy of price stability. It is considered to be the model for the **European Central Bank (ECB)**.

Since the start of stage three of **Economic and Monetary Union** on 1 January 1999, the Bundesbank has been a member of the **European System of Central Banks (ESCB)** and the **Eurosystem** and it implements the decisions of the ECB in Germany. The Bundesbank's organizational structure was altered in 2002 as a consequence of its membership of the ESCB.

Gov.: Axel A. Weber
Address: Wilhelm-Epstein-Strasse 14, 60431 Frankfurt-am-Main, or POB 10 06 02, 60006 Frankfurt-am-Main, Germany
Tel: (0)69 95663511
Fax: (0)69 95663077
E-mail: presse-information@bundesbank.de
Internet: www.bundesbank.de

Bundesgericht – *see* **Federal Court, Switzerland**

Bundesrat (Austria)

Federal Council

The Bundesrat (Federal Council) is the upper house of the bicameral parliament of Austria. It is currently made up of 64 members who are representatives of Austria's nine provinces (*Länder*). Members are elected from the legislative bodies of each province for a four-to-six-year term. The number of representatives a province can send to the Bundesrat varies from three to 12, depending on the size of its population. At least one of the seats must be given to a member of the party that won the second largest number of seats in the provincial parliament.

The Bundesrat shares legislative power with the **Nationalrat**. All legislation passed by the Nationalrat must be presented to the Bundesrat for review. The Bundesrat can at most delay legislation by sending it back to the Nationalrat. The Nationalrat can, however, override the Bundesrat's veto. A constitutional amendment in 1984 increased the powers of the Bundesrat. Now any proposed constitutional changes that alter the distribution of powers to the disadvantage of the regions require the approval of two-thirds of the Bundesrat.

Address: Bundesrat, Dr Karl Renner-Ring 3, 1017 Vienna, Austria
Tel: (0)1 401-100
Fax: (0)1 401-103-803
E-mail: services@parlinkom.gv.at
Internet: www.parlinkom.gv.at

Bundesrat (Germany)

Federal Council

The Bundesrat (Federal Council) is the upper house of the bicameral legislature in Germany. It is made up of 69 representatives of the 16 constituent German states (*Länder*). The seats are filled by members of the *Länder* governments following elections held every four or five years. Each state (or *Land*) is allocated a minimum of three and a maximum of six seats in the Bundesrat; the exact allocation depends on the size of its population. Votes must be cast as a bloc.

The Bundesrat shares legislative power with the **Bundestag** and has the right to veto bills which affect the constitutional responsibilities or financing of the *Länder*. A mediation committee (*Vermittlungsausschuss*) comprising 16 members of the Bundesrat and 16 members of the Bundestag is convened where disagreement exists between the two houses of the German parliament.

Address: Bundesrat, 11055 Berlin, Germany
Tel: (0)18 8891000
Fax: (0)18 889100198
E-mail: pressestelle@bundesrat.de
Internet: www.bundesrat.de

Bundestag

Federal Assembly

The Bundestag (Federal Assembly) is the lower house of the bicameral legislature in Germany and has been located since 1999 in the refurbished Reichstag building in Berlin. It has a basic membership of 598 parliamentarians who are directly elected for a four-year term. The most recent elections were held on 22 September 2002.

Members are elected by a system of proportional representation. Voters cast two votes: the first to decide who should represent a particular constituency and the second to determine party strength. One-half of the members represent single-member constituencies; the other half derive from party lists. Any party which gains more than 5% of votes from party lists nationally, or wins three constituencies, is entitled to an allocation of Bundestag seats. If a party gains more constituency seats in any *Land* than it is entitled to according to the party seat allocation, then surplus seats are created for that four-year Bundestag term. In the current Bundestag there are five surplus seats bringing the total membership to 603.

Following the 2002 election, four parliamentary groups (*Fraktion*) were formed (number of seats in brackets) for the **Social Democratic Party of Germany** (251), the **Christian Democratic Union** (190) with the **Christian Social Union** (58), **Alliance 90/The Greens** (55) and the **Free Democratic Party** (47). As the **Party of Democratic Socialism** only has two directly elected members, it is too small to be entitled to form a *Fraktion*. In the current Bundestag 194 members (32.2%) are **women**.

The Bundestag shares legislative powers with the **Bundesrat**. It has sole responsibility to elect the Federal Chancellor and can also remove a Chancellor through a constructive vote of no confidence. This requires the Bundestag to propose an alternative Chancellor at the same time as the old one is being removed. This procedure was used once (unsuccessfully) in 1972 and once (successfully) in 1982.

> *Address:* Deutscher Bundestag, Platz der Republik 1, 11011 Berlin, Germany
> *Tel:* (0)30 2270
> *Fax:* (0)30 22736878 or (0)30 22736979
> *E-mail:* mail@bundestag.de
> *Internet:* www.bundestag.de

Bundesverband der deutschen Industrie – *see* Confederation of German Industry

Bundesvereinigung der deutschen Arbeitgeberverbände – *see* Confederation of German Employers' Associations

Bundesverfassungsgericht – *see* **Federal Constitutional Court, Germany**

Bündnis 90/Die Grünen – *see* **Alliance 90/The Greens, Germany**

C

Camera dei Deputati

Chamber of Deputies

The Camera dei Deputati (Chamber of Deputies) is the lower house of the bicameral legislature of Italy. It is made up of 630 members who are elected by a mixed electoral system for a five-year term. Since 1994 475 deputies have been elected by a majoritarian system and a further 155 by proportional representation. The Camera dei Deputati shares its legislative role and the task of controlling the government with the **Senato della Repubblica** on an equal basis.

Since the most recent elections, held on 13 May 2001, there have been eight parliamentary groups (number of seats in brackets). These are: **Forza Italia** (178), **National Alliance** (99), **Union of Centre and Christian Democrats** (40), **Northern League** (30), **Democrats of the Left** (137), **Daisy Alliance** (80), **Communist Refoundation Party** (11), and a mixed group of nine other parties. At present, 11.5% of members of the Camera dei Deputati are **women**.

Address: Palazzo di Montecitorio, Piazza Montecitorio, 00100 Rome, Italy
Tel: (0)06 67602300
Fax: (0)06 67609950
E-mail: dlwebmast@camera.it
Internet: newenglish.camera.it

Canarian Coalition

The Canarian Coalition, or Coalición Canaria (CC), is the liberal nationalist party of the Canary Isles, Spain. Founded in 1993 as an electoral alliance of five nationalist parties, it seeks to promote the autonomy of the Canary Isles.

In the most recent regional elections CC won 33% of the vote and 23 seats in the 60-seat parliament. At national level it has entered into alliances but not coalitions with the **Popular Party**. In the most recent general elections, held on 14 March 2004, CC won 0.9% of the vote and three seats in the 350-seat **Congreso de los Diputados**.

Pres.: Paulino Rivero Baute
Address: Edif. El Drago, 1°, Calle Galcerán 7–9, 38003 Santa Cruz de Tenerife,
Spain
Tel: (0)922 279702
Fax: (0)922 280957
E-mail: agrupacion-ati@jet.es
Internet: www.coalicioncanaria.org

Centerpartiet – *see* Centre Party, Sweden

Central and Eastern European Countries (CEECs)

Central and Eastern European Countries (CEECs) is the contemporary collective name given to the region between Western Europe and **Russia**, from the Baltic to the Black Seas. It encompasses the core Visegrad states of the Czech Republic, Hungary, Poland and Slovakia and some definitions also include Bulgaria, Romania and Slovenia. Broader definitions of Eastern Europe include the Baltic states of Estonia, Latvia and Lithuania, the Balkan states of former Yugoslavia and Albania, and even the former Soviet states of Ukraine and Moldova.

An ethnically and nationally diverse region, it has over the past centuries experienced shifting borders and series of invasions and imposed rule from neighbouring empires to the west and east. In the post-Second War era the region was transformed into a number of communist 'satellite' states of the Soviet Union (USSR), trading together as COMECON (Council of Mutual Economic Assistance) and allied militarily in the Warsaw Pact. Dramatic revolutions in Poland, Hungary and Czechoslovakia in 1989 led to the fall of communist dictatorships across CEECs and to their gradual transformation into nation states with liberal democracies and market economies. The collapse of state communism revived old ethnic conflicts in some states: Czechoslovakia peacefully split into two states (Czech Republic and Slovakia) in 1993, while Yugoslavia fell into civil war and disintegrated into separate republics.

On 1 May 2004 eight CEEC states became members of the **European Union (EU)**: Czech Republic, Estonia, Hungary, Latvia, Lithuania, Poland, Slovakia and Slovenia. Bulgaria and Romania are due to join the EU in 2007. The CEEC **accession** states applied to join the EU between 1994 and 1996 and negotiations were opened in 1998 or 2000. By 2003 eight CEECs had met the **Copenhagen Criteria** and the Treaty of Accession was signed in April 2003 at a meeting of the **Council of the European Union** in Greece. Membership was endorsed by referendums held in all of the CEEC accession states.

The CEEC region experienced significant economic crises in the early stages of transition to market economies. In the late 1990s, however, there were improvements in economic stability and prosperity. The CEECs had an average economic growth rate of 4% in 1996–2002 and inflation fell from treble figures at the start of the 1990s to single figures after 1997. The region's economies benefited from a growth in foreign direct investment, a shift from **agriculture** to manufacturing production, and financial assistance from the EU. With the PHARE programme, originally established for Poland and Hungary in 1989, the EU assisted CEECs financially in their transition to stable market economies. PHARE funding was later directed to specifically help CEECs meet the Copenhagen Criteria for EU membership. Despite significant improvements the CEEC's average level of per caput gross domestic product (at purchasing power parity) remains at only 40%–50% of the EU average.

Central Bank and Financial Services Authority of Ireland

The Central Bank and Financial Services Authority of Ireland was founded as the Central Bank of Ireland in 1943. In 2003 it was restructured and renamed. The Central Bank acts as agent for and banker to the Irish government, carries out economic research and analysis, and is responsible for the production and issue of currency. Since 2003 the autonomous Irish Financial Services Regulatory Authority, established within the new Central Bank, has supervised all financial institutions operating in Ireland. Since the start of stage three of **Economic and Monetary Union** on 1 January 1999, the Central Bank of Ireland has been a member of the **European System of Central Banks** and the **Eurosystem** and has implemented the decisions of the **European Central Bank** in Ireland.

Gov.: John Hurley
Address: POB 559, Dame St, Dublin 2, Ireland
Tel: (0)1 4344000
Fax: (0)1 6716561
E-mail: enquiries@centralbank.ie
Internet: www.centralbank.ie

Central Organization of Finnish Trade Unions

The Central Organization of Finnish Trade Unions, or Suomen Ammattiliittojen Keskusjärjestö (SAK) is the central organization of the trade union movement in Finland. Founded in 1907, SAK co-ordinates the work of 24 member trade unions and is itself a member of the **ETUC**.

Gen. Sec.: Lauri Ihalainen
Address: 3rd Floor, Hakaniemenranta 1, 00530 Helsinki, Finland, or POB 157, FIN-00531 Helsinki, Finland
Tel: (0)9 77211
Fax: (0)9 7721223
E-mail: sak@sak.fi
Internet: www.sak.fi

Centrale Générale des Syndicats Libéraux de Belgique – *see* General Central Organization of Liberal Trade Unions, Belgium

Centre Démocrate Humaniste – *see* Humanist Democratic Centre, Belgium

Centre Party (Finland)

The Centre Party of Finland, or Keskusta, was established in 1906. Originally the party of the rural population, it now campaigns for the centre ground between the main left- and right-wing parties. The party campaigned for Finnish independence in 1917 and today it stands for social renewal, entrepreneurship and regional equality. It favours democratic decentralization. The Centre Party has led the majority of governments in Finland since 1917. Most recently it led the government in 1991–95 which took Finland into the **European Union** and it heads the coalition government formed following the general elections of 16 March 2003 in which it gained the status of largest party, winning 55 seats in the 200-seat **Eduskunta**. The Centre Party's president, **Matti Vanhanen**, is the Finnish Prime Minister.

Leadership: Pres. Matti Vanhanen; *Sec.-Gen.* Eero Lankia
Address: Apollonkatu 11A, 00100 Helsinki, Finland
Tel: (0)9 75144200
Fax: (0)9 75144240
E-mail: puoluetoimisto@keskusta.fi
Internet: www.keskusta.fi

Centre Party (Norway)

The Centre Party, or Senterpartiet, is a liberal green party in Norway. Founded in 1920, it was originally an agrarian party which defended rural interests. Today it is a party which promotes personal responsibility, community and solidarity and the responsible use of natural resources. It seeks to expand political participation and to decentralize power, guaranteeing equal living conditions for all citizens. The party campaigned against Norway's membership of the **European Union** in both 1972 and 1994. The Centre Party participated in a coalition government with the Liberals and the Christian Democrats in 1997–2000. It had six cabinet ministers and 11 members of parliament. The party currently occupies 10 seats in the 165-seat **Stortinget**.

Leadership: Pres. Åslaug Haga; *Gen. Sec.* Dagfinn Sundsbø
Address: POB 6734, St Olavs plass, 0130 Oslo, Norway
Tel: (0)22-98-96-00
Fax: (0)22-98-96-10
E-mail: epost@senterpartiet.no
Internet: www.senterpartiet.no

Centre Party (Sweden)

The Centre Party, or Centerpartiet, is a social liberal party covering the centre-ground of politics in Sweden. It originated in 1913 as the Agrarian Union which represented rural and farmers' interests and changed its name to the Centre Party in 1958. It promotes the free market and social responsibility and its policy is based on the ideology of ecohumanism: that people have equal rights, but that these must be organized to be compatible with environmental concerns. The party supports local-level democracy and a bottom-up **European Union**. The party is opposed to Sweden's membership of the **euro**.

The party has been represented in the **Riksdag** since 1918. It governed with the **Social Democratic Party** in the 1950s and in the non-socialist coalitions in 1976–81, with party leader Thorbjörn Fälldin as Prime Minister, and again in 1991–94. At present the Centerpartiet has 22 representatives in the 349-member Riksdag that was elected on 15 September 2002.

Party Leader: Maud Olofsson
Address: Stora Nygatan 4, Gamla Stan, 111 27 Stockholm, Sweden
Tel: (0)8 617-38-00
Fax: (0)8 617-38-10
E-mail: centerpartiet@centerpartiet.se
Internet: www.centerpartiet.se

Chambre des Députés

Chamber of Deputies

The Chambre des Députés (Chamber of Deputies) is the unicameral parliament of Luxembourg. It is made up of 60 members who are elected by a system of proportional representation for a five-year term. All legislative power is vested in the Chambre des Députés. It is advised in the drafting of legislation by the **Conseil d'État**. In the current parliament that was elected on 13 June 2004 six parties are represented. These are (number of seats in brackets) the **Christian Social People's Party** (24), the **Democratic Party** (10), the **Luxembourg Socialist Workers' Party** (14), the **Action Committee for Democracy and Pension Rights** (5), and the **Green Party** (7). At present 12 members, 20% of the total, are **women**.

Address: Hôtel de la Chambre des Députés, 9 rue du Saint-Esprit, L-1475
     Luxembourg
Tel: (0)466-966-1
Fax: (0)22-02-30
E-mail: info@chd.lu
Internet: www.chd.lu

Channel Islands

The Channel Islands are a group of islands—Jersey, Guernsey, Alderney, Herm and Sark—situated off the north-west coast of France. The islands are British dependencies, but are not part of the United Kingdom. They are self-governing and each has a legislative assembly. The Channel Islands were the only part of British soil that was occupied by Germany in the Second World War from 1940 until 1945.

The Channel Islands cover a total of 194 sq km and have a population of 90,502 (Jersey) and 65,031 (Guernsey). The economy is based predominantly on financial services such as banking, fund management and insurance, which account for 55%–60% of income. Taxation and death duties are low and the Channel Islands are considered a 'tax haven'. Tourism and **agriculture** are other important industries.

Chirac, Jacques

Jacques Chirac has been President of France since May 1995. A Gaullist, Chirac reformed his party as the **Rally for the Republic** in 1976 and is now a member of the **Popular Movement**. He was first elected as President for a seven-year term in May 1995 with 52.64% of votes cast in the second round of polling, when his opponent was the **Socialist Party (PS)** candidate, Lionel Jospin. Chirac was elected for a second term in May 2002 for a shorter five-year term (a referendum in 2000 reduced the term of the presidency) despite unpopularity caused by his decision to test nuclear weapons beneath Mururoa Atoll in French Polynesia, and financial scandals dating back to his 18 years (1977–95) as mayor of Paris. However, the poor performance of the PS candidate in the first round of polling placed the **National Front** candidate, **Jean-Marie Le Pen**, in second place. In the second round of voting Chirac obtained 82.21% of the votes cast in a united front against Le Pen. Since 2002 his popularity has risen again in France, in particular as a result of his clear statement of opposition to war in **Iraq** in 2003. He was nominated for the 2003 Nobel Peace Prize.

Born on 29 November 1932 in Paris, Chirac studied at the Institute of Political Science in Paris and at the Ecole Nationale d'Administration. Since 1965 he has held a variety of political offices at local, regional, national and European level. He was State Secretary for Social Affairs in 1967, State Secretary for Economy and Finance in 1968–71, Minister for Agriculture and Rural Development in 1972–74 and Minister for the Interior in 1974. He was appointed as Prime Minister in 1974 but resigned in 1976, and served again in 1986–88 in a period of **cohabitation**. Jacques Chirac is married to Bernadette Chodron de Courcel and has two children.

Address: Palais de l'Elysée, 55 rue du Faubourg Saint-Honoré, 75008 Paris, France
Tel: (0)1-42-92-81-00
E-mail: via www.elysee.fr/ecrire/mail.htm
Internet: www.elysee.fr

Chrëstlech Sozial Vollekspartei – *see* **Christian Social People's Party, Luxembourg**

Christelijk Nationaal Vakverbond – *see* **National Federation of Christian Trade Unions, Netherlands**

Christen Democratisch Appèl – *see* **Christian Democratic Appeal, Netherlands**

Christen-Democratisch en Vlaams – *see* **Flemish Christian Democrats, Belgium**

Christenunie – *see* **Christian Union, Netherlands**

Christian Democratic Appeal

Christian Democratic Appeal, or Christen Democratisch Appèl (CDA), is the centre-right party which has dominated politics in the Netherlands. Founded in 1980 through a fusion of three confessional parties, the CDA or its constituent parties took part in all governments in 1917–94. Following significant electoral losses in 1994 the CDA was excluded from government for the first time in its history. It re-emerged as the largest party in the **Tweede Kamer** in the elections of 15 May 2002. It returned to government forming a coalition with **List Pim Fortuyn** and the **People's Party for Freedom and Democracy**. In the most recent elections to the Tweede Kamer, held on 22 January 2003, the party won 44 of the 150 parliamentary seats, thus gaining the status of largest party. It formed a coalition government with the People's Party for Freedom and Democracy and **Democrats 66** under CDA Prime Minister **Jan Balkenende**.

Chair.: Marja van Bijsterveldt
Address: Dr Kuyperstraat 5, POB 30453, 2500 GL The Hague, Netherlands
Tel: (0)70 3424888
Fax: (0)70 3643417
E-mail: cda@bureau.cda.nl
Internet: www.cda.nl

Christian Democratic Party

The Christian Democratic Party, or Christlichdemokratische Volkspartei (CVP), in Switzerland was founded as the Schweizerische Konservative Volkspartei (Swiss Conservative Party) in 1912. It became the Konservativ-Christlichsoziale

Volkspartei (Conservative Christian Party) in 1957 and the CVP in 1970. The party seeks to preserve the national unity of Switzerland. It favours a social market economy, promotes the status of families and children and the integration of immigrants in Swiss society. The CVP has traditionally had two ministers in the permanent seven-seat coalition which has existed since 1959. However, its representation was reduced to one minister following the **Nationalrat** election of 19 October 2003. The CVP's representation fell at that election from 35 to 28 seats, while the **Swiss People's Party (SVP)** increased the number of seats it occupied from 44 to 55. The SVP made the case that its representation in the coalition should be increased to two seats. This was granted at the expense of the CVP.

Leadership: Pres. Doris Leuthard; *Gen. Sec.* Reto Nause
Address: Klaraweg 6, Postfach 5835, 3001 Bern, Switzerland
Tel: (0)313573333
Fax: (0)313522430
E-mail: info@cvp.ch
Internet: www.cvp.ch

Christian Democratic Union

The Christian Democratic Union, or Christlich-Demokratische Union (CDU), is a non-denominational Christian party in Germany. Founded in 1945 initially as a series of regional-level organizations, the party developed a broad appeal as a people's party (*Volkspartei*). Following the fall of the **Berlin Wall** in 1989, the party rapidly merged with the East German Christian Democrats and won broad support among the East German population. The CDU promotes the free development of individuals and the role of families in society. It supports the social market economy and the **welfare state**, but places more emphasis on the role of the market than of the state. The party is also committed to the project of European integration and advocates both a deepening and widening of the **European Union** in order to secure freedom, peace and economic prosperity in the continent.

The CDU dominated post-war German politics at national level until 1998. The CDU governed in coalitions with the **Free Democratic Party** in 1949–56 and 1961–66 under Konrad Adenauer and Ludwig Erhard and in 1982–98 under **Helmut Kohl**. The party also governed with the **Social Democratic Party of Germany (SPD)** in a Grand Coalition in 1966–69.

Since 1998 the CDU has been the leading opposition party in the **Bundestag**. In the most recent federal elections, held on 22 September 2002, the CDU together with the **Christian Social Union** won the same percentage of the vote as the SPD (38.5%), but it obtained three fewer seats (190). On account of its success in regional (*Land*)-level elections the party currently dominates the **Bundesrat** and has been able to veto legislation passed by the Bundestag. The current party leader, Angela Merkel, is the first woman and the first East German to hold this post.

Party Leader: Angela Merkel
Address: Klingelhöferstrasse 8, 10785 Berlin, Germany
Tel: (0)30 220700
Fax: (0)30 22070111
E-mail: post@cdu.de
Internet: www.cdu.de

Christian Democrats (Finland)

The Christian Democrats, or Kristillisdemokraatit, is a small political party in Finland. Founded in 1958, it promotes Christian democratic ideals in public and political life. The party first gained representation in the **Eduskunta** in 1970. In the most recent elections, held on 16 March 2003, the party gained 5.3% of the vote and obtained seven seats in the 200-seat parliament.

Leadership: Party Leader Päivi Räsänen; *Gen. Sec.* Annika Kokko
Address: 7th Floor, Karjalankatu 2c, 00520 Helsinki, Finland
Tel: (0)9 34882200
Fax: (0)9 34882228
E-mail: kd@kristillisdemokraatit.fi
Internet: www.kristillisdemokraatit.fi

Christian Democrats (Sweden)

The Christian Democrats, or Kristdemokraterna, are a small Christian democratic party in Sweden. Established in 1964, it gained its first seat in the **Riksdag** in 1985 when it co-operated with the **Centre Party**. The party has been represented in the national parliament continually since 1991 and it took part in the four-party non-socialist coalition government in 1991–94. The party promotes autonomy and self-determination for families and communities. It also promotes the principle of subsidiarity. The Christian Democrats currently have 33 representatives in the 349-seat parliament that was elected on 15 September 2002.

Party Leader: Göran Hägglund
Address: Munkbron 1, 111 28 Stockholm or POB 451, 103 18 Stockholm,
　　　　　Sweden
Tel: (0)8 723-25-00
Fax: (0)8 723-25-10
E-mail: brev.till@kristdemokrat.se
Internet: www.kristdemokraterna.se

Christian People's Party

The Christian People's Party, or Kristelig Folkeparti (KrF), is a centre-right political party in Norway. Founded in 1933, the party campaigns to promote Christian values in Norwegian politics. At the most recent elections to the **Stortinget**, held on 10 September 2001, the KrF won 22 seats in the 165-seat parliament. Together with the **Conservative Party** and the **Liberal Party** it formed a minority coalition government, of which **Kjell Magne Bondevik** of the KrF is Prime Minister. The KrF had previously participated in six coalition governments since 1963 and had led two under, respectively, Lars Korvald, in 1972–73, and Kjell Magne Bondevik, in 1997–2000.

Party Leader: Dagfinn Høybråten
Address: Øvre Slottsgate 18–20, POB Sentrum, 0105 Oslo, Norway
Tel: (0)23-10-28-00
Fax: (0)23-10-28-10
E-mail: krf@krf.no
Internet: www.krf.no

Christian Social People's Party

The Christian Social People's Party, or Chrëstlech Sozial Vollekspartei (CSV), is a large political party in Luxembourg which has dominated politics in the post-war era. The CSV dates back to 1914, but was officially founded in 1944 and won 25 of 51 seats in the 1945 elections to the **Chambre des Députés**. It led all coalition governments in 1946–74 with either the **Luxembourg Socialist Workers' Party (LSAP)** or the liberal **Democratic Party**. Following a short period in opposition in 1974–79, it has led all coalition governments since 1979 under the leadership, successively, of Pierre Werner (1979–84), Jacques Santer (1984–95) and, since 1995, **Jean-Claude Juncker**. At the most recent elections, held on 13 June 2002, the party won 24 seats in the 60-seat parliament and formed a coalition with LSAP.

Party Leader: François Biltgen
Address: POB 826, 2018 Luxembourg
Tel: (0)22-57-31-1
Fax: (0)47-27-16
E-mail: csv@csv.lu
Internet: www.csv.lu

Christian Social Union

The Christian Social Union, or Christlich-Soziale Union (CSU), is the Christian party in Bavaria, Germany, and the sister-party of the **Christian Democratic Union (CDU)**. Founded in 1945, the party campaigns to strengthen the voice of Bavaria within Germany and the **European Union (EU)**. The CSU seeks to preserve the *Heimat* traditions of Bavaria but to make use of new technologies to increase the competitiveness and wealth of the *Land*, or state. The party supports the social market economy and the values of freedom and self-determination. It has campaigned to strengthen the role of the regions in the EU.

The CSU has dominated politics in Bavaria in the post-war period. There has been a CSU regional (*Land*) government and Minister President for all but three years in that period (1946–54 and since 1957) and the party has had an absolute majority in the Bavarian parliament for more than 30 years. In federal elections the CSU campaigns together with the CDU and the parties have an agreement not to challenge each other's candidates. The parties campaign with a single candidate for the chancellorship and form a joint parliamentary group in the **Bundestag**. They are referred to together as the Union. The party won 58 seats in the Bundestag elected on 22 September 2002. The CSU has twice put forward candidates for the chancellorship of the Union: Franz Josef Strauss in 1980 and Edmund Stoiber in 2002. Neither was successful, however.

Party Leader: Edmund Stoiber
Address: Franz-Josef Strauss-Haus, Nymphenburger Strasse 64, 80335 München, Germany
Tel: (0)89 12430
Fax: (0)89 1243299
E-mail: info@csu-bayern.de
Internet: www.csu.de

Christian Union

The Christian Union, or ChristenUnie, is a new Christian party in the Netherlands. It was established in 2000 when two existing parties (the Reformed Political Union and Evangelical Political Federation) unified. The party aims to represent Christian views on politics and society in local and national politics and it seeks to promote co-operation between Christian movements at European level. In the general election of 22 January 2003 the party won three seats in the 150-seat **Tweede Kamer**.

Party Leader: Thijs van Daalen
Address: Puntenburgerlaan 91, 3812 CC Amersfoort, or POB 439, 3800 AK Amersfoort, Netherlands
Tel: (0)33 4226969
Fax: (0)33 4226968
E-mail: bureau@christenunie.nl
Internet: www.christenunie.nl

Christlich-Demokratische Union – *see* Christian Democratic Union, Germany

Christlichdemokratische Volkspartei – *see* Christian Democratic Party, Switzerland

Christlich-Soziale Union – *see* Christian Social Union, Germany

Churchill, Winston

Winston Churchill was a politician and statesman in the United Kingdom. He is best known as Prime Minister of the coalition government of 1940–45 during the Second World War, when he won admiration for his determination and tireless efforts to secure the defeat of Nazi Germany. In the early post-war era, in 1946, he advocated building 'a kind of United States of Europe', founded on a close partnership between Germany and France (but not the United Kingdom), and he warned in the same year of the emerging **Cold War** in Europe, observing that 'an iron curtain has descended across the Continent'.

Born on 30 November 1874 at Blenheim Palace, Oxfordshire, Winston Churchill graduated from the Royal Military College at Sandhurst and joined the Fourth Hussars in 1895. He saw battle during military service and as a war correspondent before first being elected to the **House of Commons** in 1900 for the **Conservative Party**. In 1904 switched to the Liberal Party, but rejoined the Conservatives in 1924. Churchill held a series of ministerial posts, including First Lord of the Admiralty (1911–16) and Chancellor of the Exchequer (1924–29). He was reappointed to the post of First Lord of the Admiralty in 1939 and, following the resignation of Neville Chamberlain in 1940, became Prime Minister and Minister of Defence of an all-party coalition. Churchill had been critical of Chamberlain's policy of appeasement towards Nazi Germany prior to 1939 and insisted on Hitler's unconditional surrender during the Second World War. While preparing Britain to fight alone against Germany, Churchill also developed a relationship with the USA, securing economic and military aid from that country.

In the first post-war election, held in July 1945, Churchill was replaced as Prime Minister by Clement Attlee of the **Labour Party**. He was re-elected as Prime Minister in 1951 but, having suffered a stroke in 1953, he retired from politics in 1955. Churchill's career as a parliamentarian had spanned the reigns of six monarchs. He was also an accomplished artist and a prolific writer, who was awarded the Nobel Prize for Literature in 1953. He said in November 1949, 'Writing a book was an adventure. To begin with it was a toy, an amusement; then it became a mistress, and then a master and then a tyrant. The last phase is that just as you are about to be reconciled to your servitude, you kill the monster, and fling him out to the public.' Winston Churchill died on 24 January 1965. He was married to Clementine Hozier and they had five children.

Ciampi, Carlo Azeglio

Carlo Azeglio Ciampi has been President of Italy since 13 May 1999. He was elected for a seven-year term, having obtained 70% of the vote (a two-thirds' majority is required) in the first round of voting by the parliamentary electoral college composed of the **Camera dei Deputati** and the **Senato della Repubblica** plus 58 regional representatives. Prior to this he had been Prime Minister of Italy (1993–94), overseeing a transition government, and then treasury minister (1996–99). He is credited with ensuring that Italy met the **convergence criteria** for membership of **Economic and Monetary Union**. As President, Ciampi refused in December 2003 to sign a communications bill sponsored by Prime Minister **Silvio Berlusconi** that had passed through the Italian parliament, on the grounds that it reversed a ruling of the **Constitutional Court**.

Born on 9 December 1920 in Livorno, Ciampi was awarded a degree in literature from the Scuola Normale Superiore of Pisa and a law degree from the University of Pisa. After three years serving in the Italian army in 1941–44, Ciampi joined the **Banca d'Italia** in 1946. From 1960 he worked as an economist and head of the research department of the central bank before becoming secretary-general in 1973, deputy director-general in 1976 and director-general, also in 1976. He also became deputy chairman of the Italian Foreign Exchange Office in 1976. Ciampi served as governor of the Banca d'Italia in 1979–93. He is married and has two children.

Address: Palazzo del Quirinale, 00187 Rome, Italy
Tel: (0)06 46991
Fax: (0)06 46993125
E-mail: presidenza.repubblica@quirinale.it
Internet: www.quirinale.it

Citizenship

Citizenship as an idea was revived in the 1980s. In Western Europe and North America there was a growing concern that Western individualism and consumerist lifestyles had eroded the importance of political community. In the face of new questions being raised by feminist and ecological movements, declining levels of political participation and the erosion of **welfare state** provision, there was an increasing concern to introduce a more explicitly moral language into the everyday practice of politics. In the state socialist societies of Central and Eastern Europe, questions of citizenship were also raised in connection with the imposition of state control, the exclusion of civil society and neglect of political rights. In their different ways these academic and political debates sought to recover a language of belonging, rights and obligation.

First, citizenship is concerned with questions of membership and is therefore both inclusive and exclusive. By definition, discussions of British and/or European citizenship do not include non-British or non-European citizens. In this respect, this necessitates decisions as to who is to count as a member. For example, recent debates regarding refugees have involved a discussion of citizenship in terms of the procedures which must be successfully negotiated if one is to be granted the legal status of citizen. However, questions of belonging have been further complicated recently, with some social movements arguing for a global citizenship which potentially includes all inhabitants of the planet earth. Even here decisions have to be made in respect of the status of children and the environment, as well as the weight that should be given to future generations.

Second, ideas of citizenship are often discussed in terms of rights. To have a right means to be able to make a claim on something. In its initial conception citizenship was thought to be a three-tiered model that included civil, political and social rights. Civil rights might include equality before the law and political rights freedom of assembly and the intellectual freedoms associated with supporting political parties. Yet, it has been social rights that the labour and trade union movements of the 20th century have been most concerned to protect and extend. The right to a good education, welfare benefits and health-care all had to be struggled for in the face of opposition. The breakdown of the post-war political consensus in respect of social rights has meant that this domain has become increasingly contested in recent years. The privatization of public services and welfare functions currently constitutes a key area of dispute in respect of citizenship rights. Further, many previously marginal social groups are seeking to claim cultural as well as social, political and civil rights. Cultural rights are usually concerned with the desire to have one's lifestyle recognized by the wider community. Such claims have been raised by a number of cultural 'minorities' which wish to maintain their way of life in the face of opposition or criticism from the mainstream community.

Finally, the language of obligation or duties has been central to questions of citizenship. Many argue that rights and duties are actually inseparable and that it makes little sense to have rights to welfare without the duty to pay taxes. Indeed, many critics have pointed out that Western liberal societies have forgotten the language of obligation which has in turn promoted social atomism. In particular, the ecological movement has sought to introduce a rich political language of a duty of care in respect of the environment. In this context, to be overly concerned with our entitlements or rights will mean that current political and lifestyle practices will be insufficiently concerned with our obligations towards non-human organisms, our common environment and potential citizens of the future.

Nick Stevenson
University of Nottingham

Coalición Canaria – *see* Canarian Coalition, Spain

Coalition of the Left of Movements and the Ecology

The Coalition of the Left of Movements and the Ecology, or Synaspismos, is a new left-wing party in Greece. Founded in 1992 as the Coalition of the Left and Progress, it is an electoral coalition of left-wing and progressive parties and movements. The party changed its name to Coalition of the Left of Movements and the Ecology in 2003. It campaigns for the ideas and values of democratic socialism, ecology, feminism and anti-militarism. In the most recent national elections to the **Vouli ton Ellinon**, held on 7 March 2004, the party won 3.3% of the vote and six seats in the 300-seat parliament.

Pres.: Alexandros Alavanos
Address: 1 Eleftherias Sq., 105 53 Athens, Greece
Tel: (0)210 3378400
Fax: (0)210 3219914
E-mail: grammateia@syn.gr
Internet: www.syn.gr

Coastal Party

The Coastal Party, or Kystpartiet, is a small agrarian political party in Norway. Founded in 1999, it campaigns to protect the Norwegian coastline and the rights of fishermen and whalers. In the most recent general elections, held on 10 September 2001, the Coastal Party won one seat in the 165-seat **Stortinget**.

Party Leader: Steinar Bastesen
Address: Ytre Høgåsvei 26, 8900 Brønnøysund, Norway
Tel: (0)75-02-06-93
Fax: (0)75-02-14-50
E-mail: post@kystpartiet.no
Internet: www.kystpartiet.no

Cohabitation

Cohabitation is the term used to describe the situation in French politics that occurs when the President and the government represent opposing parties. This phenomenon occurs because there are separate elections for the President and the **Assemblée Nationale**. During periods of cohabitation the power of the executive President is reduced and that of the Prime Minister enhanced.

There have been three periods of cohabitation in France's Fifth Republic (1958–). The first was in 1986–88 between the socialist President **François Mitterrand** and a right-wing government under the leadership of **Jacques Chirac**. In the years 1993–95 there was a second period of cohabitation when François Mitterrand was President and Edouard Balladur was Prime Minister. Finally, in 1997–2002 there was a period of cohabitation between a right-wing President, Chirac, and a socialist government under the leadership of Lionel Jospin.

Cold War

The Cold War describes the situation in international relations that lasted from the end of the Second World War in 1945 until 1989/90. It was characterized by an ideological conflict between communism and capitalism, and between the two dominant economic and military powers at the time, the Soviet Union (USSR) and the USA. The era of the Cold War is described as bipolar since during that time many states aligned themselves with the political and economic ideologies of one or the other of the two opposing blocs.

The continent of Europe was split in two by the Cold War. Already by 1946 **Winston Churchill** described an 'iron curtain' dividing Europe. Broadly, the continent was divided between the capitalist states of Western Europe, which were allied to the USA, and the communist **Central and Eastern Europe Countries (CEECs)**, which were referred to as satellite states of the USSR. More drastically, Germany was divided in 1949–90 into two ideologically distinct states: the Federal Republic of Germany (FRG—West Germany) and the **German Democratic Republic** (GDR—East Germany). The **Berlin Wall** and the closed border between the two states became an iconic symbol of the Cold War in Europe.

Western Europe's response to the perceived threat of communism was, economically, to pool resources through the process of European integration into what is now the **European Union (EU)**, and militarily to participate in the western alliance, the **North Atlantic Treaty Organization (NATO)**. However, during the Cold War a number of neutral states remained outside of the EU (e.g. Austria, Finland, Sweden) and NATO (e.g. Austria, Ireland, Finland and Sweden).

The Cold War ended in the late 1980s following a change in policy by the communist regime in the USSR under Mikhail Gorbachev. This brought change domestically, through the policies of *perestroika* (restructuring) and *glasnost* (openness), and also in terms of foreign policy as the USSR decided to no longer intervene in the domestic conflicts of satellite states (the Brezhnev Doctrine). In Europe, the end of the Cold War was marked by a series of revolutions in 1989 in Central and Eastern Europe, symbolized by the fall of the Berlin Wall on 9 November 1989. The communist regimes of many CEEC states were rapidly transformed into capitalist liberal democracies, and the GDR unified with the FRG on 3 October 1990.

In the post-Cold War era the continent of Europe has been both reunited and divided by conflict. Following the end of the ideological conflict three neutral western European states joined the EU and eight former communist states of Central and Eastern Europe became members on 1 May 2004. However, in south-eastern Europe, the break-up of communist Yugoslavia led to widespread conflict and ethnic cleansing. In the post-Cold War era a new conflict in international relations is emerging between freedom and security, whereby liberal democracies feel justified in defending their values against the threat—perceived or real—of conflict, **terrorism** and 'rogue' states. For example, NATO dispatched troops to defend human rights during the **Kosovo** crisis in 1999, and the USA led a war against **Iraq** in 2003, having accused that country of possessing weapons of mass destruction.

Common Foreign and Security Policy (CFSP)

The Common Foreign and Security Policy (CFSP) was established in 1992 by the **Treaty on European Union** as the second **pillar** of the **European Union (EU)**. It was further developed by the **Treaty of Amsterdam** (1997) and the **Treaty of Nice** (2001). The EU had been slow to develop a common foreign policy to match its economic profile with an international political presence. CFSP brought two important new elements into the process of European integration.

Prior to 1992 EU member states sought to consult each other on major international issues through European Political Co-operation (ECP), which was established in 1970. ECP was later formalized in the **Single European Act** (1996) but remained reactive and weak. It proved hard to develop a more institutionalized foreign and security policy because of the unique nature of the EU: it is not a state, but a union of national entities each with distinct sovereignties, identities and 'special' international relationships with other states or regions. The impetus towards a stronger and more institutionalized common foreign policy for Europe developed in the early 1990s as a result of the changing global security climate following the end of the **Cold War** and the emergence of new conflicts in south-east Europe.

The aim of CFSP is to match the EU's clout in international trade with a presence in the international political community. It seeks to define and implement foreign and security policy positions for the EU and to develop a common defence policy. It exists to protect the common values, interests, independence and integrity of the EU and to develop democracy, the rule of law, respect for human rights and basic freedoms and to strengthen the security of the Union, preserve peace and strengthen international security and co-operation.

CFSP is an intergovernmental area of policy-making. While the **European Commission** is fully associated with CFSP, it does not have the exclusive right to refer foreign policy matters to the **Council of the European Union**. The **European Council** sets the policy principles and general guide-lines of CFSP. It decides unanimously on common strategies which are implemented by the EU. The CFSP cannot use legal instruments such as directives or regulations. The main policy instruments are: common positions, joint actions, decisions and the conclusion of international agreements. The Council of the European Union formulates and implements CFSP policy following the guide-lines set by the European Council and it also ensures that the EU's CFSP is coherent. The member state which holds the rotating presidency of the EU represents the EU internationally in CFSP matters and is responsible for implementing policy.

The Treaty of Amsterdam introduced some elements of qualified majority voting (QMV) into the implementation of CFSP; since then joint actions and common positions can be decided by QMV. A member state may block a decision made by QMV for important reasons of national policy. Also, a state has the possibility to offer 'constructive abstention' and a formal declaration; it can refrain from voting and is not required to apply the decision, but it must recognize that it is binding on the EU. The Treaty of Amsterdam also introduced the post of CFSP high representative in order to give CFSP a higher and more visible profile. The high representative is the incumbent of the post of secretary-general of the Council of the European Union. His role is to assist the Council in the formulation and implementation of CFSP decisions. The first occupant of this post is **Javier Solana**; he was appointed for a five-year term in October 1999, and was reappointed in June 2004 for a second term.

Progress towards closer defence co-operation remains harder to achieve than CFSP because of the very different defence interests of member states. However, the Treaty of Amsterdam and the Treaty of Nice developed this aspect of the EU's activities and provided the EU with a common **European Security and Defence Policy**.

Commonwealth

The Commonwealth of Nations established in 1965 is a voluntary organization of 53 states which were formerly British colonies. The Commonwealth Realm is made up of 16 states of the Commonwealth that still consider Queen Elizabeth II to be their head of state. The Harare Declaration of 1991 committed the organization to democracy and good government, and allowed for action to be taken against members which breached these principles. Before then the Commonwealth's collective actions had been limited by the principle of non-interference in the internal affairs of other members. Fiji, Pakistan, Nigeria and Zimbabwe have all been suspended from the Commonwealth of Nations for failing to uphold democratic government. The British Commonwealth has a total population of 1,800m., 30% of the world's population, and covers one-quarter of the world's land mass.

> *Sec.-Gen.:* Don McKinnon
> *Address:* The Commonwealth Secretariat, Marlborough House, Pall Mall, London SW1Y 5HX, United Kingdom
> *Tel:* (0)20 7747 6500
> *Fax:* (0)20 7930 0827
> *E-mail:* info@commonwealth.int
> *Internet:* www.thecommonwealth.org

Communist Party of France

The Communist Party of France, or Parti Communiste Français (PCF), was founded in 1920 following a split in the **Socialist Party (PS)**. It was a major political force in France until the 1970s, winning 28.8% of the vote in the elections to the **Assemblée Nationale** in 1946 and around 20% of the vote in subsequent elections held over the next 20 years. In the 1960s the PCF distanced itself from Soviet communism and in the 1970s adopted Eurocommunism in an attempt to broaden its appeal.

The PCF entered into a coalition government with the PS in 1981 but left it in 1984. It also governed in two multi-party coalitions led by PS Prime Minister Lionel Jospin, in 1997–2000 and 2000–02. Despite this, in electoral terms the party has been in steady decline since the 1980s on account of a shrinking industrial working class and the collapse of Soviet communism. In the most recent general elections, held on 9 and 16 June 2002, the PCF won 4.8% of the vote and 21 seats in the 577-seat Assemblée Nationale. In the first round of the most recent presidential elections, held on 21 April 2002, the PCF candidate, Robert Hue, obtained only 3.4% of the vote.

Party Leader: Marie-George Buffet
Address: 2 place du Colonel Fabien, 75019 Paris, France
Tel: (0)1-40-40-12-12
Fax: (0)1-40-40-13-56
E-mail: pcf@pcf.fr
Internet: www.pcf.fr

Communist Party of Greece

The Communist Party of Greece, or Kommounistiko Komma Ellados (KKE), was founded in November 1918. It was, except for a few periods, a banned party until the end of the military dictatorship in 1974. KKE campaigns for Greek working people and has the ultimate goal of transforming Greek society through the elimination of capitalism and the construction of socialism and communism. It opposes Greece's membership of the **North Atlantic Treaty Organization** and the **European Union**. The KKE joined the Coalition of the Left and Progress (since 2003 **Coalition of the Left of Movements and the Ecology**) in 1989, but left it in 1991. In the most recent national elections to the **Vouli ton Ellinon**, held on 7 March 2004, the party won 5.9% of the vote and 12 seats in the 300-seat parliament.

Gen. Sec.: Aleka Paparigha
Address: 145 Leof. Irakliou, 142 31 Nea Ionia-Athens, Greece
Tel: (0)210 2592111
Fax: (0)210 2592298
E-mail: cpg@kke.gr
Internet: www.kke.gr

Communist Party of Portugal

The Communist Party of Portugal, or Partido Comunista Português (PCP), was founded in 1921 from the **General Confederation of Portuguese Workers** Intersindical trade union. A Marxist-Leninist party, it campaigns to build socialism and communism in Portugal. In the most recent general elections, held on 20 February 2005, the PCP won 12 seats in the 230-member **Assembléia da República**.

Sec.-Gen.: Jerónimo de Sousa
Address: Rua Soeiro Pereira Gomes 3, 1600-196 Lisbon, Portugal
Tel: (0)21 7813800
Fax: (0)21 7969126
E-mail: pcp@pcp.pt
Internet: www.pcp.pt

Communist Refoundation Party

The Communist Refoundation Party, or Rifondazione Comunista, was founded in 1991 when the Italian Communist Party changed its name to the Party of the Democratic Left (Partito Democratico della Sinistra), later the Democrats of the Left, or Democratici di Sinistra. The Communist Refoundation Party was formed by Communists who opposed the reorientation of the party. It campaigns today on an anti-globalization platform. At the most recent general election, held on 13 May 2001, the Communist Refoundation Party won 11 seats in the 630-seat **Camera dei Deputati**.

> *Party Leader:* Fausto Bertinotti
> *Address:* Viale del Policlinico 131, 00161 Rome, Italy
> *Tel:* (0)06 441821
> *Fax:* (0)06 44182286
> *E-mail:* internazionale@rifondazione.it
> *Internet:* www.rifondazione.it

Confederação Geral dos Trabalhadores Portugueses-Intersindical Nacional – *see* General Confederation of Portuguese Workers Intersindical

Confederação da Indústria Portuguesa – *see* Confederation of Portuguese Industry

Confederación Española de Organizaciones Empresariales – *see* Spanish Confederation of Employers' Organizations

Confederación Sindical de Comisiones Obreras – *see* Trade Union Confederation of Workers' Commissions, Spain

Confederated Ecologists for the Organization of Original Struggles

The Confederated Ecologists for the Organization of Original Struggles, or Ecologistes Confédérés pour l'Organisation de Luttes Originales (ECOLO), is the French-speaking green party in Belgium. Founded in 1980, the party campaigns to protect national resources in the Belgian and global economy and to promote social and political inclusion. ECOLO first campaigned in national elections in 1981, winning 5% of the vote and two seats in the **Kamer**. In the 1999 election ECOLO was the third largest party in the Walloon region and subsequently entered into a liberal-led coalition under **Guy Verhofstadt**, which included the Flemish Green Party and the **Socialist Party**. In the most recent election, held on 18 May 2003, ECOLO won only 3.1% of the vote and four seats in the 150-seat Kamer and was not invited to enter into a second coalition.

Party Leader: Jean-Michel Javaux
Address: avenue Marlagne 52, 5000 Namur, Belgium
Tel: (0)81 22-78-71
Fax: (0)81 23-06-03
E-mail: info@ecolo.be
Internet: www.ecolo.be

Confédération Française Démocratique du Travail – *see* French Democratic Labour Confederation

Confédération Française des Travailleurs Chrétiens – *see* French Christian Workers' Confederation

Confédération Générale du Travail – *see* General Confederation of Labour, France

Confédération Générale du Travail-Force Ouvrière – *see* General Confederation of Labour-'Force Ouvrière', France

Confederation of British Industry (CBI)

The Confederation of British Industry (CBI) is the business and employers' organization in the United Kingdom. Founded in 1965, it lobbies nationally and internationally to improve the economic environment for business in the United Kingdom and provides an information service for its members. The CBI covers some 4m. employees organized in businesses and 6m. employees across trade associations. The CBI is itself a member of the **Union of Industrial and Employers' Confederations of Europe**.

Leadership: Pres. John Sutherland; *Dir-Gen.* Digby Jones
Address: Centre Point, 103 New Oxford St, London WC1A 1DU, United
        Kingdom
Tel: (0)20 7379 7400
Fax: (0)20 7497 2596
E-mail: enquiry.desk@cbi.org.uk
Internet: www.cbi.org.uk

Confederation of Danish Industries

The Confederation of Danish Industries, or Dansk Industri (DI), is the employers' organization for all 'competition-oriented companies' in Denmark. It comprises some 6,100 members who are organized into 24 employers' associations. DI lobbies nationally and internationally for business-friendly legislation and regulation and negotiates collective wage agreements with Danish trade unions. It is a member of the Dansk Arbejdgiverforening, the **Danish Employers' Confederation**, and the **Union of Industrial and Employers' Confederations of Europe**.

Dir-Gen.: Hans Skov Christensen
Address: H. C. Andersen Blvd 18, 1787 Copenhagen V, Denmark
Tel: (0)33-77-33-77
Fax: (0)33-77-33-00
E-mail: di@di.dk
Internet: www.di.dk

Confederation of Finnish Industry

The Confederation of Finnish Industry, or Elinkeinoelämän Keskusliitto (EK), is the business organization in Finland for all private-sector companies that was founded in January 2005. EK represents around 15,000 member companies which are organized into some 41 branch associations. It lobbies nationally and internationally for its members and to promote competitiveness and the status of Finnish business in the international economy. EK also negotiates sectoral wage agreements in the collective bargaining process. It is a member of the **Union of Industrial and Employers' Confederations of Europe**.

Leadership: Pres. Christoffer Taxell; *Dir-Gen.* Leif Fasagernä
Address: Eteläranta 10, 00131 Helsinki, Finland
Tel: (0)9 42020
Fax: (0)9 42022299
E-mail: ek@ek.fi
Internet: www.ek.fi

Confederation of German Employers' Associations

The Confederation of German Employers' Associations, or Bundesvereinigung der deutschen Arbeitgeberverbände (BDA), is the employers' association in Germany. Its members are organized into regional and interprofessional groups. BDA lobbies nationally and internationally to influence labour market policy and offers services to its members. The BDA is a member of the **Union of Industrial and Employers' Confederations of Europe**.

Leadership: Pres. Peter Hundt; *Dir-Gen.* Reinhard Göhner
Address: Breite Strasse 29, 10178 Berlin, Germany

Tel: (0)30 20330
Fax: (0)30 20331055
E-mail: info@bda-online.de
Internet: www.bda-online.de

Confederation of German Industry

The Confederation of German Industry, or Bundesverband der deutschen Industrie (BDI), is the main business organization in Germany. The BDI lobbies nationally and internationally for an economic environment that favours Germany as an industrial location and promotes the internationalization of German industry. It is also a service provider for German industrial businesses. Its members are organized into 36 branches and it is itself a member of the **Union of Industrial and Employers' Confederations of Europe**.

Leadership: Pres. Jürgen Thumann; *Dir-Gen.* Ludolf von Wartenberg
Address: Breite Strasse 29, 10178 Berlin, Germany
Tel: (0)30 20281 (+ ext)
Fax: (0)30 20282 (+ ext)
E-mail: info@bdi-online.de
Internet: www.bdi-online.de

Confederation of Icelandic Employers

The Confederation of Icelandic Employers, or Samtök Atvinnulifsins (SA), is a service organization for businesses in Iceland. It negotiates collective agreements and lobbies nationally and internationally to promote the competitiveness of Icelandic business. Around 2,600 businesses are organized in seven member associations and SA is itself a member of the **Union of Industrial and Employers' Confederations of Europe**.

Pres.: Ari Edwald
Address: Borgartúni 35, 05 Reykjavík, Iceland
Tel: (0)5910000
Fax: (0)5910050
E-mail: sa@sa.is
Internet: www.sa.is

Confederation of Italian Industry

The Confederation of Italian Industry, or Confederazione Generale dell'Industria Italiana or Confindustria, is the main business organization in Italy. Founded in 1910, today it represents some 117,000 companies in the manufacturing and service industries. It lobbies nationally and internationally to promote free enterprise and economic freedom for Italian companies. It is itself a member of the **Union of Industrial and Employers' Confederations of Europe**.

Leadership: Pres. Luca di Montezemolo; *Dir-Gen.* Maurizio Beretta
Address: Viale dell'Astronomia 30, 00144 Rome, Italy
Tel: (0)06 59031
Fax: (0)06 5919615
E-mail: confindustria@confindustria.it
Internet: www.confindustria.it

Confederation of Netherlands Industry and Employers

The Confederation of Netherlands Industry and Employers, or Vereniging VNO-NCW, is the main business and employers' organization in the Netherlands. Founded in 1996, it is the result of the merger of the Verbond van Nederlandse Ondernemingen (VNO) and the Nederlands Christelijk Werkgeversverbond (NCW). It lobbies nationally and internationally for the interests of its members and acts as a service provider. Its membership comprises some 80,000 enterprises which are organized into 150 branch associations. VNO-NCW is itself a member of the **Union of Industrial and Employers' Confederations of Europe**.

Pres.: Jacques Schraven
Address: Malietoren 12, Bezuidenhoutseweg 2594 AV The Hague, or POB
93002, 2509 The Hague, Netherlands
Tel: (0)70 3490349
Fax: (0)70 3490300
E-mail: informatie@vno-ncw.nl
Internet: www.vno-ncw.nl

Confederation of Norwegian Business and Industry

The Confederation of Norwegian Business and Industry, or Næringslivets Hovedorganisasjon (NHO), is the dominant business organization in Norway, representing around 16,000 member companies. It lobbies nationally and internationally for policies which promote the competitiveness and profitability of the Norwegian economy and its position in the global economy. NHO is itself a member of the **Union of Industrial and Employers' Confederations of Europe**.

Leadership: Pres. Erling Øverland; *Dir-Gen.* Finn Bergsen
Address: Middelthuns gate 27, Majorstuen, Oslo, or POB 5250 Majorstuen, 0303
Oslo, Norway
Tel: (0)23-08-80-00
Fax: (0)23-08-80-01
E-mail: firmapost@nho.no
Internet: www.nho.no

Confederation of Portuguese Industry

The Confederation of Portuguese Industry, or Confederação da Indústria Portuguesa, is a business organization in Portugal. Founded in 1974, it lobbies nationally and internationally on behalf of a wide range of industrial enterprises for a competitive business environment. It is a member of the **Union of Industrial and Employers' Confederations of Europe**.

Leadership: Pres. Juan Gomez Esteves; *Dir-Gen.* Heitor Salgueiro
Address: Av. 5 de Outubro, 35–1, 1069 Lisbon, Portugal
Tel: (0)21 3164700
Fax: (0)21 3579986
E-mail: geral@cip.org.pt
Internet: www.cip.org.pt

Confederation of Professional Employees

The Confederation of Professional Employees, or Tjänstemännens Centralorganisation, is a trade union confederation in Sweden. Founded in 1944, today it represents some 1.2m. members from 18 affiliated trade unions. It works at national and international level to protect the interests of professional workers in the labour market and the **welfare state**, and to promote education in the workplace and a balance between work and family. It is itself a member of **ETUC**.

Pres.: Sture Nordh
Address: Linnégatan 14, 114 94 Stockholm, Sweden
Tel: (0)8 782-91-00
Fax: (0)8 663-75-20
E-mail: info@tco.se
Internet: www.tco.se

Confederation of Public Servants

The Confederation of Public Servants, or Anotati Diiskisis Enoseon Dimosion Ypallion (ADEDY), is the trade union in Greece that represents all public-sector workers. Founded in 1945, today around 70 member organizations are affiliated to ADEDY and it is itself a member of **ETUC**.

Leadership: Pres. Spyros Papaspyros; *Gen. Sec.* Ilias Iliopoulos
Address: 2 Psylla St and Filellinon St, 105 57 Athens, Greece
Tel: (0)210 3246109 or (0)210 3244677
Fax: (0)210 3246165
E-mail: adedyed@otenet.gr
Internet: www.adedy.gr

Confederation of State and Municipal Employees

The Confederation of State and Municipal Employees, or Bandalag Starfsmanna Ríkis og Bæja (BSRB), is the trade union confederation for public service employees in Iceland. BSRB engages in collective bargaining and campaigns to protect the **welfare state** and the public sector. Founded in 1942, BSRB today represents around 18,000 members who are organized in 35 affiliated unions. It is itself a member of **ETUC**.

Pres.: Ögmundur Jónasson
Address: Grettisgötu 89, 105 Reykjavík, Iceland
Tel: (0)5258300
Fax: (0)5258309
E-mail: bsrb@bsrb.is
Internet: www.bsrb.is

Confederation of Swedish Enterprise

The Confederation of Swedish Enterprise, or Svenskt Näringsliv, is the organization that represents the interests of business in Sweden. It lobbies nationally and internationally to promote competitiveness, liberalize the economy, cut taxes and make the labour market more flexible. Svenskt Näringsliv seeks to improve Sweden's ranking in the global economy. It represents around 57,000 member companies which are organized into 48 affiliated associations, and is itself a member of the **Union of Industrial and Employers' Confederations of Europe**.

Leadership: Pres. Michael Treschow; *Dir-Gen.* Ebba Lindsö
Address: Storgatan 19, 114 82 Stockholm, Sweden
Tel: (0)8 553-430-00
Fax: (0)8 553-430-99
E-mail: info@swedishenterprise.se
Internet: www.svensktnaringsliv.se

Confederation of Swiss Employers

The Confederation of Swiss Employers, or Schweizerischer Arbeitgeberverband, is the employers' organization in Switzerland. Founded in 1908, today it represents firms employing some 1m. employees. It lobbies together with **Economiesuisse** nationally and internationally to promote the Swiss economic environment and works on labour market and education policy issues. It is a member of the **Union of Industrial and Employers' Confederations of Europe**.

Leadership: Pres. Rudolf Stämfli; *Dir-Gen.* Peter Hasler
Address: Hegibachstrasse 47, 8032 Zürich, Switzerland
Tel: (0)14211717
Fax: (0)14211718

E-mail: verband@arbeitgeber.ch
Internet: www.arbeitgeber.ch

Confederation of Trade Unions

The Confederation of Trade Unions, or Confederazione Italiana Sindacati Lavoratori (CISL), is the Christian trade union confederation in Italy. It was formed in 1948 when it broke away from the **Confederazione Generale Italiana del Lavoro**. Though originally associated with the Christian Democratic party in Italy, it has campaigned for trade union independence. The second largest trade union confederation in Italy, CISL represents the interests of some 4.1m. members from 14 national sector federations. It is itself affiliated to **ETUC**. CISL works to protect the interests of its members, to extend social dialogue and participation, and to promote jobs and the reduction of working hours. It also campaigns to reduce the gap between rich Northern Italy and the poorer **Mezzogiorno**.

Sec.-Gen.: Savino Pezzotta
Address: Via Po 21, 00198 Rome, Italy
Tel: (0)06 84731
Fax: (0)06 8456076
E-mail: cisl@cisl.it
Internet: www.cisl.it

Confederation of Unions for Academic Professionals

The Confederation of Unions for Academic Professionals, or AKAVA, is the trade union confederation representing professionals with university or higher qualifications in Finland. Membership is also open to students. AKAVA currently deals with about 400,000 members in 31 affiliated organizations. It lobbies government and employees to safeguard the status and salaries of its members and conducts wage negotiations. It is itself a member of **ETUC**.

Pres.: Risto Piekka
Address: Rautatieläisenkatu 6, 00520 Helsinki, Finland
Tel: (0)9 141822
Fax: (0)9 142595
E-mail: info@akava.fi
Internet: www.akava.fi

Confederation of Vocational Unions

The Confederation of Vocational Unions, or Yrkesorganisasjonenes Sentralforbund (YS), is the confederation of vocational trade unions in Norway. Founded in 1977, YS today represents more than 200,000 members who are organized in 21 affiliated unions. It is itself a member of **ETUC**. It campaigns nationally and internationally to improve social and working conditions and the quality of life for individuals.

Leadership: Chair. Randi Bjørgen; *Dir-Gen.* Jan G. Haanæs
Address: Brugata 19 or POB G9232 Grønland, 0134 Oslo, Norway
Tel: (0)21-01-36-00
Fax: (0)21-01-37-20
E-mail: randi.bjorgen@ys.no
Internet: www.ys.no

Confederazione Generale dell'Industria Italiana – *see* Confederation of Italian Industry

Confederazione Generale Italiana del Lavoro – *see* Italian General Confederation of Labour

Confederazione Italiana Sindacati Lavoratori – *see* Confederation of Trade Unions, Italy

Congreso de los Diputados
Congress of Deputies

The Congreso de los Diputados (Congress of Deputies) is the lower house of the bicameral parliament of Spain. It is composed of 350 members who are elected for a four-year term by a system of proportional representation. A party must obtain a minimum of 3% of the vote in order to qualify for parliamentary representation. The most recent elections were held on 14 March 2004. There are eight parliamentary groups in the current legislative period. These are (number of seats in brackets) for the **Spanish Socialist Party** (164), the **Popular Party** (148), **Convergence and Union** (10), the **Republican Left of Catalonia** (8), **United Left** (5), the **Basque Nationalist Party** (7), the **Canarian Coalition** (3) and a group of smaller parties. Of the 350 members of the current Congress, 126 (36%) are **women**.

The Congress shares a legislative role and the power to control government with the **Senado**. However, the 1978 Constitution gave the lower house the power to bring down a government. Bills and draft legislation are presented to the Congress first, and it has the power to accept or reject amendments and vetoes of the upper house.

Address: Palacio del Congreso de los Diputados, Carrera de San Jerónimo, s/n,
            28071 Madrid, Spain
Tel: (0)91 3906296
Fax: (0)91 4297332

E-mail: servicio.informacion@sgral.congreso.es
Internet: www.congreso.es

Conseil Constitutionnel – *see* Constitutional Council, France

Conseil d'État – *see* Council of the State, Luxembourg

Conservative Party (Norway)

The Conservative Party, or Høyre, is a Christian conservative party in Norway. Founded in 1884, it has been the leading opposition party to the **Labour Party** in the post-war period. The party promotes personal freedom and the right of ownership. It seeks to reduce state intervention in family life, civil society and the economy. It aims to reduce the tax burden but also to improve education and welfare services. The Conservative Party is the only conservative party in Norwegian politics that campaigned for Norway's membership of the **European Union** in the 1972 and 1994 referendums.

The Conservative Party's electoral success has been variable, fluctuating between 17% and 31.7%. It led non-socialist coalition governments with the **Christian People's Party (KrF)** in 1983–86 and in 1989–90. In the most recent elections, held on 10 September 2001, the party won 21.2% of the vote. With 38 members in the 165-seat **Stortinget**, it is the second largest party in the current parliament. It currently governs in a coalition with KrF and the **Liberal Party** and occupies 10 of 19 ministerial posts.

Party Leader: Jan Tore Sanner
Address: POB 1536, Vika, 0117 Oslo, Norway
Tel: (0)22-82-90-00
Fax: (0)22-82-90-80
E-mail: politikk@hoyre.no
Internet: www.hoyre.no

Conservative Party (Great Britain)

The Conservative Party is the main right-wing party in Great Britain. The oldest party in British politics, it dates back to the 17th century as the Tory Party. The contemporary Conservative Party dominated British politics of the 20th century in both the **House of Commons** and the **House of Lords**. It provided prime ministers for a total of 57 years, but three governments suffered major defeats: Arthur James Balfour's in 1906; **Winston Churchill**'s in 1945 and John Major's in 1997. Most recently the party governed in 1979–97, under the leadership of **Margaret Thatcher** until 1990, and then under John Major.

The Conservative Party traditionally stands for social stability and the rights of property. After the Second World War it supported the post-war consensus of the **welfare state**, public ownership of key industries, government intervention in the economy and social partnership in industry. Under the leadership of Thatcher (1974–90) the party's economic policy shifted to advocate the free market and private enterprise. In government in 1979–97 it pursued neo-liberal policies of privatization and labour market liberalization, and retrenched the welfare state and cut trade union rights.

The Conservative Party also traditionally supported the British Empire and it was under Thatcher in 1982 that the last war of Empire, in the Falklands Islands, was fought. The party opposes the break-up of the United Kingdom through devolution, promoting instead a policy of 'one-nation' conservatism. This refers to its aim of structuring a nation around a unified and unitary British national culture. The party is deeply divided on the issue of European integration, though it was under Conservative governments that the United Kingdom joined the **European Economic Community** and signed the **Single European Act** and the **Treaty on European Union**.

The party suffered severe losses at the 1997 general election and was left with only 165 representatives in the 659-seat House of Commons. Its performance at the next election, in 2001, under the leadership of William Hague, was no better; it won 166 seats. Hague's successor, Iain Duncan Smith, was removed as leader by a vote of no confidence in October 2003.

Party Leader: Michael Howard
Address: Conservative Central Office, 25 Victoria St, London SW1H ODL, United Kingdom
Tel: (0)20 7222 9000
Fax: (0)20 7222 1135
E-mail: correspondence@conservatives.com
Internet: www.conservatives.com

Conservative People's Party

The Conservative People's Party, or Konservative Folkeparti, is the main conservative party in Denmark. Founded in 1915, it is the successor party of Højre (Right). At the most recent general elections, held on 8 February 2005, the party won 18 seats in the 159-seat **Folketing**. It formed a coalition government as a junior partner with the **Liberal Party** under Liberal Prime Minister **Anders Fogh Rasmussen**.

Chair.: Bendt Bendtsen
Address: Nyhavn 4, 1020 Copenhagen K, Denmark
Tel: (0)33-13-41-40
Fax: (0)33-93-37-73
E-mail: info@konservative.dk
Internet: www.konservative.dk

Constitutional Council

The Constitutional Council, or Conseil Constitutionnel, in France was founded by the Constitution of the Fifth Republic in 1958. The council is made up of nine members who are appointed for a non-renewable nine-year term by the French President and the presidents of the **Assemblée Nationale** and the **Sénat**. The Council passes judgment on the constitutionality of laws and international agreements after parliament has voted, but before they are promulgated. It also decides on the lawfulness of presidential elections and referendums. The Constitutional Council has become increasingly active since 1974 following an amendment to the Constitution which allowed 60 members of the Assemblée Nationale and the Sénat to submit legislation for scrutiny. Since then it has come to play a more important role in the legislative process in France.

> *Address:* 2 rue de Montpensier, 75001 Paris, France
> *Tel:* (0)1-40-15-30-00
> *Fax:* (0)1-40-20-93-27
> *E-mail:* info@conseil-constitutionnel.fr
> *Internet:* www.conseil-constitutionnel.fr

Constitutional Court (Austria)

The Constitutional Court, or Verfassungsgerichtshof, is the constitutional court in Austria. It is made up of 14 judges appointed by the President; eight are proposed by the government and six are proposed by parliament. It upholds the Constitution, oversees the powers as allocated among the constituent units of the federal state, and reviews the constitutionality of legislation enacted.

> *Address:* Judenplatz 11, 1010 Vienna, Austria
> *Tel:* (0)1 531-22-0
> *Fax:* (0)1 531-22-499
> *E-mail:* vfgh@vfgh.gv.at
> *Internet:* www.vfgh.gv.at

Constitutional Court (Italy)

The Constitutional Court, or Corte Costituzionale, in Italy was founded by the Constitution in 1948, but did not start work until 1956. The court is made up of 15 judges; five are appointed by the President, five by the **Camera dei Deputati** and the **Senato**, and five by ordinary and administrative supreme courts. The court passes judgment on the constitutionality of national and regional laws once they have been passed by the legislative bodies and on conflicts regarding the allocation of power in the state. The Corte Costituzionale has become increasingly active since the 1970s and has played an important role since 1993 in attempts to reduce corruption in the Italian political system.

Address: Piazza del Quirinale 41, 00187 Rome, Italy
Tel: (0)06 46981
Fax: (0)06 4698916
E-mail: ccost@cortecostituzionale.it
Internet: www.cortecostituzionale.it

Constitutional Court (Portugal)

The Constitutional Court, or Tribunal Constitucional, in Portugal was established by an amendment to the Constitution in 1982, and first formed in 1983. It is composed of 13 judges, 10 of whom are elected by the **Assembléia da República**, and three of whom are co-opted for a non-renewable term of nine years. The Court decides on the constitutionality of laws and international agreements, and on the ability of the President to undertake his functions.

Address: Rua de 'O Século' 111, 1249-117 Lisbon, Portugal
Tel: (0)21 3233600
Fax: (0)21 3233649
E-mail: tribunal@tribconstitucional.pt
Internet: www.tribunalconstitucional.pt

Constitutional Court (Spain)

The Constitutional Court, or Tribunal Constitucional, in Spain was established by the Constitution in 1978. It is composed of 12 judges who are appointed for nine years. Four are nominated by the **Congreso de los Diputados**, four by the **Senado**, two by the government and two by the general council of the judiciary. The Court protects fundamental rights, decides on the constitutionality of laws passed by central government and the autonomous communities, and presides over disputes between the state and the regions.

Address: Domenico Scarlatti 6, Madrid 28003, Spain
Tel: (0)91 5508000
Fax: (0)91 5449268
E-mail: tcgapre@tsai.es
Internet: www.tribunalconstitucional.es

Convergence and Union

Convergence and Union, or Convergència i Unió (CiU), is the liberal nationalist party in Catalonia, Spain. Founded in 1978, it is a permanent coalition of the Democratic Union of Catalonia and Democratic Convergence of Catalonia. CiU campaigns for autonomy for Catalonia and to promote Catalan culture and language.

CiU governed in Catalonia continuously from 1980, when the first regional elections were held, until 2003. The CiU regional president during these years, Jordi Pujol, led the economic and cultural revival of the region. The party lost overall control of the Catalan parliament in 1999 and entered into government alliances, but not coalitions, with the **Popular Party (PP)**. At the most recent Catalan regional elections, held on 16 November 2003, CiU was the largest party with 30.94% of the vote but was for the first time unable to form a government. Pujol stepped down as leader. At national level, CiU supported the the PP government in 1996–2000, and at the most recent elections, held on 14 March 2004, won 3.2% of the vote and 10 seats in the 350-seat **Congreso de los Diputados**.

Leadership: Pres. Jordi Pujol; *Sec.-Gen.* Artur Mas
Address: Calle Còrsega 331, 08037 Barcelona, Spain
Tel: (0)93 2363100
Fax: (0)93 2363120
E-mail: ciu@ciu.info
Internet: www.ciu.info

Convergence criteria

The convergence criteria are the four economic tests that national economies of member countries of the **European Union (EU)** were required to pass in order to be eligible for membership of the final stage of **Economic and Monetary Union** and the **euro area**. These criteria were laid out in the **Treaty on European Union** as follows:

- Price Stability. The inflation rate of a member state must be within 1.5 percentage points of the three member states with the lowest rate during the year preceding the examination of the situation.
- Government Finances. The amount owed by a government—the annual budget deficit—must be below 3% of the total output of the economy, the gross domestic product (GDP). The total amount of money owed by government—the public debt—must be less than 60% of GDP.
- Exchange Rates. These must be kept within the margins of the **exchange rate mechanism** without a break and without severe tensions for a period of two years.
- Long-term Interest Rates. These must be within 2% of the three best-performing member states in the EU.

Eleven member states met the convergence criteria to join the euro area in 1999. Greece met the criteria in 2000. Denmark, Sweden and the United Kingdom opted to keep their national currencies. The 10 states—Cyprus, the Czech Republic, Estonia, Hungary, Latvia, Lithuania, Malta, Poland, Slovakia and Slovenia—that joined the EU on 1 May 2004 will adopt the **euro** only when they have fulfilled the convergence criteria.

Convergència i Unió – *see* Convergence and Union, Spain

Copenhagen Criteria

The Copenhagen Criteria are the conditions that **accession** states are required to fulfil in order to join the **European Union (EU)**. The Criteria were drawn up by the member states of the EU at the Copenhagen **European Council** in 1993. In order to join the EU, candidate countries must:

- be stable democracies committed to the rule of law, respect for human rights and the protection of minorities;
- have functioning market economies which are able to cope with competitive pressure and market forces of the single market;
- be able to incorporate the *acquis communautaire* and adhere to the various political, economic and monetary aims of the EU, such as political, economic and monetary union.

Corte Costituzionale – *see* Constitutional Court, Italy

Council of Europe (CoE)

The Council of Europe (CoE) is a political organization in Europe. Founded in 1949 by the Treaty of London, its aims are to attain greater unity among members, defend human rights, parliamentary democracy and the rule of law, develop agreements to standardize member countries' social and legal practices, and to promote awareness of a shared European identity. The CoE has issued 196 European treaties or conventions on issues such as human rights, the fight against organized crime, the prevention of torture, data protection and cultural co-operation. These are legally binding for members. It has also issued recommendations to governments on legal matters, health, education, culture and sport. The CoE played an important role in the transition to democracy in **Central and Eastern European Countries (CEECs)** following the collapse of communism and the end of the **Cold War**. It acted as an adviser and watchdog in the areas of human rights, local democracy, education, culture and the environment. Today the organization has a membership of 46 countries, including 21 CEECs.

The organization is composed of the Committee of Ministers, which is a decision-making body comprising 46 foreign ministers or their ambassadors, the Parliamentary Assembly, comprising 630 representatives from 46 national parliaments, the Congress of Local and Regional Authorities, and the Secretariat.

Sec.-Gen.: Terry Davis
Address: ave de l'Europe, 67075 Strasbourg Cedex, France
Tel: (0)3-88-41-20-00

Fax: (0)3-88-41-27-45
E-mail: infopoint@coe.int
Internet: www.coe.int

Council of the European Union

The Council of the European Union is the main decision-making body of the **European Union (EU)**. Established by the **Treaty of Rome**, it represents the member states of the EU. Until the **Treaty on European Union (TEU)** it was referred to as the Council of Ministers of the European Communities, and is still sometimes referred to simply as the Council of Ministers.

The Council provides a forum for representatives of EU member states to meet to make decisions on EU policy. The institution is organized as 16 different Councils which correspond to key areas of EU policy (transport, economics and finance, justice and home affairs, social affairs, etc.). Each specialist Council is composed of the relevant ministers from each member state. Foreign Ministers meet in the General Affairs Committee, which provides overall policy co-ordination. Council meetings are held between once a month and twice a year, depending on the subject matter; **agriculture** and economics and finance tend to meet monthly. Preparation for ministerial meetings is carried out by the Council's Committee of Permanent Representatives (Coreper), numerous working groups, and the Council General Secretariat. Council meetings are organized and chaired by the Council presidency, which rotates every six months. The member state which holds the presidency also organizes the biannual summit meetings of the **European Council**.

The Council of the European Union has the right to decide on all areas of EU policy. In matters which fall under the first **pillar** of the **European Community** (e.g. single market, agriculture, competition policy, economic and monetary union), the Council decides on legislative proposals made by the **European Commission**. On second and third pillar issues—**Common Foreign and Security Policy (CFSP)** and **Police and Judicial Co-operation in Criminal Matters**—the Council also has the right to make policy proposals. Originally the Council had the sole right to decide legislation, and the **European Parliament (EP)** needed only to be consulted. This is still the case in policy falling under pillars two and three. However, the TEU introduced the co-decision procedure whereby the Council makes decisions jointly with the EP on an increasing number of policy issues. A conciliation committee is set up where there is disagreement.

Originally, Council decisions were made on the basis of unanimity, and member states could veto legislation with a 'no' vote. In fact, this is still the case in CFSP and Police and Judicial matters. However, the **Single European Act** extended the use of qualified majority voting (QMV) to speed up the passage of legislation needed to complete the **Single European Market** programme in 1992. Subsequently the use of QMV has extended into additional policy areas. One important exception is taxation, where states retain the power of veto. Under the system of

QMV states' votes are weighted according to population size. These weightings were altered by the **Treaty of Nice** to incorporate the 10 **accession** states which joined the EU on 1 May 2004. At present 71% of votes are required to pass legislation. In practice formal votes are rarely taken as the Council governs according to the principle of consensus.

QMV weightings Treaty of Nice (pre-Nice votes in brackets): France 29 (10); Germany 29 (10); Italy 29 (10); United Kingdom 29 (10); Poland 27; Spain 27 (8); Netherlands 13 (5); Belgium 12 (5); Czech Republic 12; Greece 12 (5); Hungary 12; Portugal 12 (5); Austria 10 (4); Sweden 10 (4); Denmark 7 (4); Finland 7 (4); Ireland 7 (4); Lithuania 7; Slovakia 7; Estonia 4; Latvia 4; Luxembourg 4 (2); Slovenia 4; Cyprus 4; Malta 3.

The TEU increased the powers of the EP to scrutinize the Council. However, it is widely criticized as an undemocratic and opaque institution. Decisions made by the Council have tended to be made behind closed doors in order to encourage frank discussion and efficient outcomes. The accession of the 10 new member states on 1 May 2004 has raised concerns about whether the efficiency and the consensual nature of decision-making in the European Council can be retained. The Constitutional Treaty drafted by the **European Convention** proposed reforms to the Council of the European Union. It was proposed that QMV should be amended so that a double majority—55% of states representing 65% of EU citizens—is required to pass EU legislation. Also, the six-month rotating presidency would be changed to an 18-month rotating presidency shared by a troika of member states. The Council for Foreign Affairs would be chaired by a new Union Minister for Foreign Affairs. This new post would combine the current portfolios of the Commissioner for External Relations in the European Commission and the secretary-general of the Council of the European Union, who would also serve as the High Representative for Common Foreign and Security Policy.

Sec.-Gen.: Javier Solana
Address: Council of the European Union, rue de la Loi 175, 1048 Brussels, Belgium
Tel: (0)2 285-61-11
Fax: (0)2 285-73-97/81
E-mail: public.info@consilium.eu.int
Internet: ue.eu.int

Council of Ministers – *see* Council of the European Union

Council of the State

The Council of the State, or Conseil d'Etat, is an organ of the Luxembourg state which advises the government and the **Chambre des Députés** on proposed legislation, draft legislation and amendments. The Council is made up of 21 members who are appointed by the Grand Duke of Luxembourg for a maximum term of 15 years. Eleven of these members are required to have a legal training.

Address: Conseil d'Etat, 5 rue Sigefroi, 2536 Luxembourg
Tel: (0)47-30-71
Fax: (0)46-43-22
E-mail: Conseil@ce.etat.lu
Internet: www.etat.lu/CE

Cour d'Arbitrage/Arbitragehof – *see* Court of Arbitration, Belgium

Court of Arbitration

The Court of Arbitration, or Cour d'Arbitrage/Arbitragehof, is the court in Belgium which supervises the balance of powers between the state, communities and regions of the federal state. It also reviews the constitutionality of state, community and regional laws. It was established by the Constitution in 1980 and inaugurated in 1984. The Court is made up of 12 judges who are appointed by the King from a list of candidates proposed by parliament. Six judges represent the French linguistic group and six the Dutch. At least one member must be able to speak German.

Address: 7 place Royale, 1000 Brussels, Belgium
Tel: (0)2-500-12-11
Fax: (0)2-500-12-01
E-mail: cabinet_president@arbitrage.be
Internet: www.arbitrage.be

Cowen, Brian

Brian Cowen has been Minister of Finance in Ireland since 29 September 2004. He took up the post when his predecessor, Charlie McCreevy, was nominated as Ireland's European Commissioner for the term 2004–09. A member of **Fianna Fáil (FF)**, he is a minister in the coalition government between FF and the **Progressive Democrats**, led by Taoiseach **Bertie Ahern**. Cowen was first elected to the **Dáil Éireann** in June 1984, winning the seat made available by the death of his father, Bernard Cowen. He previously served as Minister for Labour (1992–93), Minister for Transport, Energy and Communications (1993–94), Minister for Health and Children (1997–2000) and Minister for Foreign Affairs (2000–04).

Born in January 1960 in Tullamore, Cowen studied at University College Dublin and later trained as a solicitor. Brian Cowen is married to Mary Molloy and has two daughters.

Address: Department of Finance, Government Bldgs, Upper Merrion St, Dublin
2, Ireland
Tel: (0)1 6767571
Fax: (0)1 6789936
E-mail: webmaster@finance.gov.ie
Internet: www.finance.gov.ie

Cyprus

Cyprus is a small island at the eastern edge of the Mediterranean Sea, to the south of **Turkey**. It is a nodal point of the European, Asian and African continents. The island has been divided since 1974 between the Turkish north and the Greek south.

Area: 9,300 sq km; *capital:* Nicosia; *population:* 761,000 (2001).

Cyprus gained independence from the United Kingdom in 1960, but it remained part of the British **Commonwealth**. The 1960 Constitution of the Republic of Cyprus proved unworkable and unable to satisfy the demands of the two main communities: the Greeks who account for 80% of the population; and the Turks who make up 18%. The Greek military junta in power in Athens staged a coup in 1974 in an attempt to annex Cyprus to Greece. In response to this, Turkey invaded the north of the island, occupying 37% of the island's territory and forcing 40% of the Greek Cypriot population to leave their homes. The Turkish-occupied north declared itself an independent state—the Turkish Republic of Northern Cyprus (TRNC)—in 1983. However, Turkey was the only country to recognize the north's sovereignty and, officially, the government of the Republic of Cyprus exists for the whole island.

The Republic of Cyprus is a presidential democracy. Executive power lies with the President, who is directly elected for a five-year term. In the elections held on 16 February 2003 the President of 10 years, Glafcoc Clerides, lost to Tassos Papadopoulos, leader of the centre-right Democratic Party, who won 51.51% of the vote in the first ballot. Legislative power lies with the 80-seat House of Representatives in which 56 seats are reserved for the Greek Cypriot community and the 24 seats for the Turkish Cypriot community remain vacant. Since 1995 representatives have been elected by a system of proportional representation. The most recent elections were held on 27 May 2001. Northern Cyprus has a parliamentary system of government with a directly elected President. Rauf Denktash has been the elected President of the unrecognized TRNC since 1985.

The **United Nations (UN)** set up a peace-keeping force in Cyprus in 1963 and its troops patrol the 'green line' border which runs through the capital Nicosia. In recent years UN-sponsored peace talks, led by Kofi Annan, have sought to find a way to reunite north and south Cyprus. It was proposed to establish Cyprus as a loose federation of two constituent states, each running its own affairs but with a joint foreign policy controlled by a central government. However, the two communities have been unable to reach agreement on the proposal. The Turkish Cypriot leader Rauf Denktash argued that too much land would be ceded to the south; and the Greek Cypriots regarded the measures for refugees wishing to return to their homes in the north as inadequate.

The need for a settlement became more urgent following the Republic of Cyprus's successful application for membership of the **European Union (EU)**. An associated state since 1973, Cyprus applied for full membership in 1990 and EU states agreed to accept it as a member in November 2002. It was hoped that the prospect of membership would bring the two communities closer to an agreement; otherwise the Greek Republic of Cyprus would join on its own. Greek Cypriots signed the EU **accession** treaty in April 2003. Shortly afterwards the Turkish Cypriot authorities opened up the 'green line' so that for the first time in 30 years Cypriots were able to move freely between the two parts of the island. Within one month, 40% of the population had travelled across the border. A referendum was held on the UN plan to reunite the island on 24 April 2004. It was hoped that the referendum would be supported by both communities so that a united island could join the EU on 1 May 2004. In the event the plans were only supported by the Turkish north (yes 64.9%; turn-out 87%). The Greek south overwhelmingly rejected it (no 75.8%; turn-out 88%) and as a consequence only the Greek south became a member of the EU.

Economy: The economy of Cyprus is divided between the Greek south and the Turkish north. The Turkish invasion of Cyprus in 1974 significantly affected many sectors of the Cypriot economy, including **agriculture**, tourism, mining and quarrying. Some 70% of the island's total resources were lost: the tourist industry lost 65% of its hotels and accommodation; the industrial sector lost 46% of its facilities, and extraction industries lost 56% of production. In addition, the Republic of Cyprus lost the northern port of Famagusta, which handled 83% of cargo, and the Nicosia International Airport.

GNP: US \$9,372m. (2001); *GNP per caput:* \$12,320 (2001); *GNP at PPP:* \$16,060m. (2001); *GNP per caput at PPP:* \$21,110 (2001); *currency:* Cyprus pound; *unemployment:* 3.3% (2002).

The Greek Cypriot economy is open and market-based and relies on exports of agricultural, mineral and manufactured products, offshore services and tourism. Tourism alone accounts for 25% of the gross domestic product. The Greek Cypriot economy gained substantial benefits from its association with the **European Union (EU)** which is its largest trading partner. The Republic of Cyprus signed an Association Agreement with the EU in 1973 and this led to a Customs Union in 1988. It became a full member of the EU on 1 May 2004. The Greek Cypriot economy is marked by high rates of growth and near full employment. Inflation has tended to be high, though this has declined steadily to below 5% since a peak of 13.5% in 1980.

The Turkish Republic of Northern Cyprus (TRNC) is economically isolated and relies on subsidies from the Turkish state. The north has significantly lower economic growth and per caput incomes than the south. The Turkish Cypriot leader Rauf Denktash opened up the borders to the southern part of the island in April 2003. For the first time since the Turkish invasion in 1973, the two parts of the island have been able to trade. The unrecognized TRNC remains outside the EU.

D

Dáil Éireann

House of Representatives

The Dáil Éireann (House of Representatives) is the lower house of the bicameral parliament, the Tithe an Oireachtas, in Ireland. It is currently made up of 166 members elected to represent one of 41 constituencies for a five-year term. In the current Dáil, elected on 17 May 2002, there are seven party groups (number of seats in brackets): **Fianna Fáil** (81), **Fine Gael** (31), **Labour Party** (21), **Progressive Democrats** (8), **Green Party** (6), **Sinn Féin** (5), **Socialist Party** (1) and other parties (13). At present 22 (13.3%) of the 166 members of the Dáil are **women**. The Dáil shares legislative responsibility with the **Seanad Éireann** but has sole responsibility for holding the government to account.

> *Address:* Dáil Éireann, Houses of the Oireachtas, Leinster House, Dublin 2, Ireland
> *Tel:* (0)1 6183000
> *Fax:* (0)1 6184118
> *E-mail:* info@oireachtas.ie
> *Internet:* www.oireachtas.ie

Daisy Alliance

The Daisy Alliance, or Margherita, is a centrist political party in Italy. Formally founded in March 2002, the Daisy Alliance is the result of a merger of the Italian Popular Party (Partido Popolare Italiano, PPI—formerly the dominant Christian Democrats, DC), Italian Renewal (Rinnovamento Italiano, RI) and the Democrats (Democratici). The Daisy Alliance first contested general elections on 13 May 2001 as part of the Olive Tree Coalition (L'Ulivo) with the **Democrats of the Left**, the **Sunflower Alliance** and the Italian Communist Party. Its leader, Francesco Rutelli, was the Olive Tree Coalition's unsuccessful candidate for Prime Minister. Margherita won 80 seats in the 630-member **Camera dei Deputati**.

> *Pres.:* Francesco Rutelli
> *Address:* La Margherita, Via Sant'Andrea delle Fratte 16, 00187 Rome, Italy

Tel: (0)06 695321
Fax: (0)06 6953253
E-mail: sede@margheritaonline.it
Internet: www.margheritaonline.it

Danish Confederation of Professional Associations

The Danish Confederation of Professional Associations, or Akademikernes Centralorganisation, is the confederation for associations representing professional employees in Denmark. Founded in 1972, it represents approximately 250,000 professionals in 22 member organizations. It campaigns to protect the interests of its members in the workplace and conducts and co-ordinates collective bargaining in the public and private sectors. It is itself a member of **ETUC**.

Chair.: Sine Sunesen
Address: Nørre Voldgade 29, POB 2192, 1017 Copenhagen K, Denmark
Tel: (0)33-69-40-40
Fax: (0)33-93-85-40
E-mail: ac@ac.dk
Internet: www.ac.dk

Danish Confederation of Trade Unions

The Danish Confederation of Trade Unions, or Landsorganisationen i Danmark (LO), is the largest and oldest trade union confederation in Denmark. Founded in 1898, it today has approximately 1.5m. members across 22 affiliated private- and public-sector unions. LO represents the interests of its members to the government and employers and co-ordinates collective bargaining. It also seeks to influence public policy, especially concerning the labour market. It also co-manages **unemployment** funds. LO originally had close formal ties with the **Social Democrats**. While the organizations are no longer mutually represented on their governing bodies, close links still exist. It is a member of **ETUC**.

Pres.: Hans Jensen
Address: Islands Brygge 32 D, 2300 Copenhagen S, Denmark
Tel: (0)35-24-60-00
Fax: (0)35-24-63-02
E-mail: lo@lo.dk
Internet: www.lo.dk

Danish Employers' Confederation

The Danish Employers' Confederation, or Dansk Arbejdsgiverforening (DA), is the large employers' organization in Denmark. Founded in 1896, DA today brings together 13 employers' organizations which represent the interests of some 29,000 companies and 47% of full-time workers. It conducts collective bargaining in the retail, manufacturing, transport and service sectors. It is a member of the **Union of Industrial and Employers' Confederations of Europe**.

Leadership: Pres. Jørgen Vorsholt; *Dir-Gen.* Jørn Neergaard Larsen
Address: Vester Voldgade 113, 1790 Copenhagen V, Denmark
Tel: (0)33-38-90-00
Fax: (0)33-12-29-76
E-mail: da@da.dk
Internet: www.da.dk

Danish People's Party

The Danish People's Party, or Dansk Folkeparti, is the nationalistic right-wing party in Denmark. The party was established in 1995 after breaking away from the Fremskridtspartiet (Progress Party). The party campaigns to protect the culture and independence of Denmark. It advocates a policy of 'Denmark for the Danes' and is opposed to **immigration** and multiculturalism in Denmark. It emphasizes the importance of law and order and the need to protect its national borders. The party is opposed to Denmark's membership of the **European Union**. The party returned 13 representatives to the **Folketing** in 1998. In the general elections held on 20 November 2001 Dansk Folkeparti increased its number of seats to 22 in the 179-seat Folketing, becoming the third largest parliamentary party. Its success was in part attributed to heightened security concerns following the terrorist attacks of **11 September** 2001. In the most recent elections held on 8 February 2005 the Danish People's Party increased its representation to 24 seats.

Party Leader: Pai Kjaersgaard
Address: Christianborg, 1240 Copenhagen K, Denmark
Tel: (0)33-37-51-99
Fax: (0)33-37-51-91
E-mail: df@ft.dk
Internet: www.danskfolkeparti.dk

Danmarks Nationalbank

Danmarks Nationalbank, the central bank of Denmark, was founded in 1818. It became the sole banker to government in 1914, took over the printing of notes in 1918 and became independent in 1936. Danmarks Nationalbank is responsible for Denmark's monetary policy and seeks to support the foreign-exchange-policy target of a fixed exchange rate for the krone against the **euro**.

In September 2000 the Danes voted against membership of the euro (no 53%). As a central bank of a **European Union** state outside the **euro area**, Danmarks Nationalbank is a member of the **European System of Central Banks**. However, the governor of Danmarks Nationalbank is not entitled to be a member of the

Governing Council of the **European Central Bank** nor to participate in decision-making for the **Eurosystem**.

Gov.: Bodil Nyboe Andersen
Address: Havnegade 5, 1093 Copenhagen K, Denmark
Tel: (0)33-63-63-63
Fax: (0)33-63-71-03
E-mail: info@nationalbanken.dk
Internet: www.nationalbanken.dk

Dansk Arbejdsgiverforening – *see* **Danish Employers' Confederation**

Dansk Folkeparti – *see* **Danish People's Party**

Dansk Industri – *see* **Confederation of Danish Industries**

de Gaulle, Charles

Gen. Charles de Gaulle was a French statesman who, having escaped to London, symbolized French resistance and led a government-in-exile during Nazi occupation in 1940–44 and was the founder of the Fifth Republic in 1958. He was also the founding father of the French political movement Gaullism.

Born on 22 November 1890 in Lille, de Gaulle graduated from the Saint-Cyr Military Academy and entered the infantry. He fought in the First World War and was taken prisoner in 1916. He was promoted to the rank of colonel in 1937 and was named Secretary of State for National Defence and War in 1940. On the eve of the Nazi occupation of France, de Gaulle went to London and with the help of **Winston Churchill** made a speech on 18 June 1940 on BBC radio urging the French to offer resistance. From London he organized the Free French Forces, later the French Committee of National Liberation and Provisional Government of the French Republic.

Following the liberation of France de Gaulle resigned as President of the Provisional Government in 1946, disagreeing with the proposed Constitution of the Fourth Republic, which he thought lacked clear executive leadership. He founded the Rally of the French People movement (Rassemblement du Peuple Français) in 1947. In the midst of the Algeria crisis in 1958 de Gaulle was called to become Prime Minister, and was given full powers to draft a new constitution. The Constitution of the Fifth Republic was adopted by referendum on 28 September 1958, and de Gaulle became the Republic's first President. As President, de Gaulle favoured European integration, adopting the Common Agricultural Policy in 1963 and forging close links with the Federal Republic of Germany through the Elysée

Treaty in 1963. He blocked the United Kingdom's application to become a member of the **European Economic Community** as he considered the country too closely allied to the USA.

De Gaulle served a second term as President after winning 54.8% of the vote on the second ballot against **François Mitterrand** in 1965. Faced with the challenge of the May 1968 student protests, he dissolved the **Assemblée Nationale** and called new elections. His party made gains in the elections held in June 1968, winning 358 of 487 seats. De Gaulle resigned as President on 28 May 1969 following a failed referendum on political reform. Charles de Gaulle died on 9 November 1970. He was married to Yvonne Vendroux and had three children.

Déi Gréng – *see* Green Party, Luxembourg

Déi Lénk – *see* Left Party, Luxembourg

Democraten 66 – *see* Democrats 66, Netherlands

Demokratesch Partei – *see* Democratic Party, Luxembourg

Democratic Party

The Democratic Party, or Demokratesch Partei (DP), is the liberal party in Luxembourg. Originally established as the Groupement patriotique et démocratique in 1945, it changed its name in 1955. The DP is a market-oriented party which stands for individual freedom, solidarity with the weaker in society, and defending democracy. The party participated in a series of coalition governments with both the **Christian Social People's Party** (in 1959–64, 1969–74, 1979–84 and 1999–2004) and the **Luxembourg Socialist Workers' Party** (1974–79). In the elections held on 13 June 2003 the DP won 10 seats in the 60-seat **Chambre des Députés** and lost its role in the coalition government.

> *Leadership: Pres.* Claude Meisch; *Gen. Sec.* Agny Durdu
> *Address:* 51 rue de Strasbourg, 2561 Luxembourg
> *Tel:* (0)22-10-21
> *Fax:* (0)22-10-13
> *E-mail:* secretariat@dp.lu
> *Internet:* www.dp.lu

Democratic Unionist Party (DUP)

The Democratic Unionist Party (DUP) is traditionally the second largest unionist party in **Northern Ireland**. Established in 1971, it is a right-wing, anti-republican

Protestant party and is committed to the continued integration of Northern Ireland in the United Kingdom. The DUP currently has five seats in the **House of Commons** that was elected on 7 June 2001.

The DUP did not take part in the Northern Ireland peace negotiations that led to the **Good Friday Agreement** because of its opposition to the inclusion of **Sinn Féin** in the talks. It also campaigned against the endorsement of the Agreement in the 1999 referendum on the issue and has since sought its renegotiation. In the Northern Ireland Assembly elections held on 26 November 2003 the DUP gained the status of the strongest party, winning 30 of the 108 seats (compared to 20 of 104 seats in 1998). It found itself in the position of having to deal with its political opposite Sinn Féin, the second largest party.

Party Leader: Ian Paisley
Address: 91 Dundela Ave, Belfast BT4 3BU, United Kingdom
Tel: (0)28 9047-1155
Fax: (0)28 9047-1797
E-mail: info@dup.org.uk
Internet: www.dup.org.uk

Democratici di Sinistra – *see* Democrats of the Left, Italy

Democrats 66

Democrats 66, or Democraten 66 (D66), is the social liberal party in the Netherlands. Founded in 1966, the party stands for individual freedom in a social framework and promotes maximum participation of citizens in the political process. It proposes the privatization of schools and the reduction of state intervention in the **welfare state**, but stricter regulation of the environment and public transport. It proposes improving democratic participation by lowering the age of voting to 16, holding more referendums, abolishing the upper house of parliament **(Eerste Kamer)** and, at European level, increasing the powers of the **European Parliament** and introducing an elected president of the **European Commission**.

D66's electoral performances have been mixed. Following initial successes, it went from the brink of extinction in the mid-1970s and early 1980s to becoming a coalition partner in the so-called purple coalition between the **Labour Party**, the **People's Party for Freedom and Democracy (VVD)** and D66 in 1994–98 and 1998–2002. In the elections held on 16 May 2002 the party won seven seats in the 150-seat **Tweede Kamer**, but its representation was reduced to six seats following the elections held on 22 January 2003, but the party governs with **Christian Democratic Appeal** and VVD.

Party Chair.: Alexander Pechtold
Address: Laan van Meerdervoort 50, 2517 AM The Hague, or POB 660, 2501
      CR The Hague, Netherlands

Tel: (0)70 3566066
Fax: (0)70 3641917
E-mail: international@d66.nl
Internet: www.d66.nl (dutch) or www.democrats.nl (english)

Democrats of the Left

The Democrats of the Left, or Democratici di Sinistra (DS), is the main left-wing party in Italy. Originally founded in 1921 as the Italian Communist Party, it abandoned communism in 1991 following the collapse of communism in Eastern Europe and became the Party of the Democratic Left (Partido Democratico della Sinistra—PDS). The PDS changed its name to the DS on 14 February 1998.

In the elections held on 27 March 1994 the PDS led the eight-party Progressive Alliance (Progressista), which gained second place. In the elections held on 21 April 1996 the PDS headed the Olive Tree Coalition (L'Ulivo) which secured a narrow majority in the **Camera dei Deputati**. PDS leader Massimo D'Alema was the Olive Tree Coalition's Prime Minister in 1998–2000. In the most recent general election, held on 13 May 2001, DS again headed the Olive Tree Coalition, with the **Daisy Alliance**, the **Sunflower Alliance** and the Italian Communist Party. The DS returned 138 deputies to the 630-seat Camera dei Deputati.

Leadership: Pres. Massimo D'Alema; *Gen. Sec.* Piero Fassino
Address: Via Palermo 12, 00184 Rome, Italy
Tel: (0)06 67111
Fax: (0)06 48023590
E-mail: p.fassino@democraticidisinistra.it
Internet: www.dsonline.it

Denmark

Denmark is a small Scandinavian state to the north of Germany which has had a democratic constitution since 1849. Denmark is traditionally a neutral state; it stayed out of the First World War in 1914–18 but was occupied by Nazi Germany on 9 April 1940. A resistance movement developed from August 1943 that lasted until the end of the Second World War. In the post-war era Denmark was a founding member of the **United Nations** in 1945 and joined the **North Atlantic Treaty Organization** in 1949.

Area: 43,000 sq km; *capital:* Copenhagen; *population:* 5m. (2001).

A constitutional monarchy, Denmark's head of state is Margrethe II, who ascended the throne in 1972. The Kingdom of Denmark includes the territories of **Greenland** and the **Faroe Islands** which were granted self-government in 1948 and 1979 respectively. A parliamentary democracy, legislative power is vested in the **Folketing**, the national parliament which has been a unicameral legislature since 1953, when a constitutional reform removed the upper house of parliament, the

Landsting. Executive power lies with the government, which since 1909 has been a coalition government. The current government is a coalition between the **Liberal Party** and the **Conservative People's Party**, headed by the Liberal Prime Minister **Anders Fogh Rasmussen**.

Since 1929 until recently Danish politics were dominated by the **Social Democrats**, and were based on a culture of consensus. There is traditionally a low degree of conflict between the Social Democrats and other mainstream non-socialist parties; election campaigns have tended to be fought on the issue of administrative and economic competence. There are, however, two issues in Danish politics which have broken the consensual tradition: European integration and **immigration**.

Denmark became a member of the **European Community (EC)** in 1973 together with the United Kingdom and Ireland. It had previously applied for membership in 1961 and 1967, but withdrew its request when **Charles de Gaulle** vetoed the United Kingdom's membership. Negotiations resumed in 1969. The main political parties favour Denmark's membership of the **European Union (EU)** and the country's involvement in further integration. However, the population remains sceptical about relinquishing sovereignty to European institutions, and is concerned with defending the status of small states in the EU. Denmark manages to keep controversial European issues out of domestic politics by calling referendums on all major European issues, or dealing with them in elections to the **European Parliament**. The decision to join the EC was endorsed in a referendum held in October 1972 (yes 63.4%; turn-out 90.1%). Referendums were also held on: the **Single European Act** (February 1986: yes 56.2%; turn-out 75.4%); the **Treaty on European Union (TEU)** (June 1992: no 50.7%; 83.1% turn-out); the TEU with opt-outs (May 1993: yes 56.7%; turn-out 86.5%); the **Treaty of Amsterdam** (May 1998: yes 55.1%; turn-out 74.8%); and, most recently, on adopting the **euro** (September 2000: no 53.1%; 87.5% turn-out).

Referendums on two European issues have resulted in a no vote. The first was in 1992 when the Danes voted narrowly against the TEU. Prime Minister Poul Nyrup Rasmussen was obliged to return to the negotiating table where he managed to secure Denmark opt-outs from the single currency, defence, **justice and home affairs**, and European **citizenship**. In this way he was able to secure a yes vote less than one year later. The second issue that was rejected in a referendum (in September 2000) concerned Denmark's membership of the single currency. This proposal was rejected despite the fact that the yes campaign had been sponsored by the incumbent Social Democrat government and all mainstream political parties, employers' associations, most trade unions and daily newspapers. The yes campaign argued that membership of the single currency would be in Denmark's economic interest: it would stimulate economic and employment growth, and help contain interest rates. The no campaign, made up of the extreme right-wing **Danish People's Party** and the left-wing and extreme left-wing **Socialist People's Party** and **Unity List**, argued that the single currency meant either a further surrender of national sovereignty or more political integration that would undermine Denmark's

welfare state. The fact that the smaller and more modestly resourced no campaign was successful has been explained in three ways. The yes camp concentrated on the economic rather than political arguments for membership even though the economic benefits were deemed to be 'slight and uncertain' by independent experts. Moreover, the referendum was held at a time when the **euro** was performing very badly. Finally, the referendum followed an event in a fellow small state—Austria— which had caused alarm in Denmark. The inclusion of the populist right-wing **Freedom Party of Austria** in the 1999 Austrian government led the other 14 EU states to impose diplomatic sanctions on Austria. This move was regarded by many in Denmark as unacceptable interference by the EU in the affairs of a small member state. The no vote was considered to be a victory for a small EU state, and the Prime Minister was obliged to concede that a second referendum on the issue of the single currency would not be held for a long time.

The second controversial issue in Danish politics is immigration. Denmark was historically a multicultural state but became increasingly more homogeneous as it lost territory; today immigrants and their dependants make up about 7% of the population. In recent years the issue of immigration has come to dominate political debate. Concerns centre upon the strain that immigration allegedly imposes on the Danish welfare state. Support for anti-immigration parties grew rapidly in the 1990s and mainstream parties began to address the issue in their own campaigns.

Support for the anti-immigration Danish People's Party rose sharply at elections held in March 1998. It managed to increase its representation in the Folketing from four to 13 seats. Following the election held on 20 November 2001 the number of seats the party occupied increased to 22. In fact, that was a significant election in Danish politics in a number of ways. It was held shortly after the terrorist attacks of **11 September** 2001 and security issues dominated the campaign. A decisive shift to the right occurred and, for the first time since 1929, the non-socialist parties secured a majority in the Folketing. The Liberal Party gained the status of largest party and it formed a coalition government with the Conservative People's Party with Liberal Anders Fogh Rasmussen as Prime Minister. This is a minority government and relies on the support of the Danish People's Party. The coalition promised to cut taxation and to provide extra funding for pensioners, hospitals, education and research. It has also introduced legislation to reduce immigration. A foreign spouse of a Danish resident is no longer automatically allowed to enter the country if she/he is under the age of 24. Furthermore, immigrants will now have to wait for seven years until they are entitled to the full benefits of the Danish welfare state. Within one year of the introduction of the new legislation asylum applications had fallen by 71%. In the most recent elections, held on 8 February 2005, the Danish People's Party increased its parliamentary representation to 24 seats.

Economy: Denmark has a small but open economy which relies on foreign trade for around two-thirds of its total gross domestic product (GDP). Traditionally an agricultural economy, aid granted under the **Marshall Plan** in the early post-war era triggered a rapid phase of industrialization and by 1963 industrial exports had overtaken agricultural exports. The economy is organized as networks of craft-based, specialized small and medium-sized enterprises which produce niche products, rather than as large firms engaged in mass production. Today its main exports are pharmaceuticals and food products and its main trading partners are Germany, the United Kingdom, Sweden and, increasingly, **Central and Eastern European Countries**.

GNP: US $164,000m. (2001); *GNP per caput:* $30,600 (2001); *GNP at PPP:* $153,000m. (2001); *GNP per caput at PPP:* $28,490 (2001); *GDP:* $161,542m. (2001); *exports:* $77,856m. (2001); *imports:* $67,489m. (2001); *currency:* Danish krone; *unemployment:* 4.7% (2002).

Denmark has consistently campaigned for liberalization of world trade in the **World Trade Organization**, the **Organisation for Economic Co-operation and Development** and the **European Union (EU)**. Denmark has been a member of the EU since 1973 and, since 1982, the Danish krone has been linked to first the Deutsche Mark (DM) and then the **euro**, meaning that the krone-euro exchange rate cannot fluctuate by more than 2.25%. Despite this, a majority of voters (53.1%) opposed giving up the Danish krone for the euro in a referendum held in September 2000.

The Danish economy is a corporatist economy. Trade union involvement in governments' economic policy-making began during the First World War and developed further during the 1930s and 1940s. By the 1970s trade unions—especially the **Danish Confederation of Trade Unions**—were consulted on most important areas of economic policy, especially when socialist-led governments were in power. Trade unions are represented in the commissions which draft important legislation, they are consulted by government ministries before bills are placed before the **Folketing** and parliamentary committees consult tráde unions when they scrutinize bills. Moreover, trade union leaders meet regularly with leaders of the **Social Democrats** and are represented in the Economic Council that was established in 1962.

The dominance of the Social Democrats during the 20th century, and the involvement of the labour movement in economic policy-making, promoted the development of a social democratic **welfare state**. The Danish welfare system offers universal welfare support, and all citizens—male and female—have equal rights to social security. It provides an extensive range of cash benefits and social services, such as child-care, health-care and education, funded by the state through general taxation. Public expenditure accounts for 26% of GDP and Denmark has one of the highest taxation levels in the world. However, public support for the welfare state remains high.

The Danish economy initially coped well with the global recession of the 1970s on account of its niche-oriented industrial exports and agricultural sector which was protected by EU subsidies. However, it was subsequently harmed by high public deficits, inflation, and an increase in the rate of **unemployment** from 2% in 1973 to more than 10% in 1983. Non-socialist governments in 1982–93 raised taxes, cut spending and broke from the tradition of indexing wages to prices. Tying the krone to the DM also enforced monetary restraint. During the 1980s Denmark launched large technological development programmes in order to upgrade its industrial infrastructure. To cut unemployment the government sought to boost demand for labour through wage subsidies to both private and public firms, and to reduce the labour supply through early retirement schemes. A generous, passive welfare state safety net existed for those who remained unemployed, and the rate of unemployment remained at around 12% until the early 1990s.

The recovery of the Danish labour market—sometimes referred to as the Danish jobs miracle—took place from 1993 when a Social Democrat-led majority coalition took office. This government reduced the rate of unemployment from 12.7% in 1994 to 7.9% in 1997 and to 5% in 2001. Its strategy was to transform the welfare state from a passive safety net into an active system aiming at returning the unemployed to the labour market. The welfare-to-work scheme reduced the period of benefit entitlement from seven to five years and increased the number of schemes which offer job-placement or training for the unemployed. The level of benefits was not affected. A number of employment leave schemes were also introduced to improve the circulation of the employed and unemployed in the labour market. From 1994 insured employees were given the right to take leave for education, child-care or (until 1999) a sabbatical.

The Danish economy has performed well in recent years. Unemployment has remained low and increases in exports have led to a substantial trade surplus. The government has significantly reduced the level of public debt. Moreover, the structure of the economy coupled with government sponsored industrial and labour market policies have assisted Denmark's transformation into a successful knowledge-based economy. The election of the liberal-conservative coalition in November 2001 and its re-election in February 2005 poses no real threat to the Danish welfare state. Liberal Prime Minister Anders Fogh Rasmussen moderated his free-market and anti-welfare stance for the election in 2001 and instead promised to cut taxation, and provide extra funding for pensioners, hospitals, education and research. However, new legislation introduced by the right-wing government means that immigrants, who are disproportionately affected by unemployment, will now have to wait for seven years before they are entitled to the full benefits of the Danish welfare state.

Deutscher Gewerkschaftsbund – *see* German Trade Union Federation

Dutch Central Bank

The Dutch Central Bank, or De Nederlandsche Bank, was founded in 1814. Since the start of stage three of **Economic and Monetary Union** on 1 January 1999

De Nederlandsche Bank has been a member of the **European System of Central Banks** and the **Eurosystem**. It implements the decisions of the **European Central Bank** in the Netherlands.

Gov.: Arnout Wellink
Address: De Nederlandsche Bank, Westeinde 1, 1017 ZN Amsterdam, or POB
    98, 1000 AB Amsterdam, Netherlands
Tel: (0)20 5249111
Fax: (0)20 5242500
E-mail: info@dnb.nl
Internet: www.dnb.nl

Dutch Trade Union Confederation

Dutch Trade Union Confederation, or Federatie Nederlandse Vakbeweging (FNV), is the largest trade union confederation in the Netherlands. Founded in 1976 through the merger of the socialist Netherlands Federation of Trade Unions and the Catholic Federation of Dutch Trade Unions, FNV today represents around 1.2m. members in 14 affiliated unions. Around 60% of all trade unionists in the Netherlands belong to FNV. The organization is itself a member of **ETUC**. FNV campaigns on employment and income issues for employees, and also for social security claimants, who make up 20% of total membership. It lobbies nationally and internationally for improvements in labour legislation, and workers' rights as well as on environmental, health and pensions issues.

Pres.: Lodewijk de Waal
Address: Naritaweg 10, 1043 BX Amsterdam, Netherlands
Tel: (0)20 5816300
Fax: (0)20 6844541
E-mail: info@vc.fnv.nl
Internet: www.fnv.nl

E

Ecologistes Confédérés pour l'Organisation de Luttes Originales – *see* Confederated Ecologists for the Organization of Original Struggles, Belgium

Economic and Monetary Union (EMU)

Economic and Monetary Union (EMU) was completed in three stages during the 1990s, culminating in the introduction of **euro** notes and coins on 1 January 2002.

1. As a first stage, all **European Union** member states became involved in the **Exchange Rate Mechanism (ERM)** which began in July 1990. The United Kingdom and Italy were forced to leave the ERM in 1992. In October of that year the **European Council** agreed that the next stage of EMU would begin in January 1994 and the **Treaty on European Union** set up the institutional framework to further EMU.
2. Stage two entailed closer economic and monetary co-operation between states and the creation of the **European Monetary Institute**.
3. The third stage of EMU began in January 1999. This involved the establishment of the **European Central Bank** and the **European System of Central Banks**. The exchange rates of member state currencies were irrevocably fixed to the euro. To participate in the third stage, member states were required to meet the **convergence criteria**. When these were applied in 1998 it was decided that only Greece would not qualify immediately. In 2000 that country was able to meet the convergence criteria and joined the single currency in 2001. Denmark and the United Kingdom had been given opt-outs from the single currency, and Sweden had also decided not to join.

Earlier plans for EMU were drawn up in the Werner Report of 1970 which aimed to achieve EMU by 1980. This attempt was abandoned because of the poor economic climate of the 1970s. Proposals for a second attempt at completing EMU were laid out in the Delors Report of April 1989, and agreed by the European Council in June 1989.

Economiesuisse – *see* Swiss Business Federation

Eduskunta

The Eduskunta is the unicameral parliament of Finland. It is made up of 200 members who are elected by a system of proportional representation every four years. Finland is divided into 15 electoral districts and the number of MPs returned by each district depends on the size of its population. The most recent elections were held on 16 March 2003. The eight parties currently represented in the Eduskunta are organized in the following parliamentary groups (with numbers of seats in brackets): the **Centre Party** (55); the **Finnish Social Democratic Party** (53); the **National Coalition Party** (40); the **Left Alliance** (19); the **Green League** (14); the **Swedish People's Party** (9); the **Christian Democrats** (7) and the **True Finns Party** (3). Of the 200 members of the Eduskunta, 75 (37.5%) are **women**. The Eduskunta passes legislation and decides on the state budget. It also elects the Prime Minister and supervises the work of the government. The Finnish parliament can be dissolved early by the President if proposed by the Prime Minister.

Address: Eduskunta, Mannerheimintie 30, 00102 Helsinki, Finland
Tel: (0)9 4321
Fax: (0)9 4322274
E-mail: parliament@parliament.fi
Internet: www.eduskunta.fi

Eerste Kamer

The Eerste Kamer, or Senate, is the upper house of the bicameral parliament—the States General—in the Netherlands. It is made up of 75 part-time members who are elected every four years by the members of 12 provincial councils. The most recent elections took place on 25 May 2003. The Eerste Kamer shares legislative functions with the lower house, the **Tweede Kamer**. It does not have the right to amend legislation but can vote to accept or reject legislative proposals. The Eerste Kamer also plays a role in scrutinizing the work of the government through written questions.

Address: Eerste Kamer der Staten-Generaal, Binnenhof 22, Postbus 20017, 2500
    EA The Hague, Netherlands
Tel: (0)70 3129200
Fax: (0)70 3653868
E-mail: griffie@eerstekamer.nl
Internet: eerstekamer.cust.pdc.nl

Eichel, Hans

Hans Eichel is Minister of Finance in Germany. A modernizing social democrat, he was appointed in 1999 to replace the traditionalist Oskar Lafontaine who had disagreed with Chancellor **Gerhard Schröder** over the direction of the **Social Democratic Party**'s **(SPD)** economic policy. A member of the SPD since 1964, Eichel was an SPD councillor in Kassel city council in 1968–75 and mayor of the city in 1975–91. He was leader of the SPD in the state (*Land*) of Hesse in 1989–2001 and Minister President of Hesse in 1991–99. He has been a member of the executive of the SPD since 1984.

Born on 24 December 1941 in Kassel, Eichel studied German, philosophy, politics, education and history at the Universities of Marburg and Berlin. He qualified as a grammar school teacher and taught in Kassel in 1970–75. Hans Eichel is married and has two children.

Address: Federal Ministry of Finance, Wilhelmstrasse 97, 10117 Berlin, Germany
Fax: (0)30 22422297
E-mail: via www.bundesfinanzministerium.de
Internet: www.bundesfinanzministerium.de

Elinkeinoelämän Keskusliitto – *see* Confederation of Finnish Industry

Enhedslisten-De Rød-Grønne – *see* Unity List-The Red-Greens, Denmark

Enlargement

Enlargement refers to the process of expanding the **European Union (EU)** to accept new member states. Originally founded as the **European Economic Community** in 1957 by six countries (Belgium, France, Germany, Italy, Luxembourg and the Netherlands), the EU had by May 2004 enlarged to a membership of 25 states.

The first round of enlargement involved Denmark, Ireland and the United Kingdom in 1973. The second round, in 1981, brought in Greece and the third, in 1986, Portugal and Spain, followed by Austria, Finland and Sweden in 1995 to make the EU15. The fifth round of enlargement in May 2004 brought in Cyprus, the Czech Republic, Estonia, Hungary, Latvia, Lithuania, Malta, Poland, Slovenia and Slovakia. The current EU is referred to as EU25.

Esquerra Republicana de Catalunya – *see* Republican Left of Catalonia, Spain

ETUC – *see* **European Trade Unions Confederation**

Euro

The Euro (€) is the common currency of the **European Union (EU)**. It was agreed by the **European Council** in 1995 that the euro would replace the **European Currency Unit** at a rate of one-to-one at the start of stage three of **Economic and Monetary Union** on 1 January 1999.

The European Council unanimously decided on 25 May 1998 that 11 member states had met the **convergence criteria** for membership of the single currency. These were: Austria, Belgium, Finland, France, Germany, Ireland, Italy, Luxembourg, Portugal and Spain. In June 2000 it decided that Greece had since fulfilled the criteria and that country entered the **euro area** on 1 January 2001. Euro banknotes and coins were introduced for these 12 member states on 1 January 2002, and national currencies were gradually phased out.

Initially the performance of the euro against the US dollar was weak. Launched at US $1.17, the value of the euro fell rapidly during its first year. The **European Central Bank** intervened four times in September 2000 to support the currency, but its value nevertheless fell to a low of US $0.8225 in October 2000. Following the introduction of banknotes and coins the euro reached parity with the dollar again in July 2002 and by December 2003 its value had risen to US $1.2043. Its recovery has arguably had more to do with the problems of the US economy than with the strength of the euro economic area. Large states such as Germany and France have struggled to increase economic growth and to adhere to the conditions of the **Stability and Growth Pact**.

Three EU member states remained outside the euro area. Voters in Denmark rejected membership of the euro in a referendum in September 2000, 53% voting no. In Sweden a similar decision was made in a referendum held in September 2003 (56% voting no). The **Labour Party** government in the United Kingdom plans to hold a referendum on membership 'when the time is right'. The 10 **accession** states that joined the EU on 1 May 2004—Cyprus, the Czech Republic, Estonia, Hungary, Latvia, Lithuania, Malta, Poland, Slovakia and Slovenia—will only be able to adopt the euro when they have fulfilled the convergence criteria.

Euro area

The euro area consists of the member states of the **European Union** which participate fully in **Economic and Monetary Union** and which have adopted the **euro** as their currency. The euro area's monetary policy is managed by the **Eurosystem**.

Eurojust

Eurojust is an agency of the **European Union (EU)** which promotes judicial co-operation and co-ordination between member states. Established in 2002, it seeks to assist in investigations and prosecutions covering more than one territory of the EU. The organization is composed of 25 senior prosecutors or judges, each nominated by a member state. Eurojust forms part of the third **pillar** of the EU, **Police and Judicial Co-operation in Criminal Matters**. It has its headquarters in the Netherlands.

Pres.: Michael G. Kennedy
Address: Maanweg 174, 2516 AB The Hague, Netherlands
Tel: (0)70 4125000
Fax: (0)70 4125555
E-mail: info@eurojust.eu.int
Internet: www.eurojust.eu.int

European Central Bank (ECB)

The European Central Bank (ECB), the independent central bank of the **European Union (EU)**, was established in 1998 for the third stage of **Economic and Monetary Union (EMU)**. Together with the national central banks of all of the member states it forms the **European System of Central Banks (ESCB)** and, together with the central banks of the **euro area**, it forms the **Eurosystem**. Its role is to ensure that the functions of the ESCB and the Eurosystem are effectively carried out. A new institution, the ECB's reputation has improved with the strength of the **euro**. The first ECB president, Wim Duisenberg, was frequently criticized for the ECB's slow reaction to economic events and its poor public image. However, when he was replaced by **Jean-Claude Trichet** in November 2003, Duisenberg's work was overwhelmingly praised.

The ECB is run by the Governing Council which has responsibility for formulating monetary policy for the euro area and guide-lines for its implementation. The Governing Council is made up of the governors of the national central banks of member states participating in the euro and all of the members of the Executive Board. The Executive Board is made up of the president and vice-president of the ECB as well as four further specialists in monetary matters and banking. The Executive Board is appointed for a non-renewable term of eight years. The Executive Board is responsible for implementing the guide-lines and decisions of the Governing Council. Finally, the General Council, made up of the president, the vice-president and the governors of the national central banks of all member states, is responsible for preparing non-euro area member states for membership of the single currency.

The ECB's capital currently amounts to €5,000m. The national central banks of member states are the sole subscribers and holders of this capital. The amount of each national central bank's subscription is determined by the member state's shares in the gross domestic product and population of the EU. In 2001 the percentage shares of the national central banks of the member states in the key for ECB's capital were: Austria 2.3594; Belgium 2.8658; Denmark 1.6709; Finland 1.3970; France 16.8337; Germany 24.4935; Greece 2.0564; Ireland 0.8496; Italy 14.8950; Luxembourg 0.1492; Netherlands 4.2780; Portugal 1.9232; Spain 8.8935; Sweden 2.6537; United Kingdom 14.6811. The non-euro national central banks contribute 5% of the amount they would have had to pay if they were full members of EMU.

Pres.: Jean-Claude Trichet
Address: Kaiserstrasse 29, 60311 Frankfurt-am-Main, Germany
Tel: (0)69 13440
Fax: (0)69 13446000
E-mail: info@ecb.int
Internet: www.ecb.int

European Coal and Steel Community (ECSC)

The European Coal and Steel Community (ECSC) was established in 1952, having been provided for by the **Treaty of Paris** of 1951. Six states signed up as founding members to establish a free-trade area and a common market in the areas of coal, iron ore, steel and scrap. It was the first step in the process of European integration. The impetus for the development of an ECSC came from **Jean Monnet** and **Robert Schuman**, and was formulated in the **Schuman Plan** of 1950. The ECSC was considered to be the most effective means of rebuilding the European industrial economy, particularly in the Ruhr area, whilst at the same time preventing another war on the continent.

The ECSC was governed by four new institutions. These were: the High Authority, the **Council of Ministers**; the Common Assembly, and the **European Court of Justice**. The ECSC itself later developed into the **European Economic Community** with the **Treaty of Rome**, and was referred to as the **European Community** from 1967. The ECSC was a 50-year arrangement which expired in July 2002. By that time it had developed into the **European Union** through the **Treaty on European Union**.

Founder Members: Belgium, France, Germany, Italy, Luxembourg and the Netherlands

European Commission

The European Commission is one of the principal institutions of the **European Union (EU)**. Originally established by the **Treaty of Rome** as one of the executive bodies of the **European Economic Community**, it later took on some of the functions of the High Authority which governed the **European Coal and Steel Community** until 1967. The role of the Commission is to initiate policy formulation, monitor the implementation of policy and manage EU programmes and the EU's external relations. As such it has the characteristics of both a political executive and a civil service.

The European Commission is led by the president of the Commission and his College of Commissioners, who collectively serve a four-year term. Since 2004 the College has been composed of 25 commissioners, including the president, each nominated by one of the 25 member states. This new arrangement for the enlarged EU25 replaces the former situation whereby there were 20 commissioners, with the larger states (Germany, France, Italy, Spain and the United Kingdom) providing two commissioners, and the smaller states just one.

The president of the Commission is nominated by the **Council of the European Union** and the Council's choice is then ratified by the **European Parliament (EP)**. The commissioners are nominated by their member states, and are then approved or rejected by the president. The president allocates portfolios to the nominated commissioners—each commissioner is responsible for one of the Directorates-General (DGs)—and the EP then has the authority to approve or reject the complete College. The EP threatened to vote against the College proposed by President **José Manuel Durão Barroso** in October 2004 as many Members of the European Parliament (MEPs) objected to his choice of Commissioner for DG Justice, Freedom and Security, Rocco Buttiglione, who had expressed controversial views on homosexuality and the role of **women** in society. Barroso was forced to withdraw and reconstitute his proposed College.

The European Commission plays an important role in the policy-making process of the **European Community (EC)**, the first **pillar** of the EU. Although it is ultimately the Council of the European Union and the EP that agree legislation, the Commission is responsible for drafting legislation, overseeing its implementation and imposing sanctions on member states and firms that breach Community law. The Commission manages the EC budget and the allocation of funds to programmes such as the Common Agricultural Policy and **Structural Funds**. The Commission also represents the EU in international organizations such as the **World Trade Organization**, the **United Nations**, the **Council of Europe**, the **Organisation for Economic Co-operation and Development**, and the **G7/G8**. Even in policy areas where decisions are made on an intergovernmental basis, such as when the **European Council** agrees new treaties or agreements are reached by the inter-governmental pillars of the EU in the areas of **Common Foreign and Security Policy** or **Police and Judicial Co-operation in Criminal Matters**, the Commission plays an important role in translating general guide-lines into detailed policy. The work of the DGs is supported by a set of departments which provide services to the Commission. These include personnel, translation and interpreting and statistical services (Eurostat). The Commission has a total staff of around 22,000 (2002).

The Commission is accountable to the EP. As well as having the right to reject the president's choice of commissioners, the Parliament can dismiss the whole College, though not individual commissioners, by means of a two-thirds' majority in a vote of no confidence. President Jacques Santer, the president of the College of Commissioners in 1995–99, resigned nine months early in March 1999 after the Commission had narrowly survived an EP vote of censure (232 for, 293 against) in January 1999. The Commission was accused by an independent Committee of Experts of corruption, a lack of accountability and financial mismanagement. Specifically, the Committee of Experts accused the Commissioner for Research, Edith Cresson, of offering contracts to friends, and President Santer of not being vigilant against Commission corruption. The president of the Commission in 1999–2004, Romano Prodi, set about reforming the institution to improve standards of accountability, efficiency, transparency and responsibility. These reforms were guided by a Commission White Paper of 2000, and their implementation was overseen by vice-president and Commissioner for Administrative Reform, Neil Kinnock.

The 25 members of the 2004–09 College of the European Commission are: José Manuel Durão Barroso, president (Portugal); Günter Verheugen vice-president/DG Enterprise and Industry (Germany); Margot Wallström, vice-president/DG Institutional Relations and Communication Strategy (Sweden); Jacques Barrot, vice-president/DG Transport (France); Siim Kallas, vice-president/DG Administrative Affairs, Audit and Anti-Fraud (Estonia); Franco Frattini, vice-president/DG Justice, Freedom and Security (Italy); Viviane Reding, DG Information Society and Media (Luxembourg); Stavros Dimas, DG Environment (Greece); Joaquin Almunia, DG Economic and Monetary Affairs (Spain); Danuta Huebner, DG Regional Policy (Poland); Joe Borg, DG Fisheries and Maritime Affairs (Malta); Dalia Grybauskaite, DG Financial Programming and Budget (Lithuania); Janez Potocnik, DG Science and Research (Slovenia); Jan Figel, DG Education, Training, Culture, and Multilinguism (Slovakia); Markos Kyprianou, DG Health and Consumer Protection (Cyprus); Olli Rehn, DG Enlargement (Finland); Louis Michel, DG Development and Humanitarian Aid (Belgium); László Kovács, DG Taxation and Customs Union (Hungary); Neelie Kroes, DG Competition (Netherlands); Mariann Fischer Boel, DG Agriculture and Rural Development (Denmark); Benita Ferrero-Waldner, DG External Relations and European Neighbourhood Policy (Austria); Charlie McCreevy, DG Internal Market and Services (Ireland); Vladimir Spidla, DG Employment, Social Affairs and Equal Opportunities (Czech Republic); Peter Mandelson, DG Trade (United Kingdom); Andris Piebalgs, DG Energy (Latvia).

Address: rue de la Loi/Wetstraat 200, 1049 Brussels, Belgium
Tel: (0)2 299-11-11
E-mail: via europedirect-cc.cec.eu.int/websubmit/?lang=en
Internet: europa.eu.int/comm/index_en.htm

European Community (EC)

The European Community (EC) is the term given to the first **pillar** of the **European Union (EU)**. It was originally established as the European Communities (also EC) following the merger of the **European Economic Community**, the **European Coal and Steel Community** and Euratom into a single body in 1967.

The EC is the supranational part of the EU and policy-making procedures in the EC are subject to the community method. This means that the **European Commission** initiates a legislative proposal, which then has to be agreed by the **Council of the European Union** and, now usually, the **European Parliament**. This contrasts with intergovernmental areas where it is the Council that normally has the right to initiate and decide on legislation. The policy areas which fall under the EC include matters relating to the **Single European Market**, freedom of movement of goods, services, capital and people, **agriculture**, environment, competition and trade. It also includes **Economic and Monetary Union** and, since the **Treaty of Amsterdam**, some aspects of **Justice and Home Affairs**.

European Convention

The European Convention was charged with drafting a Constitutional Treaty for the **European Union (EU)**. The aim of the exercise was to consolidate the existing treaties of the EU and its machinery to make it better able to speak with a single voice on an international stage, to deal with the challenges of EU **enlargement** and to improve the openness, coherence, efficiency and democracy of the EU's institutions for its citizens.

The decision to institute the Convention was set out in the Laeken Declaration on the Future of the European Union of December 2001. With **Valéry Giscard d'Estaing** as its president, the European Convention held its inaugural meeting in March 2002 and the 265-page draft Constitution was published by the European Convention on 18 July 2003 and signed by EU leaders on 29 October 2004.

The Constitutional Treaty consolidates existing treaties into a single document and formalizes many aspect of existing practice. Important innovations include:

- changing the six-month rotating presidency of the **European Council** to a two-and-a-half year chairmanship, renewable once (Article I-22), whose incumbent is elected by the European Council
- reforming the use of qualified majority voting (QMV) in the **Council of the European Union** so that a double majority is required, representing 55% of member states (at least 15 states) and 65% of the EU's population. If the Council of Ministers is not acting on a proposal from the **European Commission**, then the double majority required would increase to 72% of members of the Council and 65% of the population (Article I-25). Unanimity remains in the areas of taxation, social security, foreign policy and defence.
- reducing the size of the European Commission after one full five-year term from 25 commissioners to one consisting of a number of commissioners corresponding to two-thirds of the number of EU member states (Article I-26).
- creating the Union Minister for Foreign Affairs who would also be vice-president of the **European Commission** (Article I-28).

To be adopted, the draft treaty must be ratified by all 25 EU member states either in a referendum or through a parliamentary vote. Nine countries plan to hold a referendum (the Czech Republic, Denmark, France, Ireland, Luxembourg, the Netherlands, Spain, Portugal and the United Kingdom).

> *Internet:* european-convention.eu.int or
> ue.eu.int/uedocs/cmsUpload/cg00087-re02.en04.pdf for the Treaty signed on 29 October 2004

European Council

The European Council is the biannual summit meeting of the **European Union (EU)**. It brings together the heads of government or state of all EU member states to map out the strategic direction for the EU and to agree on important matters such as institutional reform, **enlargement**, and foreign, security and defence policy. The European Council began as an informal set of meetings in the early 1970s and was later incorporated into the institutional system by the **Single European Act**. It was strengthened by the **Treaty on European Union** when it was given responsibility for the two intergovernmental **pillars** of the EU: **Common Foreign and Security Policy** and **Justice and Home Affairs** (now **Police and Judicial Co-operation in Criminal Matters**).

European Council summits are hosted by the member state which holds the rotating presidency of the **Council of the European Union**. Additional meetings are held throughout the year in Brussels, Belgium. In recent years anti-globalization protesters have held demonstrations at EU summit meetings. The Constitutional Treaty drafted by the **European Convention** proposed that the six-month rotating presidency of the **European Commission** be changed to a European Council chairmanship whose incumbent would be chosen by the heads of government for a two-and-a-half-year term.

European Court of Justice (ECJ)

The European Court of Justice (ECJ) is an institution in the **European Union (EU)** that ensures that legislation agreed by the **European Community** is interpreted and implemented identically across all member states and that such implementation is in compliance with that legislation. It deals with legal disputes between member states, EU institutions, businesses and individuals. Most cases concern common economic activity, but the ECJ increasingly makes judgments in such areas as the environment or social policy. The ECJ only deals with cases that are referred to it. Established in 1951 by the **Treaty of Paris**, the ECJ began work in 1952. It is composed of one judge per member state of the EU, currently 25 judges. The judges' work is supported by eight advocates-general who examine cases brought before the court and present their opinion to the ECJ. Both judges and advocates-general are nominated by member states and appointed for a six-year term, which is renewable. They are required to be independent and impartial.

In the late 1980s the workload of the ECJ increased substantially through the legislative programme to complete the **Single European Market**. In 1989 the Court of First Instance (CFI) was set up to deal with straightforward conflicts between the Communities and its staff members, and cases brought by private companies and individuals. Despite the creation of the CFI, the courts have been criticized for the slow progress of their proceedings; the average case takes 18–24 months. Nevertheless, the ECJ and the CFI are increasingly important institutions in the EU and some key rulings have shaped the direction of the process of European integration.

The work of the ECJ is organized into six chambers; simple cases are dealt with by a chamber with three judges, and more complex cases in a five-judge chamber. Since the **Treaty on European Union** the ECJ is only required to hold plenary sessions when requested by a member state or Community institution that is involved in the proceedings. The **Treaty of Nice** established a Grand Chamber in the ECJ so that the ECJ can sit with 13 judges rather than as a plenary session involving all judges. Court judgments are determined by majority decision and there is no right of appeal against decisions of the ECJ.

Address: European Court of Justice, 2925 Luxembourg
Tel: (0)352 43-03-1
Fax: (0)352 43-03-26-00
E-mail: via www.curia.eu.int/en/instit/presentationfr/index_cje.htm
Internet: www.curia.eu.int

European Currency Unit (ECU)

The European Currency Unit (ECU) was a theoretical European currency established with the **European Monetary System** in 1978. The ECU was a 'basket' of the currencies of states participating in the **European Economic Community (EEC)**. It was originally used for the EEC's internal budget and later became used for travellers' cheques and bank deposits, but was never issued as banknotes or coins. The ECU was replaced by the **euro** in the process of **Economic and Monetary Union**.

European Economic Area (EEA)

The European Economic Area (EEA) is the trading area between the **European Community (EC)** and the states belonging to the **European Free Trade Association (EFTA)**—Norway, Iceland and Liechtenstein. Negotiated in 1991 and signed in 1992, the agreement creating the EEA allowed the EFTA members to participate in the **Single European Market** without being full members of the then EC. The agreement originally involved seven countries. However, following a referendum, Switzerland later decided not to participate and Austria, Finland and Sweden left the EEA when they joined the **European Union** in 1995.

The EEA is required to adopt the parts of the *acquis communautaire* concerned with competition rules and freedom of movement for goods, people, services and capital. The EEA also co-operates with the EC in other areas, including research and technology, environment, education and tourism. The EEA countries have the right to be consulted by the **European Commission** on any new legislation which affects them, but they do not have any decision-making powers.

European Economic Community (EEC)

The European Economic Community (EEC) was established by the **Treaty of Rome** in 1958. The EEC institutional framework was merged with the **European Coal and Steel Community** and the European Atomic Energy Community (Euratom) in 1967. From then on the EEC was officially referred to as the European Communities or **European Community (EC)**, although the EEC was still in common use. The **Treaty on European Union** of 1992 confirmed that the EC would be the official term, and the **Treaty of Rome** was amended accordingly.

European Free Trade Association (EFTA)

The European Free Trade Association (EFTA) established a free-trade area for industrial goods in Western Europe. Founded by the EFTA or Stockholm Convention in 1960, it originally comprised seven states—Austria, Denmark, Norway, Portugal, Sweden, Switzerland and the United Kingdom—which were not members of the **European Economic Community**. Denmark and the United Kingdom left EFTA when they became members of the **European Community (EC)** in 1973, and Iceland, Finland and Liechtenstein joined, Finland as an associate member.

During the 1980s members of EFTA recognized the disadvantage of being obliged to accept the rules of the EC without having the power to shape them. This became all the more apparent following the **Single European Act** which set down the rules for the completion of the **Single European Market** by 1992. Closer co-operation between EFTA and the EC came about through the establishment of the **European Economic Area** in 1992, though Switzerland chose not to participate. Austria, Finland and Sweden left EFTA when they became members of the **European Union** in 1995. Today only Iceland, Liechtenstein, Norway and Switzerland remain members of EFTA.

European Monetary Institute (EMI)

The European Monetary Institute (EMI), established by the **Treaty on European Union**, was a temporary institution which existed from January 1994 until June 1998 during the second stage of **Economic and Monetary Union**. Based in Frankfurt-am-Main, Germany, its role was to improve co-operation between the central banks and monetary policy of member states. It also made the necessary preparations for establishing the **European System of Central Banks** and was in charge of the design of the **euro** banknotes. The EMI was closed in June 1998 as soon as the **European Central Bank** was established.

European Monetary System (EMS)

The European Monetary System (EMS) was an early attempt by the **European Community** to achieve monetary union. The EMS was established on the initiative of France and Germany on 5 December 1978 in order to stabilize exchange rates, reduce inflation and prepare for monetary integration. The EMS consisted of three elements: the **European Currency Unit**, the **Exchange Rate Mechanism** and the European Monetary Co-operation Fund for financing monetary interventions.

European Parliament (EP)

The European Parliament (EP) is the legislative body of the **European Union (EU)**. Originally established as the Assembly of the **European Coal and Steel Community** by the Treaty of Paris, it adopted its present name in 1962. The EP is based in Brussels, Belgium, though monthly plenary sessions, which all Members of the European Parliament (MEPs) attend, take place in Strasbourg, France, and the main administrative office is situated in Luxembourg. Originally a weak institution, the powers of the EP have increased significantly over the years through treaty amendments designed to strengthen the democratic credentials of the EU. Though still in many respects weaker than national parliaments, the EP does have three important functions: legislative, budgetary and controlling.

The EP participates in the legislative process of the EU through a number of different procedures. Until 1987 the EP was only permitted to give its opinion on legislation proposed by the **European Commission** through the consultation procedure. The **Single European Act** introduced the co-operation procedure and the assent procedure. The former adds a second reading to the legislative process, and the EP has the power to amend or reject a common position provided for EP by the **Council of European Union** in the first reading with an absolute majority vote. The Council then requires a unanimous vote to override the EP. The assent procedure requires the support of an absolute majority of MEPs in the first reading before a Council decision can be taken; the EP can veto decisions if this majority is not forthcoming. This procedure is used in international agreements such as the **accession** of new members to the EU. The **Treaty on European Union (TEU)** introduced the co-decision procedure which gives the EP a veto in the second reading if an absolute majority of MEPs reject it. The legislation is then referred to a conciliation committee made up of equal numbers of members of the EP and the Council. If no agreement can be reached, then the legislation falls. Since the **Treaty of Amsterdam** most EU legislation has been decided by the co-decision procedure with the exceptions of key policy areas such as **agriculture, justice and home affairs**, trade, taxation and **Economic and Monetary Union**.

The EP is responsible for supervising the EU's budget. It can propose modifications to compulsory spending, in areas such as agriculture, and amendments to non-compulsory expenditure. Since the Treaty on European Union the EP can reject a whole draft budget if backed by a majority of two-thirds of MEPs.

Third, the EP has powers to control and supervise the **European Commission**, the Council of the European Union and the **European Council**. The EP discusses the Commission's annual report and budgets, scrutinizes its work in standing and *ad hoc* committees and asks written and oral questions. The EP approves the Council's nomination for president of the European Commission; it also confirms the appointment of the College of Commissioners and can dismiss the College by a two-thirds' majority vote based on the participation of at least one-half of all MEPs. In recent years the EP has used these powers to the full. The Jacques Santer Commission College narrowly escaped a vote of censure by the EP (for 232; against 293) in January 1999 after it had been accused of corruption and mismanagement. An independent committee was set up to investigate these issues and its report severely criticized the College. The Santer Commission then decided to resign collectively in order to avoid a further vote of censure. The EP threatened to reject the new Commission College proposed by **José Manuel Durão Barroso** in October 2004 as many MEPs objected to his choice of Commisioner for Justice and Home Affairs, Rocco Buttiglione. The threat led Barroso to withdraw and reconfigure his proposed team. The EP has less power to control the Council of the European Union and the European Council, but they are required to attend plenary sessions and report to the EP.

MEPs were initially delegates from national parliaments but since 1979 they have been directly elected in member states for five-year terms by an electoral system decided by the member state. All citizens of the EU are entitled to vote in elections to the EP and, since the TEU, EU citizens have had the right to vote and stand for election to the EP in any member state. At the most recent elections, held in June 2004, 732 MEPs were elected for the 25 EU member states. MEPs are allocated to countries according to the size of their populations. As agreed in the **Treaty of Nice**, seats in the new EP are distributed as follows: Austria 18; Belgium 24; Cyprus 6; Czech Republic 24; Denmark 14; Estonia 6; Finland 14; France 78; Germany 99; Greece 24; Hungary 24; Ireland 13; Italy 78; Latvia 9; Lithuania 13; Luxembourg 6; Malta 5; Netherlands 27; Poland 54; Portugal 24; Slovakia 14; Slovenia 7; Spain 54; Sweden 19; United Kingdom 78.

The EP is organized into political groups which bring together MEPs of political 'families' from all member states. In June 2004 there were seven political groupings which had the following number of members: the European People's Party (Christian Democrats) and European Democrats 268; the Socialist Group in the European Parliament 202; the Alliance of Liberals and Democrats for Europe 88; the Greens/European Free Alliance 42, the European United Left-Nordic Green Left 41, Independence/Democracy 36, Union for Europe of the Nations 27. Additionally, 28 MEPs are unattached. Of the 732 MEPs elected in June 2004, 30.33% are **women**.

Address: rue Wiertz, 1047 Brussels, Belgium
Tel: (0)2 284-21-11
Fax: (0)2 284-69-74
Internet: www.europarl.eu.int

European Regional Development Fund (ERDF)

The European Regional Development Fund (ERDF) was established in 1975 to promote regional economic convergence and to assist regions facing severe economic problems due to the decline of traditional heavy industries. Since 1988 ERDF has been one of the **European Union**'s **(EU) Structural Funds**. The other three are the **European Social Fund (ESF)**, the guidance section of the European Agricultural Guarantee and Guidance Fund and the Financial Instrument for Fisheries Guidance (FIFG). For the period 2000–06, the Structural Funds together with the Cohesion Fund (which is targeted specifically at Greece, Ireland, Portugal and Spain) account for approximately one-third of EU expenditure.

The **Treaty of Rome** did not contain a provision for a community regional policy, although many policies have regional impacts, most notably the ESF. The ERDF was established in 1975 as the main instrument of Community regional policy. The primary purpose of the ERDF is to address regional economic disparities. It represents only a small fiscal transfer from the richest member states to the poorest regions of the EU and has a significant direct economic effect only on the very poorest regions.

The Structural Funds are equivalent to approximately 0.4% of the gross domestic product (GDP) of the EU, around €175,000m. over this period. The ERDF receives approximately two-thirds of the Structural Funds budget. Seventy per cent of this funding goes to regions whose development is lagging behind. These have per caput income that is less than 75% of average EU GDP per caput. These are termed Objective 1 regions. In addition, 11.5% of the funding assists economic and social conversion in areas experiencing structural difficulties—Objective 2 regions. Finally, 12.3% of the funding promotes the modernization of training systems and the creation of employment (termed Objective 3) outside the Objective 1 regions. The ERDF contributes funding to Objectives 1 and 2.

There are also four Community Initiatives which account for 5.35% of the Structural Funds budget. These include INTERREG III (for cross-border, transnational and interregional co-operation), URBAN II (to promote the sustainable development of cities and declining urban areas), Leader + (to support rural development through local initiatives) and Equal (to combat inequalities and discrimination through improving access to the labour market). Of these, the ERDF contributes to INTERREG III and URBAN II.

The Structural Funds and the Cohesion Fund represent the main instruments of social and economic cohesion policy for the EU. Their aim is to strengthen the structural factors which determine competitiveness and, thereby, the growth potential of the most disadvantaged regions. The broad policy framework for social and economic cohesion policy was established in 1988 with a major reform of the Structural Funds. These reforms were closely linked to the agreement of the **Single European Act** and to a recognition that closer economic integration may not bring about growth for all regions, particularly those lagging in terms of EU GDP. In addition to doubling the financial support to the Structural Funds, the 1988 reforms also brought the then three funds (FIFG was established along with the Cohesion Fund in 1993) together under a common set of regulations.

The scope of ERDF is relatively wide-ranging. For the 2000–06 period, funds may be used to support infrastructural improvements (particularly in lagging and peripheral regions) and the regeneration of industrial sites and support for rural areas (in Objective 2 areas); and also to support small and medium-sized enterprises and innovation and technological development capacity.

The implementation of the ERDF, and that of the Structural Funds as a whole, is underpinned by four principles established in the 1988 reforms. These include the concentration of funds on a few policy objectives and targeted at defined population levels, the agreement of multi-annual regional or thematic programmes to establish priorities at the local or regional level, the development and implementation of programmes through partnership of the public sector and social partners, and additionality, whereby the contribution of the EU is additional to, and not a substitute for, the contribution of the member states.

The current Structural Funds and Cohesion Fund regulations will expire in 2006. New regulations were proposed in 2004 for the period 2007–13. Following the conclusions of the Lisbon Summit in 2000, key policy priorities will be the creation of more and better jobs, greater social inclusion, equal opportunities and continued support for the knowledge-based society. Following the **accession** of countries in 2004 with significantly lower levels of GDP per caput than the average of the previous EU member states, the eligible funds will be targeted predominantly at the new member states with some transitional funding provisions made for the current recipients. The ERDF will be used in 2007–13 to support the following objectives: convergence (the economic catch up of the poorest regions); regional competitiveness and employment (support outside the poorest regions); and European territorial co-operation (to promote co-operation between all regions, specifically around sustainable development).

Internet: www.europa.ei.int/comm/regional_policy/index_en.htm
Peter Wells
Sheffield Hallam University

European Security and Defence Policy (ESDP)

European Security and Defence Policy (ESDP) is part of the **Common Foreign and Security Policy** of the **European Union (EU)**. Established by the Cologne European Council in 1999 and formalized by the **Treaty of Nice** signed in 2001,

ESDP covers all areas of EU security and seeks to gradually formulate a common defence policy for all member states.

Through ESDP, the EU has strengthened its responsibility for the four Petersberg tasks, a set of activities to which the **Western European Union (WEU)** committed itself at a summit held in Petersberg in June 1992. These are: humanitarian and rescue operations, peace-keeping tasks, and activities for combat forces in crisis management, including peace-making.

The EU also committed itself to the 'headline goal' which states that, by 2003, the EU should have been able to deploy 60,000 troops within 60 days and for at least one year in order to carry out the Petersberg tasks. Through the development of ESDP, the EU has adopted many of the roles that were originally intended for the WEU, though not the common defence clause. It is also developing its own **Rapid Reaction Force**.

European Social Fund (ESF)

The European Social Fund (ESF) was established by the **European Economic Community** to support employment and social development, particularly in regions that have faced high levels of **unemployment**. Since 1988 ESF has been one of the **European Union's (EU) Structural Funds**. The other three are the **European Regional Development Fund**, the guidance section of the European Agricultural Guarantee and Guidance Fund and the Financial Instrument for Fisheries Guidance. For the period 2000–06, the Structural Funds, together with the Cohesion Fund (which is targeted specifically at Greece, Ireland, Portugal and Spain), account for approximately one-third of expenditure of the budget of the EU. More recently ESF has been used to promote the European Employment Strategy in each of the member states.

The ESF is the main financial tool through which the EU translates its strategic employment policy aims into action. The ESF was established by the **Treaty of Rome** in 1958 with the aim of improving mobility within the labour market, primarily by providing funds for the training and retraining of workers affected by industrial restructuring. In its first decade the main beneficiaries of the ESF were Italian agricultural workers migrating to work in northern Italy and workers in the Federal Republic of Germany. It was first reformed in 1971 to place a greater focus on providing support for workers in declining industries, **women**, migrant workers, young people and those with disabilities. The next major reform of the ESF came with the signing of the **Single European Act** and the reform of it and the other Structural Funds.

Since the **Treaty of Amsterdam** the ESF has been used as the major instrument for the EU to shape the implementation of the European Employment Strategy; in particular, its focus since the Lisbon European summit has been on employment and competitiveness in the knowledge-based economy.

The primary purpose of the ESF, through Structural Funds programmes, is to develop the employability of individuals. Although the focus of the ESF is therefore on the development of work skills, it also possesses the scope to reduce barriers which individuals or groups may face in re-entering the labour market. Programmes are planned by member states together with the **European Commission** and then implemented through a wide range of provider organizations both in the public and the private sectors. These organizations include national, regional and local authorities, educational and training institutions, voluntary organizations and the social partners (trade unions and works councils, industry and professional associations, and individual companies).

During the Structural Funds 2000–06 programming period, the ESF is investing approximately €62,500m. in modernizing and reforming labour markets. Key priorities include: preventing long-term **unemployment**, reintegrating marginalized groups into society, promoting equal opportunities, and helping in the transition towards the knowledge-based economy by the promotion of lifelong learning.

During the 2000–06 programming period, ESF support has targeted the following activities: education and vocational training projects; schemes to promote and encourage employment and self-employment; initiatives to generate new sources of employment; improvements to national, regional and local employment services; schemes to foster links between the worlds of work, education and research; and innovative measures and pilot projects to create work in local communities.

The current Structural Funds and Cohesion Fund regulations will expire in 2006. New regulations were proposed in 2004 for the period 2007–13. Following the conclusions of the Lisbon summit in 2000, key policy priorities will be the creation of more and better jobs, greater social inclusion, equal opportunities and continued support for the knowledge-based society. Following the accession in 2004 of countries with significantly lower levels of per caput gross domestic product than the average of the previous EU member states, the eligible funds will be targeted predominantly at the new member states with some transitional funding provisions made for the current recipients. The ESF will be used in 2007–13 to support the following objectives: convergence (the economic catch up of the poorest regions); regional competitiveness and employment (support outside the poorest regions); and European territorial co-operation (to promote co-operation between all regions, specifically around sustainable development).

Internet: www.europa.eu.int/comm/employment_social/esf2000/index-en.htm
Peter Wells
Sheffield Hallam University

European System of Central Banks

The European System of Central Banks is made up of the **European Central Bank** and the national central banks of all member states of the **European Union (EU)**. It was set up by the **European Monetary Institute** in 1998 for the third stage of

Economic and Monetary Union. Officially, it is responsible for maintaining price stability, and defining and implementing a common monetary policy, and it supervises the foreign reserves of EU member states. However, as not all of the member states are taking part in the **euro area**, an additional institution called **Eurosystem** has been created to carry out decision-making tasks. In this way, member states not participating in the **euro** do not take part in decision-making and implementation of policy for the euro area.

European Trade Unions Confederation (ETUC)

The European Trade Unions Confederation (ETUC) is the confederation of employees' organizations at European level. Founded in 1973, it campaigns for workers' rights in the process of European integration. It is made up of some 77 member organizations from 35 European countries and represents more than 60m. members. It exists to influence decision-making in the European institutions and to ensure a presence of the trade union voice in consultation procedures. It also seeks to establish a social dialogue with employers' organizations at European level.

Leadership: Pres. Cándido Méndez Rodríguez; *Gen. Sec.* John Monks
Address: 5 blvd Roi Albert II, 1210 Brussels, Belgium
Tel: (0)2 224-04-11
Fax: (0)2 224-04-54
E-mail: ctuc@etuc.org
Internet: www.etuc.org

European Union (EU)

The European Union (EU) is the body established in 1993 by the **Treaty on European Union**. The establishment of the EU was a significant step towards achieving the aim set out in the **Treaty of Rome** of creating an 'ever closer union' among the people of Europe. Significantly, with the EU came the concept of EU **citizenship**, the **Social Chapter**, and plans to complete **Economic and Monetary Union (EMU)** and introduce a **single currency**.

However, in many ways, the EU fell short of being a true union. For one thing, a number of states secured 'opt-outs' of aspects of the EU which they opposed. For example, Denmark chose not to participate in foreign policy decision-making that had defence implications and the United Kingdom opted out of the Social Chapter. Denmark, Sweden and the United Kingdom have all opted out of EMU. This development has led to debates about whether there should be differentiated integration or enhanced forms of co-operation in the EU.

The EU is structured as three **pillars**: the **European Community**, **Common Foreign and Security Policy** and **Justice and Home Affairs**, now **Police and Judicial Co-operation in Criminal Matters**. EU decision-making is conducted on a different basis, depending on whether policy falls under the supranational first pillar or the intergovernmental second and third pillars. In some policy areas of the first pillar (e.g. taxation) states protect their right to veto proposals and in intergovernmental areas it has been notoriously difficult for the EU to speak with a single voice on foreign policy and defence issues.

The **enlargement** of the EU to 25 member states on 1 May 2004 could make the aim of creating a coherent union more difficult. While the **accession** states were obliged to adopt the *acquis communautaire* in its entirety and were permitted no opt-outs, there are concerns that they might exercise their veto rights in the **Council of the European Union** to make their voices heard and bargain for concessions.

The EU has been reformed and consolidated by the **Treaty of Amsterdam** and the **Treaty of Nice**. The decision to convene the **European Convention** to draft a Constitutional Treaty for the EU was a further step in the process of forming a coherent union.

Europeanization

Europeanization is a concept used in the study of **European Union (EU)** politics associated with the work of scholars such as Claudio Radaelli, Tanja Börzel, Chrisoph Knill and Dirk Lehmkuhl to describe the process whereby the EU influences the domestic politics, policy and polity of member and non-member states. The impact of the EU is triggered through a variety of mechanisms, such as creating new rules or regulations which explicitly alter national institutions **(Economic and Monetary Union)**, altering domestic arrangements and with them opportunity structures **(Single European Market)** or through benchmarking exercises **(Lisbon process)** which alter belief systems in the domestic setting.

The impact of Europeanization is not unitary, and the process clearly does not lead to convergence of institutions, practice or norms in EU member states. Rather, the degree of change depends on the policy area, the nation and institutions. It is widely accepted that the degree of national—or sub-national—adaptation to the process of Europeanization varies according to the ability and motivation to adapt as well as the 'goodness of fit' between EU and domestic arrangements.

Europol

Europol is the European police agency. Established in 1992, it co-ordinates criminal intelligence between the member states of the **European Union (EU)**. It is especially concerned with preventing and combating organized crime, such as drugs-trafficking, **immigration** networks, human-trafficking, child pornography, money-laundering and **terrorism**. Europol forms part of the third **pillar** of the EU, **Police and Judicial Co-operation in Criminal Matters**. It is accountable to the **Justice and Home Affairs (JHA)** ministers of EU member states, collectively the JHA Council.

Dir: Jürgen Storbeck
Address: POB 90850, NL-2509 LW The Hague, Netherlands
Tel: (0)70 3025000
Fax: (0)70 3455896
E-mail: info@europol.eu.int
Internet: www.europol.eu.int

Eurosclerosis

Eurosclerosis is a term used in the context of the politics of the **European Union (EU)** to describe the period between 1966 and the early 1980s when little progress was made in the process of European integration. To economists, Eurosclerosis is the theory that seeks to explain the poor economic performance of the European economy. The widely contested thesis argues that poor economic performance in Europe can be attributed to the over-regulation and institutional rigidity of the European economy and labour market. In order to trigger economic growth and reduce **unemployment**, proponents of the Eurosclerosis theory argue that it is necessary to cut regulation and the **welfare state**, wage equality and excessive labour costs. The term was coined by the Kiel-based German economist Herbert Giersch in the 1980s.

Eurosystem

The Eurosystem is an institution made up of the **European Central Bank (ECB)** and the national central banks of the states participating in the **euro area**. The term is used as distinct from the **European System of Central Banks** which includes all **European Union** member states.

The key aim of the Eurosystem is to maintain price stability: it aims to keep year-on-year consumer price increases below 2%. To do this it defines and implements monetary policy for the euro area. It conducts foreign exchange operations, holds and manages the official foreign reserves of euro area economies and issues banknotes for the euro area. Decision-making for the Eurosystem is conducted through the Governing Council and the Executive Board of the ECB.

Eurozone – *see* Euro area

Eusko Langileen Alkartasuna-Solidaridad de Trabajadores Vascos – *see* Basque Workers' Solidarity, Spain

Euzko Alderdi Jeltzalea-Partido Nacionalista Vasco – *see* Basque Nationalist Party, Spain

Exchange Rate Mechanism (ERM)

The Exchange Rate Mechanism (ERM), together with the **European Currency Unit (ECU)**, formed the foundations of the **European Union**'s project to achieve **Economic and Monetary Union (EMU)**. The ERM was intended to stabilize exchange rates and control inflation. The ERM gave each currency a central exchange rate against the ECU and that in turn gave them central cross-rates against each of the other participating currencies. Participating currencies were required to keep their exchange rates within a 2.25% margin above and below a bilateral rate. The Italian lira was allowed to fluctuate up to 6% either side of the central rate. The United Kingdom initially remained outside the system.

The ERM experienced difficulties in 1992 as a number of participating currencies failed to keep within the set limits. On 16 September 1992 ('Black Wednesday') the British pound and Italian lira were forced to leave the system and the Spanish peseta was devalued. Later, as the project to complete EMU progressed, a currency's ability to remain with the **European Monetary System** became one of the **convergence criteria** for membership of the **euro area**.

F

Faroe Islands

The Faroe Islands are a group of 18 islands situated between the North Atlantic Ocean and the Norwegian Sea, equidistant to Iceland and Norway. The islands cover some 1,399 sq km; the capital is Torshavn. Part of the Kingdom of Denmark, the Faroe Islands were granted a high degree of self-government in 1948. There is a strong movement for full independence on the islands and a referendum on the issue of independence was scheduled for 26 May 2001. This was shelved after the Danish government announced that a yes vote would lead to the end of the generous financial subsidy (15% of Denmark's gross domestic product) within four years.

The head of state of the Faroe Islands in Queen Margrethe II of Denmark, who is represented by the High Commissioner—since November 2001 Birgit Kleis—appointed by the monarch. The Faroe Islands returns two representatives to the **Folketing**, the national parliament of Denmark, and the Danish government is responsible for defence, foreign relations, monetary policy and policing. Domestic issues are decided in the Faroese parliament, the 32-seat Logting which is elected for a four-year term. Following the most recent elections, held on 20 January 2004, a government was formed by three of the four main parties, headed by Social Democrat Johannes Eidesgaard. The elections in fact returned the governing pro-independence coalition, but internal disagreements rendered it unable to govern. The pro-independence Republican Party is not included in the current coalition.

The Faroese economy is dominated by fishing, fish processing and shipbuilding. Economic performance has improved since 1994 on account of an increase in fish catches and high export prices. The economy has increased its budget surpluses and reduced its debt to Denmark. **Unemployment** among the population of 47,700 (2003) has also fallen, to about 1% (2000), and the standard of living is comparable to that of the Danes. Oil and gas finds just outside the Faroese territory have led to hopes that deposits could be sourced in the immediate Faroese area. This would boost the economy and reduce the Faroe Islands' dependency on economic assistance from Denmark.

Federal Constitutional Court

The Federal Constitutional Court, or Bundesverfassungsgericht (BVG), in Germany was founded in 1951 to uphold the German Constitution. The court is made up of 16 judges, eight of whom are chosen by the **Bundesrat** and eight by the **Bundestag**, for a 12-year, non-renewable term. The BVG is considered to be one of the most important and highly respected institutions in Germany, and is one of the most powerful constitutional courts in Western Europe.

The BVG makes judgments regarding the constitutionality of proposed and enacted legislation. It also rules on conflicts between the political levels in the federal system and between public authorities and members of the public, and it can also ban political parties which are deemed not to respect the values of the Basic Law. It banned an extreme right-wing party, the Sozialistische Reichspartei, in 1952 and the extreme left-wing Kommunistische Partei Deutschlands in 1956. The BVG has been criticized for some judgments that were deemed to be political and to interfere with the legislative process. It has twice (in 1975 and 1993) overruled parliamentary legislation on abortion on the grounds that it is an act of killing and does not respect the right to life provided for in the Constitution.

Address: Schlossbezirk 3, 76131 Karlsruhe, or POB 1771, 76006 Karlsruhe, Germany
Tel: (0)721 91010
E-mail: bverfg@bundesverfassungsgericht.de
Internet: www.bverfg.de

Federal Court

The Federal Court, or Bundesgericht, is the highest court in Switzerland. It is made up of 30 full-time and 30 part-time judges who represent all language and regional communities. It conducts constitutional review of laws made at cantonal levels.

Address: ave du Tribunal Fédéral 29, 1000 Lausanne 14, Switzerland
Tel: (0)213189111
Fax: (0)213233700
E-mail: direktion@bger.admin.ch
Internet: www.bger.ch

Federatie Nederlandse Vakbeweging – *see* Dutch Trade Union Confederation

Fédération des Industriels Luxembourgeois – *see* Federation of Luxembourg Industry

Fédération Générale du Travail de Belgique – *see* General Federation of Belgian Workers

Federation of Austrian Industry

The Federation of Austrian Industry, or Industriellenvereinigung, is the business organization in Austria. Founded in 1862, it lobbies nationally and internationally to promote Austrian business and it also provides services to its members. It is itself a member of the **Union of Industrial and Employers' Confederations of Europe**.

Leadership: Pres. Veit Sorger; *Gen. Sec.* Markus Beyrer
Address: Schwarzenbergplatz 4, POB 61, 1031 Vienna, Austria
Tel: (0)1 711-35-0
Fax: (0)1 711-35-2910
E-mail: iv-office@iv-net.at
Internet: www.iv-net.at

Federation of Christian Unions

The Federation of Christian Unions, or Algemeeen Christelijk Vakverbond/ Confédération des Syndicats Chrétiens, is the largest Christian trade union federation in Belgium. Founded in 1886, it represents 1.5m. workers from 13 affiliated unions in all economic sectors. It aims to improve the democratic representation of labour in the economy and the workplace.

Pres.: Luc Cortebeeck
Address: Haachtsesteenweg 579, 1031 Brussels, Belgium
Tel: (0)2 246-31-11
Fax: (0)2 246-30-10
E-mail: pers@acv-csc.be
Internet: www.acv-csc.be

Federation of Enterprises

The Federation of Enterprises, or Verbond van Belgische Ondernemingen/ Fédération des Enterprises de Belgique, is the business organization in Belgium. It lobbies nationally and internationally for a favourable business climate for all Belgian companies. The organization comprises some 30,000 businesses through 50 sectoral associations. It is itself a member of the **Union of Industrial and Employers' Confederations of Europe**.

Leadership: Pres. Luc Vansteenkiste; *CEO* Rudi Thomaes
Address: 4 rue Ravenstein, 1000 Brussels, Belgium
Tel: (0)2 515-08-11
Fax: (0)2 515-09-15

E-mail: info@vbo-feb.be
Internet: www.vbo-feb.be

Federation of Greek Industries (FGI)

The Federation of Greek Industries (FGI) in Greece was founded in 1907. It represents Greek manufacturing and service industries domestically and abroad and is itself a member of the **Union of Industrial and Employers' Confederations of Europe**.

Leadership: Chair. Ulysses Kyriacopoulos; *Dir-Gen.* Ioannis Drapaniotis
Address: Xenofontos 5 Syntagma, 105 57 Athens, Greece
Tel: (0)210 3237325
Fax: (0)210 3222929
E-mail: info@fgi.org.gr
Internet: www.fgi.org.gr

Federation of Icelandic Industries

The Federation of Icelandic Industries, or Samtök Idnadarins (SI), is the main organization for businesses in Iceland. It lobbies internationally and nationally to promote a competitive business climate and the internationalization of the Icelandic economy. It also provides services for its 15,000 member companies. Members of SI are also automatically members of the **Confederation of Icelandic Employers** and SI is itself a member of the **Union of Industrial and Employers' Confederations of Europe**.

Leadership: Pres. Vilmundur Josefsson; *Dir-Gen.* Sveinn Hannesson
Address: Borgartúni 35, 105 Reykjavík, Iceland
Tel: (0)5910100
Fax: (0)5910101
E-mail: mottaka@si.is
Internet: www.si.is

Federation of Luxembourg Industry

The Federation of Luxembourg Industry, or Fédération des Industriels Luxembourgeois, in Luxembourg was founded in 1918. It lobbies on behalf of companies in the manufacturing and construction industries and for firms providing business services. It represents some 450 firms and is itself a member of the **Union of Industrial and Employers' Confederations of Europe**.

Leadership: Pres. Charles Krombach; *Dir-Gen.* Nicolas Soisson
Address: 7 rue Alcide de Gasperi, POB 1304, 1013 Luxembourg-Kirchberg
Tel: (0)43-53-66-1
Fax: (0)43-23-28

E-mail: fedil@fedil.lu
Internet: www.fedil.lu

Federation of Managerial and Professional Staff Unions

The Federation of Managerial and Professional Staff Unions, or Vakcentrale voor Middengroepen en Hoger Personeel, is the trade union federation for professional employees in the Netherlands. Founded in 1974, it represents around 175,000 members in four affiliated unions. It is itself a member of **ETUC**.

Pres.: Ad Verhoeven
Address: Multatulilaan 12, 4103 NM Culemborg, or POB 575, 4100 AN
         Culemborg, Netherlands
Tel: (0)345 851900
Fax: (0)345 851915
E-mail: info@vc-mhp.nl
Internet: www.vakcentralemhp.nl

Fianna Fáil (FF)

Fianna Fáil (FF) is one of the two main centrist parties in the Republic of Ireland. Founded in 1926, it represents those citizens who favoured the independence of the whole of Ireland during the civil war which followed independence from the United Kingdom in 1921–22. Today the party traditionally stands for unification or co-operation with **Northern Ireland**, social-democratic economic and welfare policy and a traditional Catholic stance on social issues such as divorce and abortion.

Until the late 1980s FF governed as numerous single party governments, including continuously during the years 1957–73, 1977–81 and 1987–94. Traditionally the party chose to go into opposition rather than entering coalition governments. However, as a consequence of falling electoral support during the 1980s, FF has formed coalitions with parties on both the left and right. The first such coalition was with the neo-liberal **Progressive Democrats (PD)** in 1989–92; then FF governed with the **Labour Party**, in 1992–95. Following two years in opposition, FF formed a coalition with PD following the 1997 elections. The FF-PD coalition, led by Taoiseach **Bertie Ahern**, completed a five-year term in 1997-2002, thereby becoming the longest lasting government in the history of the Republic. In the elections held on 17 May 2002 FF increased its share of the vote and the number of seats it occupied. It currently has 81 seats in the 166-seat **Dáil Éireann** and has entered into a second coalition with PD.

Party Leader: Bertie Ahern
Address: 65–66 Lower Mount St, Dublin 2, Ireland
Tel: (0)1 6761551
E-mail: info@fiannafail.ie
Internet: www.fiannafail.ie

Fine Gael (FG)

Fine Gael (FG) is one of the two main centrist parties in the Republic of Ireland. Founded in 1933, it represents those citizens who during the civil war which followed independence from the United Kingdom in 1921–22 accepted the division of Ireland. Today the party still accepts the division of Ireland and does not campaign for unification of the Republic of Ireland with **Northern Ireland**. It promotes neo-liberal economic and welfare policy and has a liberal Catholic stance on social issues such as divorce and abortion.

The FG has traditionally alternated in government with **Fianna Fáil (FF)**, but has always formed coalitions with the **Labour Party**. Most recently the FG governed in 1995–97 in a coalition with the Labour Party and the **Democratic Left** under the leadership of John Bruton. Although the FG increased its vote in the 1997 elections, it was forced into opposition on account of the drop in support for its left-wing coalition partners. FG currently has 31 seats in the 166-seat **Dáil Éireann** which was elected on 17 May 2002.

Party Leader: Enda Kenny
Address: 51 Upper Mount St, Dublin 2, Ireland
Tel: (0)1 6198444
Fax: (0)1 6625046
E-mail: finegael@finegael.ie
Internet: www.finegael.ie

Finland

Finland is a large but sparsely populated Nordic state in the north-east of Western Europe. It gained independence in 1917 after centuries under Swedish then Russian rule. Following military conflict with the Soviet Union (USSR) during the Second World War, Finland was forced to give up 10% of its territory to its eastern neighbour, the USSR (now **Russia**), with which it has a 1,000 km border. The two states signed a Treaty of Friendship in April 1948, though this became void in 1990 at the end of the **Cold War**.

Area: 338,000 sq km; *capital:* Helsinki; *population:* 5m. (2001).

A neutral country during the Cold War, Finland remained outside of the **North Atlantic Treaty Organization** and the **European Community (EC)**. It applied for membership of the EC in 1992 and joined it in January 1995 following a successful referendum on the issue on 16 October 1994 (yes 56.9%; turn-out 70%). Despite some opposition to membership from rural interests, farmers and non-mainstream parties, Finland is the most enthusiastic Nordic member of the **European Union (EU)** and the only Nordic state to participate in **Economic and Monetary Union** in 1999 and to introduce the **euro** in 2002.

A semi-presidential democracy, in Finland the directly elected President formerly had wide-ranging constitutional powers to veto or amend government legislation, suspend bills passed by parliament and in the area of foreign policy. The President also had the power to manage the process of coalition-building following national elections. However, a constitutional amendment of 1 March 2000 reduced the President's powers to those associated with a ceremonial head of state. The President now no longer has a political input into the process of coalition-building; he must develop foreign policy together with the government; and responsibility for EU policy lies with the Prime Minister. The current President is **Tarja Halonen**, the first woman to hold this office in Finland. She was elected on 1 March 2000, in the second round of voting, for a six-year term. Legislative power lies with the **Eduskunta**. Finland has developed a distinctive model of consensus politics which, in contrast to other Nordic states, encourages broad, multi-party coalitions rather than single party minority governments. Finland is also a corporatist state and social partners are traditionally included in important aspects of policy-making. Finland enjoys the reputation of having the least corrupt political system in the world and voter participation in elections is high, although it has declined in recent elections (71.9% in 1995; 68.3% in 1999; and 69.6% in 2003), raising concerns about citizens' commitment to democracy.

Finnish politics have been dominated by the **Finnish Social Democratic Party**. Since 1937 there are have only been two periods—1957–66 and 1991–95—when the party has not participated in government. The Social Democrats went into opposition voluntarily in 1991, having lost support in two previous elections. A non-socialist coalition of the **Centre Party**, the **National Coalition Party** and the **Swedish People's Party** under the Centre Party Prime Minister Esko Aho had the task of navigating Finland out of the severe economic recession of the early 1990s with policies of spending cuts and tax rises. The Finnish Social Democratic Party returned to government following the election held in March 1995 in which it achieved its best result since the Second World War, winning 28.3% of the vote and 63 seats in the Eduskunta. The Social Democrat Paavo Lipponen became Prime Minister of the so-called 'rainbow coalition' which brought together the Finnish Social Democratic Party, the National Coalition Party, the **Left Alliance**, the Swedish People's Party and the Green League. This coalition was remarkable not only for its ideological breadth but also because it was the first time that a green party had participated in a national coalition in any European state. The 'rainbow coalition' was re-elected in March 1999, though support for the Social Democrats declined to 22.9% of the vote and 51 seats in the Eduskunta. This was the first time in Finnish history that a governing coalition had been returned to power following an election. The Green League left the coalition in the spring of 2002 in protest at the government's decision to proceed with the construction of a new nuclear power station.

In the campaign for the elections held on 16 March 2003 the opposition Centre Party criticized the 'rainbow coalition' for its failure to reduce **unemployment** and Paavo Lipponen's stance on the issue of the war in **Iraq** in 2003 and his relationship with the USA. The party accused Lipponen of giving the impression that Finland supported the US-led military intervention. The election campaign also featured a well-known candidate for the populist True Finns Party, the professional boxer and wrestler Tony Halme, who campaigned on law and order issues. In the end just 6,000 votes decided that the Centre Party had gained the status of largest party. It formed a coalition with the Finnish Social Democratic Party and the Swedish People's Party under the leadership of Centre Party leader Anneli Jaatteenmaki, who became the first female Finnish Prime Minister. For a short time, Finland was the only state to have a female President and Prime Minister in office at the same time. However, Jaatteenmaki was forced to leave office after only two months following allegations that she had leaked a confidential memorandum which detailed a meeting between Lipponen and US President George W. Bush. Jaatteenmaki was replaced by the current Prime Minister **Matti Vanhanen**.

Economy: The Finnish economy has traditionally been dominated by timber and timber-related industries which account for about one-half of exports. Finland relied until the 1990s upon close trading relations with the Soviet Union (USSR); in 1985 the USSR purchased 21.5% of Finland's exports. It suffered a deep recession in 1991 following the collapse of its eastern market, but recovered quickly as it became integrated into the economy of the **European Union (EU)**. An associate member of the **European Free Trade Association** since 1973, and a co-founder of the **European Economic Area** in 1992, it became a full member of the EU in 1995.

GNP: US $123,400m. (2001); *GNP per caput:* $23,780 (2001); *GNP at PPP:* $125,000m. (2001); *GNP per caput at PPP:* $24,030 (2001); *GDP:* $120,855m. (2001); *exports:* $48,812m. (2001); *imports:* $38,427m. (2001); *currency:* euro; *unemployment:* 9.1% (2002).

Finland has a corporatist economy. Trade union involvement in government economic policy-making began during the 1930s when the Economic Council was established, and by the 1970s trade unions were consulted on most important areas of economic policy. Corporatist agreements were reached through formal tripartite incomes policy bargains rather than direct codetermination with social democratic governments. However, trade union leaders—especially from the **Central Organization of Finnish Trade Unions**—have close links with ministers of the **Finnish Social Democratic Party**. Consultation with social partners began to decrease from 1985 onwards and the centre-right coalition in 1991–95 further restricted the access of the trade unions to the economic policy-making process.

The dominance of the Finnish Social Democratic Party in the 20th century and the involvement of the labour movement in economic policy-making promoted the development of a social democratic **welfare state**. The Finnish welfare system offers universal welfare support and all citizens—male and female—have equal rights to social security. It provides an extensive range of both social transfers and social services such as child-care, health-care and education, which are funded by the state through general taxation. In 1990 public expenditure on welfare accounted for 27.2% of gross domestic product (GDP) but public support for the welfare state remains high.

The Finnish economy fell into deep recession following the end of the **Cold War**. Between 1990 and 1993 GDP fell by 15%, the rate of **unemployment** rose from 3% to 20% and public debt increased from 11.4% to 54.3% of GDP. Spending on social welfare programmes increased from 27.2% to 37.8% of GDP. In 1991 there was a banking crisis and the Finnish markka was devalued by 14% when it broke away from the **European Currency Unit**. The centre-right coalition of 1991–95 responded to the economic situation by cutting welfare spending and raising taxes. The generosity of the Finnish welfare state has diminished, but its scope remains broad none the less.

By the late 1990s the Finnish economy was growing again by 5% a year. Finland's recovery can be largely attributed to its **accession** to the EU. In the early 1990s Finland made a rapid application to join the EU to become further integrated into Western European markets. The economy's recovery can also be attributed to a concerted policy to promote a modern, high-tech economy, especially in the area of telecommunications. The government decided in 1995 to increase spending on research and development (R&D) by 3,200,000m. markka, raised through the sale of state-owned companies, and to increase the share of R&D expenditure from 2.5% to 2.9% of GDP between 1996–99. The funds were spent on promoting academic research in Centres of Excellence and universities, industrial clusters, and regional innovation systems in both the centre of the country and in the peripheries—for example in Oulu in the north. Local innovation agreements have been negotiated with social partners according to the corporatist model of regeneration. The social partners also agreed to a policy of wage restraint during the recovery. Much of Finland's recovery has centred on the Finnish firm **Nokia**, which is the world's largest mobile phone manufacturer. The company now accounts for more than 5% of the country's GDP, and for one-quarter of exports. The success of the economy is now closely linked to international demand for its products in the high-tech sector, in particular Nokia's mobile phones. Finland's economic performance as a knowledge economy is still not wholly stable. In the year to 2001 economic growth slowed from 6.1% to 0.7%, but it nevertheless recovered faster than the other countries in the **euro area** from the economic slowdown of 2002.

Finnish Confederation of Salaried Employees

The Finnish Confederation of Salaried Employees, or Toimihenkilökeskusjärjestö (STTK), in Finland represents about 650,000 members in 21 affiliated trade unions and a wide range of public and private sectors. STTK lobbies government and employers for full employment, fair working conditions and equal opportunities. It also negotiates framework and income policy agreements.

Pres.: Mikko Mäenpää
Address: Pohjoisranta 4A, POB 248, 00171 Helsinki, Finland
Tel: (0)9 131521

Fax: (0)9 652367
E-mail: firstname.lastname@sttk.fi
Internet: www.sttk.fi

Finnish Social Democratic Party

The Finnish Social Democratic Party, or Suomen Sosialidemokraattinen Puolue, is the dominant political party in Finland. Founded as the Finnish Labour Party in 1899, it adopted its present name in 1903. Since 1937 there have only been two periods when the party has not participated in government: 1957–66 and 1991–95. The party aims to establish a society based on the values of freedom, equality and solidarity. It promotes participatory democracy at national level in parliament, at local or community level, internationally and at the workplace. It advocates democratic control of the market, regulation of the global economy and a work-oriented welfare society with an appropriate balance of rights and responsibilities.

The Finnish Social Democratic Party governed in the broad 'rainbow coalition' in 1995–2003 under Prime Minister Paavo Lipponen. Following the elections held on 16 March 2003, the party occupies 53 seats in the 200-seat **Eduskunta** and it governs as a junior partner with eight ministerial posts in a coalition with the **Centre Party** and the **Swedish People's Party**. The current President of Finland, **Tarja Halonen**, is a social democrat.

Leadership: Party Leader Paavo Lipponen; *Gen. Sec.* Eero Heinäluoma
Address: Puolue Saariniemenkatu 6, 00530 Helsinki, Finland
Tel: (0)9 478988
Fax: (0)9 712752
E-mail: palaute@sdp.fi
Internet: www.sosialidemokraatit.fi

Fischer, Heinz

Heinz Fischer has been Federal President of Austria since 2004. He was elected with 52.4% of the vote in the first round of polls held on 25 April 2004. He was sworn in as President on 8 July 2004, two days after the death of his predecessor, Thomas Klestil. A candidate for the **Social Democratic Party of Austria**, he is the first social democrat to be elected as President since 1986. Fischer was secretary (1963–75) and then executive chairman (1975–83) of the social democratic group in the Austrian parliament. He was a member of the **Nationalrat** in 1971–2004 and served as its president in 1990–2002 and as vice-president in 2002–04. He was deputy chairman of the party of European Socialists in 1992–04.

Born on 9 October 1938 in Graz, Fischer studied law and political science at the University of Vienna, gaining a doctorate in law in 1961. In his academic career as a political scientist he was appointed associate professor in 1978 and then professor in

1994 at the University of Innsbruck. Heinz Fischer is married to Margit Fischer and has two children.

Address: Office of the Federal President, Hofburg, 1014 Vienna, Austria
Tel: (0)1 534-22
Fax: (0)1 534-22-418
E-mail: Heinz.Fischer@hofburg.at
Internet: www.hofburg.at

Fischer, Joschka

Joschka Fischer has been foreign minister and Vice-Chancellor in Germany since 1998. A member of the **Alliance 90/The Greens**, he is, despite some controversy, consistently cited as the country's most popular politician and is well respected on the international stage. Fischer became foreign minister following the success of the Alliance 90/The Greens in the **Bundestag** elections held in September 1998 when his party formed a coalition with the **Social Democratic Party of Germany (SPD)**. He faced controversy in 2001 when pictures from the 1970s showing Fischer attacking a policeman during a street protest were released. He apologized but did not resign. He was also strongly criticized by pacifists in his own party for committing German troops to **Kosovo** in 1999. He was, however, vehemently opposed to the US-led military intervention in **Iraq** in 2003 and made passionate speeches at the time in the **United Nations**. In January 2005 Fischer became embroiled in a political controversy concerning the issuing of visas in Ukraine.

Fischer joined the Green Party (Die Grünen) as part of its 'realist' wing in 1982 and was elected as one of the first Green Party representatives in the **Bundestag** in 1983–85. He went on to become the first German Green to take up a government post as Minister for the Environment in the state (*Land*) government of Hesse in 1985–87. There he provoked outrage when he arrived to swear his oath wearing jeans and trainers. When the Green Party left this government, he remained in the *Land* parliament in 1987–91 and was Minister for the Environment, Energy and Federal Affairs in 1991–94. He was elected to the Bundestag again in 1994 and became parliamentary spokesman for Alliance 90/The Greens.

Fischer was born on 12 April 1948 in Gerabronn, Baden-Württemberg. He dropped out of school in 1965 and during the 1960s and 1970s he married, travelled, and worked at casual jobs. More importantly, he became active in the militant left-wing organization 'Revolutionärer Kampf', protesting among other things against the Viet Nam War. In 1971 he was sacked from a job in the Opel car plant for trying to politicize other workers. He distanced himself from the radical left in 1977 following the kidnapping and murder of the president of the employers association, Hanns-Martin Schleyer, by the Rote Armee Fraktion. Fischer has been married and divorced four times. He has two children with his second wife.

Address: Foreign Ministry, Werderscher Markt 1, 10117 Berlin, Germany
Tel: (0)30 50000
Fax: (0)30 50003402
Internet: www.auswaertiges-amt.de

Flemish Christian Democrats

The Flemish Christian Democrats, or Christen-Democratisch en Vlaams (CD&V), is the centre-right political party in Flemish-speaking Belgium. Founded in 1945 as the Christian People's Party (Christelijke Volkspartij—CVP), the party dominated politics in post-war Belgium and led coalition governments in 1949–54, 1958–73 and 1974–99. In the elections held in 1999 support for the CVP collapsed and the party went into opposition. In the most recent elections, held on 18 May 2003, the CD&V won 13.2% of the vote and 21 seats in the 150-seat **Kamer**, thereby becoming the fifth largest party.

Leadership: Pres. Jo Vandeurzen; *Gen. Sec.* Pieter Demeester
Address: Wetstraat 89, 1040 Brussels, Belgium
Tel: (0)2 238-38-11
Fax: (0)2 238-38-71
E-mail: webmaster@cdenv.be
Internet: www.cdenv.be

Flemish Liberal and Democrat Party

The Flemish Liberal and Democrat Party, or Vlaamse Liberalen en Democraten (VLD), is the liberal party in Flemish-speaking Belgium. Established from the Party for Freedom and Progress in 1992, it refers to itself as an economic and social liberal party that seeks to promote the interests of citizens independent of dogmas and pressure groups.

VLD made substantial electoral gains in 1999 and has since led two coalition governments under Prime Minister **Guy Verhofstadt**. The first was a coalition between the French-speaking liberals and socialists plus two green parties. In the most recent elections, held on 18 May 2003, VLD won 15.4% of the vote and 25 seats in the 150-seat **Kamer**. It formed a coalition with the liberal **Reformist Movement**, the **Socialist Party**, and the **Socialist Party-Anders**.

Party Chair.: Bart Somers
Address: Melsensstraat 34, 1000 Brussels, Belgium
Tel: (0)2 549-00-20
Fax: (0)2 512-60-25
E-mail: vld@vld.be
Internet: www.vld.be

Folketing

Parliament

The Folketing is the unicameral parliament of Denmark. It is made up of 179 members who are elected for a four-year term by a system of proportional representation. Elections in 17 multi-member constituencies fill 135 seats and there are 40 supplementary seats to ensure a proportional distribution of seats in relation to votes for parties. In addition, there are two seats to represent the **Faroe Islands** and two to represent **Greenland**. The Folketing is the sole organ empowered to legislate, though Acts only take effect after receiving Royal Assent.

There are seven parties represented in the current Folketing which was elected on 8 February 2005 (number of seats in brackets): the **Liberal Party** (52); the **Social Democrats** (47); the **Danish People's Party** (24); the **Conservative People's Party** (18); the **Socialist People's Party** (17); the **Socialist People's Party** (11) and the **Unity List-The Red-Greens** (6). Of the 179 members of the current Folketing, 66 (36.9%) are **women**.

Address: Folketinget, Christiansborg, 1240 Copenhagen K, Denmark
Tel: (0)33-37-55-00
Fax: (0)33-32-85-36
E-mail: folketinget@folketinget.dk
Internet: www.folketinget.dk

Folkpartiet Liberalerna – *see* Liberal Party, Sweden

Football

Football is one of the most popular sports in Europe. It is governed by national football associations and, at European level, by the Union of European Football Associations (UEFA). UEFA organizes competitions (Champions League, UEFA Cup and the EURO tournaments), seeks to increase access and participation to the game and promotes the principles of fair-play and anti-racism. UEFA has recently become more involved in lobbying the European institutions and opened an office in Brussels, Belgium, in 2003.

Football is increasingly becoming regarded as an industry or area of economic activity which should be subject to European law. The Bosman ruling of the **European Court of Justice (ECJ)** in 1995 was the first step in the **Europeanization** of football. In 1990 Jean-Marc Bosman, a Belgian professional football player with RC Liège, claimed that the transfer rules of the Belgian Football Federation and UEFA, which prevented his transfer to the French club US Dunkerque, contravened the **Treaty of Rome** provision for the freedom of movement for workers (Article 48). The case was referred to the ECJ.

Prior to the Bosman case, a professional player could only transfer to another club with the agreement of both clubs in the form of a transfer fee. Even if a player was out of contract, he was not permitted to sign a new contract until the transfer fee had been paid or he had been granted a free transfer. Also, before the Bosman ruling there were quota systems in national leagues and UEFA competitions which limited the number of foreign players in each match. In UEFA club competitions, only three foreign players per team were permitted to play.

In 1995 the ECJ ruled that the existing transfer rules contravened Article 48 of the Treaty of Rome and that a player who was out of contract would no longer be prevented from signing a contract to move to a club in another member state of the **European Union (EU)** or **European Economic Area**. It also ruled that the transfer can not be made more difficult by a demand for a transfer fee. Only in-contract players can have transfer fees paid for them. The ECJ decided that placing limits on the number of foreign players in competitions also contravened Article 48 of the Treaty of Rome and that this would no longer be allowed. Clubs are now able to field as many players from EU states as they wish.

Pres. of UEFA: Lennart Johansson
Address: route de Genève 46, Case postale, 1260 Nyon 2, Switzerland
Tel: (0)229944444
Fax: (0)229944488
E-mail: info@uefa.com
Internet: www.uefa.com

Fortuyn, Pim

Pim Fortuyn was a controversial, openly gay Dutch politician with strong anti-**immigration** and anti-Islamic views. He favoured closing the Dutch borders to new immigrants and believed that Muslim immigration damaged Dutch society's otherwise liberal views on homosexuality and gender equality. Fortuyn had a broad appeal among the young, the far right and those disillusioned with the centre-left government.

Fortuyn was assassinated on 6 May 2002, nine days before the Dutch national elections to the **Tweede Kamer** in which his newly founded party, **List Pim Fortuyn**, had been expected to perform well. Following his murder the List Pim Fortuyn party went on to win 26 of the 150 seats in the Tweede Kamer and governed in the first coalition government formed under **Jan Peter Balkende**.

Fortuyn entered politics on 26 November 2001 and was elected head of list of the radical new party **Leefbaar Nederland** (Liveable Netherlands) which had been formed to contest the elections of May 2002. He was dismissed on 9 February 2002, one day after he suggested publicly that Article One of the Dutch Constitution, which bans discrimination, should be changed to favour freedom of speech instead. He founded the List Pim Fortuyn party on 11 February 2002 and contested local elections in Rotterdam in March. In that city, governed by the **Labour Party** for more than 50 years, Fortuyn won 17 of the city council's 45 seats with 35% of the vote.

Born Wilhelmus Simon Petrus (Pim) Fortuyn on 19 February 1948 in Velsen, he studied sociology at the Free University of Amsterdam. He obtained a Ph.D. from Groningen University for his thesis on social and economic development in the Netherlands in 1945–49. He lectured on Marxist sociology at Groningen University and was a part-time professor in social sciences at Erasmus University in 1991–95.

Forza Italia

Come on, Italy!

Forza Italia (Come on, Italy!—a **football** chant) is a new right-wing populist party in Italy. It was founded in 1994 by businessman **Silvio Berlusconi** in order to fill the void created by the demise of the Christian Democrats, which had dominated Italian politics in 1945–94.

In the general elections held on 27 March 1994 Forza Italia formed two electoral alliances: the Freedom Alliance (Polo della Libertà) with the **Northern League**; and the Good Governance Alliance (Polo del Buon Governo) with the **National Alliance**. The two coalitions achieved landslide victories and won an absolute majority of seats in the **Camera dei Deputati**. The Forza Italia-led coalition under Prime Minister Silvio Berlusconi lasted until December 1994.

In the general election held on 21 April 1996 Forza Italia formed the Alliance for Freedom (Polo per la Libertà) with the **National Alliance**, the Christian Democratic Centre and United Christian Democrats (later **Union of Centre and Christian Democrats**), but came second to the left-wing Olive Tree Alliance.

At the most recent general elections, held on 13 May 2001, Forza Italia headed the House of Freedoms Coalition (Casa Delle Libertà) which included the National Alliance, the Northern League and the Christian Democratic Centre and United Christian Democrats, and the new Italian Socialist Party. Forza Italia won 178 seats in the 630-seat parliament, and Silvio Berlusconi became Prime Minister of the House of Freedoms Coalition.

Party Leader: Silvio Berlusconi
Address: Via dell'Umiltà 36, 00187 Rome, Italy
Tel: (0)06 6731276
Fax: (0)06 6731231
E-mail: fi-adesioni@forzait.org
Internet: www.forza-italia.it

Foss, Per-Kristian

Per-Kristian Foss has been Minister of Finance in Norway since 2001. A member of the **Conservative Party**, he supports cutting taxes and funding public services from North Sea oil revenues.

Born on 19 July 1950, Foss studied political science, public justice and criminology at the University of Oslo. He worked as a journalist in 1971–73 before switching to politics as a career. He was chairman of the Conservative Party's youth group in 1973–77 and has been a member of the **Storting** since 1981, acting as chairman of the standing committee of finance in 1989–93. He was head of the Conservative Party in Oslo in 2000–04 and is currently deputy chairman of the party nationally.

Address: Norwegian Ministry of Finance, POB 8008 Dep, 0030 Oslo or
Akersgata 40, 0180 Oslo, Norway
E-mail: postmottak@finans.dep.no
Internet: odin.dep.no/fin

Framsóknarflokkurinn – *see* Progressive Party, Iceland

France

France is a large state in the centre of Western Europe and includes four overseas territories known as *départements d'outre-mer* (DOM): Guyane (French Guiana) in South America; Guadeloupe and Martinique in the Caribbean Sea; and Réunion in the Indian Ocean. It was first constituted as a republic in 1792. During the Second World War most of France was occupied by Nazi German military forces. A southern sector was governed by the Vichy regime in 1940–44. After liberation the Fourth Republic was founded in 1946. This was an unstable political system characterized by a large number of polarized political parties and a high turnover of governments, beset, from 1954, by the growing cost of war in Algeria. In 1958, at the height of the Algerian crisis, Gen. **Charles de Gaulle** agreed to serve as Prime Minister of the Fourth Republic (and, later, as President of the Fifth Republic) if a new constitution was drafted to strengthen the role of the President. De Gaulle's aim for the Fifth Republic was to unite the nation by transcending the traditional divisions between left and right, offering strong national leadership through the office of President, and pursuing an independent role for France in international affairs; France is, for example, a political but not a military member of the **North Atlantic Treaty Organization**. These principles formed the core of Gaullism.

Area: 552,000 sq km; *capital:* Paris; *population:* 59m. (2001).

The state form of the Fifth Republic (1958) is unique in Western Europe, and has been referred to as French exceptionalism. The Fifth Republic is a semi-presidential political system in which executive power normally lies with the President rather than with the Prime Minister. The President has—since 1962—been directly elected for a seven-year term; though it was decided in a referendum in 2000 that the term of the French presidency would be reduced to five years from 2002. Although the President has executive power, he is, as a rule, obliged to appoint the Prime Minister and his cabinet from the ranks of the largest party in the **Assemblée Nationale**. Legislative power is shared between the weak institutions of the Assemblée

Nationale and the **Sénat**. France is traditionally a centralized state with power overwhelmingly concentrated in Paris. It is also characterized by a weak civil society.

Since 1945 French politics have been shaped by the German question. France had fought three wars with its neighbour since 1870. The country's response to this was to develop co-operative alliances with Germany and a strong Franco-German partnership which has shaped western European politics. As well as signing the Elysée Treaty of Friendship with Germany in 1963, France was a founder member of the **European Coal and Steel Community** and together with Germany has been at the forefront of the project to further European integration. Mainstream French parties and the French population are largely in favour of European integration. In September 1992 President **François Mitterrand** held a constitutionally unnecessary referendum to endorse the **Treaty on European Union** which resulted in a slim majority in favour (yes 51.05%).

In parallel to support for European integration there has been a concern to maintain the political features of French exceptionalism by seeking to transfer them to the European level. In contrast, the process of **Europeanization** has significantly altered the contours of France's centralized state and *dirigiste* political economy, and the state has been stripped of many of its functions as these have been passed up to European institutions. The centralized nature of the French state has also been altered by a domestic process of decentralization which since 1982 has passed power down to France's 22 regional councils and 96 departments. Most recently a constitutional reform of March 2003 consecrated the principle of decentralization.

The institution of the presidency remains strong though its power has been trimmed by three periods of **cohabitation**—power-sharing with a Prime Minister from an opposition party. During cohabitation domestic policy is determined by the head of government and the President leads foreign policy, though he does not have complete autonomy. In addition, the power and willingness of the **Conseil Constitutionnel** to intervene in the policy-making and legislative process has increased since 1971.

The institutional design of the Fifth Republic, which sought to represent and unite the French nation, is weakening. This is reflected in declining popular support for institutions of the Fifth Republic. There is a high rate of abstentions and spoiling of ballot papers in elections; turn-out in the first rounds of the 2002 presidential and legislative elections was only 69.18% and 64.41% respectively. At the same time, there has been a rise in social movements highlighting issues such as **unemployment**, racism and HIV/AIDS which use protests, direct action or the **media** as a means of promoting their cause. In the 1990s and early 2000s France also experienced a wave of strikes among public-sector workers who opposed austerity measures undertaken to meet the **convergence criteria** for participation in **Economic and Monetary Union** and reforms of state pension schemes. Furthermore, the issues of **immigration** and the assimilation of France's immigrant population have deeply divided the nation. Immigration and issues of law and order are now—after the economy—the second most important electoral issue.

The Gaullists, who sought to unify the French nation, and other non-Gaullist right-wing parties dominated politics in the early years of the Fifth Republic. The Gaullists and their allies in government regularly won more than 50% of the vote in the first round of elections during the first two decades of the Fifth Republic. Between 1958 and 1981 the right also provided all Presidents (**Charles de Gaulle** 1959–69, Georges Pompidou 1969–74, **Valéry Giscard d'Estaing** 1974–81) and governments. During the 1970s the left re-established itself: the **Socialist Party (PS)** was founded in 1969 and co-operated with the **Communist Party of France (PCF)** to win the presidency and a majority in the Assemblée Nationale in 1981.

In 1981 the socialist François Mitterrand was elected as President, a post which he held following re-election in 1988 until 1995. The neo-Gaullist **Jacques Chirac** was elected as President in 1995 and was re-elected in 2002. The same period has been characterized by alternation of majorities in the Assemblée Nationale—and thus governments—between the right- and left-wing political families. Until 1986 the French electorate elected a party alliance into the Assemblée Nationale that supported the President's political stance. Since 1981 no party of the left or right has managed to secure two consecutive terms in office, meaning that until 2002 neither Mitterrand nor Chirac had been able to complete a seven-year term with a parliamentary majority in his favour. Since 1981 governments of the left have been in office in 1981–86, 1988–93 and 1997–2002 while the right has governed in 1986–88, 1993–97 and since 2002.

In 1995–97 the right dominated French politics, holding the presidency, four-fifths of the Assemblée Nationale, two-thirds of the Sénat, 20 of 22 regional councils, 80% of department councils, and one-half of the large French towns. However, the right's popularity fell at national level on account of unmet electoral promises and budget cuts and, in 1997, Chirac took the unprecedented (and risky) decision of calling early parliamentary elections. The right lost control of the Assemblée Nationale and a 'pluralist' left-wing government made up of the PS, the PCF, the **Greens** and the Mouvement des Citoyens entered into office. At the same time, the right experienced a crisis and reorganized. The non-Gaullist alliance, the Union pour la Démocratie Française (UDF), split in 1998 following regional elections in which some of its constituent parties (Démocratie Libérale) entered into electoral pacts with the extreme right-wing **National Front (FN)** in order to prevent the left from coming to power. The neo-liberal Démocratie Libérale left the UDF, and the Alliance pour la France was founded in 1998 in an attempt to bring together both camps of the right. The RPR and Démocratie Libérale came together but the reconstituted UDF remained outside.

The wavering fortunes of the divided moderate right, periods of right-left cohabitation, and concern about unemployment and corruption have coincided with the steady rise of **Jean-Marie Le Pen**'s extreme right-wing FN. Since the 1980s the FN has experienced increasing electoral success at European, national, regional and municipal levels. It has also succeeded in shaping the political agendas of both the mainstream right and the left in France, especially on issues of immigration and law and order. The presence of the FN in French politics reached its peak during the presidential elections held in April 2002. In the first round of voting Jean-Marie Le Pen won 16.86% of the vote and came second to Jacques Chirac who polled 18.88% (the poorest ever first-round performance by an incumbent president). A second FN politician, Bruno Mégret, won a further 2.34%. The socialist candidate, incumbent Prime Minister Lionel Jospin, achieved third place with 16.18% of the vote, and was thus eliminated from the second round. In the next round of balloting, Chirac rallied support from the moderate right and left and gained 82.21% of the vote (the highest ever percentage in a second round) against Le Pen's 17.79%. In the parliamentary elections held in May 2002 Chirac's newly formed moderate right-wing Union pour une Majorité Présidentielle (now the **Popular Movement**) won a majority in the Assemblée Nationale so that he was no longer required to cohabit with the left. The FN won 11.12% of the vote in the first round of the parliamentary elections but no seats in the first or second ballot. Since 2002 the Gaullist right has again held the presidency and dominated the Assemblée Nationale, as was intended for the Fifth Republic.

Economy: France's economy is large and based predominantly on manufacturing. Characterized traditionally by a lack of capital and savings necessary for industrial investment, France's relatively late industrialization was led and financed by the state. As a consequence, a unique model of state-led or *dirigiste* capitalism developed. In the post-war period the state drew up five-year economic plans and nationalized industry and financial institutions. It also controlled finance, investment and monetary policy through the Treasury (Trésor) and the Ministry of Finance. The state selected strong firms and promoted these as national champions which should contribute to the development of 'grand projets' such as the TGV high-speed train, the Airbus and Concorde. Economic planning and management was conducted by an élite set of civil servants educated at the Ecole nationale d'administration or the Ecole polytechnique. In the state-led model of capitalism social partners played a minor role in economic policy-making, but they have demonstrated their influence through strikes and direct action protests.

GNP: US $1,380,700m. (2001); *GNP per caput:* $22,730 (2001); *GNP at PPP:* $1,425,000m. (2001); *GNP per caput at PPP:* $24,080 (2001); *GDP:* $1,309,807m. (2001); *exports:* $371,795m. (2001); *imports:* $351,033m. (2001); *currency:* euro; *unemployment:* 8.9% (2002).

France's state-led model of capitalism underwrote 30 years of growth in the post-war era—the so-called *Trente Glorieuse*—during which time the economy expanded at an annual rate of some 5.2%. In parallel to this economic success, France constructed a generous corporatist **welfare state** based on the principle of occupational solidarity. The welfare state was organized around the insurance principle: employees and employers contributed to distinct occupational social security schemes which until 1995 were managed by social partners, and have since been managed by the state. Social benefits in cases of **unemployment**, sickness and old age offered generous replacement rates which were calculated according to the claimant's previous income. An exception to the corporatist principle was the family allowance scheme which pays—more typically of social democratic welfare states—universal benefits to all families with two or more children. France has, in contrast to other corporatist states such as Germany, a relatively high female participation rate in the labour market.

The economic success of the *Trente Glorieuse* has also been attributed to France's inclusion from the start in the project of European integration. A founder member of the **European Coal and Steel Community**, the French economy benefited from peaceful and co-operative relations with its larger neighbour, and former enemy, Germany. In the early years France was able to influence the project of European integration to its advantage, especially in the agricultural sector. From the mid-1980s onwards, the process of **Europeanization** started to shape the contours of the *dirigiste* French political economy. France was particularly affected in the 1980s by the project to complete the **Single European Market (SEM)** by 1992 and the effort in the 1990s to achieve **Economic and Monetary Union (EMU)**. These projects altered state-market relations, macroeconomic performance and the welfare state.

From 1973 economic growth in France began to stall, averaging about half the annual rate achieved during the *Trente Glorieuse*, and unemployment began to rise. When the first socialist government of the Fifth Republic was elected in 1981, President **François Mitterrand** embarked on a Keynesian strategy to boost the economy: French firms, banks and insurance institutions were nationalized; public investment and wages were increased. In response to soaring inflation government policy changed direction two years later and from 1983 onwards a policy of sound money was pursued instead, the franc being linked to the Deutsche Mark (DM). It sought to tackle **unemployment** by reducing the working week to 39 hours and introducing early-retirement schemes. To address the problems of social exclusion, unemployment among the young and the long-term unemployed, who are often uninsured, in 1988 the government introduced a minimum income scheme, the Revenu Minimum d'Insertion. This marked the start of a gradual shift from insurance- to tax-based welfare.

Since the mid-1980s the French economy has undergone two waves of privatization. In 1986–88 the right-wing government pursued the policy of selling state-owned firms out of ideological conviction and the need to meet the criteria for the SEM project. In 1993–97 the right-wing government embarked on a second wave of privatization and this was continued by the 'pluralist' left-wing administration in 1997–2002. This second wave was less ideologically-driven and conducted more out of concern to reduce the budget deficit in order to meet the **convergence criteria** for participation in EMU by 1999 and then to try to adhere to the rules of the **stability and growth pact**.

In the early 1990s the French economy was severely affected by its policy of the *franc fort* which linked the national currency to the DM. This policy was important in the sense that it demonstrated France's commitment to the project of European integration and helped to keep the country's inflation rate in check. However, when the German **Bundesbank** adjusted its policy in response to German unification, France's interest rates soared, economic growth stalled and there were further increases in unemployment and public debt. Between 1990–95 the rate of unemployment rose from 9% to 12.5% of the workforce and public debt increased from less than 2% to 6% of gross domestic product (GDP). By 1995 the state spent 55% of GDP.

In the early 1990s France committed itself to participate in EMU as laid down in the **Treaty on European Union**. To qualify for participation, France was required to meet the convergence criteria; most significantly, it had to cut its budget deficit from 6% to 3% of GDP by 1999. The right-wing government of 1993–97 pledged to increase employment and to repair France's 'social fracture', but later changed course and sought to introduce tax increases and social security cuts. The government's plans to harmonize benefit entitlements between separate occupational schemes led to a massive wave of strikes in 1995–96, and it was eventually forced to back down. The pluralist left-wing government of 1997–2002 attempted to tackle unemployment by introducing the 35-hour working week and also introduced a public jobs scheme for the young unemployed.

France successfully met the convergence criteria and has participated in the final stage of EMU since 1999. However, it has (with Germany) struggled to adhere to the rules of the stability and growth pact. Its public debt levels have risen again to more than 3% of GDP and it has been threatened with sanctions and fines by the **European Commission**. Since 2002 the right-wing government has made a concerted effort to reform public spending and implement unpopular measures such as reform of pension entitlements for public-sector workers. No party in France is in favour of harsh welfare retrenchment.

The French state-led economy has been transformed in the last two decades by the processes of Europeanization and has become more open and present in the international economy. There is some evidence that it is transforming into both a German-style Rhineland economy and a liberal market economy like that of the United Kingdom. At the same time, in this process, the state has managed to retain influence in a wide range of areas: it directed the distribution of shares during the process of privatization, keeping control through core ownership (*noyaux durs*) and arranging a complex network of cross-holdings; and graduates of the élite civil servant schools (Enarques) dominate the management in the new privately-owned firms. Also, the state took over the management of social insurance funds in 1995 and remains the employer of some 2m. civil servants.

Free Democratic Party

The Free Democratic Party, or Freie Demokratische Partei (FDP), is the liberal party in Germany. Founded in 1948 under the leadership of Theodor Heuss, it campaigns on a platform of social liberty and support for the market economy. The FDP has traditionally served as a crucial pivot party, forming coalition governments with both the **Christian Democratic Union (CDU)** in 1949–66 and 1982–98 and the **Social Democratic Party** in 1969–82. However, since the collapse of the CDU-FDP government in 1998 and the rise of **Alliance 90/The Greens** it has continually lost support. In the most recent general elections, held on 22 September 2002, the FDP, for the first time, put up its own candidate for the chancellorship, Guido Westerwelle, and aimed to win 18% of the vote. It managed to poll only 7.4% of the vote, however, and won only 47 seats in the 603-seat **Bundestag**.

Party Leader: Guido Westerwelle
Address: Thomas-Dehler-Haus, Reinhardtstrasse 14, 10117 Berlin, Germany
Tel: (0)30 28495820
Fax: (0)30 28495822
E-mail: fdp-point@fdp.de
Internet: www.liberale.de

Freie Demokratische Partei – *see* Free Democratic Party, Germany

Freiheitliche Partei Österreichs – *see* Austrian Freedom Party

Freisinnig-Demokratische Partei/Parti Radical Démocratique – *see* Radical Free Democratic Party, Switzerland

Fremskrittspartiet – *see* Progress Party, Norway

French Christian Workers' Confederation

The French Christian Workers' Confederation, or Confédération Française des Travailleurs Chrétiens, is a Catholic trade union federation in France that was established in 1919. It survives as a small union, the majority of its members having left to form the French Democratic Labour Confederation in 1964. A traditional federation, it lobbies to defend the basic rights of workers in France and to protect the role of the family.

Pres.: Jacques Voisin
Address: 13 rue des Ecluses-St-Martin, 75483 Paris Cedex 10, France
Tel: (0)1-44-52-49-00
Fax: (0)1-44-52-49-18
E-mail: communication@cftc.fr
Internet: www.cftc.fr

French Democratic Labour Confederation

The French Democratic Labour Confederation, or Confédération Française Démocratique du Travail (CFDT), is a large trade union confederation in France. Originally the **Confédération Française des Travailleurs Chrétiens** (French Christian Workers' Confederation), it changed its name in 1964 in order to remove all religious connotations. Today the organization represents around 889,000 employees from a wide range of sectors and occupations. Over 1,500 trade unions are affiliated to the CFDT. It lobbies to improve democracy in the workplace, to promote emancipation and freedom of workers.

Gen. Sec.: François Chérèque
Address: 4 blvd de la Villette, 75955 Paris CEDEX 19, France
E-mail: confederation@cfdt.fr
Internet: www.cfdt.fr

Frjálslindi flokkurinn – *see* Liberal Party, Iceland

Front National – *see* National Front, Belgium

Front National – *see* National Front, France

Funktionærernes og Tjenestemændenes Fællesråd – *see* Salaried Employees' and Civil Servants' Confederation, Denmark

G

G7/G8

The G7 is an informal group of seven major industrial democracies: France, the USA, the United Kingdom, Germany, **Japan**, Italy and Canada. The heads of state or government meet at annual summits to discuss economic and political issues affecting the participating states and the international community.

Six countries began meeting in 1975, and Canada first attended one year later, forming the G7. In 1998 **Russia** attended the summit held in Birmingham, United Kingdom, thus forming the G8. However, on account of Russia's comparative economic weakness, some issues are still discussed in the forum of the G7. The G7/G8 summits are hosted by the country holding the rotating presidency of the group, which changes at the end of each calendar year. It was announced at the Birmingham summit in 1998 that Russia would host a summit for the first time in 2006, and thus become fully integrated into the G8. Additionally, the **European Union (EU)** is represented at summits by the president of the **European Commission** and the leader of the country that holds the presidency of the **Council of the European Union** at the time of the summit.

The aim of G7/G8 meetings is to discuss issues and tensions that arise through the increased interdependence of sovereign states in the era of globalization. Key issues that the summits address are macroeconomic management, international trade, relations with developing countries and nuclear proliferation. Since the end of the **Cold War** the agenda has grown to include issues such as east-west relations, energy and **terrorism** and security issues. Also, the G7/G8 host can propose additional themes for summit discussion, for example, employability (**Tony Blair** 1998), debt relief (**Gerhard Schröder** 1999) and information technology and the digital divide (Keizo Obuchi 2000).

G7/G8 summit meeting are traditionally prepared by personal representatives of political leaders, referred to as 'sherpas'. This system is supported by ministerial and *ad hoc* meetings throughout the year. Decisions made among the G8 are implemented by the ministerial groups and other international organizations such as the EU, the **International Monetary Fund**, the **World Bank**, and the **Organisation for Economic Co-operation and Development**.

During the 1990s G7/G8 political leaders started to include multinational companies and non-governmental organizations (NGOs) in meetings and the follow-up process. However, there exist among NGOs and civil society organizations strong concerns regarding the agenda and decisions of the élite-led G7/G8 meetings. Since the summit held in Birmingham in 1998 summit anti-globalization demonstrations have regularly been held. In Genoa, Italy, in 2001 one protester died in clashes between police and demonstrators. The anti-globalization organization ATTAC organized its own counter-G8 summit in Geneva, Switzerland, in 2003.

General Central Organization of Liberal Trade Unions

The General Central Organization of Liberal Trade Unions, or Centrale Générale des Syndicats Libéraux de Belgique (CGSLB), is a union federation in Belgium. The outcome of the merger of regional liberal unions in the first half of the 20th century, it has been called the CGSLB since 1939. Today, the organization represents around 220,000 public- and private-sector workers and social security claimants from two affiliated unions. It is itself a member of **ETUC**.

Pres.: Guy Haaze
Address: Koning Albertlaan 95, 9000 Gent, Belgium
Tel: (0)9 222-57-51
Fax: (0)9 221-04-74
E-mail: cgslb@cgslb.be
Internet: www.cgslb.be

General Confederation of Labour

The General Confederation of Labour, or Confédération Générale du Travail (CGT), is the large, left-wing trade union confederation in France. Founded in two stages, in 1895 and 1906, it is the oldest organization of its kind in the country. The CGT campaigns to transform the French economy and society. It traditionally had close links with the **Communist Party** and was only admitted to **ETUC** in May 1999.

Gen. Sec.: Bernard Thibault
Address: 263 rue de Paris, 93516 Montreuil Cedex, France
Tel: (0)1-48-18-80-00
Fax: (0)1-49-88-18-57
E-mail: info@cgt.fr
Internet: www.cgt.fr

General Confederation of Labour-'Force Ouvrière'

The General Confederation of Labour-'Force Ouvrière', or Confédération Générale du Travail-Force Ouvrière (CGT-FO), is an independent trade union confederation in France. Formed in 1948 as a breakaway group from the **General Confederation of Labour**, which had close links with the **Communist Party**, CGT-FO is independent of political parties or religious denominations and lobbies for workers' freedom and democracy and to defend public services and the **welfare state**.

Gen. Sec.: Jean-Claude Mailly
Address: 141 ave du Maine, 75680 Paris Cedex 14, France
Tel: (0)1-40-52-83-17
Fax: (0)1-40-52-83-15
E-mail: via www.force-ouvriere.fr/mail.asp?mail=0
Internet: www.force-ouvriere.fr

General Confederation of Portuguese Workers Intersindical

The General Confederation of Portuguese Workers Intersindical, or Confederação Geral dos Trabalhadores Portugueses-Intersindical Nacional, is the larger of two main trade union confederations in Portugal. Officially founded in 1974, this communist movement dates back to the informal trade union, Intersindical, that was formed in 1971. The trade union campaigns on national and international issues and has become a member of **ETUC**.

Sec.-Gen.: Manuel Carvalho da Silva
Address: R. Vitor Cordon, 1249-102 Lisbon, Portugal
Tel: (0)21 3236500
Fax: (0)21 3236695
E-mail: cgtp@cgtp.pt
Internet: www.cgtp.pt

General Federation of Belgian Workers

The General Federation of Belgian Workers, or Fédération Générale du Travail de Belgique, or Algemeen Belgisch Vakverbond, is a socialist trade union federation in Belgium. Founded in 1898, it today represents the interests of more than 1.2m. workers in seven trade unions, and also the interests of those excluded from the labour market. It campaigns to improve social justice and economic and social democracy. It is itself a member of **ETUC**.

Gen. Sec.: André Mordant
Address: rue Haute 42, 1000 Brussels, Belgium
Tel: (0)2 506-82-11
E-mail: via www.fgtb.be
Internet: www.fgtb.be

General Workers' Union (Portugal)

The General Workers' Union, or União Geral dos Trabalhadores de Portugal (UGTP), is the socialist-oriented trade union confederation in Portugal. It was founded in 1978 following an alliance between the social democratic and socialist factions of the trade union movement. Today there are 52 affiliated trade unions in the UGTP covering all sectors of activity and it is itself a member of **ETUC**. UGTP lobbies at national and international level for social reform to guarantee a minimum level of well-being for its members, the right to work for a fair and equal wage and the social integration of workers. It also seeks to eradicate regional disparities in Portugal and to promote education and training.

Leadership: Pres. João Dias da Silva; *Gen. Sec.:* João Proença
Address: R. Buenos Aires 11, 1249-067 Lisbon, Portugal
Tel: (0)21 3931200
Fax: (0)21 3974612
E-mail: ugt@mail.telepac.pt
Internet: www.ugt.pt

General Workers' Union (Spain)

The General Workers' Union, or Unión General de Trabajadores (UGT), is a large socialist trade union confederation in Spain. Founded in 1888, it worked in exile and underground in 1939–76 during the Franco dictatorship. Today UGT represents members, conducts collective bargaining and offers services for workers across a wide range of sectors, organized in 11 affiliated trade unions. It also represents the unemployed and pensioners. UGT is a founding member of **ETUC**.

Sec.-Gen.: Cándido Méndez Rodríguez
Address: Calle Hortaleza 88, 28004 Madrid, Spain
Tel: (0)91 5897601
Fax: (0)91 5897603
E-mail: info@cec.ugt.org
Internet: www.ugt.es

Geniki Synomospondia Ergaton Ellados – *see* Greek General Confederation of Labour

German Democratic Republic (GDR)

The German Democratic Republic (GDR), or East Germany, was the socialist state established in 1949 in the Soviet-occupied zone of post-war Germany. It existed alongside the Federal Republic of Germany (FRG), then West Germany, for 41 years during the **Cold War**. The GDR was a satellite state of the Soviet Union

(USSR), which took responsibility for the security of the GDR. A workers' uprising against the system on 17 June 1953 was suppressed by Soviet troops leading to around 55 deaths. The GDR regime constructed the **Berlin Wall** and closed borders to the west on 13 August 1961. These borders were not breached until the peaceful revolution of 1989. The socialist regime resigned following the fall of the Berlin Wall on 9 November 1989 and the GDR formally ceased to exist on 3 October 1990 when the Constitution and institutions of the FRG were extended to the east on the occasion of **German unification**.

Area: 108,333 sq km; *capital:* East Berlin; *population:* 16.4m. (1989).

Initially founded in 1949 with a democratic constitution, the GDR evolved into a centralized socialist state through constitutional changes in 1968 and 1974 which defined it as the socialist state of the German nation and committed it to common ownership and strong relations with the USSR. The GDR came to be dominated by one party, the Sozialistische Einheitspartei (SED—Socialist Unity Party), as in the multi-party elections the allocation of seats in the Volkskammer was fixed in advance of polling day, ensuring that the SED was always the largest party. Thus, the highest organ of the SED, the *Politbüro*, dominated decision-making in the parliament and Council of Ministers. Walter Ulbricht was head of the SED in 1949–71, Erich Honecker in 1971–89 and Egon Krenz in October–November 1989. The secret service of the GDR—the Ministry of State Security or Stasi—was also accountable to the *Politbüro*. Established in 1950, by 1989 this organization employed more than 91,000 full-time staff for a population of 16.4m.

The socialist planned economy of the GDR was the strongest economy in the COMECON (Council for Mutual Aid and Assistance), the trading bloc for the states of Eastern Europe, but it lagged behind that of the FRG, particularly in terms of productivity. The GDR lacked natural resources and suffered from a poor infra-structure and outdated capital in industrial plants. The uprising that took place in 1953 was a protest against excessive production demands imposed on workers, and the Berlin Wall was built in 1961 to stem the exodus of skilled workers and professionals.

While the GDR had close relations with the USSR, its relationship with the FRG was initially antagonistic as the FRG refused to recognize the political system and sovereignty of the GDR. This changed on the election, in 1969, of **Willy Brandt**, whose *Ostpolitik* led to *détente* and the peaceful co-existence of the two German states. In the 1980s the hardline SED resisted the Soviet leader Mikhail Gorbachev's policies of *glasnost* and *perestroika* and any kind of opening up of the political system. Thousands of GDR citizens fled to the west in the summer of 1989 via the newly opened Hungarian-Austrian border and civil rights movements began to demand freedom to travel and democratic reform of the GDR state. The regular 'Monday demonstrations' in Leipzig, which in October 1989, involving as many as 1m. protesters, overshadowed the GDR's 40th anniversary celebrations, which Gorbachev attended. On 9 November the SED announced in a press conference that it would follow the lead of other Eastern European states and open up its western border for travel. This led to the fall of the Berlin Wall, democratic elections in March 1990, reform of the GDR under Minister-President Lothar de Maizière, and German unification on 3 October 1990.

German Trade Union Federation

The German Trade Union Federation, or Deutscher Gewerkschaftsbund (DGB), was founded in 1949. Today it represents around 7.7m. employees organized in eight affiliated unions. The union is independent and non-confessional and campaigns to promote solidarity and social partnership in German society. The DGB expanded in 1990 when the trade union movement of the **German Democratic Republic**, the Freier Deutscher Gewerkschaftsbund (FDGB—Free German Trade Union Federation), was dissolved. The DGB structure was extended to the east. The DGB is itself a member of **ETUC**.

Pres.: Michael Sommer
Address: Bundesvorstand, Henriette-Herz-Platz 2, 10178 Berlin, Germany
Tel: (0)30 240600
Fax: (0)30 24060324
E-mail: info@bvv.dgb.de
Internet: www.dgb.de

German unification

German unification occurred when the **German Democratic Republic (GDR)** and the Federal Republic of Germany (FRG) were formally united on 3 October 1990. This event followed the fall of the **Berlin Wall** and the collapse of the socialist state system of the GDR in November 1989. According to the Constitution of the FRG, the Basic Law, there were two possible methods for completing German unification. Paragraph 146 provided for the termination of both German states and the drafting of a new constitution for the new, unified state. Paragraph 23 made it possible to extend the FRG to new states (*Länder*) within Germany so that they became part of the FRG. On 23–24 August 1990 the East German parliament voted by 294 of 400 votes to come under the purview of the Basic Law of the FRG and German unification was thus completed according to Paragraph 23. On the day of German unification the GDR ceased to exist and the FRG was extended to the five new *Länder* in the east.

German unification had also to be agreed by the Allies. While the USA had no reservations, the Soviet Union (USSR) at first opposed the plans on the grounds that it did not wish a unified Germany to become part of the **North Atlantic Treaty Organization**. The United Kingdom and France were concerned about the implications of having a larger and more powerful Germany in the **European Union**. German Chancellor **Helmut Kohl** reassured the Allies by promising to limit the number of German troops and to lock Germany further into the process of European integration. At the final '2 + 4 Talks' in Moscow, USSR, on 12 September 1990 the foreign ministers of the FRG, the GDR, France, the USSR, the United Kingdom and the USA signed an agreement regulating the external aspects of German unification and returning full sovereignty to unified Germany from 3 October 1990.

It took just under one year to complete the process of German unification. However, unification as an outcome was by no means inevitable. From the 1970s the two Germanys were recognized as separate states and the *Ostpolitik* of Chancellor **Willy Brandt** in 1969–74 promoted peaceful co-existence of the two states over unification. The protesters in the 1989 revolution did not initially specifically demand unification, but rather freedom to travel and democratic reform of the GDR state. Chancellor Helmut Kohl published a Ten Point Plan in November 1989 which proposed a confederation of the two German states and the idea of unification became increasingly popular. In the democratic election to the Volks-kammer held in the GDR in March 1990 the pro-unification parties of the right gained the highest number of votes (48%). GDR citizens were voting, among other things, to adopt the Deutsche Mark (DM) as their national currency. Monetary, economic and social union was completed on 1 July 1990 and the East German currency was replaced by the DM at a general rate of one-to-one.

The term German unification is often used interchangeably with German reuni-fication. However, since Germany in its present form and with its current borders has never existed before, the term unification is preferable.

Germany

Germany, officially the Federal Republic of Germany (FRG), was founded in 1949 through the inauguration of the new Constitution, the Basic Law (*Grundgesetz*). The Constitution applied initially to the territory of the military zones occupied by the western Allies—the United Kingdom, the USA and France. The Soviet-occupied zone in the east became the **German Democratic Republic (GDR)**. The Basic Law was a temporary constitution, the validity of which it was possible to extend to other German states (*Länder*). The Constitution was extended to the state of Saarland in 1957 and the process of **German unification** entailed the extension of the Basic Law to the five new *Länder* in the former GDR. During the **Cold War** the FRG's relations with the GDR were initially adversarial. They were subse-quently characterized by a policy of *détente* and co-existence brought about through **Willy Brandt**'s *Ostpolitik*. A Basic Treaty was signed between the two German states in December 1972 which obliged each to respect the authority and independ-ence of the other, though the FRG remained committed to the goal of unification. When the GDR collapsed on 9 November 1989, FRG Chancellor **Helmut Kohl** pursued a policy of formal German unification and the process was completed on 3 October 1990. German unification entailed the transfer of the Basic Law and the political institutions of the FRG to the five new *Länder* of East Germany, rather than the drafting of a new constitution. However, since unification some of the traditional characteristics of the German political system have altered.

Area: 357,000 sq km; *capital:* Berlin; *population:* 82m. (2001).

The Federal Republic of Germany is often characterized as a semi-sovereign state because Germany was an occupied state, and because sovereignty is divided between the federal government and a number of alternative political and non-political institutions. A federal state, power is shared between the federal government and the 16 German *Länder* (until 1990 there were 11). The *Länder* have autonomy in the domains of policing, culture, broadcasting and education and share responsibility with federal government in joint tasks such as higher education and regional economic development. Each state (*Land*) elects its own parliament and government to carry out these tasks. The German federal system is referred to as co-operative rather than competitive federalism as complex rules of financial equalization (*Finanzausgleich*) redistribute resources from the richer to the poorer *Länder*, and from the federal state to the *Länder*.

The head of state in the FRG is the non-executive Federal President who is elected by an electoral commission made up of members of the national **Bundestag** and the *Länder* parliaments. The incumbent President, **Horst Köhler**, was elected in June 2004. Legislative power is vested with the bicameral parliament comprising the Bundestag and the **Bundesrat**. Executive power at federal level lies with the Chancellor—since 1998 **Gerhard Schröder**—who is granted sole responsibility for setting the direction of government policy. The Chancellor is nominated by the largest party in the Bundestag, and appointed following a formal vote in the lower house.

In contrast to its democratic predecessor, the Weimar Republic of 1919–33, the political system of the FRG has been characterized by a high degree of stability. Post-war politics have been dominated by two main parties, the **Christian Democratic Union (CDU)** and the **Social Democratic Party of Germany (SPD)**—referred to as *Volksparteien* or People's Parties. The smaller, liberal **Free Democratic Party (FDP)** has traditionally acted as a pivot party, forming coalitions with parties of the left and right, and a fourth political party, The Greens (now **Alliance 90/The Greens**) entered the Bundestag in 1983 and formed a national coalition with the SPD in 1998. Following German unification the **Party of Democratic Socialism**, the successor party to the communist party of the GDR, gained significant representation in the Bundestag though its support has fallen in recent elections. The low number of parties represented in the Bundestag is the consequence of the electoral law which requires a party to gain either 5% of the vote or three direct mandates in order to be allowed to claim its full allocation of seats. Also, anti-democratic parties can be banned by the **Federal Constitutional Court** and such measures were taken in 1952 and 1956. Parties of the extreme right wing do exist, but their electoral successes have been in local and state (*Land*) elections.

The CDU dominated politics in the early years of the FRG, forming governments in 1949–66 under Konrad Adenauer and Ludwig Erhard. The CDU and SPD formed a Grand Coalition in 1966–69 until the 1969 election when the SPD, under the leadership of **Willy Brandt**, chose to govern with the FDP. Following Brandt's resignation in 1974 Helmut Schmidt was SPD Chancellor until his government was brought down by a constructive vote of no confidence in 1982. Chancellor Helmut Kohl led a CDU-FDP coalition for 16 years, in 1982–98. The end of the Kohl era was marked by the election of the SPD-Alliance 90/The Greens coalition in September 1998. This event was remarkable because it was the first time ever that a complete change of government had come about as a result of an election rather than a change in coalition preferences. It was the first time that Alliance 90/The Greens had participated in government at national level, and it was the first wholly left-of-centre coalition. The red-green coalition was re-elected on 22 September 2002. At that election the SPD gained the same share of the vote as the CDU (38.5%), but support for the Greens rose to its highest ever level (8.6%). Much of the party's success can be attributed to the popularity of its foreign minister and Vice-Chancellor, **Joschka Fischer**.

Germany has also been described as a semi-sovereign state as, initially an occupied state, it had a limited capacity to act alone on the international stage. Instead, it committed itself to multilateralism, pursuing its goals in regional and international organizations. Germany joined the **North Atlantic Treaty Organization (NATO)** in 1955. A civilian power, it has traditionally refused to commit troops to military activities. The FRG was also a founder member of the **European Coal and Steel Community** and has from the start been the largest net contributor to the European budget, though it has not had political power in European institutions commensurate with the size of its economy and population.

Although no new German constitution was written at the time of German unification in 1990, some have used the label 'the Berlin Republic' to characterize the post-1990 German state. This refers not only to the change of capital from Bonn to Berlin, agreed by the Bundestag in 1991 and completed in 1999, but also to the more confident and less consensual mode of politics in Germany. Politicians have expressed discontent at Germany's role as paymaster of the **European Union (EU)** and at the fact that it 'punches beneath its weight' in EU institutions. Moreover, the Federal Constitutional Court ruled in 1994 that it was no longer unconstitutional for German military forces to take part in NATO military missions if they were justified on humanitarian grounds. Consequently, Germany committed troops to NATO out-of-area missions in **Kosovo** in 1999 and in Afghanistan in 2001. However, the red-green government refused to participate in the US-led war against **Iraq** in 2003.

Economy: The German economy is the largest in Europe and the third largest in the world. It is an open, export-oriented economy specializing in the production of machinery, tools, cars and chemicals. Germany industrialized in two phases: the south of the country developed networks of small and medium-sized firms in the 17th century and the centre and north industrialized during the second industrial revolution in 1830–70, developing large-scale autarkic firms. The service sector in Germany has been slower to develop.

GNP: US $1,939,600m. (2001); *GNP per caput:* $23,560 (2001); *GNP at PPP:* $2,078,000m. (2001); *GNP per caput at PPP:* $25,240 (2001); *GDP:* $1,846,069m. (2001); *exports:* $657,453m. (2001); *imports:* $619,920m. (2001); *currency:* euro; *unemployment:* 8.7% (2002).

During the division of Germany in 1945–90 the German economy was separated into the command economy of the **German Democratic Republic (GDR)** and the capitalist social market economy of the Federal Republic of Germany (FRG) in the west. West Germany reconstructed its economy in the post-war era with funds from the **Marshall Plan**, the precondition of which was that it would integrate into the Western alliance. West Germany was a founder member of the **European Coal and Steel Community**, a project that allowed Germany to develop key areas of its industrial economy, without this being perceived by its neighbours as a strategy to rearm.

West Germany experienced a period of rapid economic growth and prosperity during the 1950s. With this economic miracle, or *Wirtschaftswunder*, developed a distinct model of capitalism, referred to as the Rhineland model or the social market economy. While many features of the Rhineland model predate 1933, others were innovations for the FRG. This German model of capitalism is traditionally characterized by a close, consensual relationships between industry, finance and labour. Industry is financed by long-term loans from banks which in turn sit on the supervisory board of the firms they fund. Labour is represented in the decision-making process in industry through institutions of codetermination both on supervisory boards (since 1952 and 1976) and in elected works councils (since 1972). Most trade unions reorganized in the post-war period into a unified trade union federation, the **German Trade Union Federation**, according to the principle of one union per industry. In 1948 social partners were granted the right to negotiate wages autonomously. Wage agreements are negotiated between employers' organizations and trade unions for a whole sector or industry. German industrial workers are generally highly paid. This is compensated by high levels of productivity made possible by a highly skilled labour force and investment in modern technology. Labour is also protected by workers' rights that make dismissal difficult. The German state has a minimal role in the economy except to set rules and regulate. Control over monetary policy and the German currency—until 2002 the Deutsche Mark (DM)—was handed to the independent **Bundesbank**.

In post-war Germany a comprehensive corporatist **welfare state** developed. This partially built on the legacy of Otto von Bismarck, who introduced a social security system in the late 19th century as a means of guaranteeing the loyalty of civil servants to the state and reducing the political standing of the social democrats. The welfare system in the FRG is an insurance-based scheme funded by payroll taxes levied on employers and employees. This scheme traditionally offers generous benefits calculated according to prior earnings in the event of **unemployment** or sickness, and in old age. A less generous, means-tested tax-funded scheme for non-insured citizens offers last-resort benefits. In line with the Christian democratic principle of subsidiarity—that policy should be developed as close as possible to the citizen—the welfare state in Germany relies on **women** and families to provide unpaid services such as child-care and care for the elderly. In the traditional male-breadwinner welfare state, women have, until recently, had low economic activity rates.

The German economy adapted comparatively well to the oil shock of the early 1970s. Industry was not subsidized by the state and so was forced to absorb increases in fuel prices by reducing fuel consumption and using its highly skilled workforce to adapt production methods from uniform mass production to flexible specialization. The manufacture of high-quality niche products was particularly successful in the south of the country in the *Länder* of Baden-Württemberg, Bavaria and Hesse. The German economy began to experience difficulties in the 1980s when other exporting nations—in particular **Japan**—became more efficient and innovative in the production of niche products. Demand for Germany's exports fell and the economy struggled to maintain the virtuous circle of its high-wage, high-skill, and high-productivity levels. The problems of rising unemployment and public debt in the 1980s were addressed by cutting the working week (to 38.5 hours in 1985 for metalworkers) and moderate cuts in welfare spending. More ambitious reform of the social market economy was abandoned at the time of **German unification** in 1990.

The collapse of the GDR on 9 November 1989 led to a rapid unification of the economies and polities of the two German states. Monetary, economic and social union came first and was formally completed on 1 July 1990. This introduced the DM to the GDR at the economically unviable rate of one-to-one. Also, the institutions of the Rhineland model and corporatist welfare state were transferred wholesale to the new *Länder*. The eastern economy boomed for a couple of years, mostly on the back of the construction industry, but fell into deep recession in 1993. East German industry suffered from the parity exchange rate and from the fall in demand for East German products, both domestically, as eastern Germans spent their DM on western goods, and in its former markets in **Central and Eastern European Countries**. Moreover, despite the fact that productivity in GDR industry was one-third of that of the west, trade unions demanded rapid equalization of wages to avoid the emergence of a low-wage economy in the new *Länder*. The privatization of state-owned GDR industry through the *Treuhand* also led to the closure of thousands of firms which could not compete in market conditions.

West Germany's unification policy aimed to promote, as **Helmut Kohl** put it, 'flourishing landscapes' in the east and rapid convergence of the two economies. By the mid-1990s the objective had switched from aiming for convergence to promoting innovative 'lighthouse regions' in the east around Dresden, Leipzig or Chemnitz. To achieve this, the old *Länder* made substantial transfer payments to the new *Länder*, funded partially by an income tax surcharge, and partially by increasing the public debt, which doubled within five years of unification. The aid—by 2004 a total of €1,250,000m.—has been predominantly in the form of cash payments to meet the obligations of the welfare state rather than as investment in industrial capital, human capital or research and development. As a consequence, the eastern economy has not caught up with the west. Since the recession of 1993 unemployment in unified Germany has soared in the east and currently stands at double the rate of that in the west (17.7% compared with 7.8% in 2002) and is in some regions as high as 19%. Productivity in the east remains lower than the west, and wages in most sectors have not been equalized.

The coalition of the **Social Democratic Party of Germany (SPD)** and **Alliance 90/The Greens** that took office in September 1998 made a promise to reduce unemployment by 2002. Having failed to meet this pledge, it convened a commission (the Hartz Commission) composed of politicians, businessmen and social partners to devise solutions to Germany's mass unemployment. The government stated that it would implement the commission's recommendations one by one if returned to office following the election of September 2002. Since re-election the SPD-Green coalition has implemented a series of controversial labour market and welfare reforms to speed up the transition of the unemployed from welfare to the labour market, encourage the creation of low-paid starter jobs, liberalize redundancy laws in small firms and shift some of the burden of funding healthcare to the patient.

The growth of public debt during the 1990s raised concerns that Germany would not meet the **convergence criteria** for membership of **Economic and Monetary Union (EMU)**. In the event, a series of austerity measures were adopted to reduce public spending and Germany successfully met the **convergence criteria** and participated in the final stage of EMU in 1999. With public debt levels at nearly 4% of gross domestic product, Germany has failed to adhere to the formal rules of the **stability and growth pact** and has been threatened with sanctions and fines by the **European Commission**. There is significant evidence from the late 1990s and early 2000s that the processes of unification, **Europeanization** and the intensification of competition associated with globalization have begun to erode some of the traditional key features of the German economic model and welfare state.

Gibraltar

Gibraltar is a small British dependency on the southern tip of Spain with a population of 30,000. It was ceded to Britain by Spain in the Treaty of Utrecht in 1713. The treaty states that if Britain were to leave Gibraltar, Spain would have the right to first refusal in taking over. The Constitution of 1969 granted Gibraltar widespread autonomy, but many Gibraltans favour full independence. Since full autonomy is not an option, Gibraltar's residents wish to remain British rather than be transferred to Spanish jurisdiction. In 2002 Britain and Spain entered into talks to discuss the possibility of joint sovereignty. In a referendum on the issue held on 7 November 2002 the proposal of shared sovereignty was overwhelmingly rejected by the population (no 98.97%; turn-out 87.9%).

Il Girasole – *see* Sunflower Alliance, Italy

Giscard d'Estaing, Valéry

Valéry Giscard d'Estaing is a conservative politician and former President of France who was most recently President of the **European Convention** convened in 2002 to draw up a Constitutional Treaty for the **European Union**. Giscard d'Estaing served as President of France in 1974–81, having been Minister for Finance and Economic Affairs in 1962–66 and in 1969–74. He was elected as President in 1974, having won 50.7% of the vote in the second round of elections against the socialist **François Mitterrand**. In his campaign he promised political, economic and social change and, as President, he lowered the age of voting from 21 to 18, relaxed divorce and abortion laws and introduced bills on equal pay and **women**'s rights. At European level he campaigned for the formation of the European Council in 1974. Also, together with German Chancellor Helmut Schmidt, with whom he had a close relationship, he established the **European Monetary System** in 1979.

Giscard d'Estaing founded the **Union for French Democracy** in 1978 as an alternative conservative party to the Gaullist **Rally for the Republic** and to support his second bid for the presidency in 1981. In the event, he lost the election to François Mitterrand and, following defeat, maintained a low profile on the political scene. He was, however, a member of the **European Parliament** in 1989–93 and a member of the **Assemblée Nationale** in 1993–2002.

Born on 2 February 1926 in Koblenz, Germany, Giscard d'Estaing studied at the Ecole Polytechnique and the Ecole Nationale d'Administration. He is married to Anne Aymone and they have four children.

Good Friday Agreement

The Good Friday Agreement, formally known as the Belfast Agreement, is the 1998 peace agreement for **Northern Ireland**. This 65-page document paved the way for the return of a devolved government to the province in 1999. The Northern Ireland Assembly was set up alongside a north-south ministerial council, a British-Irish council and a British-Irish intergovernmental conference. In addition to these formal institutions, other measures were introduced to address the concerns of the major political parties: Unionists were offered the repeal of the Irish Republic's constitutional claim to Northern Ireland; Nationalists were offered a new commission on policing, which led to the reform of the Royal Ulster Constabulary, replacing it with the Police Service of Northern Ireland in November 2001, and a human rights commission.

The consensual and inclusive approach of the Good Friday Agreement was reflected in the results of the 1998 referendums held to endorse the agreement. Most political parties in Northern Ireland supported the agreement and 71% of the population voted in favour of it. In the Republic of Ireland 94% of the population endorsed the agreement. David Trimble of the **Ulster Unionist Party** and John Hume of the **Social Democratic and Labour Party** won the 1998 Nobel Peace Prize for the efforts they had made to find a peaceful solution to the conflict in Northern Ireland.

Grasser, Karl Heinz

Karl Heinz Grasser has been Minister of Finance in Austria since 2000 in the coalition between the conservative **Austrian People's Party (ÖVP)** and the populist right-wing **Austrian Freedom Party (FPÖ)**. A supporter of the free market economy, Grasser was originally a member of the FPÖ but left the party following his resignation from the first ÖVP-FPÖ coalition in 2002. He was nearly forced to resign following conflicts within his party over the issue of tax cuts. In response to severe floods in the summer of 2002 the coalition decided to postpone planned tax cuts to fund the repair operations. Grasser supported the postponement of tax cuts, but the then party leader, **Jörg Haider**, tried to force the minister to resign for breaking electoral promises. Chancellor **Wolfgang Schüssel** supported Grasser and called new elections, promising to reappoint him in a new government as a non-party-affiliated minister.

Born on 2 January 1969 in Klagenfurt, Grasser took a degree in business studies in the same town. He was vice-president for human resources and public relations for the firm Magna Europe in 1998–2000 and manager of the company Sport Management International in 1999–2000.

Address: Himmelpfortgasse 8, 1015 Vienna, Austria
Tel: (0)1 514-33 + ext
Fax: (0)1 512-62-00
E-mail: karl-heinz.grasser@bmf.gv.at
Internet: www.bmf.gv.at

Greece

Greece comprises a mainland and more than 2,000 islands in the south-east periphery of Europe. Greece won independence from the Ottoman Empire in 1870. It was occupied by Nazi Germany in 1941–44 during the Second World War and was then divided by a civil war waged in 1946–49 between the political right, led by Field Marshal Alexandros Papagos, and the communist guerrilla army, which was ultimately defeated. The democratic political system of the post-war period in Greece was interrupted by a seven-year military dictatorship in 1967–74 which resulted in the termination of the monarchy.

Area: 132,000 sq km; *capital:* Athens; *population:* 11m. (2001).

During the **Cold War** Greece was the only liberal democratic state in Europe east of Austria. It received generous support from its western allies and became a committed member of the **North Atlantic Treaty Organization**. It built up a strong army to deal with the perceived threat from its former enemy **Turkey** and the issue of the divided island Cyprus. Greece became a member of the **European Community** in 1981. Originally a member state which advocated strengthening the political side of integration, in recent years it has blocked projects in the area of defence, such as the **rapid reaction force**, because of its sensitivities on the issue of Turkey.

According to the Constitution of 1975 Greece is a parliamentary republic. The head of state is the non-executive President—since 1995 **Constantinos Stephano-poulos**—who is directly elected for a five-year term. Legislative power is vested in the **Vouli ton Ellinon** and the Greek electoral system of reinforced proportional representation gives the largest party in the Vouli an exaggerated majority so that the executive is invariably a single-party government. Since the most recent elections, held on 7 March 2004, **New Democracy (ND)**, headed by Prime Minister **Konstantinos Karamanlis**, has formed the government.

Since the end of military dictatorship in 1974, Greek politics have been dominated by two parties established for the new democratic regime. Former Prime Minister Constantine Karamanlis founded the right-wing ND and Andreas Papandreou formed the socialist **Pan-Hellenic Socialist Movement (PASOK)**. Both of these parties were strongly dominated by, and oriented around, the personalities of their founders, encouraging strong personality politics in Greece. In the clientelistic political system, parties also have a tradition of offering social protection to their supporters in the form of jobs, contracts and welfare benefits such as generous pension schemes. Most election campaigns concentrate on the issues of economic responsibility of the state and the clientelistic habits of the dominant Greek parties.

Parties of the right dominated Greek politics in 1949–81. PASOK interrupted the power of the right in 1981, coming to office with 48.1% of the vote and 172 seats in the 300-seat Vouli. Subsequently PASOK governed continuously in 1981–89, and again in 1993–2004. During the 1980s PASOK governments followed an orthodox socialist path, significantly increasing public spending and expanding the public sector and public services. This led to severe economic problems, such as high public debt and a rate of inflation that reached 16%. In the 1990 elections ND came to power and, during their three years in office, pursued neo-liberal policies. It sought to reduce the role of the state and to cut government spending and debt. It froze wages in the public sector and placed a limit on the number of new public-sector workers who could be engaged (only one employee could be taken on for every three that left). It also addressed the pension problem, accelerated the privatization process and attempted to increase the government's tax revenues.

In 1993 ND was forced to call early elections following an internal party dispute over the issue of Macedonia, which led to defections from the ND parliamentary group and the loss of its parliamentary majority. The end of the Cold War meant that Greece was no longer isolated as the only liberal democracy in the south-east corner of Europe. However, it also revived old boundary issues. Greek politicians were deeply divided over the status of the new, independent state of the former Yugoslav

Republic of Macedonia which was founded following the disintegration of Yugoslavia. The ND Greek foreign minister, Antonis Samaras, clashed with Prime Minister Constantine Mitsotakis over the new name for Macedonia: Samaras belonged to those nationalistic Greeks who tried to insist that 'Macedonia' should not be included in the name of the new state.

PASOK returned to power in 1993 having won 46.88% of the vote and 170 parliamentary seats. By this time it had changed its programme to a less statist, more market-oriented form of social democracy that aimed to promote social solidarity. It planned to tackle **unemployment** not by expanding the public sector, but by promoting economic growth and it no longer opposed privatization policies. The PASOK government was re-elected in 1996, having won 41.5% of the vote and 162 parliamentary seats. Costas Simitis became Prime Minister and party leader in, respectively, January and June 1996, following the resignation and subsequent death of Andreas Papandreou. With less emphasis on a charismatic leader, Greek politics have started to focus on the competence and performance of government. Simitis set about implementing a modernization package which aimed at reforming the state, economy and Greece's international relations. His aim was to reduce clientelism in the state, secure Greece's membership of **Economic and Monetary Union** and improve relations with Turkey. Simitis succeeded in securing Greece's entry to the **euro area** by January 2001 and, despite a number of difficulties, oversaw smooth preparations for the Athens 2004 Olympic Games. Diplomatic relations between Greece and Turkey improved, especially following the earthquakes which affected both states in 1999. However, reform of the generous pension scheme was blocked by trade unions. For the next Vouli elections, held on 7 March 2004, Simitis proposed to implement a 'convergence charter' which aims to raise the standard of living from 70% of the **European Union** average to 80% by 2008. PASOK aimed to achieve this by lowering taxes and increasing spending on education, training and job creation, and pensions. Simitis resigned as leader of PASOK in January 2004 in order to transfer that office to George Papandreou (son of former Prime Minister Andreas Papandreou).

PASOK was defeated in the general elections held on 7 March 2004, winning only 40.55% of the vote and 117 seats. There was a widespread perception that PASOK had not fulfilled the promises it had made to reduce unemployment and improve public services. ND emerged as the majority party, winning 45.36% of the vote and 165 parliamentary seats. Under Prime Minister Karamanlis the government pledged to reduce the rate of unemployment from 9% to 6% through increased economic growth and by improving the structural weaknesses in the economy.

Economy: The Greek economy traditionally relies on **agriculture**, tourism and shipping; Greece has the world's third largest merchant fleet but an underdeveloped and declining manufacturing sector. Employment is concentrated in a large number of small, family-owned businesses and the large public sector. A clientelistic public sector and **welfare state** have expanded over the years to benefit and fulfil commitments to supporters of the governing party. The Greek state has high rates of public spending but a weak tax base; in the early 1990s only 8% of gross domestic product (GDP) was raised through taxation. Greece also has a large 'black' economy; in the mid 1990s it was estimated that this had grown to 40% of the size of the legal one.

GNP: US $121,000m. (2001); *GNP per caput:* $11,430 (2001); *GNP at PPP:* $186,000m. (2001); *GNP per caput at PPP:* $17,520 (2001); *GDP:* $117,169m. (2001); *exports:* $30,071m. (2001); *imports:* $41,291m. (2001); *currency:* euro; *unemployment:* 9.6% (2002).

During the **Cold War** Greece was an isolated capitalist state in the region. Benefiting from the **Marshall Plan**, Greece experienced rapid economic growth in the early post-war period. During the 1950s Greece enjoyed the fastest growth rate and the lowest inflation rate in Europe. Greece joined the **European Community** in 1981, becoming the poorest country in the region and a net recipient of European regional and structural funds. This helped further economic growth. Greece's special status among other Western democracies came to an end with the collapse of the communist regimes in **Central and Eastern European Countries**. No longer isolated, Greece has benefited from the establishment of new market economies in its neighbouring countries (especially Bulgaria and Macedonia). Greece was allocated €25,000m. in **European Union (EU)** structural aid for the period 2000–06, but will no longer gain from 2006 when aid is redirected to the new member states which joined the EU on 1 May 2004.

Greece's economic success stalled in the 1980s. The left-wing **Panhellenic Socialist Movement (PASOK)** government of 1981–90 increased public spending, nationalized ailing firms and expanded the public sector and services. This, coupled with a poor record at raising taxes, led to high levels of public debt. In the 1980s the budget deficit increased fourfold and public debt had risen to 120% of GDP by 1992. The growth rate fell and the rate of inflation soared to 20% in 1991. The **New Democracy (ND)** government of 1990–93 pursued a policy of privatization and reduced the role of the state in the economy. The government again froze wage payments in the large public sector, and ruled that only one new government employee could be appointed for every three that left the service. It brought the generous pension scheme under control and attempted to increase the tax revenue. It increased indirect taxation, lowered direct taxation and reorganized the tax-collection system in 1992. By the time that PASOK returned to power in 1993 it too was committed to reforming the economy, cutting debt, and controlling inflation. It drew up a social contract with social partners; this included agreements on prices, tax reform, social benefits and incentives for private investment. It also became more pro-EU and, following its re-election in September 1996, committed Greece to the project of **Economic and Monetary Union (EMU)**.

On 14 March 1998 the national currency, the drachma, was devalued by 12.1% to allow it to participate in the **Exchange Rate Mechanism**. Greece did not qualify to be included in the first round of EMU in 1999 as its inflation rate (around 5%) was significantly above the EU average. The PASOK government adopted a package of austerity measures and cuts in public spending in order to bring down inflation and national debt. It managed to reduce this and Greece was accepted into the EMU in 2000, entering it in the following year. PASOK successfully achieved its aim of preparing the Greek economy for entry into the **euro area** in time for the introduction of coins and banknotes on 1 January 2002.

Greece appeared to thrive in the euro area, achieving economic growth that was twice the EU average rate (3.8%). Less positively, **unemployment**, especially youth unemployment, is high and the rate of inflation is above the EU average (3.5% in mid-2002). Moreover, following the change of government in March 2004 it emerged that the PASOK government had concealed the size of the country's budget deficit, particularly spending on defence and social security. The incoming ND government revealed in September 2004 that Greece had not met the criteria of the **stability and growth pact** in any year since it had joined the euro area, and that the budget deficit in 2003 was closer to 4.6% of GDP than to the official figure of 1.7%.

Greek General Confederation of Labour

The Greek General Confederation of Labour, or Geniki Synomospondia Ergaton Ellados (GSEE), is the main trade union confederation in Greece. Founded in 1918, it represents employees at national level and negotiates wage agreements. GSEE has tended to be dominated by a range of political factions, and has generally followed the government of the day. In recent years the movement has become more independent. GSEE is affiliated to ETUC.

Pres.: Christos Polyzogopoulos
Address: Patission 69, 104 34 Athens, Greece
Tel: (0)21 088346115
Fax: (0)21 08202120
E-mail: info@gsee.gr
Internet: www.gsee.gr

Green League

The Green League, or Vihreä Liitto, is the green party in Finland. Formally established in 1988, its roots go back to the tradition of direct action of the green movement in the 1970s. The party campaigns for the environment, for alternative approaches to social policy and for rejuvenating grass roots democracy. The Finnish greens first contested parliamentary elections in 1983 when two representatives were elected to the **Eduskunta**. Further gains were made in national and local elections during the 1980s and 1990s. Despite losing a seat in the 1995 elections, the party went on to participate in the ideologically progressive 'rainbow coalition' led by the **Finnish Social Democratic Party**. A Vihreä Liitto member of parliament, Pekka Haavisto, was made Minister of Environment and Development Co-operation. In elections held in 1999 the party won 11 parliamentary seats and continued to govern in the 'rainbow coalition' with one-and-a-half ministers (the second for just two years of the four-year term). It withdrew from government in 2002 following a decision to accept a fifth nuclear power plant. In elections held on 16 March 2003 Vihreä Liitto won 14 seats in parliament, its best ever result.

Party Leader: Osmo Soininvaara
Address: 3rd Floor, Fredrikinkatu 33A, 00120 Helsinki, Finland
Tel: (0)9 58604160
Fax: (0)9 58604161
E-mail: vihreat@vihrealiitto.fi
Internet: www.vihrealiitto.fi

Green-Left

Green-Left, or GroenLinks, is a socialist environmentalist party in the Netherlands. Founded in 1989 through a fusion of four socialist parties, it campaigns primarily on peace and conservation issues. The party was first represented in the **Tweede Kamer** in 1989. The party currently has eight representatives in the 150-seat lower house which was elected on 22 January 2003.

Party Leader: Merman Meijer
Address: Oudegracht 312, 3511 PK Utrecht, or POB 8008, 3503 RA Utrecht, Netherlands
Tel: (0)30 2399900
Fax: (0)30 3300342
E-mail: info@groenlinks.nl
Internet: www.groenlinks.nl

Green Party (Austria)

The Green Party, or Grüne, in Austria began as a Green electoral list for the 1986 elections to the **Nationalrat**. Originally a left-wing ecological protest movement, the party has become more conservative since 1993 under the leadership of Alexander van der Bellen. It is no longer anti-militaristic and supports the interests of business and the reform of the **welfare state**. The party first entered parliament in 1986 with eight representatives. In elections held in November 2002 the Greens won a record 17 seats in the 183-seat **Nationalrat** and were considered as a potential coalition partner for the conservative **Austrian People's Party**.

Party Leader: Alexander van der Bellen
Address: Lindengasse 40, 1071 Vienna, Austria
Tel: (0)1-52-125-201
E-mail: infopool@gruene.at
Internet: www.gruene.at

Green Party (Ireland)

The Green Party is the ecological party in Ireland. Founded in 1981, it campaigns for sustainable development, decentralized decision-making and the introduction of a basic income. It first gained representation in the **Dáil Éireann** in 1989. Following the most recent general elections, held on 17 May 2002, the Green Party returned six members to the 166-seat Dáil.

Party Leader: Trevor Sargent
Address: 16/17 Suffolk St, Dublin 2, Ireland
Tel: (0)1 6790012
Fax: (0)1 6797168
E-mail: info@greenparty.ie
Internet: www.greenparty.ie

Green Party (Luxembourg)

The Green Party, or Déi Gréng, is the main ecological party in Luxembourg. Founded in 1983, the party campaigns on environmental and ecological matters, and against nuclear power and weapons. The party has received growing support in recent years. In the most recent general election, held on 13 June 2004, the party won 11.6% of the vote and seven seats in the 60-seat **Chambre des Députés**.

Party Representatives: Tilly Metz and Robert Rings
Address: 25 rue Notre-Dame, 2240 Luxembourg
Tel: (0)46-37-40-1
Fax: (0)46-37-43
E-mail: greng@greng.lu
Internet: www.greng.lu

Green Party (Portugal)

The Green Party, or Partido Ecologista 'Os Verdes' (OV), is the left-wing ecological party in Portugal. Founded in 1982, OV seeks to raise public awareness of ecological challenges at national and global level. OV has campaigned in national elections for the **Assembléia da República** on a platform with the **Communist Party of Portugal** and has never won more than two parliamentary seats since 1983. It currently has two deputies in the 230-seat parliament.

Address: Rua da Boavista, no. 83-3° Drt., 1200-066 Lisbon, Portugal
Tel: (0)21 3960291 or (0)21 3960308
Fax: (0)21 3960424
E-mail: osverdes@mail.telepac.pt
Internet: www.osverdes.pt

Green Party (Sweden)

The Green Party, or Miljöpartiet de Gröna, in Sweden has its roots in the environmental, anti-nuclear, peace and **women**'s movements and was established as a formal party in 1981. Following elections held in 1988 the party became the first new party to enter the **Riksdag** in 70 years and remained represented until 1991. It was re-elected in 1994 and there are currently 17 Green Party representatives in the 349-seat parliament that was elected on 15 September 2002. The minority social democratic government of **Göran Persson** relies on the support of the Green Party although it is not part of a coalition.

Party Spokespersons: Maria Wetterstrand and Peter Eriksson
Address: Gamla stan, Prästgatan 18A, POB 2136, 103 14 Stockholm, Sweden
Tel: (0)8 545-22-450
Fax: (0)8 545-224-60
E-mail: info@mp.se
Internet: www.mp.se

Green Party (Switzerland)

The Green Party, or Grüne/Les Verts, in Switzerland began as a series of regional environmental initiatives and movements and parties that emerged from the late 1960s. The party was formally established as the Grüne Partei der Schweiz in 1986 and changed its name to Grüne in 1993. The Greens won 14 seats in the 200-seat **Nationalrat** that was elected in 1991, but suffered electoral losses in 1995 when its representation fell to eight seats. This increased to nine seats in 1999 and, at the most recent national elections, held on 19 October 2003, the party won 13 seats in the Nationalrat.

Pres.: Ruth Genner
Address: Waisenhausplatz 21, 3011 Bern, Switzerland
Tel: (0)313126660
Fax: (0)313126660
E-mail: gruene@gruene.ch
Internet: www.gruene.ch

Greenland

Greenland is a large island in the North Atlantic Ocean between Canada and Europe. Its total area is 2,166,086 sq km, of which 1,755,637 sq km are covered by ice. The capital is Nuuk. The population of Greenland is 56,000 (2002) and the main languages spoken are Greenlandic and Danish. Greenland has been part of Denmark since 1721. The island was granted self-government in 1979 but the head of state is Queen Margrethe II of Denmark, Greenland sends two representatives to the Danish **Folketing** and Denmark still controls Greenland's foreign affairs.

Greenland became a member of the **European Community (EC)** with Denmark in 1973 but withdrew from it in 1985 following a controversy concerning fishing quotas. Since then relations with the EC and the **European Union** have been based on special agreements.

Greenland's legislative power lies with the unicameral Landstinget. This is made up of 31 members who are elected for a four-year term. At the most recent elections to the Landstinget, held on 3 December 2002, parties advocating independence from Denmark won more than 50% of the vote. The current Greenlandic coalition government is headed by Hans Enoksen of the social-democratic, pro-independence party, Siumut. Most political parties favour independence, but they are divided on whether this should happen immediately or when some progress has been made towards resolving the country's economic and social problems. The Greenlandic economy is dependent on exports of fish and fish products; and on annual subsidies of US \$375m. from the Danish government to fund the large public sector and comprehensive social democratic welfare system which supports the high number of unemployed (10.4% in 2003).

The Greens

The Greens, or Les Verts, is an ecological party in France. Founded in 1984, it campaigns for radical ecological politics. The party made moderate electoral gains during the 1980s with an ideological position that was characterized as lying between left and right. During the 1990s The Greens gained more support and governed in two multi-party coalitions led by the **Socialist Party**, in 1997–2000 and 2000–02, each time providing the Minister for the Environment. At the most recent general elections, held on 9 and 16 June 2002, The Greens won 4.5% of the vote and three seats in the 577-seat **Assemblée Nationale**. In the first round of the most recent presidential elections, held on 21 April 2002, the candidate for The Greens, Noël Mamère, won 5.2% of the vote.

Gen. Sec.: Yann Wehrling
Address: 247 rue du Faubourg Saint-Martin, 75010 Paris, France
Tel: (0)1-53-19-53-19
Fax: (0)1-53-19-03-93
E-mail: lesverts@lesverts.fr
Internet: www.lesverts.fr

Grímsson, Ólafur Ragnar

Ólafur Ragnar Grímsson has been President of Iceland since 1996. He was elected as the fifth President in June 1996 for a four-year term, having won 40.9% of the votes cast. An unopposed candidate in June 2000, he was reappointed for a second term, and was re-elected for a third on 26 June 2004 with 85.6% of the votes cast. Grímsson's political activities began in 1966–73 on the board of the **Progressive**

Party's Youth Federation; and on the party's executive board in 1971–73. He first stood for a seat in the **Althingi** in 1974 for the Liberal and Left Alliance and was elected as a representative of the People's Alliance Party for Reykjavík in 1978 and for Reykjanes in 1991 and 1995. He was chairman of the parliamentary group of the People's Alliance Party in 1980–83 and he was elected leader of that party in 1987, a position which he held until 1995. Grímsson was Minister of Finance in 1988–91.

Born on 14 May 1943 in Ísafjördur in north-west Iceland, Grímsson studied economics and political science at the University of Manchester, United Kingdom, and was awarded a doctorate in 1970. He then taught political science at the University of Iceland and became a professor in 1973. Grímsson married Gudrún Katrín Thorbergsdóttir, who died in 1998. He has twin daughters.

Address: Office of the President, Sóleyjargata 1, 150 Reykjavík, Iceland
Tel: (0)5404400
Fax: (0)5624802
E-mail: forseti@forseti.is
Internet: www.forseti.is (under construction)

Groenlinks – *see* **Green-Left, Netherlands**

Grüne – *see* **Green Party, Austria**

Grüne – *see* **Green Party, Switzerland**

H

Haarde, Gier

Gier Haarde has been Minister of Finance in Iceland since April 1998. A member of
the **Independence Party (SSF)**, he is part of a coalition government between the
SSF and the **Progressive Party (FSF)**, now led by FSF leader **Halldór Ásgrímsson**. Haarde has been a representative for SSF in the **Althingi** since 1987. He served
as chairman of the SSF parliamentary group in 1991–98 and chairman of the foreign
affairs committee in 1995–98. He has been vice-chairman of the SSF since 1999.
Haarde worked as an economist for the **Sedlabanki** in 1977–83 and as a political
adviser to the Minister of Finance in 1983–87.

Born on 8 April 1951, Haarde studied economics at Brandeis University and the
University of Minnesota, and International Relations at Johns Hopkins University,
in the USA. Gier Haarde is married to Inga Jona Thordardottir, and they have five
children.

Address: Ministry of Finance, Arnarhvall, 150 Reykjavík, Iceland
Tel: (0)5459200
Fax: (0)5628280
E-mail: mail@fjr.stjr.is
Internet: eng.fjarmalaraduneyti.is

Haestirettur – *see* **Supreme Court, Iceland**

Haider, Jörg

Jörg Haider is a politician for the extreme right-wing **Austrian Freedom Party
(FPÖ)** and governor of the state of Carinthia. A controversial politician, he is
credited with transforming the electoral fortunes of the FPÖ during his 14 years as
party leader but has been widely criticized for his comments on Nazi politics and
policy, and for his anti-**immigration** views.

Haider has been a member of the FPÖ since 1971 and active in FPÖ politics at
national level and in the province of Carinthia. He became head of the FPÖ in 1986,
a post which he held until 2000. He served as governor of Carinthia in 1989–91 and

has again held that office since 1999. Haider was forced to resign as governor of Carinthia in 1991 following his comment that 'in the Third Reich they had an "orderly" employment policy'. He referred to Nazi concentration camps as merely 'punishment camps' in 1995, and in that year also stated that the Nazi Waffen SS was a 'part of the Wehrmacht' and therefore 'deserves all the honour and respect of the army in public life'. While Haider has apologized for such comments, they have raised concern in Austria, the **European Union (EU)** and Israel.

In national elections held in October 1999 the FPÖ gained 27% of the vote and entered into a coalition with the conservative **Austrian People's Party**. The inclusion of Haider's FPÖ in national government in January 2000 sparked a wave of protests in Austria and across Europe. Austria's EU partners imposed diplomatic sanctions on the state. Haider was not included in the government, and he resigned as party leader in February 2000. While some perceived this as an attempt to make the party seem more moderate, others interpreted it as a shrewd move on the part of Haider, who harbours ambitions of becoming Austrian Chancellor.

Born on 26 January 1950 in Bad Goisern, Haider studied law in Vienna and was federal leader of the nationalistic youth movement 'Ring Freiheitlicher Jugend' in 1970–74. Jörg Haider is married and has two daughters.

Halonen, Tarja

Tarja Halonen was elected as President of Finland on 1 March 2000 for a six-year term. A social democrat, she received 40% of the vote in the first round of the presidential election and 51.6% in the second round. The 11th President of Finland, Halonen is the first woman to hold the post. Halonen became a member of the **Finnish Social Democratic Party** in 1971 and served as parliamentary secretary to the Prime Minister in 1974–75. She was elected to the **Eduskunta** in 1979 and held her seat through five consecutive elections until she became President.

Halonen was Minister at the Ministry for Social Affairs and Health in 1987–90, Minister of Justice in 1990–91 and Minister for Foreign Affairs in 1995–2000. While Halonen was Minister for Foreign Affairs, Finland held the presidency of the **European Union** for the first time, in July–December 1999. Tarja Halonen has also been active in the **Council of Europe**, first as deputy-chairwoman of the Finnish Delegation to the Parliamentary Assembly, in 1991–95, and then in the Ministerial Committee. She also served five terms on the Helsinki City Council, in 1977–96.

Born on 24 December 1943 in Helsinki, Halonen is a graduate of the University of Helsinki and has a master's degree in law. She began her professional career as social affairs secretary for the National Union of Finnish Students in 1969–70. In 1970 she became a lawyer with the **Central Organization of Finnish Trade Unions**. Tarja Halonen is married to Pentti Arajärvi and has one daughter.

Address: Office of the President of Finland, Mariankatu 2, 00170 Helsinki, Finland
Tel: (0)9 661133
Fax: (0)9 638247
E-mail: president@tpk.fi
Internet: www.presidentti.fi

Hoge Raad – *see* Supreme Court, Netherlands

Högsta Domstolens – *see* Supreme Court, Sweden

Højesteret – *see* Supreme Court, Denmark

Holocaust

The Holocaust is a term mainly used to describe the systematic, state-sponsored oppression and killing of about 6m. men, women and children—above all Jews—by Nazi Germany and its collaborators between 1939 and 1945. The Hebrew term *Shoah* has a similar meaning but often refers specifically to the killing of the Jewish population and could therefore to some extent be considered as one element of the 'Holocaust'.

Shortly after Adolf Hitler's Nationalsozialistische Deutsche Arbeiterpartei (NSDAP) came to power in 1933, the new rulers began to adopt increasingly barbaric methods to suppress above all Jewish citizens, but also political opponents of the Third Reich (especially social democrats and communists). Concentration camps were set up as early as 1933, a fact that was publicly known. These early camps were not death camps. However, thousands of opponents of the government and an increasing number of Jews suffered and many died because of bad conditions and the brutal treatment they received from the SS (Schutzstaffel), a paramilitary organization of the NSDAP.

The persecution of the Jews was carried out at different levels: the Nazis called for a boycott of Jewish businesses and Jews were dismissed from jobs in the public sector. Following the Nürnberg Laws of 1935, Jews were deprived of citizenship and were not allowed to marry so-called Aryan Germans. On *Kristallnacht*, the night of 9 November 1938, nearly every synagogue in Germany was set alight, and from then on thousands of Jews were imprisoned in concentration camps, mainly in Dachau and Buchenwald. Following the early German victories in the Second World War, most of the European Jewry fell under German control. The Nazis then pursued an even more barbaric strategy: *Einsatzgruppen* of the SS apprehended and killed Jews, Roma and many non-Jewish slaves across **Central and Eastern European Countries**. Furthermore, mainly in former Poland the Nazis created ghettos (the biggest in Warsaw and Lodz) and large-scale concentration camps where millions of

Jews would be killed. At the 'Wannsee Conference' on 20 January 1942 Germany decided the 'final solution'; that 11m. people should be systematically annihilated in such concentration camps as Auschwitz, Chelmno and Treblinka. By the time that Allied troops liberated the camps—which came to be referred to as 'KZ' at the end of the war—6m. people had died, mainly by being gassed.

The Holocaust remains a central, traumatic event in European history and has significant implications for European politics today. Holocaust Remembrance Days—observed on different days in different countries—secure the international commemoration of the millions of victims of Nazi Germany's extermination policies. The most important Remembrance Day lies on 27 Nisan in the Jewish calendar (shortly after Passover, April/May in the Gregorian calendar). The parliament of Israel declared the day Yom Hashoah ve Hagevurah (Holocaust Remembrance and Heroism Day), marking not only the destruction, but also the resistance of Jews. This nation-wide public holiday is observed in various ways: through candle lighting, speeches, poems, prayers and singing. Six candles are often lit to represent the 6m. victims. A major international political effort to secure the remembrance of the Holocaust was undertaken in 1998, when at the initiative of Sweden the 'Task Force for International Co-operation on Holocaust Education, Remembrance and Research' was created. The mission of this organization is 'to encourage activities on Holocaust education, remembrance, and research in member countries and in other interested countries' (taskforce.ushmm.org). Among its European members are Austria, the Czech Republic, Denmark, France, Germany, Hungary, Israel, Italy, Latvia, Lithuania, Luxembourg, the Netherlands, Norway, Poland, Sweden and the United Kingdom.

Compensation for Jewish victims of the Holocaust has mainly been negotiated since 1951 through the Jewish Claims Conference (www.claimscon.org). As a result, the German government has paid more than US \$50,000m. in indemnification for suffering and losses resulting from the Nazi persecution. In August 2000 the German government and parts of the German economy created the Foundation 'Remembrance, Responsibility and Future' (www.stiftung-evz.de) which aims to secure compensation for forced labourers and other Nazi victims in the Third Reich. The foundation was also launched to 'provide adequate legal security for German enterprises and the Federal Republic of Germany, especially in the United States of America' (Preamble, The Law on the Creation of a Foundation 'Remembrance, Responsibility and Future'). Five thousand million Deutsche Marks (DM) were made available by the companies joined together in the Foundation Initiative of German Industry, and another 5,000m. DM by the German government. The application deadline pursuant to the Law was 31 December 2001. The regulations for the payment have been sharply criticized from the very beginning since the whole process seemed too complicated and slow.

Sascha Feuchert
University of Giessen

House of Commons

The House of Commons is the lower house of the bicameral parliament of the United Kingdom. It is made up of 659 members who are elected by a first-past-the-post electoral system for a maximum five-year term. The most recent elections took place on 7 June 2001. In those elections the **Labour Party** won 412 seats. Other parties represented in the House of Commons (number of seats in brackets) are the **Conservative Party** (166), the **Liberal Democrats** (52), **Plaid Cymru** (4), the **Scottish National Party** (5), the **Ulster Unionist Party** (6), the **Democratic Unionist Party** (5), the **Social Democratic and Labour Party** (3) and **Sinn Féin** (4). At present 119 (18%) of the 659 members are **women**. The House of Commons is the main legislative body in the British parliament and it also scrutinizes the work of government. It shares these roles with the **House of Lords**, though it takes primacy over the non-elected upper house.

Address: Westminster, London SW1A 0AA, United Kingdom
Tel: (0)20 7219 4272
Fax: (0)20 7219 5839
E-mail: hcinfo@parliament.uk
Internet: www.parliament.uk

House of Lords

The House of Lords is the upper house of the parliament in the United Kingdom. Prior to a reform in 1999 there were more than 1,200 members and its membership was based predominantly on inheritance. Around two-thirds of members had inherited their peerage while the other third had been appointed by the government to serve as 'life peers' until their death. Around one-half of peers in 1997 supported the **Conservative Party**. Constitutional reform enacted by the **Labour Party** in 1999 considerably reduced the size and affected the composition of the upper house, but stopped short of making it an elected chamber and removing all hereditary peers. It is now made up of 707 members; these are 91 hereditary peers, 590 life peers, and 26 archbishops and bishops. Though much weaker than the **House of Commons**, the House of Lords shares a legislative role with the lower house and also scrutinizes the work of government, can delay legislation, and provides some government ministers. It also has an important judicial function as the United Kingdom's Supreme Court of Appeal.

Address: Westminster, London SW1A 0PW, United Kingdom
Tel: (0)20 7219 3107
Fax: (0)20 7219 0620
E-mail: hlinfo@parliament.uk
Internet: www.parliament.uk

Høyesterett – *see* **Supreme Court, Norway**

Høyre – *see* **Conservative Party, Norway**

Humanist Democratic Centre

Humanist Democratic Centre, or Centre Démocrate Humaniste (CDH), is the centre-right party in the French-speaking regions of Belgium. Founded in 1945, originally as the all-Belgian Christian People's Party (Parti Social Chrétien—PSC), it became independent of the PSC in 1972 and changed its name to Centre Démocrate Humaniste in 2002. The party promotes liberty, private initiative, social security and the family.

CDH formed coalitions with the larger **Flemish Christian Democrats (CD&V)** for most of the post-war era. It went into opposition following CD&V's poor electoral performance in 1999. In the most recent national elections, held on 18 May 2003, CDH won 5.5% of the vote and eight seats in the 150-seat **Kamer**.

Leadership: Pres. Joëlle Milquet; *Sec.-Gen.* Eric Poncin
Address: rue des Deux Eglises 41, 1000 Brussels, Belgium
Tel: (0)2 238-01-11
Fax: (0)2 238-01-29
E-mail: info@lecdh.be
Internet: www.lecdh.be

I

Iceland

Iceland is a small island located beneath the Arctic Circle in the far north-west of Europe. Geologically Iceland is a relatively new island, formed by volcanic activity. It is still regularly affected by earthquakes and volcanic eruptions. (The volcano Heimaey on the Westman Islands erupted early in the morning on 23 January 1973.) Situated in the North Atlantic Ocean, Iceland has adopted a mid-Atlantic stance, fostering relations with the USA and the **European Union (EU)**. A member of the **North Atlantic Treaty Organization**, Iceland hosts troops of the US army, but has no army of its own.

Area: 103,000 sq km; *capital:* Reykjavík; *population:* 282,000 (2001).

Iceland became an independent republic in 1944 following centuries of rule by Denmark. The Icelandic head of state is the non-executive President who is elected every four years. Since 1996 this has been **Ólafur Ragnar Grímsson**. Legislative power is vested with the **Althingi** and executive power with a coalition government which has been headed since 2004 by Prime Minister **Halldór Ásgrímsson**.

Unlike other Nordic states, politics in Iceland are not dominated by social democratic parties. For long Icelandic politics involved four main parties: the conservative **Independence Party**, the moderate **Progressive Party**, the Social Democratic Party and the left-wing People's Alliance. The conservative Independence Party has participated in the majority of coalition governments in the last 50 years. Most recently it governed continuously in 1991–2004 under Prime Minister David Oddsson, first in a coalition with the social democrats and then, from 1995, with the Progressive Party. Conservative governments have presided over high levels of economic growth and low **unemployment** and have liberalized the economy and restructured the **welfare state**.

In 1983 a significant new political force emerged. The Women's Alliance campaigned for legislation that specifically promoted **women**'s and children's interests. It campaigned on issues of equality in the workplace, to increase the representation of women in politics, and to change the political culture: the Women's Alliance was a grass roots movement that had no leader and agreed policy through consensus rather than by vote. At the height of its success in 1987 it won 10.1% of the vote and six seats in the Althingi. Since then its share of the vote and number of seats in the Althingi have fallen as mainstream parties have addressed the issues it raised. Following elections to the Althingi in 1999 a radical restructuring of the left occurred, whereby three parties—the Social Democratic Party, the People's Alliance and the Women's Alliance—combined to form the **Alliance Party**. A new party, **Left-Green Alliance**, was founded as concerns about the use of Iceland's natural resources grew; and a Liberal Party was also founded. At the most recent election to the Althingi, held on 10 May 2003, the Independence Party won 33.7% of the vote and formed a coalition with the Progressive Party. The coalition which has worked together since 1995 was initially led by David Oddsson of the Independence Party. As part of a post-election agreement he relinquished the role of head of government to Halldór Ásgrímsson on 15 September 2004.

Iceland strongly defends its independence and sovereignty and has never applied to join the EU, though it has been a member of the **European Free Trade Association** since 1970 and of the **European Economic Area** since 1 January 1994. The Independence Party is opposed to EU membership on the grounds of national independence and economic interest. It is only the social democrats and some business interests who have campaigned for Iceland to consider membership and the Progressive Party has shown some willingness to discuss membership. Iceland's opposition to EU membership can also be explained by the economy's reliance on the fishing industry. Iceland strongly protects the fishing waters around the island and has expanded its territorial waters three times since the end of the 1950s. Icelandic fishermen have exclusive rights to fish in the 322-km zone around the island. EU membership would mean adopting the EU's common fisheries policy and sharing these waters and fish stocks with fishermen from other EU states.

Economy: Iceland has a wealthy economy and its citizens enjoy one of the highest standards of living in the world. Its prosperity largely derives from the fishing industry which still employs around 10% of Iceland's workers and supplies two-thirds of the country's exports. Concerns about the sustainability of Iceland's fish stocks have led to the introduction of quotas and attempts to find alternative sources of economic growth and prosperity.

GNP: US $8,152m. (2001); *GNP per caput:* $28,910 (2001); *GNP at PPP:* $8,135m. (2001); *GNP per caput at PPP:* $28,850 (2001); *currency:* króna; *unemployment:* 3.3%(2002).

Iceland introduced quotas on major fish stocks in 1984 in order to prevent over-fishing and to maintain sufficient stocks for future generations. Owners of fishing vessels were given quotas free of charge, according to their fishing experience, but formally the fish stocks remain the joint property of the nation. The introduction of quotas led to the concentration of fishing within a smaller number of larger firms as these bought up the fishing rights of smaller companies. The number of quota holders fell by 26% in 1990–94. Iceland abandoned commercial whaling following the international moratorium in 1986, but the government reintroduced 'scientific whaling' in 1990.

As alternatives to fishing, Iceland has in recent years begun to exploit its natural resources to supply hydro-electric power to other nations, and it is also developing geothermal science, the production of aluminium and new scientific ventures. The private firm DeCODE Genetics was established in Iceland to research the genetic basis of various diseases because of the unique genetic constitution of its population. Iceland also has a booming tourist industry. A Nordic economy, Iceland has a well-developed **welfare state**, which is supported by politicians of the left and the right. With a less influential social democratic movement than other Nordic states, welfare coverage is more modest than on mainland Scandinavia. The Icelandic welfare state supports a highly educated population, with some 8,000 Islanders going abroad each year to study—mainly to the USA, the United Kingdom and Germany—and with 90% returning later to Iceland to work. Iceland has a high rate of labour-market participation among **women**.

In the 1980s the Icelandic economy experienced a series of problems. It had high levels of foreign debt and high inflation rates, which peaked at 25% in 1988. The króna was devalued three times in that year: by 6% in February, 10% in May, and 3% in September. From the early 1990s onwards Iceland underwent a process of rapid economic liberalization. This was a consequence of the country's membership of the **European Economic Area** which required member states to open up markets to all products except fish and food. Iceland also lifted capital controls, privatized banks and liberalized its telecommunications sector. The election of 1991 led to a coalition being formed between the conservative **Independence Party** and the Social Democratic Party, headed by Prime Minister David Oddsson. His governments cut public spending radically, continued the process of privatizing state industries and implemented far-reaching tax reforms. The government also reduced the scope of the welfare state, decreasing the numbers of public-sector employees, particularly in hospitals, shifting some of the responsibility for pension provision to individuals, and increasing the official retirement age to 70. A significant national agreement on the labour market was signed in 1990 between social partners. As a consequence, by the mid-1990s Iceland's rate of inflation had fallen to zero and then stabilized at around 2%. However, the country experienced **unemployment** for the first time (a rate of about 5%) as the fishing industry suffered the consequences of declining fish stocks.

Iceland's economy has experienced high levels of growth since the late 1990s. The economy grew by an average of 4.1% per year in 1994–98 and by 6% in 1999. This represented faster growth than that achieved by any other advanced industrial country for this period and it was twice the average rate of growth of the **European Union**. Unemployment fell to around 2% and Iceland even started to import labour, for example from Poland, to work in the fishing industry. The country still has a large current account deficit, however, and inflation has risen again, to around 3%. There are also increasing concerns that the rewards of economic growth are not being equally apportioned and that the profits from the nation's fishing stocks are being distributed unjustly.

Icelandic Confederation of Labour

The Icelandic Confederation of Labour, or Althydusamband Íslands (ASÍ), in Iceland promotes the interests of 111 local trade unions organized into six national federations and five national trade unions. Its constituent trade unions represent predominantly private-sector workers across a range of sectors. ASÍ is itself a member of **ETUC**.

Leadership: Pres.: Grétar Thorsteinsson; *Gen. Sec.:* Gylfi Arnbjörnsson
Address: Sætún 1, 105 Reykjavík, Iceland
Tel: (0)5355600
Fax: (0)5355601
E-mail: asi@asi.is
Internet: www.asi.is

IKEA

IKEA is a Swedish furniture company, specializing in well-designed, low-priced and functional products. Founded by Ingvar Kamprad in 1943, the IKEA franchise had expanded by 2004 to 201 stores in 35 countries across four continents. In the 2004 financial year sales totalled €12,800m. The IKEA Group is owned by the Stichting INGKA, a charitable foundation registered in the Netherlands. Stichting INGKA in turn owns INGKA Holding BV, the parent company for the IKEA Group companies.

Pres. of IKEA Group: Anders Dahling
Address: Inter IKEA Systems BV, Olof Palmestraat 1, NL-2616 LN Delft, Netherlands
Fax: (0)152153838
Internet: www.ikea.com

Immigration

Immigration is—politically and economically—one of the most controversial policy issues in Western Europe. Originally a diverse continent, Europe is being criticized for closing its doors to new citizens and becoming a 'fortress'. There was net immigration in the early post-war era to states such as the United Kingdom, France and Germany which had colonial legacies and/or expanding economies. Other states, such as Spain, Portugal and Ireland, experienced net emigration and declining populations. During the 1980s and 1990s the trend halted as national immigration rules became more restrictive. Regulations placed limits on the number of new immigrants entering countries and the reunion of family members with existing immigrants. In the same period the expanding economies of Ireland, Spain and Portugal experienced net immigration of nationals and non-nationals. Conflicts in Europe (in the former Yugoslavia and **Turkey**) and the Asian and African continents led to an increase in the number of people seeking asylum in Western Europe. According to the Geneva Convention of 1951, Western European states are obliged to accept asylum-seekers. There were 380,000 applications for asylum in 2001.

The treatment of immigrants varies greatly across the nation states of Western Europe. Although some states (e.g. the Netherlands and Sweden) have a tradition of openness towards immigrants and asylum-seekers, there exists across Western Europe a strong discourse that claims (wrongly) that immigration poses a threat to the cohesion of established communities. Recent debates have focused on the degree of integration of existing immigrants, on states' policies towards illegal immigrants and asylum-seekers, and on the status of workers from the **Central and Eastern European Countries (CEECs)** which have recently joined the **European Union (EU)**. Government policy has changed in a number of countries to promote the integration of immigrants through compulsory language or civic lessons and to restrict the inflow of new migrants—including those from CEECs. This debate is even evident in countries such as the Netherlands (which has 2% of the EU population and 10% of the region's asylum-seekers) where there has traditionally been a liberal immigration regime. There, the established consensus on the multicultural society was disturbed by the views of politician **Pim Fortuyn** who was assassinated in 2002. Moreover, since the 1970s political parties such as the **Austrian Freedom Party**, **Vlaams Blok** in Belgium, the **Swiss People's Party** and the **National Front** in France have emerged which advocate stopping new immigration to their countries and, in some cases, the repatriation of existing established immigrant populations. Some such parties have enjoyed significant electoral success—particularly, but not exclusively, in regions that have experienced industrial decline and high **unemployment**. There is evidence that such parties' policies have also influenced the debate in mainstream political parties. The Austrian Freedom Party and the Swiss People's Party participate directly in national government.

The current political debate on immigration contrasts with the views of economists. From their perspective Western Europe requires immigration to fill gaps in the labour market, to rejuvenate Europe's ageing population, and to maintain a level of competitiveness *vis-à-vis* the USA. While unemployment remains high in a number of Western European states, such as Germany and Spain, there is none the less a demand for migrant labour. European economies require both low-skilled, low-wage labour for activities, such as cleaning and **agriculture**, that nationals are increasingly unwilling to undertake, and specialists in areas such as information technology (IT) where the supply of domestic skilled workers is too low to meet demand. Moreover, demographers have indicated that EU fertility rates in Western Europe are falling, and that the region requires net immigration of 1.6m. migrants per year to maintain the population at its current level up to 2050. Immigration is also required to bring down the median age of the EU's population (this is currently 37.7 compared with 35.5 in the USA). At current fertility rates it is projected that the

EU median age will have risen to 52.7 by 2050, compared with 36.2 in the USA. National policy-makers have responded to the skills gap with *ad hoc* policies to accept certain groups of skilled workers. Germany, for example, introduced a Green Card scheme for IT workers. However, there is no systematic policy to increase fertility levels.

At the European level, the **Treaty of Amsterdam** committed EU member states to develop Europe-wide legislation on immigration. At the European Council summit in Tampere, Finland, in 1999 EU heads of state and government agreed to create, within five years, an area of 'Freedom, Security and Justice'. To this end they agreed to a common asylum system as well as to tighten controls on external borders to prevent illegal immigration. This meant harmonizing diverse sets of national rules and priorities. Spurred on by the terrorist attacks on the USA on **11 September** 2001, and the 11 March 2004 bomb attacks in Madrid, Spain, member states agreed common rules on asylum, immigration and judicial co-operation and agreed to move immigration and asylum into the first **pillar** of the **European Community** in 2004. Further discussions are being held on whether to set up asylum transit camps in North Africa. Overall, the EU strategy places an emphasis on keeping people out of the EU and reinforces the region's image as 'Fortress Europe'.

Independence Party

The Independence Party, or Sjálfstædisflokkurinn (SSF), is the liberal conservative party in Iceland. Founded in 1929 through a merger of the Conservative Party and the Liberal Party, it is the largest political party in Iceland today. The party aims to promote individual and corporate initiative and pursues a policy of reducing taxation. It promotes welfare, particularly for families and the elderly, and aims to maintain high levels of employment and education. SSF has governed in coalitions for 44 of the last 58 years. In the most recent elections, held on 10 May 2003, the party won 33.5% of the vote and 22 seats in the 63-seat **Althingi**. It now governs in coalition with the **Progressive Party**. Party leader David Oddsson was Prime Minister in 1991–2004. He relinquished office to **Halldór Ásgrímsson** of the Progressive Party on 15 September 2004 as part of the 2003 coalition agreement.

Party Leader: David Oddsson
Address: Valhöll, Háaleitisbraut 1, 108 Reykjavík, Iceland
Tel: (0)5151700
Fax: (0)5151717
E-mail: xd@xd.is
Internet: www.xd.is

Industriellenvereinigung – *see* Federation of Austrian Industry

International Monetary Fund (IMF)

The International Monetary Fund (IMF) is an international organization that was established in 1944 by the Bretton Woods conference. Part of the **United Nations** system, it aims to promote monetary co-operation, facilitate the growth of trade, promote exchange stability, help establish multilateral payments systems and offer resources to members with balance-of-payments difficulties. It carries out these tasks through surveillance—observing and advising members—and providing technical and financial assistance to member countries experiencing difficulties. In return, countries are obliged to meet certain conditions, such as economic reforms or privatization. These are referred to as Structural Adjustment Programmes.

The IMF has a membership of 184 countries. The resources of the IMF derive from quota subscriptions paid by member countries when they join. These quotas—calculated according to the member's economic output and size of trade—determine the country's subscription payments, the level of financing it can receive from the Fund, and its voting power within the organization. The USA pays 17.5% of total quotas.

The IMF is run on a day-to-day basis by the executive board which is composed of 24 executive directors and the managing director. Rodrigo de Rato has been managing director of the Fund since 2004. China, France, Germany, **Japan**, **Russia**, Saudi Arabia, the United Kingdom and the USA have their own seats on the board. The other 16 members are elected by groups of countries for a two-year term. The executive board is accountable to the board of governors, made up of a governor and an alternate governor nominated from each member state, which meets once a year. The IMF has been widely criticized for imposing austerity measures on countries in deep financial crisis, encouraging developing countries to take on additional debt, and for being unaccountable.

Man. Dir: Rodrigo de Rato
Address: 700 19th St, NW, Washington, DC 20431, USA
Tel: (0)202 623-7000
Fax: (0)202 623-4661
E-mail: publicaffairs@imf.org
Internet: www.imf.org

Iraq

Iraq is a state in the Middle East spanning the Tigris and Euphrates rivers, covering 438,317 sq km. Iraq's governing regime, led by President Saddam Hussain, was deposed three weeks after the beginning of a US-led military campaign against it, on 9 April 2003. Saddam Hussain himself was captured on 13 December 2003 and faces trial on charges of genocide, crimes against humanity and war crimes. The US-led coalition invaded Iraq on 20 March 2003 following Hussain's failure to comply with the requests of **United Nations (UN)** inspectors searching for weapons of mass destruction (WMDs). UN weapons inspectors requested more time to complete their search, but the war proceeded none the less, without UN approval. Since the fall of Saddam Hussain no WMDs have been found. US politicians justified the war as part of the USA's post-**11 September** 2001 'war on **terrorism**', although no link has been established between Saddam Hussain's regime and the terrorist network al-Qa'ida; and as an intervention that was necessary to end human rights abuses. The states of Western Europe were divided in their support for the war in Iraq. Governing parties in the United Kingdom, Spain and Italy supported it, while France and Germany were strongly opposed. The US defense secretary, Donald Rumsfeld, referred to this division in 2003 as one between 'new' and 'old' Europe.

The modern nation state of Iraq was formed through the merger of ethnically diverse provinces under British rule in 1918–32. Following independence in 1932, Iraq was governed by a monarch until 1958, when a revolution established a republic. A military coup in 1963 brought an end to the first republic and the Baath (Renaissance) Party assumed power, advocating Arab nationalism and socialism. Saddam Hussain became President for the Baath Party in 1979. The Iraqi economy is dominated by oil. In 1979 it accounted for 95% of foreign-exchange earnings. During the 1970s the Baath Party nationalized Iraqi oil fields and set five-year plans to increase industrial and agricultural production. The economy suffered as a consequence of war with Iran in 1980–88, of the Gulf War in 1991 that followed Iraq's invasion of Kuwait, and of international economic sanctions imposed from 6 August 1990 by a UN Security Council resolution.

Iraq is currently governed by an Interim Government sworn in on 1 June 2004 (and to which sovereignty was transferred on 28 June), which is led by President Sheikh Ghazi Mashal Ajil al-Yawar and Prime Minister Dr Ayad Allawi. At elections held for a Transitional National Assembly (TNA) on 30 January 2005, in which 8.5m. Iraqis (58% of the registered electorate) voted, the Shi'a United Iraqi Alliance won a clear majority (140 of 275 seats) in the interim legislature. However, the party was required to form a coalition since a two-thirds' majority is needed to pass legislation in the TNA. The Kurdistan Alliance List won 75 seats, the Iraqi List of Dr Allawi secured 40 seats and other, smaller parties won 20. The new government faces the challenge of restoring civil order, reconstruction, and the creation of a new political system for the ethnically diverse population of some 25m.

Ireland

The Republic of Ireland, founded in 1949, is composed of 26 counties in the south of Ireland. The establishment of the republic followed a conflict-ridden process of liberation from the United Kingdom. A first attempt to declare independence—the Easter Rising of 1916—was crushed by the British. The Irish Free State was later established as an independent state under the British Crown in 1921. This also led to the partition of Ireland as six counties remained part of the United Kingdom.

Irish independence was followed by a year-long civil war fought between those who accepted partition and those who wanted the whole island of Ireland to be independent of the United Kingdom. This issue remains the most significant cleavage in Irish politics. Under the leadership of Eamonn De Valera the Irish Free State was abolished, and a new constitution established Eire (Ireland) as a sovereign and democratic state in 1937. This became the Republic of Ireland in 1949.

Area: 70,000 sq km; *capital:* Dublin; *population:* 4m. (2001).

In the Republic of Ireland the head of state, the President, is directly elected for a seven-year term. Since 1997 this office has been held by **Mary McAleese**. Legislative power is vested with the bicameral parliament, the Tithe an Oireachtas, which is made up of the **Dáil Éireann** and **Senead Éireann**. The most recent elections to the Dáil were held on 17 May 2002. Executive power is given to the government, headed by the Taoiseach (Prime Minister). **Bertie Ahern** has been Taoiseach since 1997.

Irish politics are traditionally dominated by two main centrist parties, **Fianna Fáil (FF)** and **Fine Gael (FG)**. While broadly similar on economic policy, these two parties differ according to which side supporters stood on at the time of the civil war: while FG accepted division, FF wished to maintain a united Ireland. Today, FF is more committed to unification or co-operation with **Northern Ireland**, and FG is more indifferent to Irish unification. Ireland is also divided on social issues such as divorce and abortion between fundamental and liberal Catholics. On social issues FF is more fundamentalist and FG more liberal.

Originally support for FF or FG was large enough to ensure that both parties could form single party majority or minority governments. FF led governments under Taoiseach Eamonn De Valera for a total of 21 years in 1932–59. It also governed in 1957–73, 1977–81 and 1987–94. FF regularly chose to go into opposition rather than enter into coalition government. Since the 1980s support for the two main parties has declined on account of a series of party corruption scandals, and they have increasingly been unable to govern alone. Now both parties are willing to form coalition governments with the parties on the left—the **Labour Party** and the **Democratic Left**—and the right—the **Progressive Democrats (PD)**. As FF has moved from its commitment to single-party government to governing in coalitions, so the influence of the FG has gradually diminished.

Since 1997 FF had governed with the neo-liberal PD. In the 2002 election FF was re-elected, increasing its share of the vote, and continued to govern in coalition with the PD. The election in 2002 was significant for two reasons: it was the first election to be called after a government had completed a full five-year term in office; and it was the first time since 1969 that an incumbent government had been returned to office. The success of the FF-PD coalition was attributed to its successful management of the economy, the economic boom and the successful negotiation with the United Kingdom of the **Good Friday Agreement** on Northern Ireland in 1998.

Ireland joined the **European Economic Community** in 1973, together with the United Kingdom and Denmark. An enthusiastic member state, Ireland regards the project of European integration as an alternative allegiance to its traditional relationship with the United Kingdom. Ireland has also enjoyed significant financial benefits from the European Common Agricultural Policy and **structural funds**. However, as a militarily neutral country that is not a member of the **North Atlantic Treaty Organization**, Ireland opposes any **European Union** co-operation on defence issues that appears to threaten the state's neutral stance. In the referendum held on 7 June 2001 to endorse the **Treaty of Nice**, concerns were raised about whether the development of a **Rapid Reaction Force** would compromise Ireland's neutral security position. In the referendum voters rejected the Treaty of Nice (no 53.87%; turn-out 35%). Following a national debate, a second referendum was held on 19 October 2002 and a yes vote was secured (yes 62.89%; turn-out 49.47%).

Economy: The Irish economy is traditionally rural and agricultural. With a small home market, it specializes in the export of beef and dairy products. Food production employs as a rule around one-quarter of Irish workers. Ireland joined the **European Economic Community** in 1973 and benefited significantly from membership. Irish farming received large subsidies from the Common Agricultural Policy and real per caput farm incomes rose by just under 60% in 1972–78. The Irish economy had a history of mass emigration to the United Kingdom and the USA from the 1950s until the late 1980s. Since the late 1980s the Irish economy has been transformed. It has achieved rapid rates of economic growth and has been dubbed the 'Celtic Tiger'.

GNP: US $87,700m. (2001); *GNP per caput:* $22,850 (2001); *GNP at PPP:* $104,000m. (2001); *GNP per caput at PPP:* $27,170 (2001); *GDP:* $103,298m. (2001); *exports:* $98,566m. (2001); *imports:* $83,221m. (2001); *currency:* euro; *unemployment:* 4.6% (2002).

Until the 1970s Ireland's manufacturing base was weak. Industrial policy developed subsequently through the Industrial Development Authority (IDA) has sought to promote manufacturing by offering tax breaks and grants to foreign investors. In the mid-1970s the IDA persuaded a significant number of US high-tech industries to invest in Ireland. These new firms accounted for almost all of the growth in manufacturing employment in the late 1970s. By the mid-1980s multinational companies were providing around 86,000 of Ireland's 186,000 manufacturing jobs and by 1988 900 foreign firms accounted for 80% of Ireland's non-food exports.

During the 1970s Ireland built up a substantial **welfare state** and provision was comparable to that of the United Kingdom. Formerly welfare had been provided from transfer payments from family members who had emigrated. During the 1970s Ireland invested heavily in health and education. Spending on health rose to 8% of gross national product (GNP) compared to the United Kingdom's spending of 6%. In schools, average class sizes fell from 24 in the 1960s to 17 in the 1980s and Ireland possessed one of the most highly educated populations in Western Europe. By 1978 Ireland was spending more of its GNP on social security payments than

Japan and the USA. The Irish welfare state expansion was funded through taxation rather than through economic growth, but the Irish economy suffered traditionally from a weak tax base. Tax rates were high, but there was narrow coverage and many exemptions. Value added tax (VAT) was 25%, but one-third of consumer spending bore no tax, and Irish consumers were able to cross the border to **Northern Ireland** where VAT was levied at a much lower rate. Corporation tax was set at 50%, but it raised only 4% of government revenue as many inward investors were offered tax breaks, increasing the burden on domestic firms. There was generous tax relief on exports and low corporation tax on manufacturers. Income tax on the average worker was the highest in Europe.

By the mid-1980s Ireland's public debt had increased to 25,000m. punts, equivalent to 28,000 punts per household. This was at the time the highest public debt as a proportion of gross domestic product of any country in Western Europe. Servicing the debt, 40% of which was foreign debt, required one-third of annual tax revenues, and 90% of tax revenues came from income tax. In order to meet debt payments, the state increased tax from 31% of GNP in 1979 to 40% of GNP in 1984. It increased tax bills, putting pressure on pay and increasing levels of emigration, especially among the young and highly skilled. In the early 1980s a commission on taxation recommended that grants and tax subsidies should be cut, transforming Ireland from a tax haven for foreign investors to an all-round enterprise-friendly economy.

The Irish economy was transformed during the late 1980s and 1990s. It experienced unprecedented rates of growth and was compared to the boom economies of south-east Asia. Annual economic growth averaged 8.5% in 1994–99, four times the average **European Union (EU)** rate. Ireland also experienced rapid employment growth, with the rate of **unemployment** falling from 15% in 1994 to 4% in 2000. Public debt fell to 68% of GNP. Ireland's rapid economic growth has been attributed to a combination of favourable conditions. An open economy, with a highly skilled labour force, Ireland benefited from the completion of the **Single European Market** in 1992 which encouraged further inward foreign investment capital, particularly from the USA. It has also received significant amounts of financial support through the EU's regional aid programmes. In 1973–2003 Ireland received more than €17,000m. in **Structural Funds** and Cohesion Fund support. The Cohesion Fund contributed €586m. to Ireland in 2000–03. In the current programming period, 2000–06, Ireland will receive €3,350m. from the Structural Funds. These European funds have on the whole been well managed and invested in infrastructure rather than short-term projects.

Ireland's growth has also been attributed to three aspects of domestic policy. Ireland developed a consensual system of social partnership. In the late 1970s Irish trade unions, collectively the **Irish Congress of Trade Unions (ICTU)**, were strong, oppositional, and well organized—reaching a density of 60% and more in the public sector. As a consequence, wage costs in Ireland were high. From 1987 Ireland shifted to a corporatist system of national-level institutions of social partnership in the National Economic and Social Council. The social partners—the government, ICTU and the **Irish Business and Employers' Confederation**— negotiated a series of three-year wage and social policy agreements which secured wage restraint, labour peace, employment growth and improvements in the standard of living. Governments also sought to encourage indigenous industry as well as foreign investors. One significant success was the Irish airline **Ryanair**, founded in 1986. This company broke the British Airways and Aer Lingus cartel on the route between London and Dublin, leading to a reduction of the return fare by 54%, an increase in traffic by one-third in 1986–87 and a boom in tourism and tourist spending.

Moreover, as the political situation became more stable in the late 1990s, there developed a cross-party commitment to supporting Ireland's economic recovery and, later, its membership of **Economic and Monetary Union (EMU)** by 1999. A member of the **European Monetary System** since 1979, Ireland cut public spending during the 1990s to meet the **convergence criteria** for membership of the EMU. It adopted the single currency in January 2002. In 2001, however, Ireland received an 'early warning' letter from the **European Commission** which was concerned about inflationary pressures.

Irish Business and Employers' Confederation (IBEC)

The Irish Business and Employers' Confederation (IBEC) is the national voice for businesses and employers in Ireland. It lobbies nationally and internationally to improve the business climate for Irish companies, develops and reviews industrial and labour-market policy and acts as a service provider for its members. IBEC comprises some 7,000 member businesses from all sectors of the economy. It is itself a member of the **Union of Industrial and Employers' Confederations of Europe**.

> *Leadership: Pres.* Gary McGann; *Dir-Gen.* Turlough O'Sullivan
> *Address:* Confederation House, 84/86 Lower Baggot St, Dublin 2, Ireland
> *Tel:* (0)1 6601500
> *Fax:* (0)1 6381500
> *E-mail:* info@ibec.ie
> *Internet:* www.ibec.ie

Irish Congress of Trade Unions (ICTU)

The Irish Congress of Trade Unions (ICTU) is the umbrella organization for trade unions in both the Republic of Ireland and **Northern Ireland**. Founded in 1894, today it represents the interests of around 754,000 employees who are organized in 56 affiliated unions on both sides of the border. ICTU is itself affiliated to **ETUC**. ICTU currently campaigns to improve living standards and wages and to promote trade union recognition and worker participation and social partnership. It also works to promote the peace process in Northern Ireland.

Gen. Sec.: David Begg
Address: 31/32 Parnell Sq., Dublin 1, Ireland
Tel: (0)1 8897777
Fax: (0)1 8872012
E-mail: www.ictu.ie/contact.htm
Internet: www.ictu.ie

Isle of Man

The Isle of Man is a small island situated off the west coast of the United Kingdom. It is a British dependency, but not part of the United Kingdom. Its parliament, the Tynwald, is located in the capital, Douglas. It legislates on domestic issues, including tax—it has a regime of low taxation—and welfare. The UK government is responsible for foreign and defence policy.

The Isle of Man covers 588 sq km and has a population of 76,300 (2001). The Manx currency is the Isle of Man pound which is linked to the British pound. The key economic sectors are banking, which contributes around 45% of gross national product, manufacturing and tourism. The Isle of Man is neither a member nor an associate member of the **European Union (EU)**, but it does have free access to EU markets.

Italian General Confederation of Labour

The Italian General Confederation of Labour, or Confederazione Generale Italiana del Lavoro (CGIL), was founded in 1906. Today it represents more than 5.5m. members in 15 national trade union federations and 134 labour chambers. It is itself affiliated to **ETUC**. CGIL campaigns to protect workers' rights and offers a range of information and advisory services.

Gen. Sec.: Guglielmo Epifani
Address: Corso d'Italia 25, 00198 Rome, Italy
Tel: (0)06 84761
Fax: (0)06 8845683
E-mail: info@cgil.it
Internet: www.cgil.it

Italian Union of Labour

The Italian Union of Labour, or Unione Italiana del Lavoro (UIL), is the left-wing trade union federation in Italy. Founded in 1950 after having broken from the **Confederazione Generale Italiana del Lavoro**, it represents today some 1.8m. employees from 16 affiliated unions and is itself a member of **ETUC**.

Gen. Sec.: Luigi Angeletti
Address: Via Lucullo 6, 00187 Rome, Italy
Tel: (0)06 47531
Fax: (0)06 4753208
E-mail: info@uil.it
Internet: www.uil.it

Italy

Italy is a state situated on a large peninsula in southern Europe. In 1861 it was united as a kingdom, to which Venice was annexed in 1866 and Rome in 1870. A fascist dictatorship led by Benito Mussolini in 1922–43, the Italian state supported Franco in the Spanish civil war and was an ally of Hitler in the Second World War. Following the end of the Second World War, the Italian Communist Party (PCI) emerged as the largest political force. It was soon overtaken by the Christian Democratic Party (DC) which led all coalition governments in 1948–1992 and ensured that the PCI was excluded from government. Italy's political system was unstable for most of the post-war era, but reforms undertaken in the 1990s have significantly restructured the Italian political landscape.

Area: 301,000 sq km; *capital:* Rome; *population:* 58m. (2001).

The post-war Constitution that took effect on 1 January 1948 established Italy as a democratic republic. The head of state is elected by an electoral college for a seven-year term. Since 1999 this has been **Carlo Ciampi**. Legislative power is vested on equal terms in the **Camera dei Deputati** and the **Senato**. The political system of the post-war era was very democratic with frequent elections, referendums (if 500,000 or more signed a petition), high turn-outs in elections and a system of proportional representation which ensured that a large number of parties, including small parties, would gain representation in parliament. This led to a high degree of political instability and coalition governments have tended to be short-lived: there were 57 governments in 1945–97. However, the DC was represented in every government until 1994 while the second largest party, the PCI, was completely excluded during the **Cold War**. Moreover, the Italian political system developed a strong system of patronage in order to secure votes. Public-sector jobs were allocated according to a party's electoral strength, a system referred to as *lottizzazione*. This led to patronage and corruption in the political system at all levels and also meant that political reform and decision-making were slow and consensual, leading to institutional inertia.

A founder member of the **European Coal and Steel Community**, Italy has always given support for European integration. Membership is considered to have brought economic advantages to the previously agrarian society and the European institutions have frequently acted as an external force to place pressure on the Italian political system to implement necessary, but domestically unpopular, reforms. A member of the **North Atlantic Treaty Organization**, Italy has traditionally played a minor role in international affairs.

Italian politics experienced a major upheaval at the start of the 1990s and reforms marked the start of the Second Republic. The disturbance of the political system was the consequence of the end of the Cold War, which meant that it was no longer necessary to conspire to keep the PCI out of office. At the start of the 1990s a series of corruption scandals were uncovered concerning the old political establishment that had run Italy since 1948. Investigations of the Italian judiciary centred on Milan revealed instances of corruption in all major institutions; these were referred to collectively as *Tangentopoli* ('Bribesville'). It was revealed, for example, that firms had paid bribes to politicians in return for contracts. As a consequence, the DC were driven out of office and a series of reforms in 1992 marked the *mani pulite* ('clean hands') campaign.

A series of steps have been taken to address corruption and speed up the country's decision-making process since the late 1980s. In 1988 the practice of secret voting in parliament was ended, and a referendum held in June 1991 reformed the electoral system. Far-reaching reforms were agreed in a referendum held on 18–19 April 1993. Eight questions on political reform were asked and the electorate returned a yes verdict on all issues.

The eight referendum questions and results, from a turn-out of 77%, were whether: 1) to reform elections to the Senato by introducing a plurality system for three-quarters (238 of 315) of its seats, with the remaining 25% to be allocated by the former system of proportional representation (82.7% yes); 2) to abolish state funding of political parties (90.3% yes); 3) to abolish penal sanctions on drugs-users introduced in 1990 (55.3% yes); 4) to abolish ministerial nominations of presidents of banks (89.4% yes); 5) to remove the environmental protection functions of local health boards (82.5% yes); 6) to abolish the Ministry for State Participation (89.9% yes); 7) to abolish the Ministry of Agriculture (70.1% yes); and 8) to abolish the Ministry of Tourism (82.2% yes). Following the overwhelming support for these reforms, the parliament modified the electoral system for the Camera dei Deputati in August 1993. Mirroring the new system in the Senate, three-quarters of its members are now elected through a plurality system in single-member constituencies and the remainder are allocated by a system of proportional representation.

The events and reforms of the early 1990s led to a restructuring of the party system from one dominated by a party of the centre (DC) to one characterized by two distinct blocs on the left and the right. The DC collapsed in 1993 following the revelations of scandals and bribery and reformed as the Italian Popular Party (PPI). Two new right-wing parties emerged. The **Northern League**, established in 1991, won support in regional, local and national elections for its opposition to corruption in government in Rome, **immigration** and transfer payments to the **Mezzogiorno**. Media businessman and billionaire **Silvio Berlusconi** occupied the space vacated by the collapse of the DC by founding the national **Forza Italia** in January 1994. On the left, the PCI transformed itself in 1990 into the Democratic Party of the Left (PDS—since 1998 **Democrats of the Left**). The smaller **Communist Refoundation Party** was formed in 1991 by communists who opposed the social democratic reorientation of the PCI. Since this reorientation there has been regular alternation between governments of the left and right.

In the election held in March 1994—the first under the new election laws—the right-wing 'Freedom Pole' (Forza Italia, National Alliance, Lista Pannella (libertarians) and Northern League) gained an absolute majority in the Camera dei Deputati and a plurality in the Senato. Berlusconi formed his first coalition government, but this was forced to resign on 22 December 1994 when the Northern League withdrew its support in response to investigations into Prime Minister Berlusconi's business dealings. There followed a year of 'technocratic' government led by the central banker, Lamberto Dini; and then four left-wing 'Olive Tree' coalition governments (in 1996–2001), comprising the Democratic Party of the Left (PDS), which won 21% of the vote, the Greens, the Italian Socialist Party (PSI), the Italian People's Party (PPI) and Italian Renewal. The government formed following elections held in April 1996 was led for two years by Romano Prodi, who thus became the second longest serving Prime Minister since 1945. This government collapsed in October 1998 when the Communist Refoundation Party withdrew its support. Massimo D'Alema became the first former communist Prime Minister. He served until a poor performance in regional elections and a national referendum, held on 21 May 2000, on further constitutional reform, and was replaced by the socialist Giuliano Amato, who was in office for one year. Amato was replaced by the former mayor of Rome, Francesco Rutelli, who governed until the elections held on 13 May 2001.

In February 2000, in preparation for the elections of 2001, the right formed the House of Freedoms (Casa delle Libertà) alliance, comprising Forza Italia, the Northern League, the National Alliance, the Christian Democratic Centre and United Christian Democrats and the New Italian Socialist Party. In the election Berlusconi's Forza Italia gained the status of largest party with 29.5% of the vote and formed a coalition government with the regionalist Northern League and the National Alliance.

Economy: The Italian economy is regionally divided. It is characterized by networks of dynamic, export-oriented small and medium-sized firms in the north, specializing in clothing (e.g. Benetton), shoes and mechanical goods. These are typically family-run and funded through savings. In the south, the **Mezzogiorno**, the economy is underdeveloped and has traditionally relied on the state to develop large-scale industrial projects and provide generous transfer payments. As a whole, Italy traditionally has a highly regulated and closed economic system, with state ownership of large industries and political intervention in the allocation of resources and leading economic appointments. There are a few large firms (e.g. Fiat, Olivetti), but their growth has been limited by restrictions on expansion and comparatively low spending on research and development.

GNP: US $1,123,800m. (2001); *GNP per caput:* $19,390 (2001); *GNP at PPP:* $1,422,000m. (2001); *GNP per caput at PPP:* $24,530 (2001); *GDP:* $1,088,754m. (2001); *exports:* $299,978m. (2001); *imports:* $283,912m. (2001); *currency:* euro; *unemployment:* 9.0% (2002).

Under the Mussolini regime key industries (e.g. through the Instituto per la Ricostruzione Industriale) were nationalized. From the end of the Second World War until the 1950s the economy was largely an agrarian one and experienced mass emigration. More than 1m. Italian workers left for the USA and Australia in 1946–57 and a further 840,000 left for France, Germany and Switzerland. The US government awarded Italy US $1,400m. in aid through the **Marshall Plan** which assisted industrial expansion. During the 1950s the economy grew by more than 5% annually, and in the early 1960s by more than 6%. By the 1960s Italy was Europe's largest producer of goods such as washing machines and refrigerators.

Dependent on imports of raw materials and energy, the Italian economy suffered from the oil crises of the 1970s. During the 1970s it had inflation rates of 20%, high levels of industrial unrest (a high number of working days were lost to strikes), high taxes and rigid labour laws. The **welfare state** was overstretched by an ageing population and high **unemployment** in the 1980s — 12% in 1987. Generous welfare benefits introduced in the 1970s led to spiralling levels of public debt. In the mid-1980s public-sector borrowing was equivalent to 15% of gross domestic product (GDP). Attempts to reduce this were frustrated by two things: first, the lack of political will required to cut welfare entitlement in a clientalistic system heavily dominated by patronage; and, second, the difficulty in increasing tax revenues. It is estimated that Italy's 'black' or submerged economy is worth between 18%–25% of formal GDP and that one-quarter of income tax and one-third of value added tax go uncollected.

European integration led to a restructuring of the Italian economy and increased the competitiveness of Italian firms. A founder member of the **European Coal and Steel Community**, European integration gave Italian businesses a larger market. The **Single European Market** led to a liberalization of financial services, and Italy's membership of the **Exchange Rate Mechanism** from 1979 required firms to make savings by resisting wage demands rather than relying on a devaluation of the lira. In the 1980s the Italian economy underwent a 'second renaissance', recording the fastest rates of growth of the four largest European economies, and the rate of inflation declined from 20% to 5%. Public debt had been reduced to 11% of GDP by the end of the 1980s through the sale of some of Italy's state-run firms; the large state holding company, IRI, sold 17 large firms employing a total of 64,000 people in 1983–89. Alfa Romeo was sold to Fiat in 1987 and was transformed from a loss-making into a profitable business. Despite these successes, Italy's pragmatic privatization policy was limited in its success for two reasons. First, although it expanded in 1985–87, the Italian stock exchange was under-developed. Second, in a culture of family-run businesses and high savings, there was a lack of buyers of shares. The consequence was that share ownership became concentrated in the hands of a few 'tycoons', such as Gianni Agnelli (Fiat) or Silvio Berlusconi (media).

In the 1990s public debt rose to 108% of GDP, and the cost of servicing this debt accounted for around one-fifth of total government spending. On 16 September 1992 the lira left the **Exchange Rate Mechanism** and the currency had lost 24% of its value by the beginning of 1993. This crisis, together with a strong will to meet the **convergence criteria** for membership of **Economic and Monetary Union (EMU)**, triggered a concerted effort to reform the economy. An agreement was reached between three main trade unions and the employers' organization in 1992 to end the system of indexing wage rises to the cost of living (*scale mobile*). Also, Amato's budget in 1993 cut pensions payments and health expenditure and froze public-sector wages and payments to local government. At the same time, new taxes were raised and there were further attempts at privatization. Italy qualified for membership of EMU in 1998. Between 1992 and 1997 it reduced the rate of inflation from 5.7% to 1.4% and the government deficit was lowered from 12.1% of GDP to the required 3%. Concerns were raised at the time that these targets had been reached through one-off measures and would not be sustainable in the long term. The Italian government raised 5,300,000m. lira through a 'Europe Tax', it froze some payments to state employees and placed tight controls on spending for national and local government.

During the 1990s the Italian economy grew at an average annual rate of only 1.6%, the slowest rate in the **European Union**. The rate of unemployment rose to 10% of the labour force and it has been slow to fall. The economy also has a low employment rate—around 53%, compared with 63% on average in the **euro area**. There are low levels of investment in Italy from abroad. Despite political reforms to tackle corruption, the economy is still perceived as lacking flexibility, capital and infrastructure. Governments have sought to reform these weaknesses by making it easier to set up new businesses or to hire labour on a temporary basis.

Izquierda Unida – *see* United Left, Spain

J

Jan Mayen

Jan Mayen is a small volcanic island in the north Arctic Ocean covering 373 sq km. It has been a part of Norway since 1930. The island has a population, or 'crew', of 18 people who run the meteorological station and the Long Range Navigation (Loran C) base.

Japan

Japan is the world's second largest economy after the USA and a close economic partner of the **European Union (EU)**. Japan's strong economy was developed through the car and electronics industries during the post-war era and it rapidly overtook many Western European economies. The Japanese economy is characterized by close co-operation between the government and industry, technologically advanced production methods and a strong work ethic among workers who are guaranteed lifelong employment in a firm. Industrial production is organized in closely co-ordinated groups (*Keiretsu*) of manufacturers, suppliers and distributors. The Japanese economy grew on average by 10% in the 1960s, 5% in the 1970s and 4% in the 1980s. In the 1990s, however, growth slowed to an average of 1.6%. Since then many of the traditional features of the Japanese economic model have begun to erode. Economic recovery has been slow and government debt stands at 150% of gross domestic product.

GNP: US \$4,523,300m. (2001); *GNP per caput:* \$35,610 (2001); *GNP at PPP:* \$3,246,000m. (2001); *GNP per caput at PPP:* \$25,550 (2001); *GDP:* \$4,141,431m. (2001); *exports:* \$448,107m. (2001); *imports:* \$421,627m. (2001); *currency:* yen; *unemployment:* 5.4% (2002).

Japan is the EU's third largest export market and the EU is Japan's second largest export market. Japanese exports to the EU increased by more than 40% in 1993–2001, from €50,100m. to €72,300m., and EU exports to Japan nearly doubled during the same period, from €28,800m. to €53,700m. The member states of the EU have benefited from high levels of Japanese foreign direct investment (FDI) and, from the late 1990s, EU FDI in Japan increased significantly (by 24% in 1999). The

EU is now Japan's most important source of FDI. Japan and the EU co-operate closely in the **World Trade Organization**.

Area: 378,000 sq km; *capital:* Tokyo; *population:* 127m. (2001).

Japan is a constitutional monarchy and a parliamentary democracy. The head of state is Emperor Akihito who acceded to the throne in 1990. According to the Constitution of 1947, legislative power is vested with the bicameral Diet, or *Kokkai*. This comprises the House of Councillors (*Sangiin*) and the House of Representatives (*Shugiin*). The head of government is elected following parliamentary elections, held most recently on 9 November 2003. Since April 2001 this has been Prime Minister Junichiro Koizumi of the Liberal Democratic Party. In office Junichiro Koizumi has sought to revive the economy and reform the political system.

Juncker, Jean-Claude

Jean-Claude Juncker is Prime Minister and Minister of Finance in Luxembourg. He was first appointed to this office on 20 January 1995 when his predecessor, Jacques Santer, became President of the **European Commission**. Prior to this Juncker was governor of the **World Bank**, in 1989–95. Juncker was reappointed as Prime Minister following the parliamentary election of June 1999; his **Christian Social People's Party (CVP)** formed a coalition with the **Democratic Party**. He was re-elected on 31 July 2004 as head of a coalition between the CVP and the **Luxembourg Socialist Workers' Party**.

Juncker became politically active in the CVP in 1974 and was appointed as parliamentary secretary for the party in 1979 and as Secretary of State for Labour and Social Security in 1982. Juncker was first elected to the **Chambre des Députés** in June 1984 and served as Minister for Labour and Minister in charge of the Budget in Jacques Santer's first government. When re-elected to parliament in June 1989, he became Minister of Finance and Minister of Labour. As Minister of Finance in 1989–94, Juncker played a key role in the process of **Economic and Monetary Union (EMU)**. As chairman of the Council of Finance Ministers (Ecofin) in 1991, he helped shape EMU and the **Maastricht Treaty**. He is credited with having proposed an opt-out from the single currency so that the negotiations could proceed without the participation of the United Kingdom. Juncker was appointed the first 'Mr Euro' on 10 September 2004 by the finance ministers of the **euro area**. As such he chairs the group's monthly meetings and acts as a link between states participating in the **euro** and the **European Central Bank**.

Born in Rédange-sur-Attert on 9 December 1954, Juncker obtained a master's degree in law from the University of Strasbourg (France) in 1975. Although admitted to the Bar of Luxembourg in February 1980, he opted to pursue a political career. Juncker survived a serious road accident in the autumn of 1989 which left him in a coma for two weeks. Jean-Claude Juncker is married to Christiane Frising.

Address: Ministère d'Etat, 4 rue de la Congrégation, 1352 Luxembourg
Tel: (0)478-21-00
Fax: (0)46-17-20
E-mail: Minister.Etat@me.etat.lu
Internet: www.gouvernement.lu

Justice and Home Affairs (JHA)

Justice and Home Affairs (JHA) is the area of the **European Union (EU)** concerned with **immigration** and asylum, and police and judicial co-operation. Member states were originally reluctant to co-operate on these issues affecting national sovereignty and they were not included in the **Treaty of Rome**. Since the 1970s member states' co-operation in JHA issues has increased incrementally, first with the TREVI group, then the **Schengen Agreement** and the **Treaty of Amsterdam**. The effort to achieve greater JHA co-operation was triggered by the commitment to the free movement of people realized by the **Single European Market** in 1992, and by rising rates of immigration following the end of the **Cold War**.

The **Treaty on European Union (TEU)** introduced JHA as the third **pillar** of the EU. This allowed the development of JHA policy on an intergovernmental basis, meaning that member states retained the right to initiate and agree JHA policy in the **Council of the European Union**. The decision-making process in the JHA Council was a five-stage process at the end of which a decision had to be made unanimously. The result of this was that, in practice, the TEU did little to advance the JHA agenda, although it did establish **Europol**. JHA decision-making at the time was criticized for being undemocratic and opaque as the role of other supranational institutions was minimal or non-existent. The **European Commission** had only limited rights to initiate policy in this area, the **European Parliament (EP)** had only the right to be consulted, and the **European Court of Justice (ECJ)** was excluded completely.

In order to advance the JHA agenda and to improve its democratic credentials, the Treaty of Amsterdam transferred much of the JHA third pillar into the **European Community** first pillar. It was agreed that by 2004 all JHA policy would have to be initiated by the Commission, then scrutinized by the EP using the co-decision procedure and that ECJ would also be allowed to make judgments. Issues relating to **Police and Judicial Co-operation in Criminal Matters** remained in the inter-governmental third pillar.

In October 1999, following the institutional changes made at Amsterdam, a **European Council** meeting specifically dedicated to JHA was convened in Tampere, Finland. The decision made at Tampere moved JHA policy forward, committing JHA ministers to transform the EU into an 'area of freedom, security and justice', set milestones for the development of common immigration and asylum policies, and establish **Eurojust**. Further developments in JHA policy were triggered by the terrorist attacks on the USA on **11 September** 2001.

K

Kalliomäki, Antti Tapani

Antti Tapani Kalliomäki has been Deputy Prime Minister and Minister of Finance in Finland since 2003. A member of the **Finnish Social Democratic Party**, he was Minister for Trade and Industry in 1995–99. Kalliomäki served on Vantaa City Council in 1984–2000 and has been a member of the **Eduskunta** since 1983. In the national parliament he was chairman of his party's parliamentary group in 1991–95 and in 1999–2003 and has both chaired and sat on various parliamentary committees.

Born on 8 January 1947 in Siikainen, Kalliomäki worked as a physical education teacher in 1973–91. Antti Kalliomäki is married and has two children.

Address: Ministry of Finance, Snellmaninkatu 1A, POB 28, 00023 Helsinki, Finland
Tel: (0)9 16033004
Fax: (0)9 16034712
E-mail: valtiovarainministerio@vm.fi
Internet: www.financeministry.fi

Kamer/Chambre

House of Representatives

The Kamer or Chambre (House of Representatives) is the lower house of the bicameral federal parliament in Belgium. It is made up of 150 members who are elected by a system of proportional representation for a four-year fixed term. The most recent elections were held on 18 May 2003. In the current parliamentary term there are 10 party groups in the Kamer. These are (with number of seats in brackets): the **Socialist Party** (25); the **Socialist Party-Spirit** (23); the **Confederated Ecologists for the Organization of Original Struggles** (4); the **Reformist Movement** (25); the **Flemish Liberal and Democrat Party** (25); the **New Flemish Alliance** (1); the **National Front** (1); **Vlaams Blok** (18); the **Flemish Christian Democrats** (21); and the **Humanist Democratic Centre** (7). Of the 150 deputies, 53 (35%) are **women**.

The Kamer shares legislative responsibility with the upper house of parliament, the **Sénat**. It alone is responsible for the budget, army quotas, naturalization and laws concerning the responsibilities of ministers and for holding the government to account.

Address: Chambre des Représentants, 1008 Brussels, Belgium
Tel: (0)2 549-81-36
Fax: (0)2 549-83-02
E-mail: PRI@lachambre.be
Internet: www.lachambre.be

Karamanlis, Konstantinos

Konstantinos Karamanlis has been Prime Minister of Greece since 10 March 2004. His appointment followed the general election of 7 March 2004 in which his party, **New Democracy (ND)**, won 45.36% of the vote and 164 seats in the 300-seat **Vouli ton Ellinon**. This brought an end to 20 years of government by the **Panhellenic Socialist Movement**.

Karamanlis was a leading member of the ND youth wing in 1974–79. He was elected as a member of parliament for the district of Thessaloniki in 1989 and served as secretary of the parliament's board and secretary of political planning for the party in 1989. He took over as president of ND in March 1997. Born in September 1956 in Athens, Karamanlis studied law at the Athens School of Law and Tufts University, USA. He practised as a lawyer in 1984–89. Konstantinos Karamanlis is married to Natasa Pazaiti and is the father of twins.

Address: Maximos Mansion 19, Herodou Attikou str, 106 74 Athens, Greece
Tel: (0)210 6710571
E-mail: info@primeminister.gr
Internet: www.primeminister.gr

Keskusta – *see* Centre Party, Finland

Kohl, Helmut

Helmut Kohl is a Christian Democratic politician and statesman in Germany. He was Chancellor of the coalition of the **Christian Democratic Union (CDU)**, the **Christian Social Union (CSU)** and the **Free Democratic Party (FDP)** in 1982–98, a record 16 years. As Chancellor he oversaw **German unification** in 1990 and, a committed European, he strove to achieve deeper European integration through the establishment of the **European Union (EU)** and **Economic and Monetary Union (EMU)**. He was awarded the title of Honorary Citizen of Europe by EU heads of state and government shortly after he was voted out of office in 1998. Kohl's political career has been tarnished by financial corruption scandals, however. He has been accused of accepting anonymous and therefore illegal donations for the CDU which are not recorded in the party's accounts. He admitted in December 1999 that he had accepted between 1.5m. and 2m. Deutsche Mark in donations to his party, but has refused to reveal the name of the donors.

Born on 2 April 1930 in Ludwigshafen, Rhineland-Palatinate, Kohl studied history, law and constitutional studies at the University of Frankfurt-am-Main and Heidelberg University, receiving his doctorate from Heidelberg University in 1958. He worked in the chemistry industry in 1958–69 and developed his political career initially in the youth wing of the CDU which he had joined in 1947. Kohl was elected to the Rhineland-Palatinate state (*Land*) parliament in 1959 and was leader of the CDU at *Land* level in 1966–73. An informal agreement was made in 1967 between Helmut Kohl and Peter Altmeier, the then Minister President for Rhineland-Palatinate, that Altmeier would stand for another term, but that Kohl would take over from him after two years. In this way, Kohl became Minister President for Rhineland-Palatinate in 1969 and was re-elected in 1971 and 1975. Kohl became vice-chairman of the federal CDU in 1969, and chairman in 1973.

Kohl was the CDU's candidate for the chancellorship in **Bundestag** elections for the first time in 1976. Although unsuccessful, the CDU did make substantial electoral gains. Kohl gave up his office as Minister President of Rhineland-Palatinate in order to take up his seat in the Bundestag and become leader of the opposition and chairman of the CDU/CSU parliamentary group. In opposition Kohl began coalition negotiations with the FDP in 1982. The party agreed to transfer its allegiance from the **Social Democratic Party of Germany (SPD)** to the CDU and the government of Helmut Schmidt was subsequently defeated in the first successful constructive vote of no confidence in the history of the FRG on 1 October 1982. Kohl became Chancellor on the same day. He called new elections to secure his mandate in March 1983, and the CDU/CSU won its second highest vote ever. Kohl was re-elected as Chancellor following elections in 1987, 1990 and 1994.

Kohl's first two terms as Chancellor were unremarkable. He announced polices to improve Germany's economic position and reduce **unemployment**, but the turn-around (*Wende*) he promised in the early 1980s never materialized. His party suffered severe defeats in *Land* elections in the late 1980s and Kohl struggled to be allowed to contest the chancellorship in the forthcoming elections. Kohl's political career was saved by the fall of the **Berlin Wall** on 9 November 1989 and by the collapse of the socialist regime in the **German Democratic Republic (GDR)**, those and subsequent events enabling him to secure a place in history as the Chancellor of German unification. Sensing the mood of the East Germans, Kohl promised rapid economic and social union and the introduction of the West German currency at a one-to-one rate. In the GDR Volkskammer elections in March 1990 parties supporting Kohl's plans won 48% of the vote. Kohl and his advisers negotiated unification with the leaders of the four Allied countries and managed to persuade them that German unification would not be a threat to the stability of Europe. He promised to lock Germany further into the process of European integration through EMU. Following the first all-German Bundestag elections in December 1990 the CDU/CSU formed another coalition government with the FDP.

In the last phase of his chancellorship, Kohl struggled to keep the promises he had made to the East Germans at the time of unification. Instead of the 'flourishing landscapes' he had famously promised, the east experienced economic decline and soaring levels of unemployment. Kohl was narrowly re-elected in 1994, but in 1998 his government was voted out of office and replaced by an SPD-Alliance 90/The Greens coalition headed by **Gerhard Schröder**. Kohl resigned as leader of the CDU. He was later required to relinquish his post as honorary chairman of the CDU after the financial scandals had been revealed. Helmut Kohl was married to Hannelore Kohl, who committed suicide on 5 July 2001, and has two sons.

Internet: www.helmut-kohl.de

Köhler, Horst

Horst Köhler has been the Federal President of Germany since July 2004 following the indirect election of 23 May 2004. Supported by the **Christian Democratic Union**, the **Christian Social Union** and the **Free Democratic Party**, Köhler secured an absolute majority of 604 votes in the Bundesversammlung (electoral college) that elects the President. The Bundesversammlung is made up of 601 members of the **Bundestag** and 601 members drawn from the parliaments of the *Länder*. Prior to this Köhler served as managing director of the **International Monetary Fund** in Washington, DC, in 2000–04. As President, Köhler has caused some controversy by making political statements when his role is supposed to be purely ceremonial.

An economist, Köhler worked in the Federal Economics Ministry in 1976–81 in Bonn and then, for one year, in the office of the Minister President for Schleswig-Holstein. In 1982 he returned to Bonn, where he worked in the Ministry of Finance. In 1990 he was appointed as Under Secretary of State, with responsibility for negotiating economic and currency union with the **German Democratic Republic** (1990), and for those aspects of the **Treaty on European Union** concerning **Economic and Monetary Union** (1992). Köhler left government in 1993 and was first appointed president of the Association of German Savings and Giro Banks and then, in 1998, as president of the European Bank for Reconstruction and Development in London.

Born on 22 February 1943 in Skierbieszów, Poland, Köhler's family moved to Leipzig in 1944 and then, in 1953, to West Berlin, settling in Ludwigsburg in 1957. He studied economics at the University of Tübingen, gaining his doctorate in 1977. He was made an honorary professor at Tübingen University in 2003. Horst Köhler is married to Eva Köhler and has two children.

Address: Bundespräsidialamt, Spreeweg 1, 10557 Berlin, Germany
Tel: (0)30 20000
Fax: (0)30 20001999
E-mail: poststelle@bpra.bund.de
Internet: www.bundespraesident.de

Kokoomus – *see* National Coalition Party, Finland

Kommounistiko Komma Ellados – *see* Communist Party of Greece

Konservative Folkeparti – *see* Conservative People's Party, Denmark

Korkein Oikeus – *see* Supreme Court, Finland

Kosovo

Kosovo is a land-locked region within Serbia and Montenegro. It was an autono-mous province in the Socialist Republic of Yugoslavia in 1945–89, but under the rule of the Serb President Slobodan Milošević in 1987–2000 its powers were significantly reduced: the Serbs closed the Kosovan Assembly in 1990. During the 1990s resentment grew between the ethnic Albanians, who today make up 88% of the region's 1.9m. population, and the governing Serbs.

In 1998 a major civil conflict erupted between the two ethnic groups. Milošević was internationally condemned for his oppressive policies towards the Albanians in March 1998 and the Kosovo Liberation Army targeted attacks on Serb officials. By September fighting had broken out and atrocities committed by the Serbs against ethnic Albanians created tens of thousands of refugees. A major turning-point in the conflict was the massacre of 45 ethnic Albanian men and women in the village of Racak on 15 January 1999.

As all attempts by the international community to secure an end to the civil conflict failed, the **North Atlantic Treaty Organization (NATO)** decided to intervene with a series of air strikes on Serb targets from 24 March 1999. This action was a significant step because NATO's intervention in a civil conflict was unjustified under international law. Despite the lack of a **United Nations (UN)** mandate to act, NATO felt that its intervention was morally justified to prevent humanitarian tragedy. The NATO air campaign lasted until 10 June 1999 when Milošević withdrew his army from Kosovo. By that time thousands of Albanians had been massacred and some 500,000 forced to leave the country for Albania and Macedonia. Today it is estimated that the conflict cost 10,000 lives.

Following the conflict NATO deployed peace-keepers—the Kosovo Force (KFOR). KFOR included Russian troops; this marked the first time since the end of the **Cold War** that Russians had served in a NATO-led force. The Milošević regime collapsed in October 2000 and the former leader, who was indicted for war crimes by the UN in May 1999, was surrendered to the UN International Criminal Tribunal for the Former Yugoslavia in The Hague, Netherlands, in 2001. Kosovo is now a UN-administered province.

Kristdemokraterna – *see* **Christian Democrats, Sweden**

Kristelig Folkeparti – *see* **Christian People's Party, Norway**

Kristillisdemokraatit – *see* **Christian Democrats, Finland**

Kystpartiet – *see* **Coastal Party, Norway**

L

Labour Party (Ireland)

The Labour Party is the largest left-wing party in the Republic of Ireland. Founded in 1920, it stands for social democratic economic and welfare policy, including corporatism, incomes policies and an active governmental industrial policy. It is a socially secularist party and adopts a liberal position on issues such as divorce and abortion. The party tends to favour a unified Ireland.

Labour has governed as junior partner in coalitions with both **Fianna Fáil (FF)** and **Fine Gael (FG)**. Most recently it governed with FF in 1992–95 and then switched to a coalition with FG and the Democratic Left in 1995–97. The Democratic Left merged with the Labour Party in January 1999. The Labour Party currently has 21 seats in the 166-seat **Dáil Éireann** that was elected on 17 May 2002.

Party Leader: Pat Rabbitte
Address: 17 Ely Place, Dublin 2, Ireland
Tel: (0)1 6784700
Fax: (0)1 6612640
E-mail: head_office@labour.ie
Internet: www.labour.ie

Labour Party (Netherlands)

The Labour Party, or Partij van de Arbeid (PvdA), is the social democratic party in the Netherlands. Founded in 1946 through the merger of three parties, the PvdA seeks to promote social, political, and economic equality for all citizens. It has been the second party in the Netherlands for most of the post-war era, but led coalition governments with PvdA Prime Ministers in 1945–46, 1948–58 and 1973–77. Most recently it governed under Wim Kok in the so-called 'purple coalition' with the **People's Party for Freedom and Democracy** and **Democrats 66** in 1994–98 and 1998–2002. In the most recent elections, held on 22 January 2003, the party won 42 seats in the 150-seat **Tweede Kamer**.

Party Leader: Ruud Koole
Address: Herengracht 54, 1015 BN Amsterdam, or POB 1310, 1000 BH
      Amsterdam, Netherlands
Tel: (0)20 5512155
Fax: (0)20 5512250
E-mail: pvda@pvda.nl
Internet: www.pvda.nl

Labour Party (Norway)

The Labour Party, or Arbeiderpartiet, is the reformist social democratic party in
Norway. It promotes liberty, democracy, social justice and solidarity at national and
international levels. Established in 1887, it first entered the **Stortinget** in 1903 and
formed its first government in 1928. Since then the party has dominated Norwegian
politics, governing for a total of 44 years. In the post-war period there were Labour
Party Prime Ministers in 1945–65, 1971–81, 1987–97 and 2000–2001. The party is
credited with constructing the Norwegian **welfare state** and sustaining low levels of
unemployment and a small gap between income groups.

In September 2001 the Labour Party recorded its poorest electoral performance
since 1924. Its representation in the 165-seat Stortinget fell from 65 to only 43 seats
and, although still the largest party, it was unable to muster a parliamentary majority
to form a government. It now leads the opposition. In the election campaign the
party was criticized for high rates of taxation and inadequate public services.

Party Leader: Jens Stoltenberg
Address: POB 8743, Youngstorget, 0028 Oslo, Norway
Tel: (0)24-14-40-00
Fax: (0)24-14-40-01
E-mail: dna@dna.no
Internet: www.dna.no

Labour Party (Great Britain)

The Labour Party is the dominant left-wing party of Great Britain. Established in
1900, it originally campaigned for common ownership of the means of production
and redistribution of wealth. A reform to Clause 4 of the party constitution in 1995
ended the party's commitment to collective ownership and transformed it into a
democratic socialist party which promotes social justice, reward for hard work,
decency, and rights matched with responsibilities. Although the party governed for
only 23 years in the 20th century, its policies transformed British society. In 1945–
51, under Clement Attlee, Labour's first majority government took a number of
British industries into public ownership and expanded the provision of the **welfare
state**, including the establishment of the National Health Service (NHS). In 1964–
70 the second government, under Harold Wilson, implemented social measures,

including reforms of the laws relating to divorce, homosexuality and abortion, and abolished capital punishment.

Labour spent 18 years in opposition, 1979–97. During this time party policy first moved to the left under the leadership of Michael Foot, and then, from the late 1980s, underwent a series of reviews, first under the leadership of Neil Kinnock in 1983–92, and then under that of John Smith, in 1992–94. Following the sudden death of John Smith in 1994, **Tony Blair** took over as leader of the party. As a result of Blair's pragmatic and less ideological approach to politics, the party has come to be referred to as New Labour.

In 1997 New Labour was elected with a landslide victory. It won a total of 418 seats in the **House of Commons**, a majority of 179 seats. It was re-elected in 2001 with 412 seats and a marginally reduced majority of 167. In office New Labour has introduced a national minimum wage and reforms to the welfare state. New Labour has increased spending on the NHS and education and its chancellor, **Gordon Brown**, has won Labour a reputation for sound economic management. New Labour has also undertaken a radical reform of the British constitution. It held referendums on devolution for **Scotland**, **Wales** and—following the **Good Friday Agreement**—**Northern Ireland**. It has also reformed the **House of Lords**. By August 2003 the Labour Party had been in government for longer than at any other time in its history.

Party Leader: Tony Blair
Address: 16 Old Queen St, London SW1H 9HP, United Kingdom
Tel: (0)870 5900200
E-mail: info@new.labour.org.uk
Internet: www.labour.org.uk

Landsorganisasjonen i Norge – *see* Norwegian Confederation of Trade Unions

Landsorganisationen i Danmark – *see* Danish Confederation of Trade Unions

Landsorganisationen i Sverige – *see* Swedish Confederation of Trade Unions

Language

Language shapes cultural identity and bonds political communities. In Western European states such as Belgium and Switzerland distinct linguistic communities are given political representation. In other regions minority linguistic groups, such as in the **Basque Country** in Spain or **Wales** in the United Kingdom, campaign for linguistic and political rights.

The **European Union (EU)** brings together 25 member states and a total of 20 official languages: Czech, Danish, Dutch, English, Estonian, Finnish, French, German, Greek, Hungarian, Italian, Latvian, Lithuanian, Maltese, Polish, Portuguese, Slovak, Slovenian, Spanish and Swedish. The main working languages of the EU are English, French and German. However, the EU treaties recognize the importance of respecting language as part of member states' identities and of preserving cultural diversity. Each member state has the right to state which language will be its official language. To ensure democracy the EU guarantees that all official documents are translated into all combinations of languages. EU citizens have the right to correspond with EU institutions in the official language of their member state. To achieve these aims all official documents are translated into all languages and, at meetings of the **European Parliament** and the **European Council**, interpretation between all languages is arranged. With 20 official languages this means that there are, theoretically, 380 combinations of languages to translate or interpret. The **European Commission**'s Directorate-Generals for Translation (DGT) and Interpretation (DG-SCIC) provide the linguistic services to make this possible. The cost of EU linguistic services with 11 languages prior to enlargement in 2004 was €2 per citizen per year. This figure is set to rise following the **accession** of 10 new member states—and nine new languages—on 1 May 2004.

With the increase in the number of member states and official languages in 2004, several existing member states launched campaigns to obtain recognition of their minority languages as official EU languages. Ireland is campaigning to obtain such recognition for Irish, and Spain for Catalan, Basque and Galician to be granted that status. The Welsh nationalist party, **Plaid Cymru**, announced in September 2004 that it will seek to obtain recognition of Welsh as an official language, claiming that more EU citizens speak Welsh than Maltese.

Left Alliance

The Left Alliance, or Vasemmistoliitto, is a small left-wing party in Finland. Founded in 1990, it campaigns for economic and social justice as well as for sustainable development. The party currently has 19 seats in the 200-seat **Eduskunta** that was elected on 16 March 2003.

Party Leader: Suvi-Anne Siimes
Address: Viherniemenkatu 5A, 00530 Helsinki, Finland
Tel: (0)9 774741
Fax: (0)9 77474200
E-mail: raisa.rasilainen@vasemmistoliitto.fi
Internet: www.vasemmistoliitto.fi

Left Bloc

The Left Bloc, or Bloco de Esquerda, is a small left-wing party in Portugal. Formed in 1999, it is a coalition of left-wing parties and organizations. It won 6.4% of the vote and eight seats in elections to the 230-seat **Assembléia da República** held on 20 February 2005.

Leadership: Francisco Louca
Address: Av. Almirante Reis 131, 2° andar, Lisbon, Portugal
Tel: (0)21 3510510
Internet: www.bloco.org

Left-Green Alliance

The Left-Green Alliance, or Vinstrihreyfingin-Grænt Frambod (VG), is a new left-wing political party in Iceland which unites socialist and conservationist groups. The party stands for the common ownership of Iceland's natural resources and promotes sustainable development and equality and justice for all citizens, especially the elderly and disabled and those in rural areas. VG was established in 1999 prior to general elections in May of that year. Following the election held on 10 May 2003 the party has five representatives in the 63-seat **Althingi**.

Leadership: Party Leader Steingrímur Sigfússon; *Gen. Sec.* Kristín Halldórsdóttir
Address: Sudurgötu 3, POB 175, 121 Reykjavík, Iceland
Tel: (0)5228872
E-mail: vg@vg.is
Internet: www.vg.is

Left Party

The Left Party, or Vänsterpartiet, is a small socialist party in Sweden. It has its origins in the Swedish Social Democratic Left Party which was established in 1917 but split in two in 1921. The larger part, it became the Communist Party of Sweden which reoriented from a pro-Soviet communist party in 1967, changing its name to Left Party-The Communists. In 1990 it became the Left Party. The party is a radical socialist party which promotes feminism, internationalism and anti-militarism. The party has 30 representatives in the 349-seat **Riksdag** that was elected on 15 September 2002. The Left Party is not part of a coalition, but the minority **Social Democratic Party** government headed by **Göran Persson** relies on its support.

Party Leader: Lars Ohly
Address: Kungsgatan 84, POB 12660, 112 93 Stockholm, Sweden
Tel: (0)8 654-08-20
Fax: (0)8 653-23-85
E-mail: partikansliet@vansterpartiet.se
Internet: www.vansterpartiet.se

Lega Nord – *see* Northern League, Italy

Le Pen, Jean-Marie

Jean-Marie Le Pen is the controversial founder and leader of the extreme right-wing **National Front (FN)** party in France. He campaigns to cut crime and **unemployment** by reducing **immigration**. In 1987 he referred to the Nazi gas chambers as a 'detail of history' and has proposed isolating people infected with HIV/AIDS. Born on 20 June 1928 in La Trinité-sur-Mer, he served as a paratrooper in 1954 before entering politics in 1956. He campaigned for Pierre Poujade's shopkeepers' party, becoming the youngest member of the **Assemblée Nationale** in 1956. In 1972 he founded the FN. Le Pen has campaigned in regional and European elections, winning seats in the **European Parliament** in 1984 and 1999. He has contested the French presidential elections four times and his share of the vote has risen consistently, from 0.74% in 1974 to 14% in 1988, 15% in 1995 and 16.86% in 2002. He came second to **Jacques Chirac** in the first round of the 2002 presidential elections, defeating the socialist candidate, Lionel Jospin. Jean-Marie Le Pen has been married twice and has three daughters.

Lëtzebuerger Chrëschtleche Gewerkschaftsbond – *see* Luxembourg Confederation of Christian Trade Unions

Lëtzebuergesch Sozialistesch Arbechterpartei – *see* Luxembourg Socialist Workers' Party

Liberal Democrats

The Liberal Democrats, the third largest political party in Great Britain, were established in 1988 following the merger of the Liberal Party and the Social Democratic Party. Initially known as the Social and Liberal Democrats, the party came to be referred to as the Liberal Democrats. The Liberal Democrats promote freedom and fairness in British and international politics, and increased citizen involvement in politics. The party supports the democratization of the economy and redistribution of wealth, and favours increasing taxes to improve aspects of the **welfare state**. Originally 'equidistant' to the **Labour Party** and the **Conservative Party**, the Liberal Democrats moved to the left in 1992 to help to remove the Conservatives from office.

Disadvantaged by the first-past-the-post electoral system, the Liberal Democrats have traditionally struggled to make significant electoral gains. However, the party won 20 seats in the **House of Commons** in 1992, 46 seats in 1997, and 52 seats in 2001.

Party Leader: Charles Kennedy
Address: 4 Cowley St, London SW1P 3NB, United Kingdom
Tel: (0)20 7222 7999
Fax: (0)20 7799 2170
E-mail: info@libdems.org.uk
Internet: www.libdems.org.uk

Liberal Party (Denmark)

The Liberal Party, or Venstre, is a major party in Denmark. Founded in 1870 from a federation of Venstre groups in the **Folketing**, it is the oldest political party in Denmark. Venstre campaigned for parliamentary democracy and universal suffrage until this was granted to men in 1901 and to **women** in 1915. Today the party stands for individual freedom and choice, together with respect for and tolerance of the difference of others. The party campaigns for the decentralization of democratic power to local level and for involving citizens in decision-making processes. It supports the free market and the Danish **welfare state**, but emphasizes that citizens should have choice over the provision of services. Venstre supported the campaign for Denmark to adopt the **euro**.

Venstre currently has 52 representatives in the 179-seat **Folketing** that was elected on 8 February 2005 and is the largest party. Following the elections it formed a second coalition government with the **Conservative People's Party**. Venstre's leader, **Anders Fogh Rasmussen**, is Prime Minister of the current government.

Party Leader: Anders Fogh Rasmussen
Address: Søllerødvej 30, 2840 Holte, Denmark
Tel: (0)45-80-22-33
Fax: (0)45-80-38-30
E-mail: venstre@venstre.dk
Internet: www.venstre.dk

Liberal Party (Iceland)

The Liberal Party, or Frjálslindi flokkurinn, is a new liberal party in Iceland. Established in 1998, the party promotes democracy and equal citizens' rights. It is in favour of the free market and the reduction of income tax, increasing tax on consumption instead. It promotes investment in education in Iceland and seeks to liberalize the country's fisheries industry. The party won two seats in elections to the 63-seat **Althingi** in 1999. In elections held on 10 May 2003 the party increased its representation to four seats.

Party Leader: Gudjon A. Kristjansson
Address: Adalstræti 9, 101 Reykjavík, Iceland
Tel: (0)5522600

Fax: (0)5630780
E-mail: xf@xf.is
Internet: www.xf.is

Liberal Party (Sweden)

The Liberal Party, or Folkpartiet Liberalerna, is a social liberal party in Sweden. It was founded in 1934 through the merger of a number of liberal parties. It promotes the freedom of individuals and opposes state intervention. It advocates eliminating barriers to opportunity, but develops its policies from the perspective of the weakest. The party formed part of the non-socialist coalitions of 1976–78 and 1979–81. In the intervening period the party was in power as a minority government, of which Ola Ullstein was Prime Minister. The party was also a member of the non-socialist coalition in 1991–94. In the election to the **Riksdag** held on 15 September 2002 the party increased the number of seats it won threefold, to 48. Its campaign had focused on controversial proposals concerning **immigration** and the integration of non-Swedish nationals.

Party Leader: Lars Leijonborg
Address: Drottninggatan 97, POB 6508, 113 83 Stockholm, Sweden
Tel: (0)8 410-242-00
Fax: (0)8 509-116-60
E-mail: info@liberal.se
Internet: www.folkpartiet.se

The Liberals

The Liberals, or Venstre, is a party of the centre in Norway. Founded in 1884, it is today the oldest party in the country. It campaigns for the rights of individuals, and to reduce bureaucracy and regulation. It also campaigns for lower rates of taxation and to stimulate private enterprise. Venstre has had mixed electoral success in the post-war era. It had no representation in the **Stortinget** in 1985–93, but has participated in four coalition governments. Most recently, in 1997–2000 and since 2001, this has been in two non-socialist coalitions. At the most recent elections to the Stortinget, held on 10 September 2001, Venstre won two seats in the 165-seat parliament. It governs in a coalition with the **Conservative Party** and the **Christian People's Party**. This minority government relies on the support of the extreme right-wing party, the **Progress Party**.

Party Leader: Lars Henrik Michelsen
Address: Møllergt. 16, 0179 Oslo, Norway
Tel: (0)22-40-43-50
Fax: (0)22-40-43-51
E-mail: venstre@venstre.no
Internet: www.venstre.no

Liechtenstein

Liechtenstein is a principality situated between Austria and Switzerland. It was established in 1719 and became a sovereign state in 1806. The capital is Vaduz. A constitutional monarchy, the head of state is Prince Alois. Legislative power lies with the 25-seat Landtag. Members of the Landtag are elected by a system of proportional representation for a four year term; the most recent elections were held on 11 February 2001. The current head of government is Otmar Hasler.

Prince Alois acceded to the throne on 15 August 2004 following the abdication of his father, Prince Hans Adam II, who had been monarch for 15 years. During his reign Prince Hans Adam II succeeded in increasing the powers of the monarchy. In a referendum held in March 2003, 64.3% of voters agreed to grant more power to the Prince. He is now able to appoint and dismiss the government, to appoint judges and to veto decisions made by the Landtag. These constitutional reforms were criticized on the grounds that they turn Liechtenstein into an absolute monarchy. At the same time, however, the monarch's right to rule by emergency decree was removed.

Liechtenstein is a small state covering 160 sq km with a population of 33,000 (2001). It has a strong, industrialized economy and some 75,000 small businesses have been attracted to the principality by the low taxation regime. It has a thriving financial services sector. The state has recently tightened the regulation of financial services in order to prevent money-laundering; customers opening bank accounts may no longer enjoy anonymity. The state participates in a customs union with Switzerland and the national currency is the Swiss Franc. It has been a member of the **European Economic Area** since May 1995.

Lijst Pim Fortuyn – *see* List Pim Fortuyn, Netherlands

Lindh, Anna

Anna Lindh was the foreign minister for the **Social Democratic Party** in Sweden in 1998–2003. On 10 September 2003, however, Lindh, aged 46, was brutally attacked in the NK department store in central Stockholm. She was rushed to hospital but, after several attempts to save her life, she died on the following day. Many Swedes found it hard to believe that their most popular minister in recent years had been violently murdered in a similar way to the late Prime Minister, Olof Palme, 17 years earlier.

Anna Lindh was born on 19 June 1957. Her father, Staffan Lindh, an artist, and her mother, Nancy Lindh, a teacher who was born in Canada, brought their daughter up in a family environment characterized by radicalism. As a child Anna was encouraged to question truisms and not to be afraid of speaking her mind or to be political. She showed an interest in politics early in life and, at the age of 12, she became the president of her local Swedish Social Democratic youth club, Unga Örnarna. During this period she demonstrated an interest in international issues that was exceptional for a child of her age. At the age of 13 she organized an exhibition in her local school which portrayed the atrocities of the Viet Nam War. By the age of 20 she had become a local councillor in her home town, Enköping. She studied law at Uppsala University and graduated in 1982. Lindh worked as a court clerk in the Stockholm city court in 1982–83. In 1982, at the age of 25, she was elected to the Swedish parliament, the **Riksdag**, and before long she became a member of the committee on taxation.

During the early period of her political career Lindh undertook several 'solidarity' trips to Chile and Argentina in order to establish contacts with young opponents to the military regimes there. Lindh became the first woman president of the Swedish Social Democratic Youth League (SSU) in 1984, a position that she held until 1990. In 1987–89 she was also the vice-president of the International Union of Socialist Youth. As president of the SSU, Lindh was engaged in issues of international justice and development, her opposition to the South African apartheid regime being a notable example. During this period she also became a close friend of the former Norwegian Prime Minister, Jens Stoltenberg, and other European social-democratic politicians who shared her passion for internationalism and issues of global justice. Curiously for a politician who later became one of the most active foreign ministers within the **European Union (EU)**, Lindh's early political career was marked by opposition to Sweden's membership of the **European Community**. She believed that the project of European integration was undemocratic and based upon capitalist economic ideas that were in stark conflict with the wider social democratic objectives of international justice and the global redistribution of income.

Lindh became Minister for the Environment in 1994. This was followed by her appointment as Minister for Foreign Affairs, in 1998. It was on the international stage that Anna Lindh made her mark, inspired by the internationalist ideas of Olof Palme. Like Palme, Lindh placed international solidarity, human rights and peace at the heart of Swedish foreign policy and believed that these values should also govern European foreign policy. For this she gained widespread respect amongst her colleagues in Europe and elsewhere. Lindh was an advocate of global human rights and was not afraid of criticizing regimes that abused the human rights of their own citizens. Her argument that **Turkey** should only be granted EU membership if it succeeded in improving its human rights record gave rise to widespread debate across Europe. Moreover, she criticized the US-led invasion of **Iraq** in 2003, arguing that the **United Nations (UN)**, multilateral diplomacy and international law were the most appropriate means of resolving violent conflict and human rights abuses. She pursued similar objectives within the EU where she actively participated in the development and formulation of European foreign policy, not least by attempting to strengthen the ties between the EU and the UN. She was also a great believer in the creation of an independent EU crisis management capability. During the Swedish presidency of the EU in 2001 Lindh played a key role in preventing a violent conflict from breaking out in the Democratic Republic of Macedonia, in particular by ensuring that the EU member states pursued a unified approach towards the region.

Prior to her assassination Lindh campaigned strongly for a yes vote in the Swedish referendum on membership of **Economic and Monetary Union (EMU)** and the **euro**. Her enthusiasm emerged from her general support for the European peace project and her conviction that only by being a full member of the EU could Sweden influence the future shape of Europe. In contrast to some of her social democratic colleagues, Lindh did not consider EMU membership to be a threat to the Swedish **welfare state**, but a guarantee for its future existence.

Not only was Anna Lindh known for her international activism, she was also regarded as a significant symbol of gender equality in Sweden and abroad. She was a role model to many young Swedish **women**, who admired her support for global gender equality as well as her ability to successfully combine married life and motherhood (she had two children) with the demanding task of being the foreign minister of Sweden. Lindh was widely expected to become the first female Prime Minister of Sweden.

In January 2004 Mijailo Mijailovic confessed to the murder of Anna Lindh. According to Mijailovic, his act of violence was not politically motivated, but a consequence of his fragile mental health. Even so, the assassination of Anna Lindh might still have a damaging effect on Swedish political life, in particular by curbing the freedom of the country's politicians and by jeopardizing the openness of Swedish society more generally. Perhaps a sign of the continuing vitality of the Swedish polity, however, was the decisive rejection of Sweden's entry into the EMU in a referendum (no 56%) a few days after Lindh's death in spite of a very visible and widespread public outpouring of grief at her death.

Annika Bergman
University of Edinburgh

Lisbon Strategy

The Lisbon Strategy is an initiative of the **European Union (EU)** agreed at the Lisbon **European Council** in 2000 to make the region the most dynamic and competitive knowledge-based economy in the world. It seeks to secure sustainable economic growth, more and better jobs, social cohesion and environmental protection. The Lisbon Strategy aims to achieve this by setting targets for member states to meet by 2010. The employment rate in the EU should increase to 70% and the activity rate of **women** to 60% by this date. A High Level Group, chaired by Wim Kok, has reviewed the progress of the member states on meeting the targets of the Lisbon Strategy. Its report in 2004 found that there had been slow progress and predicted that many of the targets would not be met by 2010. This predicted failure was attributed to an overloaded agenda, poor co-ordination, conflicting priorities, and a lack of determined political action.

List Pim Fortuyn

List Pim Fortuyn, or Lijst Pim Fortuyn (LPF), is the populist right-wing party in the Netherlands that was founded in February 2002 by **Pim Fortuyn**. The party campaigns for tough action against immigrants who do not assimilate into Dutch society, stronger measures to reduce crime and less state bureaucracy. It has also proposed a reform of the section of the Dutch Constitution that prohibits discrimination.

The party performed well in elections held on 15 May 2002, nine days after the assassination of Pim Fortuyn. It won 26 of 150 seats, thereby becoming the second largest party in the **Tweede Kamer**, and formed part of the first coalition of **Jan Peter Balkenende** together with the **Christian Democratic Appeal** and the **People's Party for Freedom and Democracy**, providing four ministers. However, the coalition collapsed following the resignation of two ministers in October 2002. The LPF has eight seats in the current Tweede Kamer that was elected on 22 January 2003.

Party Leader: Mat Herben
Address: Albert Plesmanweg 43 M, 3088 GB Rotterdam, Netherlands
Tel: (0)10 7891140
Fax: (0)10 7891141
E-mail: info@lijstpimfortuyn.nl
Internet: www.lijstpimfortuyn.nl

Luxembourg

The Grand Duchy of Luxembourg was founded in 1815 and gained full independence in 1867. It is a small, land-locked state which has borders with Belgium, France and Germany. It was occupied by Germany during the World Wars of 1914–18 and 1939–45. After the Second World War Luxembourg abandoned its traditional neutrality, forming in 1948 the Benelux economic union with Belgium and the Netherlands that was formalized in a treaty in 1958. It was a founder member of the **North Atlantic Treaty Organization** in 1948 and of the **European Coal and Steel Community** in 1952.

Area: 2,600 sq km; *capital:* Luxembourg; *population:* 441,000 (2001).

A constitutional monarchy, the head of state is Grand Duke Henri, who acceded to the throne in October 2000 following the abdication of his father, Jean. Legislative power is vested with the **Chambre des Députés** which is elected every four years. The head of the government formed following elections held on 13 June 2004 is **Jean-Claude Juncker** of the **Christian Social People's Party (CSV)**. He first became Prime Minister in 1995, replacing Jacques Santer who reluctantly became president of the **European Commission** after having been identified as a compromise candidate for that office by the member states of the **European Union**. Juncker was later reappointed following elections held in June 1999 and June 2004.

In 1999–2004 he led a coalition between the CSV and the **Democratic Party (DP)**, which in 1999 overtook the **Luxembourg Socialist Workers' Party (LSAP)** as Luxembourg's second party. In elections held on 13 June 2004 the CSV won 36.11% of the vote and 24 parliamentary seats. It formed a coalition with the LSAP, which had regained the status of second party by winning 24.37% of the vote and 14 parliamentary seats. Voting in national and European elections is compulsory and the turn-out at the elections held in 2004 was 91.68%.

The political system of Luxembourg has been remarkably stable in the post-war period. Most governing coalitions have included the CSV, with the notable exception of that formed between the LSAP and the DP in 1974–79. During the 1980s the three main parties ceded about 10% of the vote to two new smaller parties that had emerged: the **Green Party** and the **Action Committee for Democracy and Pension Rights (ADR)**. These parties increased their presence in parliament. In elections held on 13 June 2004 both the Green Party and the ADR won seven seats in the Chambre des Députés and, between them, 21.5% of the vote.

Economy: Luxembourg enjoys the highest per caput incomes in Europe. A small, regional economy, it has always been characterized by a high degree of specialization. Until the 1970s this was in steel production, but following the recessions of the 1970s it switched to emphasize banking, financial services, transportation and the media. The transformation from an industrial economy to one providing high value added services is accounted for by its unique regulatory framework and light taxation regime.

GNP: US $17,571m. (2001); *GNP per caput:* $39,840 (2001); *GNP at PPP:* $21,416m. (2001); *GNP per caput at PPP:* $48,560 (2001); *currency:* euro; *unemployment:* 3.0% (2002).

Luxembourg's strength in banking and financial management developed during the 1980s and now accounts for around 20% of gross domestic product. This growth has been attributed to Luxembourg's regime which offers tax-free savings and strict laws guaranteeing banking secrecy. The financial sector is centred on private banking, investment fund management and insurance. Today around 180 banks are based in Luxembourg and it has grown to become the sixth largest financial centre in the world. In investment fund management it is the second largest centre in the world. Luxembourg's specialization in banking and financial services since the 1980s has more than compensated for the decline in the steel industry and has contributed to high rates of economic growth (around 5.5% per year) and low rates of inflation and **unemployment**.

The Luxembourg economy enjoys high rates of employment. Some 80,000 employees in Luxembourg are cross-border workers living in Germany, France and Belgium; 62% of total employment is undertaken by cross-border workers and resident foreigners. It is a regulated economy, and 95% of jobs are permanent contracts. However, as is typical for a corporatist economy, workers are largely male and young. **Women** and older workers have significantly lower rates of employment. Generous disability and early retirement pensions have encouraged large numbers of those aged over 55 to leave the labour market. Welfare benefits are generous and both wages and social security benefits are indexed to consumer prices.

Luxembourg formed an economic union with Belgium in 1921 and until **Economic and Monetary Union (EMU)** Luxembourg and Belgian francs had the same value and were interchangeable. The state formed an economic union with Belgium and the Netherlands in 1948 and was a founder member of the **European Coal and Steel Community** in 1952. Luxembourg was one of the first member states of the **European Union (EU)** to meet the **convergence criteria** for EMU. Until the late 1990s Luxembourg was slow at transposing directives of the **Single European Market** into law, particularly in the areas of transport, motor vehicles and social policy. However, to support its key financial services sector, financial market directives have been implemented quickly. In 2000 Luxembourg was the only country to oppose EU plans to end banking secrecy laws. It also opposed a further directive in 2003 on the taxation of savings income. In both cases Luxembourg (together with Austria and Belgium) was given a special ruling for a transitional period.

Luxembourg Confederation of Christian Trade Unions

The Luxembourg Confederation of Christian Trade Unions, or Lëtzebuerger Chrëschtleche Gewerkschaftsbond (LCGB), is the Christian trade union confederation in Luxembourg. Founded in 1921, it represents the interests of some 38,000 members organized in 10 professional organizations. It is itself a member of **ETUC**. LCGB campaigns to improve salaries, working conditions and social protection. It also offers services for the children of its members.

Leadership: Pres. Robert Weber; *Sec.-Gen.* Marc Spautz
Address: 11 rue du Commerce, 1351 Luxembourg
Tel: (0)49-94-24-1
Fax: (0)49-94-24-49
E-mail: mschou@lcgb.lu
Internet: www.lcgb.lu

Luxembourg Confederation of Free Trade Unions

The Luxembourg Confederation of Free Trade Unions, or Onofhängege Gewerkschaftsbond Lëtzebuerg (OGB-L), is the independent trade union federation in Luxembourg. Founded in 1979, it represents the interests some 55,000 employees in 15 affiliated trade unions. It is itself affiliated to **ETUC**. OGB-L's main aims are to promote equal rights for all employees and the improvement of living and working conditions. It also works to improve the situation of children and families in Luxembourg.

Pres.: Jean-Claude Reding
Address: POB 149, or 60 blvd J. F. Kennedy, 4002 Esch/Alzette, Luxembourg
Tel: (0)54-05-45
Fax: (0)54-16-20
E-mail: ogb-l@ogb-l.lu
Internet: www.ogb-l.lu

Luxembourg Process

The Luxembourg Process is a **European Union (EU)** benchmarking exercise that aims to reduce **unemployment** and promote economic activity in Europe. Agreed by the Luxembourg **European Council** in 1997, it co-ordinates the employment policies of EU member states through employment guide-lines set by the **European Commission**, and National Action Plans prepared by the member states. The first set of guide-lines in 1998 requested details of national policy relating to entrepreneurship, employability, adaptability and equal opportunities. This approach to EU policy-making, as an alternative to regulation, is referred to as the open method of co-ordination.

Luxembourg Socialist Workers' Party

The Luxembourg Socialist Workers' Party, or Lëtzebuergesch Sozialistesch Arbechterpartei (LSAP), is the large socialist party in Luxembourg. From its origins in 1896 it grew to become the second party for the majority of the post-war era. The party stands for the promotion of democracy and social justice as well as freedom, solidarity and security. A modernizing party, it seeks to promote these values in the current global economic era. The LSAP has participated in coalition governments with the Christian Democrat **Christian Social People's Party (CSV)**—in 1951–59 and 1984–99—and with the liberal **Democratic Party**—in 1974–79. In parliamentary elections held in June 1999 the LSAP won 13 seats in the 60-seat **Chambre des Députés** and, as third party, failed to enter into coalition negotiations. At the next election, held on 13 June 2004, it regained the status of second party by winning 24.37% of the vote and 14 parliamentary seats. It subsequently entered into a coalition with the CSV.

Party Leader: Alex Bodry
Address: 37 rue du St. Esprit, 1364 Luxembourg
Tel: (0)45-65-73-1
Fax: (0)45-65-75
E-mail: info@lsap.lu
Internet: www.lsap.lu

M

Maastricht Treaty – *see* Treaty on European Union

Malta

Malta is a small archipelago in the Mediterranean Sea. During British rule, in 1800–1964, the Malta Labour Party (MLP) sought full integration with the United Kingdom in the late 1950s. The state was granted independence on 21 September 1964 and became a republic in 1974.

Area: 300 sq km; *capital:* Valletta; *population:* 395,000 (2001).

The head of state is President Guido de Marco, who was elected by the parliament for a five-year term on 29 March 2004. Legislative power lies with the 65-seat parliament, the House of Representatives, which is elected by a system of proportional representation every five years. Following the most recent election, held on 12 April 2003, a government was formed by the conservative Nationalist Party (NP), which won 51.7% of the vote. The NP government, first elected in 1998, is led by Prime Minister Eddie Fenech Adami.

The Maltese political system is dominated by two main parties. The NP is a conservative party supported by farmers, entrepreneurs and civil servants. It favours liberal economic policy and has supported Malta's **accession** to the **European Union (EU)**. The MLP is a socialist party which governed under Dom Mintoff in 1971–87. It promoted a closed economy and indigenous economic activity. MLP opposed Malta's membership of the EU, promoting sovereignty and neutrality instead. Malta is a neutral state and is not a member of the **North Atlantic Treaty Organization (NATO)**, though it participates in NATO's Partnership for Peace programme.

Malta became a member of the EU on 1 May 2004. It had signed an Association Agreement with the **European Community** in 1971, but successive MLP governments failed to take the next step of forming a customs union. The NP government that was elected in 1987 prepared an application for EU membership in 1990. The MLP, elected in 1996, suspended the application, supporting instead the idea of Malta as a 'Switzerland in the Mediterranean'. The NP government that was elected in 1998 launched accession negotiations in February 2000. A non-binding referendum on Malta's membership of the EU was held on 8 March 2003 and the result was in favour of membership of the EU (yes 53.6%; turn-out 91%). This result needed to be endorsed in the general election that was held on 12 April 2003. In the election the pro-accession NP won 51.7% of the vote.

Economy: Malta has traditionally been a trading post between the European and Arab economies. Its rural economy has traditionally been dominated by **agriculture** and fishing, but there is also an important shipping industry. Manufacturing is dominated by small and medium-sized enterprises, and Malta has recently been developing a service economy. Around 25% of Malta's gross domestic product (GDP) derives from tourism, and a further 12% from financial services. There is a large public sector.

GNP: US $3,637m. (2001); *GNP per caput:* $9,210 (2001); *GNP at PPP:* $5,192m. (2001); *GNP per caput at PPP:* $13,140 (2001); *currency:* Maltese lira; *unemployment:* 6.8% (2002).

The governments of the Malta Labour Party in 1971–87 favoured a closed or 'fortress' economy in order to promote indigenous industry. The Nationalist Party government that came to power in 1987 sought to liberalize the economy and remove strict import and export controls. Malta applied to join the **European Union (EU)** in 1990. In 1992–96 the Maltese economy grew by an average rate of 5%, compared with an EU average of 2.5% in 1995. It has low levels of public debt— only 36% of GDP. Around three-quarters of Malta's international trade is with the EU. By the time that it joined the EU in 2004 Malta's GDP was around 69% of the EU average.

Margherita – *see* **Daisy Alliance, Italy**

Marshall Plan

The Marshall Plan was a programme of aid provided by the USA to facilitate the economic reconstruction of Western Europe following the Second World War. The plan, also known as the European Recovery Programme, was announced on 5 June 1947 by US Secretary of State George Marshall. The US $13,300m. fund was allocated to 16 states over a four-year period. The main recipients were the United Kingdom, France, Italy and West Germany.

The USA offered aid to Europe via the Marshall Plan for a variety of reasons. It was recognized that US domestic economic development depended on the growth of US trade and investment abroad. It was necessary to provide funds to European countries so that they could purchase imports from the USA, which produced one-half of the world's manufactured goods in 1945. Moreover, it was thought that investing in the reconstruction of the European economy would improve the standard of living and make it more difficult for communists to take control of Western Europe. Third, by linking a target of European integration to the receipt of funds, the USA aimed to lock Germany into the Western Alliance and reduce the security risk attached to German economic recovery.

Aid under the Marshall Plan was originally made available to the whole of Europe and the Soviet Union (USSR) was invited to attend the Paris conference in June 1947 to discuss George Marshall's offer. However, Soviet demands were not met and the USSR interpreted the plan as one to create an anti-Soviet bloc in Europe, which would include the western part of occupied Germany. The Soviet foreign minister, Vyacheslav Molotov, left the meetings, and urged **Central and Eastern European Countries** not to become involved in the plan. In this way, aid from the Marshall Plan cemented the ideological division that developed into the **Cold War** in Europe.

The Marshall Plan facilitated a period of rapid economic growth in Western Europe, in 1948–52. It also promoted the process of European integration, marked initially by the establishment of the **European Coal and Steel Community** by the **Treaty of Paris** of 1951. The **Organisation for Economic Co-operation and Development** was originally established as the Organisation for European Economic Development to manage the fund.

McAleese, Mary

Mary McAleese has been President of Ireland since 1997. A presidential candidate of the **Fianna Fáil** party, she was inaugurated for a seven-year term of office on 11 November 1997 and reappointed in November 2004. She was elected for her first term with a majority of 58.67% under the single transferable vote system after second preference votes had been transferred from eliminated candidates. Her share of first preference votes was 45.24%. She was inaugurated for a second term in November 2004, without an election as no other candidates were nominated. McAleese's main campaigning issues include justice, equality, social inclusion, rights for the disabled (she is fluent in sign language), anti-sectarianism and reconciliation. The theme of her presidency is 'Building Bridges'; she issued an official invitation in September 2003 for the British Queen to visit the Republic of Ireland.

Born Mary Leneghan on 27 June 1951 in Belfast, United Kingdom, McAleese is the first Irish President to come from **Northern Ireland**. She graduated in law from Queen's University, Belfast, in 1973 and was called to the Northern Ireland Bar in 1974. In 1975 she was appointed Reid Professor of Criminal Law, Criminology and Penology at Trinity College Dublin, where she concentrated on the Irish Constitution, prisons, and attitudes to crime. She became director of the Institute of Professional Legal Studies at Queen's University in 1987 and the first pro-vice chancellor of Queen's University in 1994. McAleese has also worked in radio and television broadcasting as a current affairs journalist with the Irish Radio Telefís Éireann. Mary McAleese is married to Martin McAleese and has three children.

Address: Áras an Uachtaráin, Phoenix Park, Dublin 8, Ireland
Tel: (0)1 6171000
Fax: (0)1 6171001
E-mail: webmaster@aras.irlgov.ie
Internet: www.irlgov.ie/aras

Media

The development of genuinely mass media was one of the huge social and cultural changes that occurred in the 20th century. At the end of the 19th century there existed a small and largely metropolitan press. This was, after 1870, increasingly owned and controlled by large corporations. In liberal political thought this fact gained added legitimacy from concerns that the press should be free from state control. Yet in many Western European societies, in order to correct the obvious biases of the capitalist-controlled press, both television and radio were introduced in more regulated ways. The governing logic for television and radio for most of the 20th century has been linked to the idea of national public-service broadcasting. The principles of quality, equality of reception and diversity sought to bring the broadcasting media under more democratic forms of control. However, Eastern European and North American societies adopted, respectively, more statist and market-driven models.

On a number of grounds it is argued that the golden age of public-service broadcasting is now over. The rapid development of new media forms, from the internet to magazine culture, has meant that radio and television have increasingly to compete with new forms of information. Also, the rapid commercialization of television since the 1980s has undermined the governing logic of public-service broadcasting. Further, many viewed the old culture of public-service broadcasting as serving the tastes of a liberal educated élite, with little provision being made for ethnic minorities, diverse lifestyle groups or working-class people. In this respect, the media have never been a truly mass phenomenon as audiences are always culturally differentiated and communicated to in different ways by programme makers. This sociological fact has also been compounded by the development of new technology which has allowed audiences to become more explicitly targeted by the television industry.

Despite continued audience fragmentation in respect of the new media and television, the media remain a powerful force within contemporary societies. It is likely that the development of the media will continue to be an ambivalent feature of modern societies. The provision of up-to-the-minute news, reporting from distant countries and the 'appearance' of many minorities that were previously invisible from social life have arguably helped to foster both more global and culturally-inclusive orientations on the part of the community. However, concerns remain over the way in which the media promote consumerism and reduce the concerns of **citizenship** to easily digestible categories; and are increasingly controlled by the interests of large transnational corporations. This has meant that 'the media' are both celebrated for the provision of information and popular entertainment and derided for undermining social values. As a consequence it is likely that the mass media will remain at the centre of cultural controversy for many years to come.

Nick Stevenson
University of Nottingham

Mezzogiorno

Mezzogiorno, meaning land of the midday sun, is the collective name given to eight regions of southern Italy—Abruzzi, Apulia, Basilicata, Calabria, Campania, Molise, Sardinia and Sicily—which lag behind the centre and north of the country in terms of economic development and prosperity. The Mezzogiorno area covers 40% of Italy's land area and is occupied by 35% of its population, but at the end of the 1990s per caput gross domestic product there was only 70% of the Italian average.

Government policies to reduce the gap between the north and centre and the Mezzogiorno were largely successful until the mid-1970s; the income gap narrowed in the 25 years to 1975 but then began to widen as demand for products such as steel and chemicals slumped. Large numbers of southern Italians migrated to the north to work in the flexible small firms that thrived in the 1980s by investing in new technologies and responding rapidly to changes in market tastes. In the 1990s resentment among northern Italians at the levels of subsidy granted to the region grew. Organizations such as the Lombard League, the Venetian League and Free Piedmont called for southerners and foreigners to leave their regions.

The Mezzogiorno has benefited since the 1980s from policies to support new firms, extend aid to parts of the service sector, such as tourism, develop public works projects, and deliver generous early retirement. This strategy had some success in the regions located along the Adriatic coast—Abruzzi, Molise and Apulia—but in others inward investors have been discouraged by corruption and organized crime. The region received support from the Mezzogiorno Programme of the **European Regional Development Fund** in 1994–99 to promote economic development and improve legality and security. This support was continued in 2000–06.

Miljöpartiet de Gröna – *see* **Green Party, Sweden**

Mitterrand, François

François Mitterrand was a French statesman and, in 1981–95, socialist President of France. Born on 26 October 1916 in Jarnac, Mitterrand was a soldier and prisoner of war during the Second World War. He escaped from captivity to Vichy France, where he first worked as a clerk for the government, and subsequently, in 1943, following occupation, formed a resistance group. Mitterrand was elected to the

Assemblée Nationale in 1946 and served as Minister for French Overseas Territories in 1946–53, as Minister for the Interior in 1954–55 and as *garde des sceaux* (Keeper of the Seals) in 1956. He then left government, opposing its policies in Algeria and the new Fifth Republic founded in 1958. Following the constitutional amendment in 1962 that introduced a directly elected presidency, Mitterrand contested that office as the left-wing candidate in 1965 and 1974. He was elected as President in 1981 and was re-elected in 1988.

As President, Mitterrand first shifted policy to the left with a programme of nationalization, government spending and higher taxation, in 1981–83. His 14 years in office were also marked by social and institutional reforms to, for example, strengthen regional government and abolish the death penalty. During periods of **cohabitation** with right-wing governments in 1986–88 and 1993–95 Mitterrand ensured a sound separation of powers. He worked on the international stage to improve relations with Germany and to promote European integration, and at home he initiated a number of architectural projects in Paris. Towards the end of his second term of office, which ended in May 1995, Mitterrand suffered from prostate cancer. He died on 8 January 1996 in Paris. François Mitterrand was married to Danielle Mitterrand, with whom he had two sons. He also had a daughter with Anne Pingeot.

Moderata Samlingspartiet – *see* Moderate Party, Sweden

Moderate Party

The Moderate Party, or Moderata Samlingspartiet, is a large conservative party in Sweden. It evolved from a group of conservative interests in the **Riksdag** and was established as an electoral association in 1904. It became a formal party—the Conservative Party—in 1938 and changed its name to the Moderate Party in 1969. The party promotes the market economy, free enterprise and the empowerment of the individual. It advocates lowering taxation and limiting public spending. It is in favour of European integration and Sweden's membership of the **euro**.

The party governed in 1906, and again in 1928–30. In the post-war period it was part of the non-socialist coalitions of 1976–78, 1979–81 and, most recently, of that of 1991–94 under Carl Bildt. The party has 55 representatives in the 349-seat Riksdag that was elected on 15 September 2002. The governing minority **Social Democratic Party** government relies on the Moderate Party for support in international affairs.

Leadership: Party Leader Frederik Reinfeldt; *Sec.-Gen.* Sven Otto Littorin
Address: Stora Nygatan 30, Box 2080, 103 12 Stockholm, Sweden
Tel: (0)8 676-80-00
Fax: (0)8 786-54-30
E-mail: info@moderat.se
Internet: www.moderat.se

Monaco

The Principality of Monaco is an independent state situated on the Mediterranean coast, bordering France to the north. A tiny state, it occupies just 1.95 sq km but has an official population of 32,000 (2002). A constitutional monarchy, the head of state is Prince Rainer III who has reigned since 9 May 1949. Legislative power lies jointly with the Prince and the unicameral Conseil National. Elections to the 18-seat parliament are held every five years, most recently on 9 February 2003. Executive power lies with the Council of Government and the Prime Minister, or Minister of State, must be a French citizen. The office has been held by Patrick Leclercq since 5 January 2000.

The Monacan economy is based predominantly on tourism; it is renowned for its casinos. It is also an important banking centre (the currency is the **euro**), though its banks have been criticized for guarding the identity of their customers. Monaco is a tax haven: it does not levy income tax on its residents and business taxes are low. There has been an increase in the number of small and medium-sized enterprises in recent years. The rate of **unemployment** is around 3.1% (1999) and the standard of living is comparable to that of the wealthy metropolitan areas of neighbouring France.

Monnet, Jean

Jean Monnet was a French economist and planner. He is commonly regarded as the instigator and architect of the project of European integration through the **European Coal and Steel Community (ECSC).**

Born on 9 November 1888 in Cognac, the son of a brandy distiller, Monnet left school at the age of 16 and travelled the world selling the products of the family firm and establishing international contacts. During the First World War he was appointed to represent France on the Inter-Allied Maritime Commission, an international committee that allocated war resources. He served as deputy secretary-general and financial adviser of the League of Nations in 1919–23. Following the death of his father in 1923, he took over and reorganized the family business, and then worked as a freelance economist and adviser to foreign governments.

During the Second World War Monnet served as supply and reconstruction co-ordinator for the exiled French government, chairman of the Franco-British Economic Co-ordination Committee in London, and as economic liaison officer to the USA. In London he worked closely with **Winston Churchill** and in Washington, DC, he established close links with the advisers of Franklin D. Roosevelt. He managed to persuade the USA to draw up production and supply plans for its war effort in 1942–45, to make the country the 'arsenal of democracy'.

When Monnet returned to France following the end of the Second World War he strongly advocated the need for plans for the reconstruction and modernization of the French economy, and drew up the Monnet Plan in 1947. This envisaged setting investment targets and allocating investment funds for the reconstruction of key industries. His recommendations were accepted and Monnet established the Commissariat Général du Plan, serving as its first commissioner-general in 1947–55.

Monnet's next important idea was to create a single market in the coal and steel industries of Europe so that European economies could rebuild these economic sectors free of concerns that they might be used to prepare a war economy. He developed these plans with French foreign minister **Robert Schuman** and German Chancellor Konrad Adenauer and the ECSC was established in 1952, in accordance with the **Treaty of Paris** of 1951. Jean Monnet served as the first president of the High Authority, the governing body of the ECSC, in 1952–55. Monnet remained a strong advocate of further European integration until his death in 1979. He married Silvia di Bondini in 1929 and they had two children.

Mouvement des Entreprises de France – *see* Movement for French Enterprise

Mouvement Réformateur – *see* Reformist Movement, Belgium

Movement for French Enterprise

The Movement for French Enterprise, or Mouvement des Entreprises de France, is the business organization in France. Founded in 1998, it is the successor of the Conseil National du Patronat Français. It lobbies nationally and internationally to promote the interests of French business and encourages entrepreneurship. It represents some 750,000 member companies across all economic sectors, and is itself a member of the **Union of Industrial and Employers' Confederations of Europe**.

Leadership: Pres. Ernest Antoine Seillière; *Dir-Gen.* Jacques Creyssel
Address: 55 ave Bosquet, 75007 Paris CEDEX 07, France
Tel: (0)1-53-59-19-19
Fax: (0)1-45-51-20-44
E-mail: via www.medef.fr/staging/site/page.php?pag_id=1998
Internet: www.medef.fr

Multi-Level governance (MLG)

Multi-Level governance (MLG) is a term used in the context of **European Union (EU)** politics to describe the way that decision-making in the EU is dispersed across a number of territorial levels. The claim is that during the process of European integration a degree of authority has shifted from nation states in an upwards direction to the EU institutions and downwards though a process of **regionalism**. MLG highlights the fact that the process of policy-making in the EU today operates at European, national and regional levels.

N

Næringslivets Hovedorganisasjon – *see* **Confederation of Norwegian Business and Industry**

National Alliance

The National Alliance, or Alleanza Nazionale (AN), is a right-wing party in Italy. Originally founded as the extreme right-wing Italian Social Movement (Movimiento Sociale Italiano), it changed its name to AN in 1995 in order to distance itself from its neo-fascist origins and to broaden its electoral appeal, and it has enjoyed electoral successes in electoral alliances with other right-wing parties.

In the general elections held on 27 March 1994, AN joined the Good Governance Alliance (Polo del Buon Governo) with **Forza Italia**. This alliance, together with the Freedom Alliance (Polo delle Libertà), achieved a landslide victory and won an absolute majority of seats in the **Camera dei Deputati**. The Forza Italia-led coalition under Prime Minister **Silvio Berlusconi** lasted until December 1994. AN joined the Alliance for Freedom (Polo per la Libertà) with Forza Italia, the Christian Democratic Centre and the United Christian Democrats (later **Union of Centre and Christian Democrats**) in the general election held on 21 April 1996, but the alliance came second to the left-wing Olive Tree Alliance.

AN contested the general elections held in May 2001 as part of the House of Freedoms Coalition (Casa delle Libertà), which included Forza Italia, the **Northern League**, the Christian Democratic Centre, the United Christian Democrats and the New Italian Socialist Party. AN won 99 seats in the 630-seat parliament and became part of the House of Freedoms Coalition.

Party Leader: Gianfranco Fini
Address: 39 Via della Scrofa, 00186 Rome, Italy
Tel: (0)06 68817300
Fax: (0)06 6892953
E-mail: aninternational@alleanzanazionale.it
Internet: www.alleanzanazionale.it

National Coalition Party

The National Coalition Party, Kokoomus, is the moderate conservative party of Finland. Founded in 1918, one year after Finnish independence, it is an ideologically diverse party with social reformist, conservative and liberal wings. It has campaigned against extreme right-wing movements, for cutting bureaucracy and for the transfer of power to the local level, closer to citizens. It also led the pro-European campaigns on the issues of membership of the **European Union** and the single currency.

Since its establishment the party has participated in 20 governments. Following 21 years in opposition, it governed in four coalitions in 1987–2003: one led by the Centre Party and three with the **Finnish Social Democratic Party**. It returned to opposition following the elections held on 16 March 2003, when the National Coalition Party returned 40 representatives to the 200-seat **Eduskunta**.

Leadership: Party Leader Jyrki Katainen; *Gen. Sec.:* Harri Jaskari
Address: Pohjoinen Rautayiekatu 21B, 00100 Helsinki, Finland
Tel: (0)207488488
Fax: (0)9 6938206
E-mail: jyrki.katainen@eduskunta.fi
Internet: www.kokoomus.fi

National Federation of Christian Trade Unions

The National Federation of Christian Trade Unions, or Christelijk Nationaal Vakverbond (CNV), is the Christian trade union federation in the Netherlands. Founded in 1910, today it has more than 360,000 members in 11 affiliated trade unions. CNV is itself a member of **ETUC**. CNV campaigns to improve working conditions, worker participation, social security and education and training facilities.

Leadership: Pres. Doekle Terpstra; *Gen. Sec.* Bert van Boggelen
Address: Ravellaan 1, 3533 JE Utrecht, Netherlands
Tel: (0)30 2913911
Fax: (0)30 2946544
E-mail: cnvinfo@cnv.nl
Internet: www.cnv.nl

National Front (Belgium)

The National Front, or Front National (FN), is the extreme right-wing political party in French-speaking Belgium. Its campaigns are racist and xenophobic. FN president, Daniel Féret, is a member of the European Parliament and of the Brussels regional parliament. In the most recent Belgian elections, held on 18 May 2003, FN won one seat in the 150-seat **Kamer**, having obtained 2% of the vote.

Pres.: Daniel Féret
Internet: www.frontnational.be (site administratively closed)

National Front (France)

The National Front, or Front National (FN), is the extreme right-wing party in France. Founded in 1972, the FN is an anti-democratic party which opposes **immigration**, state intervention and European integration. It promotes policies that favour the family and community, the free-market economy and the repatriation of non-European 'foreigners'—even those who are French citizens—to their country of origin.

The FN became electorally significant in the 1980s when it obtained 11% of the vote in the 1984 European elections. In the 1990s it won 15% of the vote in the first round of the presidential elections held in 1995 and 15.24% of the vote and one seat in elections to the **Assemblée Nationale** held in 1997. The FN won 275 seats in regional councils in 1998 and some elements of the moderate right in the **Union for French Democracy** were prepared to enter into electoral pacts with the FN to reduce the success of the left-wing parties. The FN has also shaped the mainstream political agenda, especially around such issues as immigration and **unemployment**.

In 1999 the FN split into two parties following a power struggle between its leader, **Jean-Marie Le Pen**, and Bruno Mégret. Le Pen's FN officially became the National Front for French Unity (Front National pour l'Unité Française) and in January 1999 Mégret founded the National Republican Movement (Mouvement Républican National—MRN). While the parties were ideologically similar, Mégret's MRN declared itself more open to co-operation with mainstream right-wing parties.

Le Pen won 16.86% of the vote in the first round of the presidential elections held in April 2002, coming second to **Jacques Chirac** who obtained 18.88% of the vote. In the second round of voting one week later, Chirac secured 82.21% of the vote and Le Pen 17.79%. In the first round of elections to the 577-seat Assemblée Nationale, held on 9 June 2002, the FN won 11.12% of the vote but no parliamentary seats.

Party Leader: Jean-Marie Le Pen
Address: 4 rue Vauguyon, 92210 Saint-Cloud, France
Tel: (0)1-41-12-10-00
E-mail: internet@frontnational.com
Internet: www.frontnational.com

Nationalrat (Austria)

National Council

The Nationalrat (National Council) is the lower house of the bicameral parliament of Austria. It is made up of 183 members who are directly elected by a system of proportional representation for a four-year term. The most recent elections to it were held on 24 November 2002. In the current Nationalrat there are four parliamentary groups, or 'Klubs' (number of seats in brackets): the **Austrian People's Party** (79), the **Social Democratic Party of Austria** (69), the **Austrian Freedom Party** (18) and the **Green Party** (17). Of the 183 current members of the Nationalrat, 62 (33.9%) are **women**.

The Nationalrat shares the legislative role at national level with the **Bundesrat**, but the Nationalrat has sole responsibility for holding the government to account. The Nationalrat may be dissolved early by itself or by the Federal President upon a proposal by the federal government.

Address: Parliament, Dr Karl Renner-Ring 1–3, 1017 Vienna, Austria
Tel: (0)1-401-100
Fax: (0)1-401-103-803
E-mail: services@parlinkom.gv.at
Internet: www.parlinkom.gv.at

Nationalrat (Switzerland)

National Council

The Nationalrat (National Council) is the lower house of the United Federal Assembly, the bicameral parliament of Switzerland. It is made up of 200 members who are directly elected by a system of proportional representation for a four-year term. The most recent elections to it were held on 19 October 2003. In the current Nationalrat there are five main parliamentary groups (number of seats in brackets): the **Swiss People's Party** (55), the **Social Democratic Party of Switzerland** (52), the **Radical Free Democratic Party** (36), the **Christian Democratic Party** (28) and the **Green Party** (13). Of the 200 current members of the Nationalrat, 50 (25%) are **women**. The Nationalrat shares a legislative role at national level with the **Ständerat**.

Address: Nationalrat, Parlamentsgebäude, 3003 Bern, Switzerland
Tel: (0)31-322-21-11 or (0)31-322-53-74
Fax: (0)31-322-37-06
E-mail: allgemeine.dienste@pd.admin.ch
Internet: www.parlament.ch

National Union of Independent Trade Unions

The National Union of Independent Trade Unions, or Union Nationale des Syndicats Autonomes, is a new trade union federation in France. Founded in 1993, it represents around 360,000 members from a broad range of professions. It campaigns for social progress, tackles social exclusion and protects public-sector employment through the means of social dialogue.

Sec.-Gen.: Alain Olive
Address: 21 rue Jules Ferry, 93177 Bagnolet Cedex, France

Tel: (0)1-48-18-88-57
Fax: (0)1-48-18-88-99
E-mail: unsa@unsa.org
Internet: www.unsa.org

Nea Demokratia – *see* New Democracy, Greece

Netherlands

The Netherlands is a small state on the north coast of mainland Western Europe, bordering Germany to the east and Belgium to the west. After occupation by Nazi Germany in 1940–45 the state abandoned its traditionally neutral political stance in favour of international co-operation with Western alliances. A founder member of the **European Coal and Steel Community**, the Netherlands is one of the strongest advocates of European integration, but has also adopted an Atlanticist stance as a member of the **North Atlantic Treaty Organization**.

Dutch society and politics are characterized as 'pillarized'—*verzuiling* in Dutch. The population is divided into four distinct pillars or subcultures—Roman Catholic, orthodox Calvinist, Socialist and neutral/liberal—and each has its own closed organizational network. Yet, despite these strong cultural divisions, Dutch democracy is based on a stable culture of consensus and mutual tolerance in social and political issues. National government and the state bureaucracy bring together élites from each pillar to barter consensual agreements acceptable to all four blocs. Under this consensual model government opposition tends to be pacified and accommodated, rather than excluded. Social and political consensus has extended into many issues, including **immigration**. Traditionally an open country, the Netherlands accepted 10% of those seeking asylum in the **European Union (EU)** in 2000 although the Dutch population at that time represented only 4% of the total population of the EU. However, in recent years the Dutch consensus on issues such as immigration has appeared to be breaking down.

Area: 42,000 sq km; *capital:* Amsterdam; *population:* 16m. (2001).

A constitutional monarchy, the head of state is Queen Beatrix who acceded to the throne in 1980. Legislative power is divided between two houses of parliament: the **Eerste Kamer** and the **Tweede Kamer**. Elections to the Tweede Kamer are governed by a system of pure proportional representation. It can take many months to form a coalition government following elections. The most recent elections were held on 22 January 2003 and they resulted in the formation of a coalition between the **Christian Democratic Appeal (CDA)**, the free-market **People's Party for Freedom and Democracy (VVD)** and the social liberal **Democrats 66 (D66)**. The coalition is headed by CDA Prime Minister **Jan Peter Balkenende**.

Christian democratic parties dominated Dutch politics in the 20th century. The CDA or its three founding parties participated in all coalition governments in

1917–94. In the 1994 elections the CDA suffered heavy losses and was for the first time in its history excluded from government. The **Labour Party (PvdA)**, which also lost votes in the 1994 election, was able to form the so-called 'purple coalition' with the liberal parties VVD and D66 under the leadership of Wim Kok. The secular coalition was re-elected in 1998 and governed until the elections held on 15 May 2002. Wim Kok's 'purple coalition' resigned shortly before the May 2002 elections when it was revealed that Dutch troops had failed to prevent the massacre of more than 7,000 Muslim men and boys in the **United Nations** 'safe area' in Srebreniča, Bosnia, in 1995.

The stable consensus of Dutch politics was disrupted in 2002 by the anti-immigration, populist politician **Pim Fortuyn**. In local elections in Rotterdam held on 6 March 2002 the party list that Fortuyn headed won 35% of the vote, thereby relegating the PvdA, which had governed there for some 40 years, into second place. The general election of 15 May 2002 took place nine days after Pim Fortuyn had been assassinated by an animal rights activist. Without its founder the **List Pim Fortuyn (LPF)** none the less won 17% of the vote and 26 seats in the 150-seat Tweede Kamer, obtaining the status of second largest party. The LPF subsequently entered into a coalition with the CDA, which re-emerged as the strongest party with 27.9% of the vote, and the VVD. However, the coalition formed in July 2002 collapsed in October when two LPF ministers resigned.

The success of the political movement founded by Pim Fortuyn is indicative of the Dutch population's dissatisfaction with certain aspects of consensus democracy. By addressing the immigration issue, Fortuyn sought to break a taboo of established politics which traditionally attempted to accommodate difference rather than high-light it as a social problem. Although the LPF will not have enduring appeal, its contribution to Dutch politics could be that it marked the definitive end of the peaceful coexistence of the Dutch pillars managed by the political élite—a process referred to since the 1960s as depillarization or, in Dutch, *ontzuiling*.

Economy: The Dutch economy is open and outward-looking. A nation of merchants, the Netherlands is the location of the world's largest port (Rotterdam) and a large number of Dutch-based multinational companies, such as Philips. Dutch economic strength traditionally lies in services rather than manufacturing and the service economy accounts for around two-thirds of gross domestic product (GDP); particular strengths are in banking and finance. The Dutch economy is supported by a large number of small businesses involved in food processing, petrochemicals, engineering and software. It is also one of the world's largest exporters of flowers. The Netherlands was a founder member of what is now the **European Union (EU)** and of the **euro**. Prior to **Economic and Monetary Union**, the Dutch guilder had been linked to the German Deutsche Mark.

GNP: US $390,300m. (2001); *GNP per caput:* $35,630 (2001); *GNP at PPP:* $132,000m. (2001); *GNP per caput at PPP:* $29,340 (2001); *GDP:* $380,137m. (2001); *exports:* $255,875m. (2001); *imports:* $237,984m. (2001); *currency:* euro; *unemployment:* 2.7% (2002).

Economic and social policy-making in the Netherlands is traditionally based on the principle of consensus and in the post-1945 era the Dutch economy has been strongly regulated by social partners. A system of corporatist economic policy-making was founded in 1950 with the establishment of the Social and Economic Council (Sociaal-Economische Raad—SER). The SER consists of 45 members: 15 trade union representatives, 15 members of employers' organizations and 15 independent experts appointed by the cabinet. Two *ex officio* members of the council are the governor of **Dutch Central Bank** and the director of the independent Central Planning Bureau. According to the Industrial Organization Act of 1950, the SER must be consulted by the government on all significant economic and social policy questions. The government is not obliged to follow its recommendations, but if there is consensus among the members of the SER, its recommendations tend to be accepted. In addition, trade union and employers' organizations consult via the Foundation for Labour (Stichting van de Arbeid) founded in 1945.

The Netherlands corporatist economy developed a wide-ranging system of protection in the labour market and through the provisions of the **welfare state**. Workers were offered strong protection against redundancy and the social security system offered generous benefits for the unemployed, retired and sick. Typically for corporatist economic systems, **unemployment** was avoided by prioritizing core male workers and encouraging the young, old and **women** to exit the labour market. The employment rate as a proportion of the total working-age population was only 52% in 1982, compared with nearly 74% today.

Following the recessions of the 1970s the economy could no longer sustain its generous welfare state and the budget deficit rose to more than 7% of GDP by 1982. The so-called 'Dutch disease'—welfare without work—was addressed with a consensus formula agreed by social partners. In 1982, under the Wassenaar agreement, trade unions agreed to pay restraint and more decentralized wage-bargaining in exchange for an emphasis on job creation. The government undertook to reduce taxes to increase purchasing power. This new consensual approach, which came to be referred to as the Polder Model, led to an economic revival for two consecutive decades. Most significantly, the Polder Model led to above-average economic growth compared with other EU countries—an annual average of 3%. This was matched by low inflation and a reduction of the budget deficit. Unemployment fell from 11% in 1983 to less than 2% in 2002. There was a rapid influx of women into the labour market and much new employment was part time and in the service sector. Part-time work now accounts for one-third of total employment. At the same time, public spending was cut and the power of the social partners to manage social security was reduced. The SER plays an ever decreasing role in the Polder Model.

After nearly two decades of healthy performance, the Polder Model appears to be faltering: economic growth has slowed and inflation and unemployment are rising. While some attribute this to the general deceleration of the global economy, into which the Netherlands is well integrated, others interpret it as evidence that the Polder Model has reached its limits and needs to be further liberalized. Regular criticism is directed towards the still generous level of welfare provision and high levels of welfare dependency. According to some figures, nine people receive benefit for every 10 who are working and although life expectancy in the Netherlands is high—76 years and 81 years, respectively, for men and women—almost 1m. people in a total working-age population of 7m. qualify for the generous disability scheme—the WAO—which has been used as a way of removing surplus labour.

New Democracy

The New Democracy, or Nea Demokratia (ND), is one of the two main political parties in Greece. Founded in 1974 following the military dictatorship (1967–74), ND is a progressive conservative party which campaigns to promote the Greek nation. It is an advocate of the free market but also favours state intervention in the economy to promote social justice. It seeks to preserve the independence and sovereignty of democratic Greece, but is also an advocate of promoting Greece's position in Europe. In the first free elections following the dictatorship, held in November 1974, ND won a landslide victory, obtaining 54.37% of the vote. It was re-elected in 1977 and governed until 1981. ND returned to power as the strongest member of a coalition government in 1989, and one year later it secured a majority government in new elections. This government lasted until 1993. In the national elections to the **Vouli ton Ellinon**, held on 7 March 2004, the party won 45.37% of the vote and 165 seats in the 300-seat parliament. It subsequently formed a government, with **Konstantinos Karamanlis** as Prime Minister.

Pres.: Kostas Karamanlis
Address: Rigillis St 18, Athens, Greece
Tel: (0)210 72900719
Fax: (0)210 7236017
E-mail: ir@nd.gr
Internet: www.nd.gr

New Flemish Alliance

The New Flemish Alliance, or Nieuw-Vlaamse Alliantie (N-VA), is a democratic nationalist party in Flanders, Belgium. Founded in 2001 following the split of the People's Union (Volksunie) party, it campaigns for an independent state of Flanders. In the national elections held on 18 May 2003 N-VA won 3.1% of the vote and one seat in the 150-seat **Kamer**.

Party Leader: Bart De Wever
Address: Barrikadenplein 12, 1000 Brussels, Belgium
Tel: (0)2 219-49-30
Fax: (0)2 217-35-10
E-mail: info@n-va.be
Internet: www.n-va.be

Nice Treaty – *see* Treaty of Nice

Nieuw-Vlaamse Alliantie – *see* New Flemish Alliance, Belgium

Nokia

The Finnish company Nokia is the largest manufacturer of mobile phones in the world, having overtaken the US company Motorola in 1998. Founded in 1865, Nokia originally specialized in the manufacture of paper products and rubber boots. Until the 1990s Nokia's markets were mainly in Europe, especially the Nordic countries, and the Soviet Union (USSR). In the late 1970s Nokia bought some of Finland's numerous telephone companies and manufactured its first mobile phone in 1982. In the early 1990s, following the collapse of the USSR and the deep recession in the Finnish economy, the head of the company's mobile phone division, Jorma Ollila, became CEO. He focused Nokia's strategy on the production of mobile phones and on reaching new markets in North and South America and the Asia-Pacific region. The company now sells its products in 140 countries, has 16 manufacturing facilities in nine countries, and research and development (R&D) centres in 11. The company spends US $3,500m. annually on R&D and the development of new products. Nokia played a major role in the recovery of the Finnish economy in the 1990s. The company accounts for almost one-quarter of Finland's total exports and for around 10% of its gross domestic product.

Chair. and CEO: Jorma Ollila
Address: Nokia Head Office, Keilalahdentie 2–4, 02150 Espoo, Finland, or POB
    226, 00045 Nokia Group, Finland
Tel: (0)7180 08000
Fax: (0)7180 38226
Internet: www.nokia.com

Norges Bank

Norges Bank, the central bank in Norway, was founded in 1816. It works to promote a monetary policy that ensures price and financial stability. It manages the issue and circulation of coins and banknotes, and is also responsible for the operational management of the government's Petroleum Fund, which provides a buffer against fluctuating revenues in the petroleum sector.

Gov.: Svein Gjedrem
Address: Bankplassen 2, POB 1179, Sentrum, 0107 Oslo, Norway
Tel: (0)22-31-6000
Fax: (0)22-41-31-05
E-mail: central.bank@norges-bank.no
Internet: www.norges-bank.no

North Atlantic Treaty Organization (NATO)

The North Atlantic Treaty Organization (NATO) is an alliance of 26 countries that are committed to protecting, by political and military means, the freedom, common heritage and civilizations of its members' liberal democracies. NATO was founded by the North Atlantic Treaty, signed in Washington, DC, USA on 4 April 1949. This document committed NATO's 12 founder states (marked * below) to defend the NATO territory collectively. Article 5 of the treaty stated that 'an armed attack against one or more of [NATO's members] in Europe or North America shall be considered an attack against them all'. This meant that Western Europe could draw on the military power of the USA in the event of its countries being attacked.

NATO was founded shortly after the Soviet Union's (USSR) blockade of the city of Berlin in 1948. The establishment of NATO was the West's response to the perceived military threat of the USSR at the start of the **Cold War**. However, alternative assessments have proposed that the likelihood of a Soviet attack was exaggerated, and that NATO's key objective was in fact a political one: to mobilize popular resistance to communism in Western Europe. During the Cold War NATO developed its military capability to match that of the USSR. Its membership was also expanded to include Greece and **Turkey** (1952), West Germany (1955) and Spain (1982). Following the end of the Cold War, four states of the Warsaw Pact, the Soviet Bloc's military alliance, joined NATO. The **German Democratic Republic** became part of NATO through unification with the Federal Republic of Germany in 1990 and the Czech Republic, Poland and Hungary joined in 1999. Seven other **Central and Eastern European Countries** became members in 2004.

Since the end of the Cold War NATO has been involved in a number of military conflicts. Significantly, NATO intervened with air strikes against Serb targets in **Kosovo** in 1999 in order to prevent the massacre of ethnic Albanians. This was the first time that NATO had intervened in a civil conflict, a move that was not sanctioned by international law. NATO felt that its intervention to prevent humanitarian tragedy was morally justified. Following the terrorist attacks in the USA on **11 September** 2001, NATO for the first time invoked Article 5 of the North Atlantic Treaty, maintaining that the attack on the USA was an attack on the whole alliance.

Membership: Belgium*, Bulgaria, Canada*, Czech Republic, Denmark*, Estonia, France*, Germany, Greece, Hungary, Iceland*, Italy*, Latvia, Lithuania, Luxembourg*, Netherlands*, Norway*, Poland, Portugal*, Romania, Slovakia, Slovenia, Spain, Turkey, United Kingdom*, USA*.

Sec.-Gen.: Jaap de Hoop Scheffer
Address: NATO Headquarters, blvd Leopold III, 1110 Brussels, Belgium
Tel: (0)2707-41-11
Fax: (0)2 707-41-17
E-mail: natodoc@hq.nato.int
Internet: www.nato.int

Northern Ireland

Northern Ireland is a province which forms part of the United Kingdom. It was formed when Ireland was divided in 1921: six counties of Ireland formed Northern Ireland, and the rest formed the Republic of Ireland in 1922. Ireland had been part of the United Kingdom since 1800 through the Act of Union and this Act was amended to the United Kingdom of Great Britain and Northern Ireland Act in 1927.

Since the division of Ireland there has been deep and often violent conflict among the 1.68m. population (2001) of Northern Ireland which is characterized by competing ethnic and religious identities. Northern Ireland is divided between the Protestant Unionists, who wish to remain part of the United Kingdom, and the Catholic nationalists who regard Ireland as a single state. The Unionists make up the majority of the population—about two-thirds—and are represented politically by the **Ulster Unionist Party (UUP)**, the **Democratic Unionist Party (DUP)**, and also the United Kingdom Unionist Party and the Progressive Unionist Party. Nationalists form a sizeable minority and their interests are represented in the **Social Democratic and Labour Party (SDLP)** and **Sinn Féin**. The Irish Republican party Sinn Féin's objective is to end British rule in Ireland and to achieve national self-determination and the unity and independence of Ireland as a sovereign state. Sinn Féin has been often referred to as the political wing of the terrorist group the Irish Republican Army (IRA).

Conflict in Northern Ireland arose from the domination of the Unionist majority in the political, economic and legal spheres. In response to concerns about discrimination against the Catholic minority, the Northern Ireland Civil Rights Association was established in 1967. Sectarian fighting in the summer of 1969 led the British Government to deploy troops in the province to restore order. These troops were initially welcomed by the Catholic population, but the relationship subsequently deteriorated. The IRA was revived and some Nationalists began to use force to remove the British presence from Ireland. Unionist-dominated rule in Northern Ireland was ended by the imposition of direct rule from Westminster in 1972. What followed were 25 years of conflict interspersed with a number of unsuccessful attempts at resolution. Between 1973 and 1985 there were six attempts to secure a political solution to the conflicts in Northern Ireland. These began with the Sunningdale Agreement in 1973 and continued until the Anglo-Irish Agreement of 1985. All of these initiatives failed because Unionists would not accept any proposal that contained an all-Ireland dimension, and Nationalists would not support any set of arrangements into which the Irish Government had little input.

A seventh attempt to secure peace was made in the 1990s and a successful conclusion was reached in 1998 in the form of the **Good Friday Agreement**. This led to the re-establishment of a Northern Ireland Assembly and devolved government in 1999, and the establishment of a north-south ministerial council, a British-Irish council and a British-Irish intergovernmental conference. In addition to these formal institutions, other measures were introduced to address the concerns of each party: Unionists were offered the repeal of the Republic of Ireland's constitutional claim to Northern Ireland; Nationalists were offered a new commission on policing, which led to the reform of the Royal Ulster Constabulary and its replacement by the Police Service of Northern Ireland in November 2001 and a human rights commission.

The first elections to the 108-seat Northern Ireland Assembly were held in September 1998. The UUP won the largest share of the vote and 28 seats. The SDLP won 24 seats and Sinn Féin 18. David Trimble was nominated as First Minister and a power-sharing government was formed on 1 December 1999 with the help of US senator George Mitchell, who had chaired the Good Friday talks. Devolved government to Northern Ireland has not proved durable. The Assembly was suspended on 11 February 2000 because of the failure of the IRA to prove that it had made progress in decommissioning of weapons. It was restored on 29 May 2000, but suspended again on 14 October 2002. Since then attempts have been made to elect a new executive. Elections to the Assembly were held on 26 November 2003, but it proved impossible to create a power-sharing government as the two largest parties elected—the DUP and Sinn Féin—are not prepared to work together.

The economy of Northern Ireland has traditionally been dominated by textile and shipbuilding industries. These experienced a decline from the 1970s, but Northern Ireland's economy revived in the 1990s and was, with the help of large subsidies from the UK government (£3,340m. in 1995/96), the fastest growing region of the United Kingdom. In hi-tech manufacturing the province outperforms the mainland United Kingdom, and a large service sector, which accounts for 70% of gross domestic product (GDP), has also developed. The rate of **unemployment** fell from 16.8% in 1986 to 5.7% in 2002. While GDP growth is above the UK average, per caput GDP in Northern Ireland remains below the average for the whole of the United Kingdom. The improving economic situation has been attributed to the growth of inward investment encouraged by a more stable political situation, and the boom in the Republic of Ireland, Northern Ireland's largest export market.

Northern League

The Northern League, or Lega Nord, is a regionalist party in Italy. Founded in 1991 as an alliance of smaller regionalist movements, it campaigns for devolution of powers to the Northern Italian regions, which it refers to collectively as Padania.

In the general elections held on 27 March 1994 Lega Nord formed the Freedom Alliance (Polo della Libertà) with **Forza Italia**. This alliance, together with the Good Governance Alliance (Polo del Buon Governo), achieved a landslide victory and won an absolute majority of seats in the **Camera dei Deputati**. The Forza Italia-led coalition under Prime Minister **Silvio Berlusconi** collapsed in December 1994 when the Lega Nord deserted it. Lega Nord contested the general election held on 21 April 1996 alone, and the election was won by the left-wing Olive Tree Alliance. For the general elections held on 13 May 2001 Lega Nord joined the

House of Freedoms Coalition (Casa delle Libertà) which included Forza Italia, the **National Alliance**, the Christian Democratic Centre and United Christian Democrats, and the New Italian Socialist Party. The Lega Nord won 30 seats in the 630-seat parliament, and became part of the House of Freedoms Coalition headed by Silvio Berlusconi.

Pres.: Umberto Bossi
Address: Via Bellerio, 41 20161 Milan, Italy
Tel: (0)02 66234236
Fax: (0)02 66234402
E-mail: segreteria.federale@leganord.org
Internet: www.leganord.org

Norway

Norway, which is located in Scandinavia, to the west of Sweden, has been an independent state since 1905 (though it was occupied by Nazi Germany in 1941–45) following a 400-year union with Denmark and a century-long union with Sweden. Norway is an enthusiastic member of the **North Atlantic Treaty Organization** and provides more **United Nations** peace-keepers relative to its population size than any other country. However, Norway has twice (in 1972 and 1994) voted against joining the **European Union (EU)**. In 1972, in the first referendum, 53.5% (turn-out 79%) of voters rejected membership, and in 1994 the no vote was 52.2% (turn-out 88.8%).

Area: 324,000 sq km; *capital:* Oslo; *population:* 5m. (2001).

Opposition to EU membership derives predominantly from the perceived impact of membership on the Norwegian state capitalist economic system. Politically, Norwegians are reluctant to relinquish independence and sovereignty to the EU. At the time of the referendum held in 1994 the main political parties—the **Labour Party** and the **Conservative Party**—as well as the low-taxation party, the **Liberals**, favoured membership. The **Centre Party**, which traditionally represents farmers and fishermen, was the party most strongly opposed to membership. The **Christian People's Party**, which is supported by rural voters, and the **Socialist Left Party** also opposed EU membership. The issue of EU membership remains on the political agenda and, since the most recent referendum, some opinion polls have indicated that a majority of Norwegians in favour of membership is developing.

A constitutional monarchy, Norway's head of state is King Harald V who has reigned since 1991. Legislative power is vested with the **Storting** for which elections are held at fixed four-year intervals. The minority indigenous Sami population, a community of some 45,000 in the Arctic north, has it own 39-member assembly and some powers of self-government. The most recent elections to the Storting were held on 10 September 2001, following which a minority coalition government was formed between the Conservative Party and the Liberals with **Kjell Magne Bondevik** as Prime Minister. This is the second government led by

Conservative Bondevik and it marks a significant shift to the right in Norwegian politics. The government relies on the support of the extreme right-wing **Progress Party**.

Norwegian politics have traditionally been dominated by the Labour Party in the last 75 years. The Labour Party governed continuously (except for three weeks) as majority governments in 1945–65 and as minority governments in 1973–81 following the referendum on membership of the **European Community** in 1972, over which the left-wing vote in Norway split. Non-socialist or 'bourgeois' centre-right coalitions governed in 1965–72 and 1981–86. Labour returned to power, with Gro Brundtland as Prime Minister, for a first term in 1986–89, and then again in 1990–93 after the collapse of Jan P. Syse's government, elected in 1989, which fell after one year in power. The Labour Party was re-elected on 13 September 1993 and remained in power until 1997, when it was voted out of office, having governed as a minority for 10 of the previous 11 years, and despite the fact that it had presided over a period of strong economic growth. The party's electoral performance in 2001 was its worst in 90 years.

The 1994 election was dominated by the issue of Norway's membership of the EU, and there was a rapid rise in support for the anti-EU Centre Party which won 21 seats. In the elections held on 10 September 2001 there was a rise in support for the extreme right-wing, anti-**immigration** Progress Party. It won 26 seats in the 165-seat parliament, thereby becoming the third largest party. Although not part of the Conservative-Liberal coalition, the influence of the Progress Party is strong as the minority government relies on its support for parliamentary majorities. Support for the party increased after the election.

Economy: The Norwegian economy is dominated by its natural resources. Originally reliant on the fishing industry, in the late 1960s Norway discovered rich oil and gas reserves in the North Sea and it is now one of the world's largest exporters of fuel and fuel products. More than one-half of Norway's exports derive from this sector. It is, after Saudi Arabia, the world's second largest exporter of oil. High revenues from oil have guaranteed Norwegians the world's third highest standard of living in terms of income per person. In the mid-1990s, in order to control inflation, the Labour Party established a Petroleum Fund, a huge state savings account funded from surplus North Sea oil revenues. The money, which is being saved to meet spending commitments in the years when the oil reserves become exhausted, is now worth almost US $90,000m. (2002), equivalent to $20,000 per Norwegian citizen. The state is increasingly under political pressure to use these reserves to fund investment in public services or tax cuts.

GNP: US $160,800m. (2001); *GNP per caput:* $35,630 (2001); *GNP at PPP:* $132,000m. (2001); *GNP per caput at PPP:* $29,340 (2001); *GDP:* $166,145m. (2001); *exports:* $77,657m. (2001); *imports:* $49,073m. (2001); *currency:* krone; *unemployment:* 3.9% (2002).

The Norwegian economic system is often referred to as 'state capitalism' as the state dominates the oil industry, and most other economic sectors. At the start of the

21st century the Norwegian public sector still controlled 35% of industrial production. The country has a far-reaching social-democratic **welfare state** and a large public sector: one in three Norwegians works in the public sector. The social democratic welfare state developed a substantial provision of welfare benefits and services for children, parents and the elderly. It has the third highest employment rate and one of the lowest **unemployment** rates within the **Organisation for Economic Co-operation and Development**.

There has been no strong discussion in Norway about the privatization of state-owned resources. The economy is administered on a consensus basis, there is little private capital available and strong resistance to allowing foreign capital to take over Norwegian firms. Moreover, the state-managed economy ensures adequate subsidies to the rural regions in the fjords and Arctic north. The reluctance to privatize nationalized industries drives the widespread opposition to membership of the **European Union (EU)**. Norway is reluctant to share natural resources such as fish, to cut government subsidies or open state-run forms to competition. Norway gains the benefits of the EU free-market through its membership of the **European Economic Area**, and it has signed the **Schengen Agreement** which allows for open borders.

Norwegian Confederation of Trade Unions

The Norwegian Confederation of Trade Unions, or Landsorganisasjonen i Norge (LO), is the main trade union confederation in Norway. Founded in 1899, the LO today has more than 800,000 members organized in 25 affiliated national unions. It is itself a member of **ETUC**. A social partner in economic and social policy-making, LO lobbies nationally and internationally to combat **unemployment**, to improve conditions of pay and work, promote social security and equality and for international solidarity and co-operation. LO has close links with the Norwegian **Labour Party**, but is politically independent.

Pres.: Gerd-Liv Valle
Address: Youngs gate 11, 0181 Oslo, Norway
Tel: (0)23-06-10-50
Fax: (0)23-06-17-43
E-mail: lo@lo.no
Internet: www.lo.no

Nuder, Pär

Pär Nuder has been Minister of Finance in Sweden since 2004. A member of the **Social Democratic Party (SAP)**, he was Minister for Policy Co-ordination in 2002–04 and State Secretary in the Office of the Prime Minister in 1997–2002. Nuder has been a member of the **Riksdag** for the SAP since 1994 and served as political secretary to the SAP parliamentary group in 1992–94. Born on 27 February 1963 in Täby, he holds a bachelor's degree in law and is married with two daughters.

Address: Ministry of Finance, Drottinggatan 21, 103 33 Stockholm, Sweden
Tel: (0)8 405-10-00
Fax: (0)8 21-73-86
E-mail: registrator@finance.ministry.se
Internet: www.finans.regeringen.se

O

Onofhängege Gewerkschaftsbond Lëtzebuerg – *see* **Luxembourg Confederation of Free Trade Unions**

Organisation for Economic Co-operation and Development (OECD)

The Organisation for Economic Co-operation and Development (OECD) is an organization that produces data and analysis in order to develop economic and social policy. Originally founded as the Organisation for European Economic Co-operation in 1948 to manage the funds provided by the **Marshall Plan**, it became the OECD in 1961.

Today the OECD has 30 members, all of which are committed to democratic government and the market economy. The OECD develops policies to achieve sustainable economic growth and improvements in standards of living. Key areas include good governance, multilateral trade, education and environmental protection. The OECD also has relations with 70 other states and many non-governmental organizations. It seeks to assist economic expansion in developing countries. However, unlike the **World Bank** or the **International Monetary Fund**, it does not dispense funds.

> *Membership:* Australia, Austria, Belgium, Canada, Czech Republic, Denmark, Finland, France, Germany, Greece, Hungary, Iceland, Ireland, Italy, **Japan**, Republic of Korea, Luxembourg, Mexico, Netherlands, New Zealand, Norway, Poland, Portugal, Slovak Republic, Spain, Sweden, Switzerland, **Turkey**, United Kingdom and USA.

Sec.-Gen.: Donald J. Johnston
Address: 2, rue André Pascal, 75775 Paris Cedex 16, France
Tel: (0)1-45-24-82-00
Fax: (0)1-45-24-85-00
E-mail: webmaster@oecd.org
Internet: www.oecd.org

Österreichische Volkspartei – *see* Austrian People's Party

Österreichischer Gewerkschaftsbund – *see* Austrian Trade Union Federation

Österreichischer National Bank

The Österreichischer National Bank, the central bank of Austria, was originally founded in 1922. Its activities and assets were taken over by the German Reich in 1938 and the bank resumed its activities in 1945. The National Bank Act of 1955 was amended in 1984, and again in 1998, to prepare Austria for membership of **Economic and Monetary Union (EMU)**. Since the start of stage three of EMU, on 1 January 1999, the Österreichischer National Bank has been a member of the **European System of Central Banks** and, as a member of the **euro area**, of the **Eurosystem**. It implements the decisions of the **European Central Bank** in Austria.

Gov.: Klaus Liebscher
Address: Otto-Wagner-Platz 3, 1090 Vienna, or POB 61, 1011 Vienna, Austria
Tel: (0)1-404-20
Fax: (0)1-404-20-2399
E-mail: oenb.info@oenb.co.at
Internet: www.oenb.at

P

Panellino Socialistiko Kinima – *see* Panhellenic Socialist Movement, Greece

Panhellenic Socialist Movement

The Panhellenic Socialist Movement, or Panellino Socialistiko Kinima (PASOK), is one of the two main political parties in Greece. PASOK was founded in 1974, following the military dictatorship of 1967–74, to promote national independence, popular domination, social emancipation and democratic procedures. Today it describes itself as an open socialist, patriotic and democratic movement which campaigns for the universal values of freedom, democracy, peace and solidarity.

In the first free elections after the end of the dictatorship, held in November 1974, PASOK won 13.5% of the vote and 15 parliamentary seats, thereby becoming the third largest party after **New Democracy (ND)** and the liberals. It became the official opposition in the 1977 elections and won 48% of the vote and 173 parliamentary seats in 1981, when it formed the first socialist government in Greece. PASOK governed in 1981–90, and again in 1993–2004. In the national elections to the **Vouli ton Ellinon**, held on 7 March 2004, the party obtained 40.55% of the vote and 117 seats in the 300-seat parliament. It became the main opposition party to the ND government.

Pres.: George Papandreou
Address: Charilaou Trikoupi, Athens 106 80, Greece
Tel: (0)210 3644148 or (0)210 3609636
Fax: (0)210 3603879
E-mail: pasok@pasok.gr
Internet: www.pasok.gr/en

Partei des Demokratischen Sozialismus – *see* Party of Democratic Socialism, Germany

Parti Communiste – *see* **Communist Party, France**

Parti Socialiste – *see* **Socialist Party, Belgium**

Parti Socialiste – *see* **Socialist Party, France**

Partido Comunista Português – *see* **Communist Party, Portugal**

Partido Ecologista 'Os Verdes' – *see* **Green Party, Portugal**

Partido Popular – *see* **Popular Party, Portugal**

Partido Popular – *see* **Popular Party, Spain**

Partido Social Democrata – *see* **Social Democratic Party, Portugal**

Partido Socialista – *see* **Socialist Party, Portugal**

Partido Socialista Obrero Español – *see* **Spanish Socialist Party, Spain**

Partij van de Arbeid – *see* **Labour Party, Netherlands**

Party of Democratic Socialism

The Party of Democratic Socialism, or Partei des Demokratischen Sozialismus (PDS), is a socialist party in Germany. It is the successor party of the ruling Socialist Unity Party (Sozialistische Einheitspartei Deutschlands—SED) of the **German Democratic Republic (GDR)**. The PDS was established in December 1989 following the fall of the **Berlin Wall** and the collapse of the socialist regime in the GDR. Instead of dissolving the SED, it was decided to transform the party and to distance it from the SED dictatorship. The PDS is a democratic socialist party which promotes freedom, peace, equality, justice and solidarity. The party is an anti-capitalist party and seeks to strengthen the **welfare state** and the democratic process in Germany. Its electoral successes have been almost solely in the eastern part of Germany and it is often considered to be a regional party. The party governs in two coalitions at regional (*Land*) level (Berlin and Mecklenburg-Vorpommern).

In elections held in March 1990 to the People's Chamber in the GDR the PDS won 16.4% of the vote. In the first all-German **Bundestag** elections, held in December 1990, its share of the vote was 11.1% in the east and the party won 17 seats. In that election the PDS performed well because the 5% hurdle (i.e. the minimum share of the vote a party must win in order to obtain representation) was applied separately in the east and west. It was widely anticipated that the PDS would disappear from the political scene as soon as a single 5% hurdle was applied. Indeed, in 1994 the PDS won only 4.4% of the vote, but it won four constituency seats and because of this was awarded its allocation of seats in the Bundestag. In the elections held in 1998 the PDS won 5.1% of the vote and was able to form a parliamentary party for the first time. In the most recent elections, held on 22 September 2002, the party won 4% of the vote and with only two (not the required three) constituency seats it was not permitted to convert its allocation of votes into seats.

Party Leader: Lothar Bisky
Address: Kleine Alexanderstrasse 28, 10178 Berlin, Germany
Tel: (0)30 240000
Fax: (0)30 2411046
E-mail: parteivorstand@pds-online.de
Internet: www.sozialisten.de

Pedersen, Thor

Thor Pedersen has been Minister of Finance in Denmark since 2001. A member of the **Liberal Party**, he stands for low taxation and the free market. Pedersen has been a member of the **Folketing** since 1985. He served as Minister for Housing in 1986–89, Minister of the Interior in 1987–88 and Minister of the Interior and Economy in 1992–93. Prior to that, he was member of the Helsingør local council in 1974–86, and the town's mayor in 1978–86.

Born on 14 June 1945 in Gentofte, Pedersen studied politics at Copenhagen University. He was a sergeant in the Royal Lifeguards in 1964–66 and director of a private business in 1975–81 and 1994–2001.

Address: Ministry of Finance, Christiansborgs Slotsplads 1, 1218 Copenhagen K, Denmark
Tel: (0)33-92-33-33
Fax: (0)33-32-80-30
E-mail: fm@fm.dk
Internet: www.fm.dk

People's Party for Freedom and Democracy

The People's Party for Freedom and Democracy, or Volkspartij voor Vrijheid en Democratie (VVD), is the main liberal party in the Netherlands. Founded in 1948, it brought together three liberal political movements. The party is non-confessional and promotes the freedom of individuals, pluralism in society, and respect for human rights. It supports the decentralization of democratic participation and the social market economy.

The third party in Dutch politics, VVD was a coalition partner in 1977–81, 1982–86 and 1986–89. Following a collapse of the vote for the **Christian Democratic Appeal (CDA)** in 1994, VVD governed again in 1994–98 and 1998–2002 as the second party in the Netherlands in the so-called 'purple coalitions' between the Labour Party, VVD and **Democrats 66 (D66)**. These were the first coalition governments in which the Christian Democrats were not included since 1918. In the 2002 elections the Christian Democrats and VVD entered into a coalition with the CDA and the **List Pim Fortuyn** that lasted for only 87 days. In elections held on 22 January 2003 the party won 27 seats in the 150-seat **Tweede Kamer** and entered into a coalition with the CDA and D66.

Party Leader: Jan van Zanen
Address: Laan Copes van Cattenburch 52, 2585 GV The Hague, or POB 30836,
            2500 The Hague, Netherlands
Tel: (0)70 3613061
Fax: (0)70 3608276
E-mail: alg.sec@vvd.nl
Internet: www.vvd.nl

Persson, Göran

Göran Persson is the social democratic Prime Minister of Sweden. First elected in 1996, he began his third term of office in September 2002 as head of a **Social Democratic Party (SAP)** government that relies on the support of the **Left Party** and the **Green Party**. Persson campaigned in the election held on 15 September 2002 for the Swedish **welfare state** and generous funding for education. He also supports the **euro** and sponsored but lost the referendum held on 14 September 2003 on the issue (no 56%; turn-out 81%).

Persson first served as a member of the **Riksdag** in 1979–84 and, again, in 1991. He was Minister at the Ministry of Education in 1989–91 and Minister of Finance in 1994–96. He has been leader of the SAP since 1996.

Born on 29 January 1949 in Vingå, Persson studied at the University College of Örebro. Göran Persson has two daughters from a previous marriage.

Address: Rosenbad 4, 103 33 Stockholm, Sweden
Tel: (0)8 405-10-00
Fax: (0)8 24-64-19
E-mail: registrator@primeminister.ministry.se
Internet: www.sweden.gov.se

Perussuomalaiset – *see* **True Finns Party, Finland**

Pillar(s)

Pillar(s) in the context of European politics describes the structure of the **European Union (EU)**. The **Treaty on European Union** (1992) established the EU as three distinct pillars. The first pillar is the traditional area of activity of the **European Community**. This includes matters relating to the **Single European Market**, freedom of movement of goods, services, capital and people, **agriculture**, environment, competition and trade. It also includes **Economic and Monetary Union** and some aspects of **Justice and Home Affairs (JHA)**. Decision-making in the first pillar is subject to the community method of decision-making, meaning that the supranational institutions—the **European Commission**, the **European Parliament** and the **European Court of Justice**—play a full role in the process.

The second pillar is **Common Foreign and Security Policy**; the third, **Police and Judicial Co-operation in Criminal Matters**, formerly JHA. The second and third pillars concern matters and policy issues over which member states wish to retain sovereignty and decision-making is conducted on an intergovernmental basis via the **Council of the European Union** and the **European Council**.

In the context of the Netherlands the term pillar(s), or pillarization, is used to describe the manner in which Dutch society is divided into four distinct pillars or subcultures—Roman Catholic, orthodox Calvinist, Socialist and neutral/liberal—and each has its own closed organizational network.

Plaid Cymru

Plaid Cymru, or the Party of Wales, is a socialist party which campaigns for the full national status of **Wales** within the United Kingdom and the **European Union**. It aims to create an independent Wales, and promote equality between individuals, cultures and **languages** in that nation.

Established in 1925, Plaid Cymru won its first seat in the **House of Commons** in 1966. At present the party has four elected representatives in the House of Commons and 17 in the **Welsh Assembly**.

Party Leaders: Ieuan Wyn Jones and Elfyn Llwyn
Address: Ty Gwynfor, 18 Park Grove, Cardiff CF10 3BN, United Kingdom
Tel: (0)29 2064 6001
Fax: (0)29 2064 6001
E-mail: post@plaidcymru.org
Internet: www.plaidcymru.org

Police and Judicial Co-operation in Criminal Matters

Police and Judicial Co-operation in Criminal Matters is the third **pillar** of the **European Union**. Originally, the third pillar was **Justice and Home Affairs (JHA)**, established by the **Treaty on European Union**. With the **Treaty of Amsterdam** (1997) many aspects of JHA were transferred to the first **European Community** pillar. What remained were issues of policing and criminal justice.

Political Reformed Party

The Political Reformed Party, or Staatkundig Gereformeerde Partij (SGP), is a radical conservative Christian party in the Netherlands which has adopted a hardline position on issues of morality and ethics. Founded in 1918, the SGP has been represented in parliament since 1922. In elections held on 22 January 2003 the party won two seats in the 150-seat **Tweede Kamer**.

> *Party Chair.:* A. van Heteren
> *Address:* Laan van Meerdervoort 165, 2517 AZ The Hague, Netherlands
> *Tel:* (0)70 3029060
> *Fax:* (0)70 3655959
> *E-mail:* partijbureau@sgp.nl
> *Internet:* www.sgp.nl

Popular Movement

The Popular Movement, or Union pour un Mouvement Populaire (UMP), is a political alliance in France. It was founded as the Union for a Presidential Majority (Union pour une Majorité Presidentielle) shortly before elections to the **Assemblée Nationale** in May 2002. The merger was initiated to unify France's moderate right-wing parties as a means of rallying against the success of the extreme right-wing **National Front** candidate, **Jean-Marie Le Pen**, in the first round of the presidential elections in April 2002.

The UMP brought together the right-wing, neo-Gaullist **Rally for the Republic**, founded by **Jacques Chirac** in 1976, and the neo-liberal Démocratie Libérale which split from the **Union for French Democracy (UDF)** in 1998. The non-Gaullist right-wing UDF decided not to take part in the merger, but some centrist elements from the party switched to the UMP. In June 2002 the UMP won 357 seats in the 575-seat Assemblée Nationale and formed the government, with **Jean-Pierre Raffarin** as Prime Minister.

> *Leadership: Party Leader* Nicolas Sarkozy; *Gen. Sec.* Pierre Méhaignerie
> *Address:* 55 rue La Boétie, 75384 Paris Cedex 08, France
> *Tel:* (0)1-40-76-60-00
> *E-mail:* via www.u-m-p.org/site/Contactez.php
> *Internet:* www.u-m-p.org

Popular Party (Portugal)

The Popular Party, or Partido Popular (PP), is a populist-conservative party in Portugal. Founded in 1974 as Democratic and Social Centre, it is today the main party of the political right. PP has governed with both the **Socialist Party** and the centre-right **Social Democratic Party (PSD)**. In the elections to the **Assembléia da República** held on 20 February 2005 the PP won 7.3% of the vote and 12 seats in the 230-seat parliament.

Pres.: Paulo Portas
Address: Largo Adelino Amaro da Costa 5, 1149-063 Lisbon, Portugal
Tel: (0)21 8814720
Fax: (0)21 8879030
E-mail: cds_pp@estoterica.pt
Internet: www.cds.pt

Popular Party (Spain)

The Popular Party, or Partido Popular (PP), is the main liberal-conservative party in Spain (the right-wing Popular Alliance was refounded as the PP in the late 1980s). The PP was the main opposition party during the 1980s and 1990s, but governed as a minority administration in 1996–2000 under Prime Minister José María Aznar, relying on the support of two nationalist parties, **Convergence and Union** and the **Basque Nationalist Party**, for majorities in the **Congreso de los Diputados**. In the election held in March 2000 it won the highest number of votes obtained by any party in democratic Spain, and increased its number of seats in parliament from 156 to 183. It governed as a majority administration in 2000–04. In the most recent elections, held on 14 March 2004, the PP was voted out of office. It won 37.7% of the vote and has 148 seats in the 350-seat Congreso de los Diputados.

Leadership: Pres. Mariano Rajoy; *Sec.-Gen.* Ángel Acebes
Address: Calle Génova 13, 28004 Madrid, Spain
Tel: (0)91 5577300
Fax: (0)91 3192322
E-mail: atencion@pp.es
Internet: www.pp.es

Portugal

Portugal, situated on the Iberian Peninsula between Spain and the Atlantic Ocean, has been an independent state since 1640. The state was governed by a dictatorship in 1928–74 under António Salazar (1928–68) and Marcello Caetano (1968–74). Caetano was overthrown in 1974 in the 'carnations revolution' led by a group of professional soldiers. Following this left-wing revolution Portugal's democratic constitution came into force in 1976. The transitional phase was characterized by a left-wing political agenda of nationalization and social reform as well as the liberation of Portugal's colonies in Africa (Angola, Guinea-Bissau, Mozambique) and Asia (East Timor and Macao). Portugal subsequently underwent a gradual transition to stable democracy. The country joined the **European Community (EC)** in 1986 and has benefited politically and economically from membership. The two main political parties—the **Socialist Party (PS)** and the **Social Democratic Party (PSD)**—are both strong advocates of membership and have directed domestic policy since the early 1980s to meet the criteria for membership first of the EC and then of **Economic and Monetary Union (EMU)**.

Area: 92,000 sq km; *capital:* Lisbon; *population:* 10m. (2001).

According to its Constitution, Portugal is a democratic republic. The country is often referred to as a semi-presidential state: the head of state, directly elected every five years, exercises a direct influence on politics. The President can veto legislation and has the power to dismiss a government and dissolve parliament. The current President is the socialist **Jorge Sampaio** who was first elected in 1996. Legislative power lies with the **Assembléia da República** which is elected by a system of proportional representation every four years unless parliament is dissolved and early elections are called. This happened in December 2004 and new elections were held on February 2005. Executive power lies with the government, which since 2005 has been an PS single party majority government headed by **José Sócrates**. Portugal is a unitary and centralized state. The socialist government's proposal to establish eight regional authorities was rejected by the public in a government-sponsored referendum in November 1998. Some 63.3% of voters rejected regional devolution as a general issue and 64% rejected the proposal as a good idea for their own region. The turn-out was 48.3%. The proposal was supported by the PS and the **Communist Party of Portugal**, but opposed by the PSD and the **Popular Party (PP)**.

Portugal's first 10 years of parliamentary democracy were marked by unstable coalition and minority governments, of which there were no fewer than 16 in 1974–87. These included a government of the left in 1974–79 and a government of the centre-right, dominated by the PSD, in 1979–83. Under Prime Minister Mário Soares the PS led the 'Centre Bloc' coalition in 1983–85 and effected tough economic reforms recommended by the **International Monetary Fund**. The PS was punished for these policies in the general election of October 1985, which the PSD won. PSD Prime Minister Aníbal Cavaco Silva governed for one-and-a-half years, leading a minority government, and was re-elected in 1987 with an absolute majority. This followed a vote of censure in April 1987 and early elections in July of that year. The government of 1987–91 was the first to serve the full four-year term of office. Cavaco Silva, who governed until 1995, presided over reform of the economy and Portugal's **accession** to the EC in 1986, and sought to undo the post-revolution laws, such as employment laws and nationalization laws. He announced that he would not stand for re-election in 1995.

The PS won the elections held in 1995 and Prime Minister António Guterres led a minority government that relied on the Communists and the PP to pass legislation.

The government was re-elected in 1999 with exactly one-half of the seats in the Assembléia da República; its success was attributable to the political and economic policies it had pursued and to Portugal's qualification for entry into the first wave of EMU. Guterres resigned as Prime Minister and PS party leader in 2001 after his party's had performed poorly in local elections. New elections were called, 18 months early. In these, held on 17 March 2002, the PSD, led by **José Manuel Durão Barroso**, won 40.2% of the vote and 105 parliamentary seats, and subsequently formed a coalition government with the PP, which won 8.7% of the vote and 14 seats. As Prime Minister, Durão Barroso intended to cut taxes. However, in 2002 he was forced to raise them when it emerged that Portugal had breached the **Stability and Growth Pact** which obliged members of the **euro area** to maintain their budget deficit at less than 3% of gross domestic product (it was 3.9% in Portugal in 2001). Durão Barroso resigned as Prime Minister and leader of the PSD in 2004 following his appointment as President of the **European Commission**. The government of Pedro Santana Lopes was plagued by **unemployment** and other economic problems, and lasted for only five months. The PS won an overwhelming victory on 20 February 2005 on a promise to improve economic growth, reduce unemployment and transform Portugal into a technology-rich economy.

Economy: The Portuguese economy is traditionally dominated by **agriculture**, fishing and tourism in the south, and by textiles, shoes, ceramics and wine in the north. Apart from some large industrial companies, at the end of the 1970s most firms in the north—where three-quarters of industrial firms are located—employed fewer than 10 workers. Portugal has one-third of the world's cork trees and provides 55% of world's output. Portugal has benefited economically from membership of the **European Union (EU)**. In the 15 years to 2000 the gap in living standards between Portugal and the rest of the EU halved. Gross domestic product (GDP) per caput (at PPP) in 1986 was 53% of the EU average. By 2000 it had risen to 75%. However, regional disparities still exist: per caput GDP is 90% of the EU average in Lisbon, but only 50% in the Azores.

GNP: US \$109,300m. (2001); *GNP per caput:* \$10,900 (2001); *GNP at PPP:* \$178,000m. (2001); *GNP per caput at PPP:* \$17,710 (2001); *GDP:* \$109,803m. (2001); *exports:* \$51,419m. (2001); *imports:* \$58,275m. (2001); *currency:* euro; *unemployment:* 5.1% (2002).

Portugal has an open economy that is reliant on foreign trade, and has been a member of the **European Free Trade Association** since its foundation in 1974. Portugal was late to industrialize and its dictator António Salazar (1928–68) originally promoted the ideal of a rural economy and society. Industry and trade was encouraged from the 1950s onwards and industrial output increased throughout the 1960s at 14% per annum. In the same period there was mass emigration as some 2m. left the country. Following the revolution in 1974, the state took charge of one-quarter of the economy, and financial services, steel, shipbuilding and beer production were nationalized. The left-wing revolutionary regime developed a large public sector and **welfare state**. It offered generous subsidises to nationalized industries and strict laws to protect labour. Government spending increased significantly, not least because wages rose by 35% in 1975–76 . The Portuguese public sector remains large, with 708,000 workers, some 15% of the workforce, employed by the state. The government still spends more than 50% of the country's GDP.

Portugal experienced slow economic development for the first decade after the revolution and the economy suffered from a number of weaknesses. The country had relied on its colonies for cheap raw materials and revenue and was deprived of these when the colonies were liberated. Domestically, there was insufficient investment in infrastructure and productive and human resources. There were low levels of education and the rate of illiteracy among the population aged 15 years and over was 16%. The business sector was based on family businesses and undercapitalized. The banking sector was highly regulated until 1984 and the stock market remained dormant until 1985. During the late 1980s and early 1990s the Portuguese economy underwent a significant and rapid transformation. Portugal had the fastest rate of economic growth in Europe in 1986–88: the economy grew by 4.3% in 1986 and by 5% in 1987. The rate of inflation, which was 25% in 1983 and 1984, fell to 8.2% in 1988, and the rate of **unemployment** declined from 9% to 6.6% in the same period. Moreover, the state halved the public deficit in the two years to 1987.

The transformation of the Portuguese economy has been attributed to three things. Portugal sought assistance from the **International Monetary Fund** on two occasions, in 1977 and 1983; the adjustment requirements imposed on the second occasion were taken particularly seriously by the 'Centre Bloc' coalition government at the time which was made up of the two main political parties (the **Socialist Party** and the **Social Democratic Party**). Portugal applied to join the **European Community (EC)** in 1977 and became a member in 1986. It was required to adjust its economy to meet the conditions of the **Single European Market** in 1992, though some sectors were granted transition periods of between five and 10 years. From 1985 successive Portuguese governments undertook a programme of privatization. The Constitution was changed twice: first to allow the privatization of industries which had been nationalized in the revolutionary years, and then to permit the reduction of the state's share of ownership of the economy to less than 50%. The highly regulated banking sector was liberalized from 1984: the state privatized many banks, 90% of which had been state-owned, and foreign banks were allowed to establish themselves in the country. The removal of credit controls at the start of the 1990s also fuelled a massive consumer boom. Foreign direct investment increased and trade and investment opened up, particularly with neighbouring Spain.

Portugal also benefited financially as a poor member of the EC. In the first two years of its membership it received 137,000m. escudos from the EC in the form of **structural funds** and cohesion funds. Transfers from the EC were equivalent to 4% of the country's GDP in 1992. Some 30% of EC funding was spent on agriculture and the rest was invested in infrastructural projects such as the improvement of telecommunications facilities, motorways and bridges, as well as to improve skills and new technology. EC membership also gave Portugal macroeconomic cred-ibility. It joined the **Exchange Rate Mechanism** in 1992, but was forced to devalue the escudo in November 1992 and May 1993. By means of strong political determination to join the first wave of **Economic and Monetary Union (EMU)** it succeeded in meeting the **convergence criteria** for membership by cutting its budget deficit and public-sector deficit, tightened fiscal policy and used revenues from privatization to eliminate debt. The rate of inflation fell from 12.6% in 1991 to 2.5% in 1999. Macroeconomic stability was also secured by a system of national social bargaining that was established in 1984 through the Conselho Permanente de Concertação Social (CPCS). The CPCS—made up of the government, trade unions, and employers' organizations—agreed wage policies, working conditions and working hours. The institution led to moderate wage claims, which helped keep inflation under control, and social peace.

The rate of convergence between Portugal and the EU slowed from the late 1990s and by 2001 Portugal was growing at a slower rate than other EU countries. It also experienced difficulty in adhering to the conditions of the **Stability and Growth Pact** for membership of EMU. In 2001 the country narrowly avoided being officially reprimanded by the **European Commission** on account of its high level of public spending that led to a budget deficit equivalent to 3.9% of GDP in 2001. Portugal was able to avoid fines and denial of access to cohesion funds by reducing public spending and raising taxes. The budget deficit was equivalent to slightly less than 3% of GDP in 2004.

Portuguese Industrial Association

The Portuguese Industrial Association, or Associação Industrial Portuguesa (AIP), is the main employers' organization in Portugal. Originally founded in 1837, the organization provides services for its members in the areas of economic informa-tion, education and training, consultancy, information technology and fairs and congresses. AIP owns the Lisbon International Fair and the Lisbon Congress Centre. It is itself a member of the **Union of Industrial and Employers' Confederations of Europe**.

> *Pres.:* Jorge Rocha de Matos
> *Address:* Praça das Indústrias, 1399 Lisbon Codex, Portugal
> *Tel:* (0)21 3601000
> *Fax:* (0)21 3641301
> *E-mail:* aip@aip.pt
> *Internet:* www.aip.pt

Progress Party

The Progress Party, or Fremskrittspartiet, is the extreme right-wing party in Norway. Established in 1973, the party advocates a restrictive **immigration** policy for

Norway, limiting the annual number of immigrants to the country to 1,000; the repatriation of any asylum-seekers who break the law; and HIV/AIDS tests for new arrivals. The party is in favour of calling a referendum on whether any more foreigners at all should be admitted to Norway. The party also campaigns to abolish aid to developing countries and to cut direct and indirect taxation, using the country's oil revenues to improve public services for Norwegians instead. In elections held in September 2001 the party won 26 seats in the 165-seat **Stortinget** and is now the third largest party in the national parliament. Though it is not a member of the three-party conservative coalition, its influence is strong because the minority government relies on its support in parliament. Since the election popular support for the Fremskrittspartiet has increased further.

Party Leader: Carl Hagen
Address: Youngstorget 1, 0181 Oslo, Norway
Tel: (0)23-13-54-00
Fax: (0)23-13-54-01
E-mail: frp@frp.no
Internet: www.frp.no

Progressive Democrats (PD)

The Progressive Democrats (PD) is the market liberal party in Ireland. Founded in 1985, it is the only party to the right of the two main centrist parties, **Fianna Fáil (FF)** and **Fine Gael**. The party stands for low taxation, privatization of enterprise and a minimalist **welfare state**. It is a secularist party which, in contrast to the Catholic parties in Ireland, adopts a liberal position on issues such as divorce and abortion. It is a non-nationalistic party and does not campaign for the unification of the Republic of Ireland and **Northern Ireland**.

Since 1997 PD has been junior partner in a coalition with FF, with leader Mary Harney as Tanaiste (Deputy Prime Minister). The FF-PD coalition completed a five-year term of office (1997–2002), the longest term of any government in the history of the Republic. In elections held on 17 May 2002 the FF-PD coalition was re-elected, with PD increasing its share of the vote and its parliamentary representation. PD currently has eight seats in the 166-seat **Dáil Éireann**.

Party Leader: Mary Harney
Address: 25 South Frederick St, Dublin 2, Ireland
Tel: (0)1 6794399
Fax: (0)1 6794757
E-mail: info@progressivedemocrats.ie
Internet: www.progressivedemocrats.ie

Progressive Party

The Progressive Party, or Framsóknarflokkurinn (FSF), is a moderate liberal party in Iceland. Founded in 1916 by the merger of two agrarian parties, it still wins support from Icelandic farmers and fishermen. The party governed in coalition with the **Independence Party** in 1995–2003, and again following elections to the **Althingi** on 10 May 2003. In that election the party won 17.2% of the vote and 12 seats in the 63-seat parliament. FSF leader **Halldór Ásgrímsson** took over from David Oddsson as Prime Minister on 15 September 2004 as part of the coalition agreement.

Party Leader: Halldór Ásgrímsson
Address: Hverfisgata 33, 101 Reykjavík, Iceland
Tel: (0)5404300
Fax: (0)5404301
E-mail: framsokn@framsokn.is
Internet: www.framsokn.is

R

Radical Free Democratic Party

The Radical Free Democratic Party, or Freisinnig-Demokratische Partei/Parti Radical Démocratique (FDP/PRD), is the liberal party in Switzerland. Founded in 1894, the party stands for individual responsibility and the liberal economy. It was formerly a dominant party in the Swiss **Nationalrat**, but its status was reduced to that of third largest party at elections held in 1999 and 2003. The FDP won 36 seats in the 200-seat Nationalrat that was elected on 19 October 2003. This was seven fewer than the number it won in 1999. It has, however, retained its two ministers on the seven-seat permanent coalition despite the coalition's first reconfiguration since 1959.

> *Leadership: Pres.* Marianne Kleiner-Schläpfer (to be changed in March 2005); *Gen. Sec.* Guido Schommer
> *Address:* Neuengasse 20, Postfach 6136, 3001 Bern, Switzerland
> *Tel:* (0)313203535
> *Fax:* (0)313203500
> *E-mail:* info@fdp.ch
> *Internet:* www.fdp.ch (German) or www.prd.ch (French)

Radikale Venstre – *see* Social Liberal Party, Denmark

Raffarin, Jean-Pierre

Jean-Pierre Raffarin has been Prime Minister of France since May 2002 for the **Popular Movement** coalition. His political background is predominantly in local politics. He was a member of Poitiers municipal council in 1977–95, and then deputy mayor of Chasseneuil-du-Poitou, in 1995–2001. He was also elected to, and since 1988 has been chairman of, Poitou-Charentes regional council. In 1989 he was elected as a member of the **European Parliament** on the combined **Rally for the Republic-Union for French Democracy** list. At national level, he was elected to the **Sénat** in 1995 and 1997 to represent Vienne, and served as minister for small and medium enterprises in 1995–97.

Born on 3 August 1948 in Poitiers, Raffarin graduated from the Paris Ecole Supérieure de Commerce. He was senior lecturer at the Paris Institut d'Etudes Politiques in 1979–88, though his main career was in marketing and public relations. Jean-Pierre Raffarin is married and has one daughter.

Address: Hôtel de Matignon, 57 rue de Varenne, 75700 Paris, France
Tel: (0)1-42-75-80-00
Fax: (0)1-42-75-75-04
E-mail: via www.premier-ministre.gouv.fr/acteurs/premier_ministre/ecrire
Internet: www.premier-ministre.gouv.fr

Rally for the Republic

Rally for the Republic, or Rassemblement pour la République (RPR), was the dominant right-wing party in France in 1976–2002. Founded by **Jacques Chirac** in 1976 following the death of **Charles de Gaulle**, the neo-Gaullist RPR led governments in 1986–88 and 1993–97.

In April 2002, in preparation for elections to the **Assemblée Nationale** scheduled for June, the RPR merged with the neo-liberal Démocratie Libérale to form the Union for a Presidential Majority (Union pour une Majorité Presidentielle) which later became the **Popular Movement** (Union pour un Mouvement Populaire). The merger was triggered by the results of the first round of presidential elections held in April 2002 in which the extreme right-wing **National Front** candidate, **Jean-Marie Le Pen**, won 16.86% of the vote.

Rapid Reaction Force (RRF)

The European Rapid Reaction Force (RRF) is a rapid reaction mechanism aimed at fulfilling the Petersberg Tasks that was formed by the pooling of the military capabilities of member states of the **European Union (EU)**. At the meeting of the **European Council** held in Helsinki, Finland, in December 1999 a military capability target, the Headline Goal, was set. It requires EU member states to be able to deploy 60,000 troops within 60 days, and that deployment to be sustainable for one year in support of Petersberg missions. The Petersberg Tasks include humanitarian and rescue tasks, peace-keeping tasks and the tasks of combat forces in crisis management, including peace enforcement.

The Berlin Plus Agreement of December 2002 established the modalities of cooperation with the **North Atlantic Treaty Organization (NATO)** and allows the RRF to draw on common NATO assets if needed. Within the **Council of the European Union** a Political and Security Committee has been set up to assume the day-to-day direction of military operations if the Council agrees to deploy the RRF.

Jocelyn Mawdsley
University of Manchester

Rasmussen, Anders Rogh

Anders Rogh Rasmussen has been Prime Minister of Denmark since November 2001. He leads a coalition between the **Liberal Party**, of which he has been chairman since 1998, and the **Conservative People's Party**. This was re-elected on 8 February 2005. Rasmussen replaced Poul Nyrup Rasmussen, who was Prime Minister for the **Social Democratic Party** in 1993–2001. (The two are not related.) In the 2001 election campaign Rasmussen attracted voters by promising stricter controls on **immigration**, harder sentences for criminals and not to raise taxes. He also played down his anti-welfare stance. A supporter of the **European Union**, Rasmussen is likely to seek another referendum on Denmark's opt-outs following the Danes' rejection of membership of the **euro** in a referendum held on 28 September 2000.

Rasmussen became chairman of the Young Liberals in 1974 and has been a member of the **Folketing** since 1978. He was Minister for Taxation in 1987–92 and Minister for Economic Affairs in 1990–92, but resigned following opposition claims that he had misled parliament.

Born on 26 January 1953 in Ginnerup, Anders Rogh Rasmussen grew up on a farm and graduated with a master's degree in economics from Aarhus University in 1974. In 1978–87 he worked as a consultant with the Danish Federation of Crafts and Small Industries. Anders Rogh Rasmussen is married to Anne Mette and they have three children.

> *Address:* The Prime Minister's Office, Christiansborg, Prins Jørgens Gård 11, 1218 Copenhagen K, Denmark
> *Tel:* (0)33-92-33-00
> *Fax:* (0)33-11-16-65
> *E-mail:* stm@stm.dk
> *Internet:* www.stm.dk

Rassemblement pour la République – *see* Rally for the Republic, France

Reformist Movement

The Reformist Movement, or Mouvement Réformateur (MR), is the main liberal party in French-speaking Belgium. Formed in 2002, the MR brings together four established parties: the Liberal Reformist Party, the Party of Freedom and Progress, the Francophone Democratic Front and the Citizens' Change Movement. MR campaigns to increase the political and economic influence of the individual. In elections held on 18 May 2003 the MR won 11.4% of the vote and 25 seats in the 150-seat **Kamer**. In the current liberal-socialist government, led by **Guy Verhofstadt**, MR has six ministers, including finance minister **Didier Reynders**.

Pres: Didier Reynders
Address: rue de Naples 39, 1050 Brussels, Belgium
Tel: (0)2 500-35-43
Fax: (0)2 500-35-00
E-mail: mr@mr.be
Internet: www.mr.be

Regionalism

Regionalism relates primarily to the processes by which sub-national geographical entities, or regions, are formed by economic, social, political and cultural interests. Three broad strands of regionalism can be identified: *old regionalism*, whereby the nation state orchestrates the formation (and control or management) of sub-national territory; *new regionalism*, whereby the hegemony of the nation state in the construction of sub-national territory is challenged by economic, social, political and cultural forces; and *theoretical* insights which conceptualize the reterritorialization of space as represented by new regionalism. A fourth, *supra-national*, definition of regionalism relates to the processes by which regional blocs (e.g. the **European Union (EU)**, Asia-Pacific Economic Co-operation and the North American Free Trade Agreement) are formed. The following relates solely to the first three forms of regionalism.

Old regionalism is based on fixed geographic units, normally defined by the nation state, but often reflecting historical and culturally defined territories. This form of regionalism dates from the 19th century and the construction of nation states in Western Europe and was concerned with establishing the primacy of the nation state over its territory. Issues of ethnic, cultural and economic differences were regarded as a hindrance to this process. However, in the second half of the 20th century, and in particular in the aftermath of the Second World War, regionalism became a project of new modern nation states concerned with issues of economic equity and redistribution between regions, but also as a fundamental part of the reconstruction of the nation state itself. For example, regionalism was part of the formation of new democratic states with inter-regional systems for fiscal redistribution and systems of government based along federal or regional lines, such as in the Federal Republic of Germany and Spain.

Three main forces have challenged this form of old regionalism in the late 20th and early 21st century and form a new regionalism. First, the intensification of international economic competition and, in particular, globalization has compromised the ability of the nation state to effectively intervene in its economy. Fiscal redistribution, co-ordinated by the nation state, based on Keynesian principles of demand management has become less effective in achieving the goal of equity between regions. Second, driven by globalization, nation states have sought both to pool sovereignty, for example through the creation of regional blocs such as the EU, and to decentralize responsibility for policy formation and implementation to regions and localities, through hollowing-out the nation state, but also through notions of shifting political decision-making closer to citizens and service users. Finally, political mobilization in regions, particularly along cultural or historical nationalist lines, such as in **Scotland** and the **Basque Country**, has put pressure on nation states to cede sovereignty.

Except for supporters of a Europe of the Regions and other proponents of theses that anticipate the atrophy of the nation state, new regionalism provides a basis for identifying the forces which are challenging the nation state. However, a particular concern with new regionalism is whether new forms of regional collective action, which it espouses, will emerge to counteract economic and social inequality within and between regions.

The analysis of new regionalism has been informed and contested by advances across academic disciplines. Within political science **multi-level governance** has highlighted the ways in which regional political actors in concert with supranational bodies such as the **European Commission** can challenge the supremacy of the nation state and inter-governmental systems (such as the **Council of the European Union**) in particular areas of policy, such as regional development and cohesion policy. Work within geography and political economy has considered the capacity of regional actors and institutions to establish structures which can draw upon indigenous economic and non-economic resources and assets, most typically to promote economic growth. However, these approaches have been challenged for their tendency to generalize from specific regional case studies and for the capacity of new regionalism to provide balanced and sustainable economic and social development.

Peter Wells
Sheffield Hallam University

Republican Left of Catalonia

The Republican Left of Catalonia, or Esquerra Republicana de Catalunya (ERC), is a socialist nationalist party in the region of Catalonia in Spain. Founded in 1931, ERC campaigns for independence for Catalonia. In the first elections for the Catalan parliament, held in 1980, ERC won 8.9% of the vote and 14 seats. At its 1995 Congress the party shifted its orientation from the single issue of independence to a more diverse left-wing politics. The party won 16.44% of the vote and 23 seats in the Catalan elections held in 2003 and has eight seats (from 2.5% of the vote) in the national parliament, the **Congreso de los Diputados**, that was elected on 14 March 2004.

Leadership: Pres. Josep-Lluís Carod-Rovira; *Sec.-Gen.* Joan Puigcercós
Address: Villarroel, 45 entresòl, 08011 Barcelona, Spain
Tel: (0)93 4536005
Fax: (0)93 3237122
E-mail: info@esquerra.org
Internet: www.esquerra.org

Reynders, Didier

Didier Reynders has been Minister of Finance in Belgium since July 1999. A member of the **Reformist Movement**, he is part of the liberal-socialist coalition government headed by the liberal Prime Minister **Guy Verhofstadt**. Reynders has been a member of the **Kamer** since 1992, and led his liberal political group in parliament in 1995–99. Prior to that, in 1987–88, he administered the Office of the Deputy Prime Minister, and in 1988 was a town councillor in Liège.

Born on 6 August 1958 in Liège, Reynders studied law at the University of Liège and practised as a lawyer in 1981–85. He was general manager of the local authority department, Ministry of the Walloon Region, in 1985–88, chairman of the Belgian National Railway Co in 1986–91, and chairman of the national airline, Sabena, in 1991–93.

Address: Ministry of Finance, Wetstraat 12, 1000 Brussels, Belgium
Tel: (0)2 233-80-11
Fax. (0)2 233-80-03
E-mail: contact@ckfin.minfin.be
Internet: www.minfin.fgov.be

Rifondazione Comunista – *see* Communist Refoundation Party, Italy

Riksbank

The Riksbank, established in 1656, is the central bank in Sweden. It is responsible for safeguarding the value of the Swedish currency, the krona, with a targeted rate of inflation of 2%. It also promotes a safe and efficient payment system, supplying banknotes and coins and managing Sweden's reserves of gold and foreign currency. The Riksbank Act of 1999 reformed the structure of the Riksbank.

On 14 September 2003 Swedish citizens voted against adopting the **euro** (no 56%; turn-out 81%) and the Riksbank continues to pursue its own objectives. As a central bank of a state outside the **euro area**, the Riksbank is a member of the **European System of Central Banks**. However, the governor of the Riksbank is not entitled to be a member of the governing council of the European Central Bank, nor to participate in decision-making for the **Eurosystem**.

Gov.: Lars Heikensten
Address: Brunkebergstorg 11, 103 37 Stockholm, Sweden
Tel: (0)8 787-00-00
Fax: (0)8 21-05-31
E-mail: registratorn@riksbank.se
Internet: www.riksbank.se

Riksdag

Parliament

The Riksdag is the unicameral parliament of Sweden. It is made up of 349 members who are directly elected for a four-year term of office on the basis of proportional representation. Voters vote for a political party, but it is also possible to cast a personalized vote by marking the name of a particular candidate on the ballot paper. The Riksdag is responsible for passing laws and scrutinizing the Swedish government. It also has powers to determine the state budget. The Riksdag is also responsible for appointing an ombudsman.

There are seven parties represented in the Riksdag that was elected on 15 September 2002 (number of seats in brackets): the **Social Democratic Party** (144), the **Moderate Party** (55), the **Liberal Party** (48), the **Christian Democrats** (33), the **Left Party** (30), the **Centre Party** (22) and the **Green Party** (17). In the 2002 Riksdag 47% of parliamentarians are **women**. This is the highest percentage of female representatives ever returned to any national parliament or assembly in Western Europe.

Address: Sveriges Riksdag, 100 12 Stockholm, Sweden
Tel: (0)8 786-40-00
Fax: (0)8 786-61-45
E-mail: riksdagsinformation@riksdagen.se
Internet: www.riksdagen.se

Russia

Russia is a large state to the east of Western Europe and the **Central and Eastern European Countries**. Formerly part of the Soviet Union (USSR), it became an independent state in 1991 when the USSR collapsed. Together with Ukraine and Belarus, it formed the Commonwealth of Independent States, which was later joined by all of the former Soviet republics except the Baltic states. Since independence Russia has made much progress towards democracy and a market economy. However, concerns have been raised in recent years about the state's interference in both the democratic process and the market economy.

Area: 17,075,000 sq km; *capital:* Moscow; *population:* 145m. (2001).

Russia is, according to the Constitution of 12 December 1993, a federation comprising 89 administrative units (49 oblasts, 21 republics, 10 autonomous okrugs, six krays, two federal cities and one autonomous oblast). Executive power is vested in the President, who is elected for a four-year term. Since 31 December 1999 this has been Vladimir Putin; he first served as acting President following the sudden resignation of Boris Yeltsin and was first elected on 26 March 2000. Putin was re-elected for a second and final term on 14 March 2004, having won 71.2% of the vote. Legislative power is vested with the bicameral Federal Assembly. Its upper house, the Federation Council, represents the units of the Russian Federation;

178 members are appointed by the heads of 89 units every four years. The lower house, the State Duma, is elected every four years. One-half of the 450 deputies are elected by a system of proportional representation with a 5% threshold, and the other half are elected directly in constituencies. At the most recent election, held on 7 December 2003, United Russia, the party which supports Putin, became the largest party in the Duma, winning 222 seats. Following the elections of December 2003 Putin appointed Mikhail Fradkov as Premier and head of government.

Putin has been criticized for centralizing Russian politics and for interfering in the free democratic process. He has the power to appoint and dismiss governments, and since 2003 the Duma has been dominated by a party that supports the President, limiting the checks and balances of the political system. On 29 October 2004 the State Duma approved plans to reform the way in which heads of federal units are appointed. The changes mean that, instead of gaining office through regional elections, heads will be nominated by the President and then endorsed by the regional parliaments. Moreover, Putin suspended broadcasts by the private television network, TV-6, in 2002, and those of its successor station, TVS, in 2003, allegedly for financial reasons, raising concerns about free speech.

A regionally and ethnically diverse state, Russia has been in conflict with the break-away region of Chechnya since 1994. President Boris Yeltsin deployed troops in Chechnya in 1994 and signed a peace treaty in 1996. Conflict arose again in 1999 when militants attacked the neighbouring region of Dagestan. Russia has been the target of a series of terrorist attacks that have been attributed to Chechen separatists. In Moscow 800 people were held hostage in a theatre, and 120 died. In Beslan, North Ossieta, 360 people died when a school was occupied in 2004. Of the dead, 172 were children. President Putin has committed himself to supporting the war on **terrorism**, led by the USA. He refused to back the US-led attack on **Iraq** in 2003, however, on the grounds that **United Nations** weapons inspectors should have been given more time to complete their work.

Economy: The large Russian economy is dominated by extractive industries, producing coal, gas, oil and chemicals. The economy is dependent on oil prices as oil accounts for 80% of exports. Following the collapse of communism and the process of adjustment to an open economy, Russia lost around one-half of its gross domestic product, and price liberalization in 1992 led to high rates of inflation.

GNP: US $588,000m. (2001); *GNP per caput:* $14,300 (2001); *GNP at PPP:* $816,000m. (2001); *GNP per caput at PPP:* $19,860 (2001); *GDP:* $309,951m. (2001); *exports:* $112,507 (2001); *imports:* $73,168m. (2001); *currency:* rouble; *unemployment:* 8.9% (2001).

During the 1990s much of the state-run economy was privatized. Energy and **media** interests in particular were bought by a small group of entrepreneurs, referred to as oligarchs. The Russian economy has a weak banking system, and there is a widespread lack of trust in institutions which discourages business. Under President Putin there has been a series of investigations into the Russian oil company, Yukos. The head of the company, billionaire Mikhail Khodorkovskiy, was arrested in 2003 after the investigation of alleged fraud and tax evasion. He had also funded political campaigns opposing Putin.

In 1998 the Russian economy suffered a financial crisis and the rouble was devalued, but it subsequently made a rapid recovery. In the five years to 2003 the economy grew at an average annual rate of 6.5%, driven by investment and consumer spending. This was Russia's first period of economic stability, with low inflation and cuts in public expenditure. This also led to growth in disposable income and to a fall in the number of those in poverty from about 40% of the population in 1999 to about 25% in 2003.

Russia is the **European Union**'s **(EU)** fifth largest trading partner (after the USA, Switzerland, China and **Japan**), and more than 50% of Russia's trade is with the EU25. Total Russia-EU trade amounted to €84,000m. in 2003. Russia's main exports to the EU are machinery, chemicals, agricultural products and transport materials. The EU is in favour of Russia's accession to the **World Trade Organization**. Since 1991, through the TACIS programme, the EU has provided Russia with technical assistance and know-how to assist the transition to democracy, a market economy and the rule of law. Since 1997 EU-Russia economic relations have been governed by the Partnership and Co-operation Agreement. This encourages co-operation in the areas of trade and economic development, science and technology, and politics and policies in the areas of **Justice and Home Affairs**.

Ryanair

Ryanair is an Irish airline. Founded in 1985, it originally operated on two routes between Ireland and the United Kingdom. The company relaunched itself as a low fares/'no frills' airline in 1990/91 and, following the full deregulation of **air transport** in 1997, increased the number of services it offered to continental Europe. By the summer of 2003 Ryanair was operating on 127 routes that cover 84 destinations across 16 countries. Its annual traffic amounts to more than 15m. passengers.

To maintain its status as a low fares/'no frills' airline Ryanair has concluded agreements with small, underused airports which are able to charge the airline low landing fees and provide subsidies from regional government to encourage their use. The Bas-Rhin Chamber of Commerce and Industry, which manages Strasbourg airport, paid €1.4m. (US $1.5m.) to Ryanair to help the carrier launch two daily round trip flights from London's Stansted airport. In response to a complaint by Air France, a court in France ruled in September 2003 that this payment had amounted to illegal state aid to Ryanair. The airline suspended its service and launched one to Baden-Baden in Germany instead.

In February 2004 the **European Commission** ruled that Ryanair had received illegal incentives from the Wallonian regional government in Belgium to use Charleroi airport, south of Brussels. The Commission claimed that such incentives were incompatible with the proper functioning of the internal market. Ryanair was ordered to repay 25%–30% of the subsidy it had received, a sum of some €1.4m.

CEO: Michael O'Leary
Address: Ryanair Corporate Head Office, Dublin Airport, Co. Dublin, Ireland
Tel: (0)1 8121212
Internet: www.ryanair.com

S

Salaried Employees' and Civil Servants' Confederation

The Salaried Employees' and Civil Servants' Confederation, or Funktionærernes og Tjenestemændenes Fællesråd (FTF), is the trade union confederation in Denmark which represents salaried employees and civil servants. Founded in 1952, today it organizes 400,000 members from more than 100 independent affiliated unions and is itself a member of **ETUC**. A predominantly public-sector union, the FTF is a social partner with ministries, councils and employers.

Pres.: Bente Sorgenfrey
Address: Niels Hemmingsensgade 12, POB 1169, 1010 Copenhagen K, Denmark
Tel: (0)33-36-8800
Fax: (0)33-36-88-80
E-mail: ftf@ftf.dk
Internet: www.ftf.dk

Samfylkinginflokkurinn – *see* Alliance Party, Iceland

Sampaio, Jorge

Jorge Sampaio is the President of Portugal. A socialist, he was elected for his first five-year term of office on 14 January 1996, having won a majority of 52.57% of the vote in the first ballot. He was re-elected on 14 January 2001 after winning 55.76% of the vote in the first round.

Born on 18 September 1939 in Lisbon, Sampaio spent much of his childhood in the USA and the United Kingdom. He studied law at Lisbon University and began a legal career, working to defend political prisoners. Before the revolution of 25 April 1974 Sampaio actively opposed the dictatorship in the student movement, in the resistance movement and by standing for parliamentary elections to the National Assembly in 1969. Following the revolution in 1974 he was involved in establishing the socialist movement, MES, though his involvement ceased at the founding conference owing to ideological differences.

In 1978 Sampaio joined the **Socialist Party**. He was elected to the **Assembléia da República** in 1979 and was re-elected for four subsequent terms, most recently in 1991. He was elected as mayor of Lisbon in 1991, and re-elected in 1993. Sampaio served as president of the Union of Portuguese-speaking Cities in 1990–95, as vice-president of the Union of Iberian-American Cities in 1990, as president of the Eurocities Movement in 1990 and president of the World Federation of United Cities in 1992. Jorge Sampaio is married to Maria José Ritta and has two children.

Address: Palácio de Belém, Calçada da Ajuda, 1349-022 Lisbon, Portugal
Tel: (0)21 3614600 and (0)21 3610570
Fax: (0)21 3614611 and (0)21 3614612
E-mail: presidente@presidenciarepublica.pt
Internet: www.presidenciarepublica.pt

Samtök Atvinnulifsins – *see* Confederation of Icelandic Employers

Samtök Idnadarins – *see* Federation of Icelandic Industries

San Marino

San Marino is a small, land-locked republic situated in eastern Italy that is said to have been founded by the devout Christian stonemason Marinus in AD 301. Legislative power lies with a 60-member Great and General Council which is elected every five years. The legislature elects two Captains Regent every six months to act as the heads of state. Executive power is held by a 10-member Congress of State elected by the Great and General Councils. The current head of government is the Secretary of State for Foreign and Political Affairs, Fiorenzo Stolfi, who took office on 17 December 2002.

The population of San Marino—27,000 (2003)—is Italian-speaking. The area of the republic is 61 sq km and its capital is San Marino. The Sammarinese economy is dominated by tourism, which contributes more than 50% of the gross domestic product. More than 3m. tourists visit San Marino annually. Other areas of economic activity include banking, electronics, ceramics and wine. The rate of **unemployment** is 2.6% (2001) and the standard of living is comparable to that of the wealthy northern regions of Italy. The currency is the **euro**.

Sarkozy, Nicolas

Nicolas Sarkozy is a French politician for the **Popular Movement (UMP)**. He served as Minister of the Interior in 2002–04, and in 2004 was appointed Minister of Finance in the government headed by **Jean-Pierre Raffarin**. As Minister of

Finance, he had the task of balancing the national budget and reducing the public deficit to meet the conditions of the **stability and growth pact**. An ambitious politician whose goal is to succeed his political rival, **Jacques Chirac**, as President of France, he resigned as Minister of Finance and became president of the UMP in November 2004. President Chirac had insisted that the two posts were not compatible and that Sarkozy could only take up the party leadership if he resigned his ministerial post.

Sarkozy began his political career with the **Rally for the Republic** party at local level. He was elected as a councillor in Neuilly-sur-Seine in 1997 and as mayor of the town in 1983. In 1983–85 he served as a regional councillor for the Ile-de-France. He was first elected to the **Assemblée Nationale** in 1988, and again in 1993, 1995 and 1997. Born on 28 January 1955 in Paris, Nicolas Sarkozy studied public law and political science, and is a trained lawyer.

Schengen Agreement

The Schengen Agreement, signed on 14 June 1985 by Belgium, France, Germany, Luxembourg and the Netherlands, created a territory with no internal borders, within which the free movement of people was guaranteed. The Schengen Agreement abolished the internal borders of the signatory states and created a single external border where **immigration** checks are carried out. Members of the Schengen area agreed a single set of rules regarding visas and some aspects of asylum policy for the external border. The Schengen Agreement also established co-ordination networks between police and customs officials to combat **terrorism** and organized crime. The Schengen Information System (SIS) was also established to allow the police stations and consular agents of participating states to exchange information on individuals and missing property.

A Convention on implementing the Schengen Agreement was signed on 19 June 1990 and came into practical effect on 26 March 1995. By then the Schengen area included the five original member states plus Portugal and Spain. Since 1995 Italy, Greece, Austria, Denmark, Finland and Sweden have acceded to the Convention. In 1996 a Schengen co-operation agreement was concluded with Norway and Iceland which are not members of the **European Union (EU)**, but are members of the Nordic Passport Union. The five Nordic states had fully implemented the Schengen regime as of 25 March 2001.

The Schengen Agreement was brought into the legal and institutional framework of the EU by a protocol attached to the **Treaty of Amsterdam** (1997). The United Kingdom and Ireland have both opted to remain out of the Schengen area, but can join it provided that the area's member states agree to their doing so. The United Kingdom requested participation in some aspects of Schengen in March 1999, namely police and legal co-operation in criminal matters, the fight against drugs and the SIS. Ireland applied in June 2000 and November 2001 to take part in some aspects of Schengen. The 10 new member states which joined the EU on 1 May

2004 were required to comply with the Schengen Agreement as it is considered to be a part of the *acquis communautaire*.

Schröder, Gerhard

Gerhard Schröder is the Chancellor of Germany. He was elected by the **Bundestag** in 1998 following elections in September of that year in which his **Social Democratic Party of Germany (SPD)** achieved the status of largest party, thus bringing to an end 16 years' of government by a coalition between the **Christian Democratic Union**, the **Christian Social Union** and the **Free Democratic Party** under **Helmut Kohl**. His victory in 1998 was significant in that it was the first time in the history of post-war Germany that a change of government had resulted from an electoral defeat rather than from changes in coalition choices. The new government was also the first national coalition between the SPD and **Alliance 90/ The Greens**, and the first purely left-of-centre government. Schröder was reappointed as Chancellor of a second red-green coalition following a narrow victory in elections to the Bundestag held on 22 September 2002. His re-election was secured by his principled opposition to the involvement of German troops in the anticipated war in **Iraq** in 2003, his management of the East German flood crisis in the summer of 2002, and his concrete plans to tackle Germany's high rate of **unemployment**.

Labelled as a modernizer and a reformer in the SPD, Schröder campaigned for office in 1998 by appealing to the 'Neue Mitte' (new centre) political ground. This position was much criticized among the traditional left of the SPD and led to conflict with his party. Schröder's position within his party was strengthened in 1999 when he was elected as its leader following the resignation of left-wing party leader and finance minister Oskar Lafontaine. Schröder appointed Franz Müntefering as chairman of the SPD in February 2004 in order to concentrate on managing the government. As Chancellor, Schröder has struggled to secure the support of traditionalists in his party and of the green coalition partners on a number of controversial issues. His decision to dispatch German troops to **Kosovo** in 1999 and to Afghanistan in 2001 met with opposition from the greens, and the second deployment was only endorsed after a vote of confidence in his government had been held in the Bundestag in November 2001. Schröder encountered opposition from the traditional wing of his own party for his policies to reduce unemployment and reform the **welfare state**—the so-called Hartz reforms.

A member of the SPD since 1966, Schröder's political career began in 1978 when he was elected as national leader of Jusos, the youth movement of the SPD. In 1980 he was elected to the Bundestag. Following the defeat of the SPD government in 1982, Schröder's political focus shifted to Hanover where he became leader of the city party in 1983 and of the SPD in the state (*Land*) parliament of Lower Saxony in 1986. He became Minister President of Lower Saxony in 1990, heading a coalition between the SPD and the Green Party, and led the SPD to two further victories in the

Land, in 1994 and 1998, before becoming the SPD's candidate for the chancellorship for the 1998 Bundestag elections.

Born on 7 April 1944 in Mossenberg, Schröder completed a commercial apprenticeship and finished his secondary education at night school. He later studied law at Göttingen University from 1966, and worked for a law firm in Hanover from 1976. Gerhard Schröder has been married to his fourth wife, Doris Köpf, since 1997. The couple adopted a child in 2004.

Address: Bundeskanzleramt, Willy-Brandt-Strasse 1, 10557 Berlin, Germany
Tel: (0)1888 4000
Fax: (0)1888 4002357
E-mail: internetpost@bundeskanzler.de
Internet: www.bundeskanzler.de and www.gerhard-schroeder.de

Schuman, Robert

Robert Schuman was a Luxembourg-born politician and statesman. As foreign minister of France, he drew up the Schuman Plan which led to the establishment of the **European Coal and Steel Community** in 1951. In the Schuman Declaration of 9 May 1950 it was proposed that French and German production of coal and steel should be pooled and managed by a single High Authority. Schuman also announced that this arrangement should be opened to other countries as a first step towards economic integration in Europe, and as a way of preventing future wars. Robert Schuman is, with **Jean Monnet**, considered to be one of the founding fathers of the **European Union**.

Born in 1886 in Clausen, Luxembourg, into a bilingual family, Schuman studied law at the Universities of Berlin, Munich, Bonn and Strasbourg. He worked as a lawyer in Alsace-Lorraine and became active in French politics as a member of parliament first for Moselle, and then for Thionville East. Following the Second World War, Schuman served as Prime Minister of France in 1947–48, and was foreign minister in 1948–53.

Schüssel, Wolfgang

Wolfgang Schüssel is the Federal Chancellor of Austria. He heads a coalition between his **Austrian People's Party (ÖPV)** and the extreme right-wing **Austrian Freedom Party**. The controversial coalition was first established in February 2000. Schüssel chose to form a second coalition between these parties in February 2003 following months of fruitless negotiations with the **Social Democratic Party of Austria (SPÖ)** and the **Green Party**.

Schüssel was Minister for Economic Affairs in the first SPÖ-ÖPV coalition government in 1989 and served as Vice-Chancellor and as Minister for Foreign Affairs in three successive governments in 1995–2000. Schüssel has been leader of the ÖVP since 1995. From 1968 until 1975 he was Secretary of the ÖPV parliamentary party, or 'Klub', in the **Nationalrat**.

Born on 7 June 1945 in Vienna, Schüssel studied at the University of Vienna and gained a doctorate in law in 1968. He was general secretary of the Austrian Business Federation in 1975–91.

Address: Office of the Federal Chancellor, Ballhausplatz 2, 01014 Vienna, Austria
Tel: (0)1-531-15-0
Fax: (0)1-535-03-38
E-mail: wolfgang.schuessel@bka.gv.at
Internet: www.bka.gv.at

Schweizerische Nationalbank

The Schweizerische Nationalbank, the independent central bank of Switzerland, was founded in 1907. According to the Swiss Constitution, it conducts Switzerland's monetary and currency policy in the interest of the whole country and its main aim is to ensure price stability. It is also in charge of issuing banknotes and offering financial and statistical services to the state.

Gov.: Jean-Pierre Roth
Address: Börsenstrasse 15, POB 2800, 8022 Zürich, Switzerland
Tel: (0)16313111
Fax: (0)16313911
E mail: snb@snb.ch
Internet: www.snb.ch

Schweizerische Volkspartei – *see* Swiss People's Party

Schweizerischer Arbeitgeberverband – *see* Confederation of Swiss Employers

Schweizerischer Gewerkschaftsbund/L'Union Syndicale Suisse – *see* Swiss Trade Union Confederation

Scotland

Scotland is a nation that forms part of the United Kingdom. It became part of the United Kingdom in 1707 through the Act of Union and, until the creation of a Scottish Parliament in 1999, legislative power resided in the **House of Commons**. Scottish home rule first became a political issue in the 1880s, and since the 1930s the **Scottish National Party** has campaigned for full independence. In the referendum on devolution held on 1 May 1979, the Scots narrowly supported the proposal (yes 51.6%; turn-out 63.6%), but the result failed to win the required support of 40% of the total electorate. Following the election of the **Labour Party** on 1 May 1997 a second referendum was held on 11 September of that year. The Scottish electorate were asked both if they supported proposals for devolution (yes 74.3%; turn-out 60.4%) and whether Scotland should have its own tax-raising powers (yes 63.5%). The Scottish Parliament was established in the capital Edinburgh and the first elections to it were held in 1999. The Scottish Parliament has powers to legislate in such matters as education, health, prisons, tourism and transport. The 129-seat parliament is elected every four years by a system of proportional representation. The Parliament then elects a First Minister; at the most recent elections, held on 1 May 2003, Jack McConnell of the Labour Party was re-elected as First Minister of Scotland. He leads a second Labour-Liberal coalition. At present 39% of the Members of the Scottish Parliament are **women**.

Economy: The Scottish economy has traditionally been dominated by the coal and steel industries. Heavy industry suffered a number of periods of decline and, since the 1970s, there has been no revival. During the 1980s deindustrialization led to high rates of **unemployment**—more than 15% in 1984—and poverty. The economy is now concentrated on the North Sea oil reserves first discovered in the 1970s 150 km east of Aberdeen, as well as the growing service, finance and tourism industries. Unemployment has fallen to around 6% (2002), though it remains higher than the UK average. Wages in Scotland are around 91% of the UK average (2002). The population of Scotland—5.05m.—is in decline; the country has a lower birth rate than the UK average and the lowest life expectancy in Western Europe.

Scottish National Party (SNP)

The Scottish National Party (SNP) is a left-wing party committed to Scottish independence. It maintains that autonomy for **Scotland** and control of its natural resources would allow more appropriate policy-making for the country. It also aims to strengthen the position of Scotland within the **European Union**. Established in 1934, the SNP has enjoyed some electoral successes at national level and won five seats in elections to the **House of Commons** held on 7 June 2001. It has 27 members in the 129-seat Scottish Parliament that was elected on 1 May 2003, but has not succeeded in gaining the status of largest party.

Party Leader: Alex Salmond
Address: 107 McDonald Rd, Edinburgh EH7 4NW, United Kingdom
Tel: (0)131 525 8900
Fax: (0)131 525 8901
E-mail: snp.hq@snp.org
Internet: www.snp.org

Seanad Éireann

Senate

The Seanad Éireann (Senate) is the upper house of the bicameral parliament, the Tithe an Oireachtas, in Ireland. It is composed of 60 members who must be selected within 90 days of the dissolution of the Dáil Éireann and who are appointed by three different procedures. Eleven are nominated by the Taoiseach (Prime Minister), six are elected by the graduates of two universities (the National University of Ireland and Trinity College Dublin) and 43 are elected by five panels representing vocational interests of culture and education, **agriculture**, labour, industry and commerce and public administration. The electorate for these panels is made up of members of the incoming **Dáil Éireann**, the outgoing Seanad, county councils and county borough councils.

The Seanad shares a legislative role with the Dáil: its main function is to debate and revise legislation submitted by the lower house. The Seanad has the power to revise and initiate legislation in all areas except financial legislation, and it can not initiate bills to amend the Constitution. Increasingly the government has tended to make use of the Seanad for initiating legislation. The appointments procedure means that the composition of the Seanad will tend to reflect party strengths in the Dáil.

Address: Seanad Éireann, Houses of the Oireachtas, Leinster House, Dublin 2, Ireland
Tel: (0)1 6183000
Fax: (0)1 618 4118
E-mail: info@oireachtas.ie
Internet: www.oireachtas.ie

Sedlabanki

Sedlabanki, the central bank of Iceland, was established in 1961. It is an independent institution owned by the Icelandic state, but under separate administration. Sedlabanki is in charge of monetary policy and its main objective is price stability. It is obliged to contribute towards the government's main economic policy objectives as long as this does not conflict with the bank's own goal of price stability. In addition, it maintains external reserves and is responsible for the issue of notes and coins, and for exchange-rate matters.

Gov.: Birgir Ísleifur Gunnarsson
Address: Kalkofnsvegi 1, 150 Reykjavík, Iceland
Tel: (0)5699600
Fax: (0)5699605
E-mail: sedlabanki@sedlabanki.is
Internet: www.sedlabanki.is

Senado

Senate

The Senado is the upper house of the bicameral parliament, the Cortes, in Spain. The Senado is theoretically Spain's territorial chamber; however, a mere 51 of 259 senators are appointed from autonomous parliaments, and they have little influence on national decision-making. The Senado currently has a total membership of 259 senators, who are selected in two ways. The majority (208) are directly elected by the provinces: each mainland province elects four senators, the larger islands of the Balearics and the Canaries—Mallorca, Gran Canaria, and Tenerife—are assigned three seats each, and the smaller islands—Menorca, Ibiza-Formentera, Fuerteventura, Gomera, Hierro, Lanzarote and La Palma—one each. Ceuta and Melilla are assigned two seats each. An additional 51 senators are appointed by the legislative assemblies of each autonomous community. Each region appoints one senator plus an additional senator for every 1m. inhabitants. The Senado shares legislative competence with the **Congreso de los Diputados**.

Address: Plaza de la Marina Española 8, 28071 Madrid, Spain
Tel: (0)91 5381000
Fax: (0)91 5381003
E-mail: webmaster@senado.es
Internet: www.senado.es

Sénat/Senaat (Belgium)

Senate

The Sénat/Senaat (Senate) is the upper house of the bicameral federal parliament in Belgium. It is in the Sénat that conflicts between the interests of the federal state, the Communities and the Regions are resolved. The Sénat is made up of 71 senators who are elected or appointed for a four-year term by three different procedures. The first 40 senators are directly elected by a system of proportional representation on the same day that elections to the **Kamer/Chambre** are held. The electorate is divided into a French and a Flemish electoral college and these elect a fixed number of senators: the French college elects 15; the Flemish 25. A further 21 senators are appointed by the parliaments of the French-, Flemish- and German-speaking Communities. The French and the Flemish Communities appoint 10 senators each and the German-speaking Community appoints one senator. Of these 21 Community senators, at least one Flemish- and six French-speaking senators must be from the bilingual Brussels-Capital region. Ten additional senators are co-opted by the directly elected and nominated Community senators: the elected and the French Community senators appoint four co-opted senators; and the elected and Flemish Community senators appoint six co-opted senators. Finally, the children of the monarch become *ex officio* members of the Sénat when they reach the age of 18, and are entitled to a seat and to vote at the age of 21. Currently three of the King of Belgium's children are senators.

Until 1994 the upper house had the same powers and functions as the **Kamer**. Since the Constitution was revised on 17 February 1994 the upper house has had only equal powers in 'fundamental' federal legislation, such as constitutional revisions, laws on the structure of the Belgian state, laws affecting co-operation between the federal state, the Communities and the Regions, and laws on international treaties. Any other 'ordinary' legislation is examined and may be amended by the Sénat, but the Kamer makes the final decision.

Address: Paleis der Natie/Natieplein/Palais de la Nation, place de la Nation 1,
       1009 Brussels, Belgium
Tel: (0)2 501-70-70
Fax: (0)2 515-82-16
E-mail: webmaster@senate.be
Internet: www.senate.be

Sénat (France)

Senate

The Sénat (Senate) is the upper house of the bicameral parliament in France. It is made up of 321 members who represent the local regions (*départements*). Senators are elected indirectly for a term of nine years through electoral colleges in the *départements*; one-third of the Sénat's members being replaced every three years. Reforms under way will reduce senators' term of office to six years. The Sénat shares a legislative role with the **Assemblée Nationale**. Draft bills pass between houses until agreement is reached in a process known as the 'shuttle'. If there is no consensus after two readings in each house, the final decision rests with the lower house.

Address: Sénat, 15 rue de Vaugirard, 75291 Paris Cedex 06, France
Tel: (0)1-42-34-20-00
Fax: (0)1-42-34-26-77
E-mail: communication@senat.fr
Internet: www.senat.fr

Senato della Repubblica

Senate

The Senato della Repubblica (Senate) is the upper house of the bicameral parliament in Italy. It has a basic membership of 315 senators who are elected by a mixed electoral system for a five-year term: 75% are elected by a majoritarian system and 25% by a system of proportional representation. In addition, former Presidents are senators for life (there are currently two) and the incumbent President can make other life appointments (currently four). There is currently a total of 321 senators. In a system of perfect bicameralism, the Senate has the same powers to legislate and control the government as the lower house of parliament, the **Camera dei Deputati**.

Address: Senato della Repubblica, Piazza Madama, 00186 Rome, Italy
Tel: (0)06 67061
E-mail: infopoint@senato.it
Internet: www.senato.it

Senterpartiet – *see* Centre Party, Norway

11 September

On 11 September 2001 four terrorist attacks were carried out on the USA. In total four planes were hijacked: American Airlines Flight 11 and United Airlines Flight 175 were flown into the twin towers of the World Trade Center in New York; American Airlines Flight 75 crashed on the Pentagon in Washington, DC; and American Airlines Flight 77 crashed in Somerset County, some 210 km south-east of Pittsburgh, Pennsylvania. About 2,750 people were killed in New York, 184 at the Pentagon, and 40 in Pennsylvania. The attacks were orchestrated by the al-Qa'ida network under the leadership of Osama bin Laden. This was the first time since the civil war (1861–65) that an act of warfare had occurred within the boundaries of continental USA.

The USA and its allies responded to the attacks by launching a 'war on terror'. US-led troops invaded Afghanistan in 2001 and **Iraq** in 2003 to overturn regimes that were assumed to have harboured or have had associations with terrorists. While the states of Western Europe were united in their condemnation of the 11 September attacks, they were divided in their response to the subsequent 'war on **terrorism**'. While governing parties in the United Kingdom, Spain and Italy supported the US-led invasion of Iraq in 2003, France and Germany strongly opposed it. In 2003 the US Secretary of Defense, Donald Rumsfeld, referred to this division as one between 'old' and 'new' Europe.

Single Currency – *see* Euro

Single European Act (SEA)

The Single European Act (SEA) was signed in 1986 by the 12 member states of the **European Community (EC)** and came into force in 1987. An important development in the process of European integration, the SEA provided a treaty basis for the programme to complete the **Single European Market (SEM)** by 1992. The SEA introduced reforms to improve the efficiency and speed of decision-making in the **Council of the European Union** by extending the use of qualified majority voting, and also to improve accountability by enhancing the role of the **European Parliament (EP)**. A key development was the introduction of the co-operation procedure which gave the EP a greater role in decision-making. It meant that if the EP rejected a decision made by the Council of the European Union, the Council would require a unanimous vote in order to overrule the parliament. This procedure was used predominantly for passing measures to complete the SEM, but also in areas relating to social policy, regional funds and research and technology.

Other changes introduced by the SEA included bringing the policy areas of environment, research and technological development and economic and social cohesion into the EC domain, giving European Political Co-operation (the forerunner of **Common Foreign and Security Policy**) a legal basis, and setting up the Court of First Instance to take some of the burden off the overloaded **European Court of Justice**. The SEA also increased the EC's capacity in the areas of environment and economic and social cohesion to correct the impact of the market-building exercise. It introduced **structural funds** for poor regions and allowed for EC harmonization of health and safety policy.

Single European Market (SEM)

The Single European Market (SEM) is a single economic area in the **European Union** free of national barriers to trade. The aim of the SEM was to improve the economic efficiency of the **European Community (EC)**, intensify competition, and reduce the costs of trade. The objective of establishing an internal or common market was set out by the **Treaty of Rome**, but limited progress was made in the 1960s and 1970s. A programme to complete core aspects of the SEM was drawn up in a **European Commission** White Paper in 1985 and completed in 1992. The White Paper identified 300 measures that needed to be taken to complete the single market and these were translated into 282 items of legislation. The measures related to the removal of physical, technical and fiscal barriers to trade in order to promote the freedom of movement of goods, services, capital and labour.

The impetus to complete the SEM in 1985 was a response to lobbying from the European business community, the policy initiative of the European Commission and a shift in ideological orientations of national governments in favour of the market. It was motivated by a common concern that the economies of the EC were falling behind those of the USA, **Japan** and newly industrializing countries in south-east Asia. The **Single European Act** provided political and institutional reforms to the institutions of the EC to complete the SEM.

Siniscalco, Domenico

Domenico Siniscalco has been the Minister of Economics and Finance in Italy since 2004. He was appointed to this office following the resignation of Giulio Tremonti and replaced **Silvio Berlusconi** who had acted as Minister of Economics and

Finance until a replacement for Tremonti could be found. Prior to his appointment, Siniscalco served as director-general of the Treasury, in 2001–04.

Born on 15 July 1954 in Turin, Domenico Siniscalco studied law at Turin University and gained a Ph.D. in economics from Cambridge University in the United Kingdom. He lectured at Luiss University, the University of Cagliari, Johns Hopkins University, the University of Cambridge, and the Catholic University of Louvain. He currently holds a full professorship at the University of Turin. Domenico Siniscalco is married and has two sons.

Address: Ministry of Economics and Finance, Via XX Settembre 97, 00187
　　　　Rome, Italy
Tel: (0)06 47614606 or (0)06 47614360
Fax: (0)06 4881247
E-mail: portavoce@tesoro.it
Internet: www.tesoro.it

Sinn Féin

Sinn Féin, established in 1905, is Ireland's oldest Irish political party. An Irish nationalist party, it campaigns today in both **Northern Ireland** and the Republic of Ireland for a united sovereign state of Ireland, national self-determination and the end of British rule. Sinn Féin is regarded as the political wing of the Irish Republican Army. The party supported the **Good Friday Agreement**, but has since refused to renegotiate it on the grounds that it has been endorsed by all Irish voters in a referendum.

Sinn Féin has representatives in the **House of Commons** of the United Kingdom and in the Republic of Ireland's **Dáil Éireann**, as well as at local level and in the Northern Ireland Assembly. At the most recent elections to the House of Commons, held on 7 June 2001, Sinn Féin returned four members. It also won five seats in the most recent elections to the Dáil, held on 17 May 2002. In elections to the Northern Ireland Assembly, held in December 2003, it overtook the **Social Democratic and Labour Party** as the largest nationalist party, and became the second largest party overall, winning 24 of the 108 seats (compared to 18 of 104 seats in 1998). It now finds itself in the position of having to deal with its political opponent, the **Democratic Unionist Party**, which is the largest party.

Party Leader: Gerry Adams
Address: 51/55 Falls Rd, Belfast BT12 4PD, United Kingdom
Tel: (0)2890 223 0000
Fax: (0)2890 223 001
E-mail: info@sinnfein.org
Internet: www.sinnfein.org

Sjálfstædisflokkurinn – *see* Independence Party, Iceland

Social Chapter

The Social Chapter established minimum social conditions within the **European Union**. An innovation of the **Treaty on European Union (TEU)**, the Social Chapter allows the **European Community** to develop policy in such areas as health and safety in the workplace, working conditions, the informing and consultation of employees, the equality of men and **women** with regard to labour-market participation, and the integration of unemployed people into working life.

Initially, the Chapter had to be annexed to the TEU as a protocol as the **Conservative Party** government of the United Kingdom negotiated an opt-out. The protocol was brought into the main treaty by the **Treaty of Amsterdam** as the **Labour Party** government in the United Kingdom that was elected in 1997 signed the Social Chapter.

Social Democratic and Labour Party (SDLP)

The Social Democratic and Labour Party (SDLP) is traditionally the main nationalist party in **Northern Ireland**. Established in 1970 by John Hume and Gerry Fitt, the party was born out of the civil rights movement. It promotes left-of-centre principles and an eventual reunification of Ireland by popular consent and constitutional methods. It fully supported the **Good Friday Agreement**.

The party had three representatives in the **House of Commons** following elections held on 7 June 2001. In elections to the Northern Ireland Assembly held in December 2003 the SDLP lost a significant number of seats to **Sinn Féin**, forfeiting its status as the most significant nationalist party in Northern Ireland. It won only 18 of 108 seats (compared to 24 of 104 in 1998), triggering a discussion about the future of the party.

Party Leader: Mark Durkan
Address: 121 Ormeau Rd, Belfast BT7 1SH, United Kingdom
Tel: (0)2890 247700
Fax: (0)2890 236699
E-mail: sdlp@indigo.ie
Internet: www.sdlp.ie

Social Democratic Party (Portugal)

The Social Democratic Party, or Partido Social Democrata (PSD), is the main centre-right party in Portugal. Founded in 1974, originally as the People's Democratic Party, it is not a social democratic party in the conventional sense: the PSD campaigns to promote economic and social freedom.

The PSD led various coalitions of the right in 1979–83 and participated in a Centre Bloc coalition with the **Socialist Party** in 1983–85. Under Prime Minister Aníbal Cavaco Silva the party governed as a minority administration in 1985–87, and won an absolute majority for the period 1987–95 following a vote of censure in

1987. The PSD was in opposition in 1995–2002. In elections held on 17 March 2002 the PSD won 40.5% of the vote and 105 seats in the 230-seat **Assembléia da República**. It formed a coalition with the smaller **People's Party**, first under Prime Minister **José Manuel Durão Barroso** and, from 2004, under Pedro Santana Lopes. In the elections held on 20 February 2005 the PSD won 28.7% of the vote and 72 seats and became the main opposition party.

Pres.: Pedro Miguel Santana Lopes
Address: Rua de São Caetano 9, 1249-087 Lisbon, Portugal
Tel: (0)21 3952140
Fax: (0)21 3976967
E-mail: psd@psd.pt
Internet: www.psd.pt

Social Democratic Party (Sweden)

The Social Democratic Party, or Socialdemokratiska Arbetarpartiet (SAP), founded in 1889, is the social-democratic party in Sweden. The SAP has dominated Swedish politics in the 20th century: it governed for 44 consecutive years in 1932–76, with the exception of one short period, and has been in power again in 1982–91 and since 1994. The SAP has 144 representatives in the 349-seat **Riksdag** that was elected on 15 September 2002 and governs as a minority government under **Göran Persson** as Prime Minister.

The SAP is credited for constructing Sweden's extensive **welfare state**. It promotes the values of freedom, justice and solidarity and aims for the maximum participation of Swedish citizens in the democratic process at all levels, and in the workplace. It promotes full employment on the grounds that it supports the Swedish welfare state and is the nation's most valuable asset. Work is perceived as a strategy for creating equality between different groups of the population. The party has close links with the **Swedish Confederation of Trade Unions**.

Party Leader: Göran Persson
Address: Sveavägen 68, 105 60 Stockholm, Sweden
Tel: (0)8 700-26-00
Fax: (0)8 20-42-57
E-mail: info@sap.se
Internet: www.sap.se

Social Democratic Party of Austria

The Social Democratic Party of Austria, or Sozialdemokratische Partei Österreichs (SPÖ), is the country's main left-wing party. Established in 1888/89, it was until 1999 the dominant party in post-war Austrian politics. The party governed in grand coalitions with the **Austrian People's Party (ÖPV)** in 1945–66, 1986–2000 and, alone, in 1970–86. Following the general election of 1999 the SPÖ failed to provide the Austrian Chancellor for the first time since 1970. In elections held on 24 November 2002 the party won 36.5% of the vote and 69 seats in the 183-seat **Nationalrat**, thereby becoming the second largest party. This was the first time that it had failed to gain the status of largest party in the Nationalrat since 1966.

Party Leader: Alfred Gusenbauer
Address: Löwelstrasse 18, 1014 Vienna, Austria
Tel: (0)1-53-427-0
Fax: (0)1-53-59-683
E-mail: spoe@spoe.at
Internet: www.spoe.at

Social Democratic Party of Germany

The Social Democratic Party of Germany, or Sozialdemokratische Partei Deutschlands (SPD), is the main party of the left in the Federal Republic of Germany. Originally founded as a socialist party in 1863, the SPD was banned in 1933–45. After the Second World War the party was re-established under the leadership of Kurt Schumacher and transformed itself into a *Volkspartei* (People's Party) at the Bad Godesberg Conference in 1959. Today the party pursues a reformist agenda, campaigning to promote social justice and democracy.

The SPD governed in the post-war period in a grand coalition with the **Christian Democratic Union** in 1966–69, and led a coalition with the **Free Democratic Party** in 1969–82, first under **Willy Brandt** and then under Helmut Schmidt. The party returned to government in 1998 in a coalition with **Alliance 90/The Greens** under Chancellor **Gerhard Schröder**.

The coalition was re-elected in the general elections held on 22 September 2002, when the SPD won 38.5% of the vote and 251 seats in the 603-seat **Bundestag**, thereby becoming the largest party by a margin of three seats. Since 2002 the SPD Chancellor **Gerhard Schröder** has been widely criticized by the left wing of the party for his economic and welfare reforms, though he was widely praised for his decision not to commit German troops to the war in **Iraq** in 2003. Schröder resigned as party leader in February 2004 in order to concentrate on his role as Chancellor.

Party Leader: Franz Müntefering
Address: Willy-Brandt-Haus, Wilhelmstrasse 141, 10963 Berlin, Germany
Tel: (0)30259910
Fax: (0)3025991410
E-mail: parteivorstand@spd.de
Internet: www.spd.de

Social Democratic Party of Switzerland

The Social Democratic Party of Switzerland, or Sozialdemokratische Partei der Schweiz (SP), was founded in 1888. The party campaigns for social reform, democracy, and full employment. A dominant party in Swiss politics, in elections held on 19 October 2003 the party lost its status as the largest party in the **Nationalrat**. In the elections held in 1999 it had won 22.5% of the vote and 51 seats. In 2003 it gained one extra seat, but was overtaken by the populist right-wing **Swiss People's Party**, which won 26.65% of the vote and 55 seats. The SP has two ministers in the permanent seven-seat coalition that was established in 1959 and reconfigured in 2003.

> *Leadership: Pres.* Hans-Jürg Fehr; *Gen. Sec.* Reto Gamma
> *Address:* Spitalgasse 34, Postfach 7876, 3001 Bern, Switzerland
> *Tel:* (0)313296969
> *Fax:* (0)313296970
> *E-mail:* info@spschweiz.ch
> *Internet:* www.spschweiz.ch

Social Democrats

The Social Democrats, or Socialdemokraterne, is the social democratic party in Denmark. Founded in 1871, it is the country's largest party and has dominated Danish politics in the 20th century. It has governed in minority or coalition governments for most of the post-war period except in 1982–93 and since 2001. It is credited with the construction of the Danish **welfare state**. The party had 52 representatives in the 179-seat **Folketing** that was elected on 20 September 2001, and was the second largest parliamentary party. This was the first time since 1929 that the Social Democrats was not returned as the largest party. Its representation in parliament was reduced to 47 seats following the election held on 8 February 2005.

> *Party Leader:* Mogens Lykketoft
> *Address:* Danasvej 7, 1910 Frederiksberg C, Denmark
> *Tel:* (0)72-30-08-00
> *Fax:* (0)72-30-08-50
> *E-mail:* partikontoret@net.dialog.dk
> *Internet:* www.socialdemokratiet.dk

Socialdemokraterne – *see* **Social Democrats, Denmark**

Socialdemokratiska Arbetarpartiet – *see* **Social Democratic Party, Sweden**

Socialistisk Folkeparti – *see* **Socialist People's Party, Denmark**

Socialistische Partij – *see* **Socialist Party, Netherlands**

Socialistische Partij-Anders – *see* Socialist Party-Spirit, Belgium

Socialist Left Party

The Socialist Left Party, or Sosialistisk Venstreparti, is a socialist party in Norway. It was established in 1975 from a coalition of socialists, communists and **Labour Party** members who had contested the 1973 election on a joint list. In that election the electoral coalition won 16 seats in the **Stortinget**. The party's electoral success has been erratic over the years, but in elections held on 10 September 2001 it won its highest ever number of seats: 23 in the 165-seat parliament.

Since the late 1990s the party has campaigned for improvements in standards of pre-school care and education and against child poverty. It also promotes sustainable development and aims to move Norway away from its status as an oil economy. It promotes renewable energy sources and improvements in public transport provision. Internationally, the party is opposed to Norwegian membership of the **European Union** and campaigns for restraining global capital.

Leadership: Party Leader Kristin Halvorsen; *Gen. Sec.* Bård Vegar Solhjell
Address: Akersgata 35, 0158 Oslo, Norway
Tel: (0)21-93-33-00
Fax: (0)21-93-33-01
E-mail: post@sv.no
Internet: www.sv.no

Socialist Party (Belgium)

The Socialist Party, or Parti Socialiste (PS), is the social democratic party in the French-speaking part of Belgium. Originally founded as the Belgian Socialist Party in 1893, it was established as the PS in 1978. The party campaigns to promote the principles of freedom, liberty, solidarity, equality and justice in Belgian society and the international community.

The PS governed in 1988–99 with the **Socialist Party-Spirit** and the French and Flemish Christian Democrats. It campaigned for constitutional reform and the development of Belgium into a federal state in 1993. Following elections held in 1999, it entered into coalition with liberal and green parties, under liberal Prime Minister **Guy Verhofstadt**. In the most recent election, held on 18 May 2003, the PS won 13% of the vote and returned 25 representatives to the 150-seat **Kamer**. It subsequently formed a second coalition with the liberal parties.

Leadership: Pres. Elio Di Rupo; *Sec.-Gen.* Jean-Pol Baras
Address: 13 blvd de l'Empereur, 1000 Brussels, Belgium
Tel: (0)2 548-32-11
Fax: (0)2 548-33-80

E-mail: info@ps.be
Internet: www.ps.be

Socialist Party (France)

The Socialist Party, or Parti Socialiste (PS), is the dominant party of the left in France. The party has its origins as the French section of the Socialist International, the Section française de l'internationale ouvrière. It was founded as a separate party in 1969 and **François Mitterrand** joined at the Congress held in Epinay in June 1971. The PS is a democratic party which seeks to promote freedom and equality of citizens, regardless of gender, race, religion or sexual orientation. It seeks to transform society to mitigate the effects of capitalism in the era of globalization.

The PS formed an electoral pact with the **Communist Party of France (PCF)** during the 1970s and won both the presidential and **Assemblée Nationale** elections in 1981. François Mitterrand served two terms as President, in 1981–88 and 1988–95, and the PS has led governments and provided Prime Ministers in 1981–86, 1988–93 and 1997–2002. During the first two years in power, in 1981–83, Mitterrand and the PS-led government pursued a Keynesian economic policy of nationalization, wage rises and increased public spending. As inflation and **unemployment** rose, the government performed a massive policy about-turn, linking the franc to the German currency, the Deutsche Mark, gradually reducing the state's involvement in the economy and pursuing a policy of **Europeanization**. The 'pluralist' left-wing government made up of the PS, the **Communist Party**, the **Greens** and the Mouvement des Citoyens in 1997–2002 continued its right-wing predecessor's policy of privatization, but also sought to reduce unemployment. It introduced a 35-hour working week, a welfare-to-work scheme to create public-sector jobs for the young unemployed, and measures to tackle social exclusion.

In the first round of the presidential elections held on 21 April 2002 the PS candidate, Lionel Jospin, was placed third, winning only 16.18% of the vote. In the general election held on 9 and 16 June 2002 the PS won 140 seats in the 577-seat Assemblée Nationale.

Party Leader: François Hollande
Address: 10 rue de Solférino, 75333 Paris Cedex 07, France
Tel: (0)1-45-56-77-00
Fax: (0)1-47-05-15-78
E-mail: via www.parti-socialiste.fr
Internet: www.parti-socialiste.fr

Socialist Party (Ireland)

The Socialist Party is a new party in Ireland. Formerly known as Militant Labour, the party changed its name in 1996. It campaigns to promote the interests of working people in Ireland. At the most recent elections to the **Dáil Éireann**, held on 17 May 2002, the party won one seat.

Public Representative: Joe Higgins
Address: 141 Thomas St, Dublin 8, Ireland
Tel: (0)1 6772686
Fax: (0)1 6772592
E-mail: info@socialistparty.net
Internet: www.socialistparty.net

Socialist Party (Netherlands)

The Socialist Party, or Socialistische Partij (SP), is the socialist party in the Netherlands. Founded in 1972, the party has undergone a series of transformations from a grass roots movements to a national party, growing to become the fourth largest party in the **Tweede Kamer** today. The SP decided to focus again on local-level campaigning in 1999. The party promotes a fairer distribution of knowledge, power and income in the Netherlands and internationally, and it opposes neo-liberal economic policies. It campaigns for renationalization, to improve the state of the environment and for investment in programmes to integrate immigrants into Dutch society.

Following some success in local politics, the party first entered the Tweede Kamer in 1994, when it won two seats. Its representation increased to eight seats following elections held in 2003. During the so-called 'purple coalition' between the **Labour Party**, the **People's Party for Freedom and Democracy** and **Democrats 66** in 1994–2002, it presented itself as the red alternative to 'advancing neo-liberalism' under the social-liberal coalition.

Party Leader: Jan Marijnissen
Address: Vijverhofstraat 65, 3032 SC Rotterdam, Netherlands
Tel: (0)10 2435555
Fax: (0)10 2435566
E-mail: sp@sp.nl
Internet: www.sp.nl

Socialist Party (Portugal)

The Socialist Party, or Partido Socialista (PS), is the main social democratic party in Portugal. Originally founded in 1875, it was re-formed in 1973 under the leadership of Mário Soares. The PS campaigns to promote solidarity and social justice in Portugal. In government in the early 1980s and late 1990s the PS pursued centrist policies and liberal economic reform. Soares led a 'Centre Bloc' coalition with the **Social Democratic Party (PSD)** in 1983–85. The PS governed as a minority administration in 1995–2002 under Prime Minister António Guterres, relying on the **Communist Party of Portugal** and the **People's Party** for majorities in the **Assembléia da República**. Guterres resigned as Prime Minister and party leader in 2001 following the PS's poor performance in local elections. In the general elections held on 17 March 2002 the PS won 37.9% of the vote and 95 seats in the 230-seat parliament, coming second to the PSD. In the election held on 20 February 2005 the party won 45.1% of the vote and 120 seats and was able for the first time to form a majority single party government. Party leader **José Sócrates** became Prime Minister.

Sec-Gen.: José Sócrates
Address: Largo do Rato 2, 1269-143 Lisbon, Portugal
Tel: (0)21 3822000
Fax: (0)21 3822022
E-mail: portal@ps.pt
Internet: www.ps.pt

Socialist Party-Spirit

The Socialist Party-Spirit, or Socialistische Partij-Anders (SP.A), is the socialist party in the Flemish-speaking part of Belgium. The party separated from the former Belgian Socialist Party in 1978 and became known as the Socialist Party (SP). It changed its name to SP.A in 2000. It is also known as Social Progressive Alternative, or Sociaal Progressief Alternatief.

As SP, the party governed in coalition with the French-speaking **Socialist Party** and the Christian Democrats in 1988–99. At the most recent election, held on 18 May 2003, SP.A formed an alliance with the social-liberal Spirit party. Together they won 14.9% of the vote and 23 representatives in the 150-seat **Kamer**. SP.A-Spirit subsequently joined a liberal-led coalition under **Guy Verhofstadt**.

Party Leader: Steve Stevaert
Address: Grasmarkt 105/37, 1000 Brussels, Belgium
Tel: (0)2 552-02-00
Fax: (0)2 552-02-55
E-mail: info@s-p-a.be
Internet: www.s-p-a.be

Socialist People's Party

The Socialist People's Party, or Socialistisk Folkeparti (SF), is a socialist party in Denmark. Established in 1959 following a conflict within the Danish Communist Party, SF campaigns to promote democratic socialist change in Denmark and abroad. The party has 11 members in the 179-seat **Folketing** that was elected on 8 February 2005.

Party Leader: Holger K. Nielsen
Address: Christianborg, 1240 Copenhagen K, Denmark
Tel: (0)33-37-44-44

Fax: (0)33-12-72-48
E-mail: sf@sf.dk
Internet: www.sf.dk

Social-Liberal Party

The Social-Liberal Party, or Radikale Venstre, is a liberal party in Denmark. Founded in 1905 by a group which broke away from the **Liberal Party** (Venstre) to emphasize social issues, the party today occupies the centre ground in Danish politics. It stands for liberalism with social responsibility, and is anti-military. It has entered into numerous coalition governments with parties on the left and right, most recently with the **Social Democrats** until 2001. At the general election held on 8 February 2005 the Social-Liberal Party won 17 seats in the 179-seat **Folketing**.

Party Leader: Søren Bald
Address: Christiansborg, 1240 Copenhagen K, Denmark
Tel: (0)33-37-47-47
Fax: (0)33-13-72-51
E-mail: radikale@radikale.dk
Internet: www.drv.dk

Sócrates, José

José Sócrates has been Prime Minister of Portugal since 20 February 2005 when the **Socialist Party (PS)** secured a decisive victory in the election held then and was able to form its first single party majority government. Characterized as a modernizer, Sócrates was elected on a promise to implement economic reform, cut **unemployment** and improve social cohesion. He had previously served as Secretary of State in the Ministry of Environment in 1995–97, as Deputy Prime Minister in 1997–99 and as Minister of the Environment in 1999–2002. He was first elected to the **Assembléia da República** in 1987–95 and was re-elected in 2002. A member of the PS since 1981, he became its general secretary in September 2004.

José Sócrates was born on 6 September 1957 in Vilar de Maçada and studied civil engineering and, later, health engineering at the National School of Public Health. He is married and has two children.

Address: Rua da Imprensa à Estrela 4, 1200-888 Lisbon, Portugal
Tel: (0)21 3923500
Fax: (0)21 3951616
E-mail: gpm@pm.gov.pt
Internet: www.portugal.gov.pt/Portal/EN/Primeiro_Ministro

Solana, Javier

Javier Solana has been secretary-general of the **Council of the European Union** and high representative for **Common Foreign and Security Policy (CFSP)** since

18 October 1999. This post was an innovation of the **Treaty of Amsterdam**, and Solana was the first person to occupy it. Solana's role is to assist the Council in CFSP matters and to conduct political dialogue with third parties on behalf of the Council presidency. He was appointed for a second five-year term in July 2004, and is to become the Union Minister for Foreign Affairs in the event of the Constitutional Treaty for Europe coming into force. Solana has also been secretary-general of the **Western European Union** since 25 November 1999. In his first five years as high representative for the CFSP Solana has overseen the development of **European Security and Defence Policy**, of a European Security Strategy and a **European Union** strategy against **terrorism**.

Born on 14 July 1942 in Madrid, Spain, Solana gained a doctorate in physics, studying as a Fulbright scholar in the USA. He worked as professor of physics at the Madrid Complutense University. Solana joined the **Spanish Socialist Party (PSOE)** in 1964 and was first elected to the **Congreso de los Diputados** in 1977. He served continually in the PSOE governments of Felipe González, as Minister for Culture in 1982–88, Minister for Education and Science in 1988–92 and Minister for Foreign Affairs in 1992–95. Subsequently, in 1995–99, he served as secretary-general of the **North Atlantic Treaty Organization**.

Address: Council of the European Union, rue de la Loi 175, 1048 Brussels, Belgium
Tel: (0)2 285-61-11
Fax: (0)2 285-73-97-81
E-mail: public.info@consilium.eu.int
Internet: ue.eu.int

Solbes, Pedro

Pedro Solbes has been Minister of the Economy in Spain since 2004. A member of the **Spanish Socialist Party**, he is part of the minority socialist government formed following the general elections held on 14 March 2004. Prior to this, in 1999–2004, Pedro Solbes was European commissioner for Economic and Monetary Affairs. In this role he oversaw the final stages of **Economic and Monetary Union**, including the introduction of **euro** notes and coins on 1 January 2002. He strongly defended the euro currency in its troubled first months and the widely criticized **Stability and Growth Pact**.

Born on 31 August 1942 in Pinoso, Solbes studied economics and law in Spain and Brussels, and has a Ph.D. in political science from the University of Madrid. He worked as a civil servant in the Ministry of Foreign Trade and later helped negotiate Spain's **accession** to the **European Community**, in 1986. He served as Minister of Agriculture, Fisheries and Food in 1991–93, and as Minister of the Economy in1993–96. Following the electoral success of the **Popular Party** in 1996, Solbes was a member of parliament in 1996–99. Pedro Solbes is married with two children.

Address: Ministry of Finance, Paseo de la Castellana 162, 28046 Madrid, Spain
Tel: (0)91 5837400
E-mail: portal@mineco.es
Internet: www2.mineco.es/mineco

Sosialistisk Venstreparti – *see* Socialist Left Party, Norway

Sozialdemokratische Partei Deutschlands – *see* Social Democratic Party of Germany

Sozialdemokratische Partei Österreichs – *see* Social Democratic Party of Austria

Sozialdemokratische Partei der Schweiz – *see* Social Democratic Party of Switzerland

Spain

Spain, located in the Iberian peninsula between France and Portugal, is Western Europe's second largest country in surface area. Its political history has been turbulent, with nearly 45 *coups d'état* in 1814–1923, a short-lived Second Republic in the early 1930s, a civil war in 1936–39, and an authoritarian regime under Gen. Francisco Franco in 1939–75. Following Franco's death in 1975 his chosen successor, King Juan Carlos, oversaw Spain's successful transition to democracy. An attempted military coup in 1981 was quashed by King Juan Carlos. Since then Spain's transition to democracy has been held up as a model for other fledgling democracies and it is now considered a fully integrated member of Western Europe.

Area: 506,000 sq km; *capital:* Madrid; *population:* 41m. (2001).

Spain's 1978 Constitution provided for a system of parliamentary democracy. The bicameral parliament, the Cortes, is made up of the lower house, the **Congreso de los Diputados**, and the upper house, the **Senado**. The head of state is King Juan Carlos. The head of government is currently **José Luis Rodríguez Zapatero** of the **Spanish Socialist Party (PSOE)**. The Socialists were elected as a minority government on 14 March 2004, winning 164 seats in the 350-seat Congreso de los Diputados. The election of the PSOE, following eight years in opposition, came three days after terrorist bombings in Madrid in which 191 people died. Until the attacks it had been anticipated that the **Popular Party (PP)** under José María Aznar would be re-elected.

Spain is a unitary state, but the Constitution allows for regional devolution. Since 1979 Spain has been divided into 17 regions, or autonomous communities, each of which has a Statute of Autonomy which regulates its autonomous status and its relations with central government. The system is characterized by asymmetric levels of autonomy, with historical regions such as Catalonia and the **Basque Country** enjoying the highest degree of autonomy. Each autonomous community has its own parliament, executive and judiciary. In many regions, regional or nationalist political parties campaign to increase their region's autonomy (e.g. **Convergence and Union (CiU)** in Catalonia). Additionally, nationalist parties, such as the **Basque Nationalist Party**, campaign for independence for their region. Although the Spanish Senado is supposed to be Spain's territorial chamber, only 51 of 259 senators are appointed directly by autonomous parliaments and they have little influence on national decision-making.

Spanish politics have been dominated by left-wing parties since Franco's death in 1975. Following a short period of transition to democracy under Adolfo Suarez's Union of Democratic Centre and an attempted military coup in 1981, the PSOE gained the status of largest party in the Congreso de los Diputados and formed four successive governments in 1982–96 under Felipe González. The first three administrations (in 1982–93) were majority governments, but during its next three years in office the PSOE governed as a minority government, relying on the support of the Catalan nationalist party CiU in parliament.

The PSOE governments under González oversaw Spain's accession to the **North Atlantic Treaty Organization (NATO)** in 1982 and a much-disputed referendum on NATO membership in 1986. Membership of the **European Community** followed in 1986. An enthusiastic member of the **European Union (EU)**, integration into Europe is for Spain a symbol of democracy, freedom and a reconnection with the continent after years of isolation under Franco. Spain has benefited immensely from the EU's **structural funds**. It has acted as champion of poorer countries in the EU as well as a bridge to North Africa and Latin America.

The González years were also characterized by rapid economic growth. However, during the 1980s Spain continued to suffer from high **unemployment** caused by the structural economic reforms brought by the modernization of the Spanish economy and EU membership. Towards the mid-1990s the PSOE government was undermined by a series of corruption and political scandals. The governor of the **Banco de España**, Mariano Rubio, was convicted of tax evasion. It was later alleged that the Spanish government had sponsored the anti-terrorist agency GAL, which was responsible for the death of some 27 supporters of the Basque terrorist organization ETA in the 1980s.

In the general election held on 3 March 1996 a shift to the right occurred when the PP, under José María Aznar, gained the status of largest party in the Congreso de los Diputados. It initially governed without a majority, relying on the support of the Catalan, Basque and other, smaller nationalist parties. The PP's reliance on regionalist and nationalist political parties prevented it from following its instinct to pursue a more centralizing political programme. In his first term Aznar's primary political objective was to ensure that Spain qualified in the first wave for membership of **Economic and Monetary Union**, cutting 250,000m. pesetas from the first budget. In elections held on 12 March 2000 Aznar won an overall majority and no longer needed the support of other parties to govern. Although the PP government pursued a hardline policy against ETA and Basque nationalists, it agreed to allow the autonomous communities to retain 30% rather than 15% of tax revenues. A more controversial policy was a closer relationship with the USA, particularly following the terrorist attacks of **11 September** 2001. Spain committed troops to the war in **Iraq** in 2003, even though 90% of the Spanish population opposed Spain's involvement.

Despite Aznar's unpopular policy on Iraq, it was anticipated that the PP would be re-elected in the general election held on 14 March 2004. However, on 11 March 2004 terrorists detonated three bombs in Madrid. The PP government immediately blamed the attacks on ETA, which had claimed some 800 victims in 30 years. The government was then strongly criticized for this premature conclusion when it emerged that the attacks were more probably the work of terrorists linked to al-Qa'ida. Critics claimed that the PP had sought to make political capital from the attacks: had it been ETA, voters would have supported the PP's tough measures on the Basque terrorists; if the bombs were in any way linked to the war in Iraq, this would have benefited the PSOE. As a consequence, there was a large transfer of support from the PP to the PSOE in the elections, and a high turn-out (77.2%). The PSOE won 42.6% of the vote and currently has 164 seats in the 350-seat Congreso de los Diputados, governing as a minority administration under José Luis Rodríguez Zapatero. Immediately following the election, Zapatero withdrew Spanish troops from Iraq and began to pursue a European rather than an Atlanticist foreign policy. The new PSOE government also pledged to bring about a social revolution, proposing to relax abortion laws, tighten legislation on domestic violence and enact legislation that would allow **women** to accede to the Spanish throne.

Economy: The Spanish economy is dominated by car manufacturing, tourism, textiles and steel. Spain is the fourth largest car producer in Europe, though all firms in the sector are foreign-owned. Traditionally a rural economy, Spain experienced some industrialization at the start of the 20th century, before the civil war of 1936–39. During the Franco era (1939–75) industry was protected by the state and Franco's corporatist economy developed rapidly during the 1960s. Today the Spanish economy draws its strength from main industrial areas in Catalonia, Madrid and the **Basque Country**. Catalonia hosts small and medium-sized industries specializing in textiles and shoes, and the Basque Country is oriented towards steel, shipbuilding, machine tools and aerospace. Other regions, such as Andalucía, still have largely rural economies and well-developed tourist industries.

GNP: US $588,000m. (2001); *GNP per caput:* $14,300 (2001); *GNP at PPP:* $816,000m. (2001); *GNP per caput at PPP:* $19,860 (2001); *GDP:* $581,823m. (2001); *exports:* $175,336m. (2001); *imports:* $182,577m. (2001); *currency:* euro; *unemployment:* 11.4% (2002).

During the transition to democracy, economic stability was initially maintained through a series of social agreements between the government, employers and the socialist and communist trade unions. The first was the Moncloa Pact of 1977. This process of social concertation provided for social peace and economic stability in the early years of democracy. Until 1987 wage increases were fixed by national negotiationss, led by the government. This forum also discussed broader issues about how the economy should be run. Social concertation broke down after 1986 when trade unions opposed the **Spanish Socialist Party (PSOE)** government's proposals on pensions and social benefits. The unions staged a general strike on 14 December 1988, and two further strikes in the late 1980s. Social concertation was resumed following the election of the conservative **Popular Party** in 1996, and during the 1990s a series of tripartite agreements were signed which fostered social peace, wage moderation and economic growth. This process helped keep inflation in check. Spain's inflation rate was 25% in 1977 and 14.5% in 1981. As a result of wage moderation, collective agreements and tight monetary policy, inflation has fallen and now oscillates around 3%.

The Spanish **welfare state** expanded rapidly following the election of the PSOE in 1982. Social spending initially rose, but later stagnated as public spending priorities shifted towards improving Spain's infrastructure. Since democratization Spain has continuously suffered from high rates of **unemployment**. During the recession of the mid-1990s unemployment reached a high of 23.4%, but it has since fallen to around 12%. Spanish unemployment is higher in regions such as rural Andalucía and the once heavily industrial Basque Country. **Women** and the under-25s are also disproportionately affected by unemployment. It is believed that a large number of the unemployed work in the informal economy, the size of which is estimated at 15%–20% of official gross domestic product (GDP).

The Spanish labour market is highly regulated and slow to create new employment. Workers have traditionally been protected by strict rules on hiring and firing and employers have been obliged to pay generous severance pay when there are lay-offs. To encourage the creation of new jobs the labour law was liberalized during the 1980s and 1990s, introducing and expanding the use of temporary contracts. Now around one-quarter of Spanish employees are on temporary contracts. Spain also has a large public sector; public-sector employment grew by 20% in 1986–91 and many new jobs were in regional governments.

Spain's rapid economic growth in the late 1980s coincided with the country's **accession** to the **European Community (EC)**. This brought many benefits to the economy: it triggered a general opening-up and modernization and improved the management of the economy; it forced successive Spanish governments to implement programmes of tough economic measures to promote competitiveness and a larger market; and it led to a programme of privatization to meet the requirements of the **Single European Market** in 1992. EC membership also brought significant cash benefits from Brussels in the form of **structural funds** (160,000m. pesetas in 1988). Until recently Spain was the **European Union's (EU)** largest recipient of regional development funds.

As a consequence of EC membership, the Spanish economy has converged with its Community counterparts. Spain's per caput GDP was only 70% of the EC average in 1983, but it had risen to 75% of the average by 1994 and to 80% by 2000. In 1981–85 the Spanish economy grew at an average annual rate of 1.5%. Following EC membership, the rate of growth increased to 5% in 1988 and 1989. The period of rapid economic expansion, 1986–94, was followed by a short recession in 1994–95 during which unemployment rose as high as 23.4% and the budget deficit to 5.5% of GDP. Spain's rapid recovery was aided by the PSOE and then PP government's determination that the country would participate in the first wave of **Economic and Monetary Union**. Spain met the **convergence criteria** for the first wave of membership in 1999 and adopted the **euro** as its currency in 2002. As a member of the **euro area**, Spain's economy has performed comparatively well. It has grown steadily, even during the general slow-down that occurred from 2001 onwards (by 2% in 2002), and faster than the EU average for nearly 10 consecutive years. There has also been a growth in employment. However, the rates of unemployment and inflation remain above the EU average.

Spanish Confederation of Employers' Organizations

The Spanish Confederation of Employers' Organizations, or Confederación Española de Organizaciones Empresariales, is the major representative institution of the business community in Spain. Founded in 1977, it represents 1m. public and private companies in all sectors through 200 regional and trade organizations and 2,000 primary associations. It is itself a member of the **Union of Industrial and Employers' Confederations of Europe**.

Leadership: Pres. José María Cuevas-Salvador; *Gen. Sec.* Juan Jiménez Aguilar
Address: C/Diego de León 50, 28006 Madrid, Spain
Tel: (0)91 5663400
Fax: (0)91 5628023
E-mail: ceoe@ceoe.es
Internet: www.ceoe.es

Spanish Socialist Party

The Spanish Socialist Party, or Partido Socialista Obrero Español (PSOE), is the large left-wing political party in Spain. Founded in 1879, it seeks to promote the principles of liberty, equality and solidarity in Spanish society. The PSOE has dominated politics in post-Franco Spain. It governed in the post-Franco period in 1982–96 under Felipe González. During this time it pursued centrist, modernizing policies, for two terms as majority governments, and then in coalition with **Convergence and Union (CiU)**. The PSOE government's shift to the centre caused problems with trade unions and there were three general strikes in the 1980s. The party was also involved in scandals in the 1990s and went into opposition in 1996–2004. At elections held on 14 March 2004 the PSOE won 42.6% of the vote and currently has 164 seats in the 350-seat parliament, the **Congreso de los Diputados**.

It governs as a minority administration under Prime Minister **José Luis Rodríguez Zapatero**.

Leadership: Pres. Manuel Chaves González; *Gen. Sec.* José Luis Rodríguez
    Zapatero
Address: Calle Ferraz 70, 28008 Madrid, Spain
Tel: (0)91 5820444
E-mail: infopsoe@psoe.es
Internet: www.psoe.es

Special Supreme Tribunal

The Special Supreme Tribunal is the constitutional court in Greece. Established by the 1975 Constitution, it is made up of the president of the Council of State, the presidents of the Supreme Court and the Council of Comptrollers, four councillors of the Council of State and four members of the Supreme Court. It examines the validity of referendums, deals with conflicts between courts and clarifies constitutional matters. The decisions of the court are irrevocable.

Address: 47–49 Panepistimiou St, 105 64 Athens, Greece
Tel: (0)210 3710092
Fax: (0)210 3710137

Staatkundig Gereformeerde Partij – *see* Political Reformed Party, Netherlands

Stability and Growth Pact (SGP)

The Stability and Growth Pact (SGP) was agreed on 7 July 1997. As a part of stage three of **European and Monetary Union** launched on 1 January 1999, it commits member states that met the **convergence criteria** for participation in the **euro area** to maintain budgetary discipline. The SGP was introduced following concerns, particularly in Germany, that member states which manage to meet the convergence criteria would later circumvent the strict monetary policy of the **European Central Bank** by accumulating high budget deficits which would threaten the stability of the euro area.

The SGP sets out detailed arrangements for the surveillance of states' fiscal performance, and for the co-ordination of economic policies, and establishes the procedures for dealing with budget deficits which breach the rule that they must not exceed 3% of gross domestic product (GDP). Participating states are required to submit annual reports on their economic performance to the **European Commission** and the **European Council**. If a report provides evidence of an excessive deficit, then the Council can request that action be taken to correct the deficit. If this is not taken, sanctions can be applied. These first take the form of a non-interest-bearing deposit with the Commission. The value of this deposit comprises a fixed component of 0.2% of GDP and a variable component linked to the size of the deficit. The deposit would be converted into a fine if the excessive deficit has not been corrected within two years. If it is deemed that an excessive budget deficit results from unusual events outside the control of the member state, or from a severe economic downturn (defined as an annual fall in real GDP of at least 2%), then no sanctions are imposed.

In practice the rules are interpreted more flexibly. Since 1999 Ireland, Portugal, France and Germany have shown evidence of deficits greater than the 3% threshold, but no sanctions have been imposed. In November 2003 the Council decided that it would not fine France and Germany. There have been widespread calls to reform the SGP.

Ständerat

Council of States

The Ständerat (Council of States) is the upper house of the bicameral parliament of Switzerland which represents the cantons at federal level. It is made up of 46 members who represent the 26 Swiss Cantons. Most Cantons select two senators each, though the half Cantons (Obwald, Nidwald, Basel-City, Basel-Country, Appenzell Outer Rhodes and Appenzell Inner Rhodes) elect only one. The Ständerat shares a legislative role at national level with the **Nationalrat**.

Address: Ständerat, Parlamentsgebäude, 3003 Bern, Switzerland
Tel: (0)313222111
Fax: (0)313223706
E-mail: webmaster@admin.ch
Internet: www.parlament.ch

Stephanopoulos, Constantinos

Constantinos Stephanopoulos has been the President of Greece since 1995. He was re-elected for his second, and final, five-year term by the **Vouli ton Ellinon** in February 2000. In 1995 Stephanopoulos was nominated for the post of President by the Politiki Anixi (Political Spring) party and was supported by the ruling **Panhellenic Socialist Movement (PASOK)**. In 2000 his nomination was supported by the two main political parties—PASOK and **New Democracy (ND)**.

Born in 1926 in Patras, Constantinos Stephanopoulos graduated in law from the University of Athens. He was elected as a member of parliament in 1964 for the National Radical Union. In 1974 he joined ND and became its spokesman. Stephanopoulos was Minister for Commerce in 1974, Minister for the Interior in 1974–76, Minister for Social Services in 1976–77 and Minister for the Presidency in 1977–81. Stephanopoulos left ND in 1985 and became one of the co-founders of the Democratic Renewal Party. When this was disbanded in 1994 Stephanopoulos took the decision to leave politics.

Address: Presidential Palace, 2 Vas. Georghiou B' St, Athens 100 28, Greece
Tel: (0)210 7238111
Fax: (0)210 7248938
Internet: www.presidency.gr

Stortinget

Parliament

The Stortinget is the unicameral parliament of Norway. It is made up of 165 members who are elected by a system of proportional representation for a fixed term of four years. Norway's 19 counties serve as the constituencies and these are divided into polling districts. In addition to 157 constituency representatives elected to the Stortinget, a further eight are distributed among the counties after an election has been held. The most recent elections were held on 10 September 2001. Eight political parties are represented in the current Stortinget. These are (with number of seats in brackets): the **Labour Party** (43); the **Conservative Party** (38); the **Progress Party** (26); the **Socialist Left Party** (23); the **Christian People's Party** (22); the **Centre Party** (10); the **Liberals** (2) and the **Coastal Party** (1). At present, 36.4% of members of the Stortinget are **women**. The Stortinget is responsible for passing and amending laws. It is the final authority in matters concerning state finances and it exercises control over government activities.

Address: Karl Johans Gate 22, 0026 Oslo, Norway
Tel: (0)23-31-30-50
E-mail: stortinget.postmottak@stortinget.no
Internet: www.stortinget.no

Structural Funds

The Structural Funds of the **European Union (EU)** are paid to the least advantaged parts of the EU in order to promote social and economic cohesion. There are four structural funds: the **European Social Fund**; the **European Regional Development Fund**; the European Agricultural Guarantee and Guidance Fund; and the Financial Instrument for Fisheries Guidance.

Sunflower Alliance

The Sunflower Alliance, or Il Girasole, is an electoral alliance in Italy comprising the Italian Democratic Socialists (Socialisti Democratici Italiani—SDI) and the Federation of Greens (Federazione dei Verdi—Verdi). Formed for the general elections held on 13 May 2001, the Sunflower Alliance returned 18 deputies to the **Camera dei Deputati** as part of the Olive Tree Alliance (L'Ulivo) with the **Democrats of the Left**, the **Daisy Alliance** and the Italian Communist Party.

Internet: www.ilgirasole.org

Suomen Ammattiliittojen Keskusjärjestö – *see* **Central Organization of Finnish Trade Unions**

Suomen Pankki

Suomen Pankki, the central bank of Finland, was founded in 1811. The Act governing the Bank of Finland was revised in 1997, and, again, in 1998, as the first set of amendments did not meet all of the requirements for entering stage three of **Economic and Monetary Union (EMU)**. Since the start of stage three of EMU, on 1 January 1999, the Suomen Pankki has been a member of the **European System of Central Banks** and, as a member of the **euro area**, of the **Eurosystem**. It implements the decisions of the **European Central Bank** in Finland. Suomen Pankki also hosts the Institute for Economics in Transition which conducts research on transition economics and the Russian, Baltic and Chinese cases in particular.

Gov.: Erkki Liikanen
Address: POB 160, 00101 Helsinki, Finland
Tel: (0)108311
Fax: (0)9174872
E-mail: info@bof.fi
Internet: www.bof.fi

Suomen Sosialidemokraattinen Puolue – *see* **Finnish Social Democratic Party**

Supreme Court (Denmark)

The Supreme Court, or Højesteret, is the highest court in Denmark. Founded in 1661 by King Frederik III, it has been an independent institution since 1849. It is made up of a president and 18 other judges who are appointed by the Minister of Justice. The Højesteret has the right to determine whether the decisions of the executive are in accordance with the law, and whether bills passed by the **Folketing** are constitutional.

Address: Prins Jørgens Gård 13, 1218 Copenhagen K, Denmark
Tel: (0)33-63-27-50
Fax: (0)70-10-44-55
E-mail: lsm@domstolsstyrelsen.dk
Internet: www.domstol.dk

Supreme Court (Finland)

The Supreme Court, the Korkein Oikeus, is the highest court in Finland. The court consists of a president and at least 15 other judges who are appointed by the President of Finland; at present there are 18 members. The Korkein Oikeus gives advice to the President in cases regarding the right to pardon. It also provides legal opinions on the constitutionality of government bills during the legislative process. It can initiate new laws or recommend amendments to existing ones.

Address: Pohjoisesplanadi 3, POB 301, 00171 Helsinki, Finland
Tel: (0)103640000
Fax: (0)103640154
E-mail: korkein.oikeus@om.fi
Internet: www.kko.fi

Supreme Court (Iceland)

The Supreme Court, or the Haestirettur, of Iceland was founded in 1919. The court is made up of nine judges who are appointed for life by the President. It holds the highest judicial power in Iceland.

Address: Dómhúsinu v/Arnarhól, 101 Reykjavík, Iceland
Tel: (0)5103030
Fax: (0)5623995
E-mail: haestirettur@haestirettur.is
Internet: www.haestirettur.is

Supreme Court (Ireland)

The Supreme Court in Ireland is known as An Chúirt Uachtarach. Originally founded in 1924, the court consists of a chief justice and seven additional ordinary judges who are appointed by the President on the advice of the government. As well as being the highest court in Ireland, the Supreme Court has the power to decide whether bills passed by the **Dáil Éireann** and the **Seanad Éireann** are constitutional.

Address: Four Courts, Inns Quay, Dublin 7, Ireland
Tel: (0)1 8886569
Fax: (0)1 8732332
E-mail: SupremePublic@courts.ie
Internet: www.courts.ie

Supreme Court (Netherlands)

The Supreme Court, or Hoge Raad, is the highest court in the Netherlands. Its judges are appointed for life by the monarch and it conducts judicial review of legislation.

Address: Kazernestraat 52, 2514 CV 's-Gravenhage, Netherlands
Tel: (0)70 3611311
E-mail: via www.rechtspraak.nl/over+deze+site/reageren.html
Internet: www.hogeraad.nl

Supreme Court (Norway)

The Supreme Court, or Høyesterett, is the highest court in Norway. Founded in 1814, the court is made up of 18 judges who are appointed by the monarch on behalf of the government. It has the power to review the legality of government decisions and the constitutionality of legislation adopted by the **Storting**.

Address: Høyesteretts plass, POB 8016 Dep., 0030 Oslo, Norway
Tel: (0)22-03-59-00
Fax: (0)22-33-23-55
E-mail: post@hoyesterett.no
Internet: www.hoyesterett.no

Supreme Court (Sweden)

The Supreme Court, or Högsta Domstolens, is the highest court in Sweden. Founded in 1789 by King Gustav III, decisions of the court were until 1975 made in the name of the monarch. Today the court is made up of 16 judges who are appointed by the government. The Högsta Domstolens is the third, and final, instance in civil and criminal cases. The Council on Legislation in the court gives its opinion on draft law before it is submitted to the **Riksdag**.

Address: Riddarhustorget 8, or POB 2066, 103 12 Stockholm, Sweden
Tel: (0)8 617-64-00
Fax: (0)8 617-65-21
E-mail: registrator@hogstadomstolen.se
Internet: www.hogstadomstolen.se

Svalbard

Svalbard is a group of islands located between the Arctic Ocean, the Barents Sea, the Greenland Sea and the Norwegian Sea, to the north of Norway. The Spitsbergen Treaty of 1920 recognized Svalbard as a part of Norway, and it formally became a part of the state in 1925. The Svalbard islands cover a total of 63,000 sq km, though 60% of the territory is covered by glaciers. The main areas of economic activity are coal mining, research and tourism. Svalbard has a population of 2,750, mainly Norwegians and Russians.

Svenska Folkpartiet – *see* Swedish People's Party, Finland

Svenskt Näringsliv – *see* Confederation of Swedish Enterprise

Sveriges Akademikers Centralorganisation – *see* Swedish Confederation of Professional Associations

Sweden

Sweden is a Scandinavian state with a strong tradition of social democracy and military neutrality. It is a constitutional monarchy—King Carl XVI Gustaf has reigned since 1973—and political power lies with the **Riksdag**. The most recent elections were held on 15 September 2002 when the **Social Democratic Party (SAP)** was re-elected, returning **Göran Persson** as Prime Minister. The SAP won 40% of the vote and governs as a minority government, relying on the **Left Party** and the **Green Party** for parliamentary majorities.

Area: 450,000 sq km; *capital:* Stockholm; *population:* 9m. (2001).

The SAP has dominated Swedish politics for more than 70 years. It governed continuously in 1932–76 and the only periods when it was not in government were 1976–82 and 1991–94. The SAP Prime Minister in 1932–46, Per Albin Hansson, pioneered the introduction of the Swedish **welfare state** based on his concept of *Folkhemmet* (People's Home). The idea behind the *Folkhemmet* was to establish an extensive, universal social welfare system which would end class conflict and promote democracy based on openness, participation and compromise. Sweden also strongly promotes equal rights between men and **women**. The Swedish welfare state was expanded during the boom years between the 1940s and the 1970s. Non-socialist (or bourgeois) coalitions led by the **Moderate Party**, which governed in 1976–82, following the oil crisis, and again in 1991–94, during the country's worst recession since the 1930s, did little to dismantle the social democratic *Folkhem*.

The SAP has undergone a series of programmatic reforms and has readily adapted its policies to address socio-economic conditions. During the 1980s SAP Prime Ministers Olof Palme (1982–86) and Invar Carlsson (1986–91) were willing to adjust the welfare state and, following the recession of 1991–94, Carlsson, in 1994–96, and then Persson, from 1996, implemented necessary cuts in the social state in order to direct Sweden's economic recovery. These measures were unpopular with voters and the 1998 election, when it won only 36.6% of the vote, marked the SAP's worst electoral performance in 77 years. However, voters trusted the SAP more than the bourgeois coalition to return the country to the path of growth and stability. The SAP was able to continue as a minority government with the support of the Left Party and the Green Party, whose votes had significantly increased. Between the elections held in 1998 and 2002 Sweden made a substantial economic recovery, and in the 2002 election the SAP's share of the vote rose again to 40%.

Sweden is a neutral and militarily non-aligned state. During the **Cold War** it refused to join the **North Atlantic Treaty Organization (NATO)** military alliance and remains outside it today. Sweden does provide troops for peace-keeping operations and is an active member of NATO's Partnership for Peace Programme.

In recent years it has attenuated its policy of neutrality, and in 2001 the late foreign minister, **Anna Lindh**, offered unreserved support for retaliation for the terrorist attacks on the USA of **11 September**.

Following the end of the Cold War Sweden became a member of the **European Union (EU)** on 1 January 1995. Membership followed a referendum, held on 13 November 1994, in which voters narrowly endorsed EU **accession** (yes 52.3%; turn-out 83%). While the leadership of the SAP government supported joining the EU, the SAP's membership, trade unions and women remained sceptical. There was widespread concern that EU membership would lead to a worsening of the social standards associated with the Swedish welfare model.

Sweden remains a sceptical member of the EU, supporting policies of **enlargement** rather than deepening. In a referendum held on 14 September 2003 the country voted against joining the **euro** (no 56%; turn-out 83%). Although the yes campaign was well organized and well funded, the rejection of the single currency was triggered by voters' concerns about the democratic deficit and lack of transparency in EU institutions, and the poor performance of economies in the **euro area** compared to Sweden. The outcome may also have been affected by the shocking stabbing on 10 September 2003 in a Stockholm department store of foreign minister Anna Lindh, who had been a key figure in the yes campaign. This was the second time in recent years that a Swedish politician had been murdered. Olof Palme, Prime Minister in 1982–86, was murdered on 28 February 1986 while returning home from a cinema in Stockholm.

Economy: The Swedish economy is the biggest in Scandinavia. Late to industrialize, its development was fostered by a strong central government, a good stock of raw materials and a well-educated workforce. An open and export-oriented economy, it developed a series of large multinational companies in transport (Volvo), machinery and electronics (Ericsson and Electrolux), wood and paper products **(IKEA)** and chemicals. It grew faster in 1870–1970 than that of any other country, except **Japan**, and by the 1970s Sweden was one of the richest countries in the world, ranked fourth in the list of the **Organisation for Economic Co-operation and Development** that measures (at PPP) per caput gross domestic product (GDP). Its success was attributed to the Swedish model of economic management.

GNP: US $225,900m. (2001); *GNP per caput:* $25,400 (2001); *GNP at PPP:* $212,000m. (2001); *GNP per caput at PPP:* $23,800 (2001); *GDP:* $209,814m. (2001); *exports:* $98,197m. (2001); *imports:* $85,388m. (2001); *currency:* krona; *unemployment:* 4.0% (2002).

A mixed and corporatist political economy, Sweden is traditionally characterized by co-operative relationships between the private sector, employers, trade unions and the state. Labour is strongly organized in trade unions (81.9% in 2000) and there is a strong system of centralized wage-bargaining which aims at minimizing wage differentials. There is little direct state intervention in the private sector and there are few nationalized industries. However, government spending on the

welfare state is high. The Swedish welfare state was conceived in the 1930s and constructed by social democrats during the 1950s, 1960s and 1970s. An archetypal social democratic welfare state, Sweden provides universal welfare benefits for citizens such as parents, pensioners and the unemployed, plus a broad range of social services, such as child-care, health-care and housing. Sweden significantly expanded the public sector from the 1960s in order to bring **women** into the labour market, and sponsors active labour-market policies to meet the aim of full employment. The welfare state is funded through high direct taxation. Public support for the welfare state and welfare spending in Sweden is high as some 60% of citizens rely on the state for either jobs or benefits.

After the oil crisis of the 1970s economic growth in Sweden stalled. The government responded to the recession and rising **unemployment** with fiscal expansion. It developed a series of active labour-market policies to limit the rate of unemployment to 1%–3% and invested in industries and building projects to boost demand. This led to a rapid rise in public spending and government debt. The foreign balance of payments was rescued by a series of devaluations of the krona, but at the cost of rising inflation. When the economy was booming in 1950 Sweden had one of the lowest ratios of public spending to GDP in the industrial world. By 1983 it was some 25 percentage points above the average of other industrial states. The economy expanded in 1985–91, but Sweden was then struck, in 1991, by the worst recession since the 1930s. Industrial production fell by 17%–18% in the years 1990–93 and unemployment soared to 9%–14%. Public spending increased to 73% of GDP in 1993 and tax revenues fell, plunging Sweden into budget deficit. Public borrowing placed pressure on interest rates which the **Riksbank** briefly raised, in 1992, to 500%. The krona, which was tied to the **European Currency Unit** in 1991 in order to halt inflation, had to be decoupled from it in 1992 following a currency crisis. This led to a 20% depreciation of the Swedish currency.

The strength of Sweden's recovery from 1994 was proportionate to the depth of the recession it had suffered. The economy grew at an average annual rate of 3% in 1994–98 and of 4% in 1999–2000. By 1998 the budget had been balanced and unemployment had fallen to 4%. The non-socialist coalition government and the opposition social democrats used the recession and financial crisis as an opportunity to agree and implement a programme of austerity measures and fiscal restraint in order to fuel Sweden's recovery. The Swedish recovery coincided with the country's **accession** to the **European Union** in 1995.

By 2002 many aspects of the strong Swedish economic model had been restored. Unemployment and inflation were low, growth had been steady at an average rate of 3.2% over four years and there was a balance-of-payments surplus. Much of the recovery was based on the growth of the information technology industry. Sweden had established itself by 2000 as Europe's strongest market for internet set-ups. Stockholm alone had some 900 internet companies in 2000 and more than 50% of Swedes have access to the internet.

However, during the recovery some observers identified a breakdown of the principles of consensus and wage restraint that had formerly characterized the Swedish model. Some large firms (e.g. Ericsson) have threatened job cuts in Sweden and managers are demanding higher executive salaries. At the same time, Swedish company tax is relatively low in comparison with other Western European states.

Swedish Confederation of Professional Associations

The Swedish Confederation of Professional Associations, or Sveriges Akademikers Centralorganisation (SACO), is an organization that represents academics and graduate professionals in Sweden. Founded in 1943, SACO today represents more than 500,000 professionals who are members of 26 affiliated associations. It is itself affiliated to **ETUC**. SACO offers advice services to its members and campaigns to stimulate economic growth, raise levels of education and strengthen the position of individuals in the workplace.

Pres.: Anna Ekström
Address: Lilla Nygatan 14, Gamla Stan, Sweden, or POB 2206, 103 15
    Stockholm, Sweden
Tel: (0)8 613-48-00
Fax: (0)8 24-77-01
E-mail: kansli@saco.se
Internet: www.saco.se

Swedish Confederation of Trade Unions

The Swedish Confederation of Trade Unions, or Landsorganisationen i Sverige (LO), is the main confederation of trade unions in Sweden. Founded in 1898, it today represents the interests of some 1.9m. workers who are members of 16 affiliated trade unions. LO has close links with the **Social Democratic Party** and is a member of **ETUC**. LO lobbies nationally and internationally on labour market and social security issues. It also conducts wage-bargaining and trade union and youth education.

Pres.: Wanja Lundby-Wedin
Address: Barnhusgatan 18, 105 53 Stockholm, Sweden
Tel: (0)8 796-25-00
Fax: (0)8 21-97-11
E-mail: info@lo.se
Internet: www.lo.se

Swedish People's Party (Finland)

The Swedish People's Party, or Svenska Folkpartiet (Sfp), is a moderate liberal party which represents the Swedish-speaking minority in Finland (6% of the

Finnish population). Established in 1906, the party generally obtains around three-quarters of its votes from Swedish-speaking Finns and the rest from Finnish-speaking voters. The party campaigns for bilingualism in Finland as well as Nordic and European integration. The party advocates private initiative and an education system that promotes individual achievement. It defends a comprehensive but active **welfare state**.

The Sfp has participated in more than 43 governments since 1906. The party returned nine representatives to the 200-seat **Eduskunta** that was elected on 16 March 2003 and entered into a coalition with the **Centre Party** and the **Finnish Social Democratic Party**.

Party Leader: Jan-Erik Enestam
Address: Simonsgatan 8A, POB 430, 00101 Helsingfors, Finland
Tel: (0)9693070
Fax: (0)96931968
E-mail: info@sfp.fi
Internet: www.sfp.fi

Swiss Business Federation

The Swiss Business Federation, or Economiesuisse, is the main business organization in Switzerland. Founded in 2000, it is the result of a merger between the Swiss Federation of Commerce and Industry and the Society for the Promotion of the Swiss Economy. Economiesuisse represents more than 30,000 businesses from a wide range of sectors which are organized in 100 trade associations. It works closely with the Schweizerischer Arbeitgeberverband and is a member of the **Union of Industrial and Employers' Confederations of Europe**.

Leadership: Pres. Ueli Forster; *Dir.-Gen.* Rudolf Ramsauer
Address: Hegibachstrasse 47, 8032 Zürich, Switzerland
Tel: (0)14213535
Fax: (0)14213434
E-mail: info@economiesuisse.ch
Internet: www.economiesuisse.ch

Swiss People's Party

The Swiss People's Party, or Schweizerische Volkspartei (SVP), is the populist right-wing party in Switzerland. It was founded in 1971 following the merger of two rural farmers' parties. The SVP campaigns to limit the immigrant population in Switzerland, and is opposed to the country joining the **European Union**. It is also against the setting up of a Swiss 'Solidarity Foundation' to help the world's poor.

The party made electoral gains at federal level throughout the 1990s and following the 1999 election was the second largest party, occupying 44 seats in the 200-seat **Nationalrat**. In the elections held on 19 October 2003 the party won

26.6% of the vote and 55 parliamentary seats, overtaking the **Social Democratic Party of Switzerland** to become the largest party.

The SVP had just one seat in the permanent seven-member coalition established in 1959. Following its electoral success in 2003 the party negotiated the transfer of an additional seat to it, at the expense of the **Christian Democratic Party**, which was taken by the SVP's controversial politician Christoph Blocher. During the 2003 election campaign the SVP was criticized by the **United Nations** High Commissioner for Refugees for appearing to blame crime and drugs problems on asylum-seekers.

Leadership: Pres. Ueli Maurer; *Gen. Sec.* Gregor Rutz
Address: Brückfeldstrasse 18, 3000 Bern 26, Switzerland
Tel: (0)313005858
Fax: (0)313005859
E-mail: info@svp.ch
Internet: www.svp.ch

Swiss Trade Union Confederation

The Swiss Trade Union Confederation, or Schweizerischer Gewerkschaftsbund, is the main trade union confederation in Switzerland. It is composed of 17 trade unions representing some 390,000 members. It is confessionally and politically independent and is itself a member of **ETUC**.

Leadership: Pres. Paul Rechsteiner; *Gen. Sec.* Serge Gaillard
Address: Monbijoustrasse 61, 3000 Bern 23, Switzerland
Tel: (0)313770101
Fax. (0)313770102
E-mail: info@sgb.ch
Internet: www.sgb.ch

Switzerland

Switzerland is a small, land-locked country with a long tradition of direct democracy and as a politically neutral state. The modern Swiss federal state, which dates back to 1843, has a unique federal political system which emphasizes consensus and includes a strong dimension of direct democracy through referendums.

Area: 41,000 sq km; *capital:* Bern; *population:* 7m. (2001).

Switzerland is divided into 26 cantons, six of which are half-cantons. The federal government is responsible for foreign relations, defence, banking and currency, railways and **immigration**, while the cantons govern in most other areas, including taxation, policing, education, law-making and many areas of welfare spending. Additionally, within each canton there are communes, 2,842 in total. The bicameral Swiss parliament, or Federal Assembly, is elected for a fixed term every four years. The **Nationalrat** comprises members elected by universal suffrage, and the

Ständerat is made up of nominees of the cantons: each canton returns two representatives each, though half-cantons return just one. Following parliamentary elections, the Federal Assembly elects the cabinet, or Federal Council (Bundesrat), for the same, fixed four-year term. The Federal Council is a permanent coalition of seven ministers who tend to be re-elected until they retire.

According to a 'magic formula' agreed in 1959, coalitions comprised two ministers from the **Social Democratic Party of Switzerland**, two from the **Radical Free Democratic Party**, two from the **Christian Democratic Party** and one from the **Swiss People's Party (SVP)**. The coalition also strikes a balance between representatives of linguistic groups (German, French, Italian and Romansch) and religious denominations (Catholic and Protestant). In the Swiss political tradition the permanent coalition processes or administers the demands of conflicting groups, rather than leading public opinion. Since the cabinet is a representative coalition, Switzerland has no tradition of opposition politics in parliament. Moreover, Switzerland has a rotating, non-executive presidency. The head of state is drawn annually from among the seven federal ministers.

The election held on 19 October 2003 led to a readjustment of the stable model of permanent coalitions. The right-wing populist and anti-immigration party, the SVP, won 26.6% of the vote and 55 seats in the 200-seat Nationalrat, thereby becoming the largest party. The SVP's share of the vote increased by 11% in 2003 compared with 1999, when it was the second largest party. The SVP's most prominent politician, the industrialist Christoph Blocher, immediately demanded, and obtained, a second seat in the Federal Council at the expense of a cabinet member from the Christian Democratic Party. A controversial party, the SVP's anti-immigration campaign literature had even attracted strong criticism from the **United Nations (UN)** High Commissioner for Refugees. Blocher had stated that the SVP would resign from the cabinet and increase opposition if it was not granted an additional seat.

Switzerland has a strong tradition of direct democracy. Since 1866 Swiss voters have had the right to submit parliamentary laws and independent laws to a national vote. (**Women** were granted the right to vote in 1971.) With 50,000 voters' signatures, citizens can request a vote on a parliamentary law; with 100,000 votes, a referendum can be called to introduce a new law to parliament. Around one-half of parliamentary laws are accepted, while almost all such new laws (90%) are rejected by the voters. In 1866–1996 some 450 national referendums were held. Referendums are also regularly held at canton and commune level, on issues such as public-spending plans, so that voters were called to cast a vote 10 times a year during the 1990s. Voter turn-out has fallen from 50%–60% in the 1950s to around 40% at present.

A permanently neutral state, Switzerland for long opted to remain outside of international organizations such as the United Nations and the **European Union (EU)**. Following the end of the **Cold War**, this stance weakened and in the 1990s and early 2000s the Swiss conducted a series of referendums on membership of international organizations. The Swiss agreed in May 1992 to join the **World Bank** and the **International Monetary Fund**. In a referendum held in June 2001 voters agreed to allow Swiss troops to carry weapons during peace-keeping missions abroad, and in March 2002 Switzerland's membership of the UN was approved. However, EU membership remains off the agenda. Though Switzerland is a member of the **European Free Trade Association**, Swiss citizens decided against joining the new **European Economic Area** in 1992, opting instead for a series of bilateral agreements with the EU in May 2000. Switzerland decided in 2001 not to open membership negotiations with the EU when 77% of voters rejected the proposal. Opposition to EU membership arises from the concern that it would endanger Switzerland's neutrality and tradition of direct democracy. With the strengthened presence of the nationalistic SVP in the federal government, the issue of membership is unlikely to be raised again for some time.

A number of controversial issues have been subject to referendums in Switzerland in recent years. The country was criticized in the late 1990s for its neutrality in the Second World War and for its treatment of victims of the **Holocaust**. One report, commissioned by the Swiss parliament and written by an independent commission of experts (headed by the historian Jean-François Bergier), found that in 1942 Switzerland had refused entry to some 24,000 refugees from Nazi Germany. The Swiss state was also accused of bolstering the Nazi war economy, and banks and art galleries were found to have been negligent in respect of the restoration of property to victims of the Holocaust. A separate report revealed the existence of 54,000 Swiss bank accounts that may have belonged to victims of the Holocaust. The Swiss banks had previously admitted to 800 such accounts. On the day that the Bergier report was published in 2002 the Swiss parliament agreed to establish a fund known as the 'Solidarity Foundation' for the world's poor by selling 450 tons of Switzerland's gold reserves. The 'Solidarity Foundation' proposal was rejected in a referendum held in 2002 by 51.8% of voters.

With the rise of the anti-immigration SVP, the size of the immigrant population in Switzerland became a key issue. In September 2000 voters rejected an initiative to reduce the upper limit applied to the immigrant population from 19% to 18%. In this vote, 63.7% opposed the proposal. In November 2002 a referendum was held on a right-wing proposal to refuse entry to any asylum-seeker who had already passed through a neighbouring safe country. The proposal was narrowly rejected, by 50.1% of the electorate.

Economy: Switzerland is the second richest country in Europe (after Luxembourg) in terms of gross national product (GNP) per caput (at PPP), and its citizens enjoy one of the highest qualities of life in the world. Its economic strength is based on banking and finance (e.g. Credit Suisse, Zürich Financial Services), machinery and electronics, chemicals, watches (e.g. Swatch) as well as food production (e.g. Nestlé).

GNP: US $277,200m. (2001); *GNP per caput:* $38,330 (2001); *GNP at PPP:* $224,000m. (2001); *GNP per caput at PPP:* $30,970 (2001); *GDP:* $247,091m. (2001); *exports:* $123,552m. (2001); *imports:* $109,531m. (2001); *currency:* Swiss franc; *unemployment:* 2.9% (2002).

Switzerland's open, independent economy has sought to benefit from the economic advantages of globalization without the country becoming a member of international organizations. Switzerland was a founder member of the **European Free Trade Association**, but it refused to join the **European Economic Area (EEA)** in 1992 as this new arrangement obliged members to accept the past decisions of the **European Community (EC)**. Instead, it signed a series of bilateral agreements with the EC. It did, however, opt to join the **International Monetary Fund** and the **World Bank** in 1992. The Swiss government has not ruled out membership of the **European Union (EU)** and there is strong support for this among multinational companies, large banks and companies. In 2001, in a referendum initiated by pro-European citizens, voters were asked whether membership negotiations with the EU should be initiated. The proposal was rejected by 77% of voters.

Switzerland prospered in the post-Second World War era outside of regional and international organizations. In the early 1990s it was argued that Switzerland's decision not to join the EEA would be detrimental to the economy since two-thirds of Swiss exports are to the EU; it was estimated that the decision might cut 4%–6% from the country's gross domestic product. Indeed, the Swiss economy barely grew at all in 1991–98 and the rate of **unemployment** rose to 5% (1997). However, by 2000 the economy was growing again at a rate of 3% and the rate of unemployment had fallen to 2.9% by 2002. Switzerland also enjoys a current account surplus of US \$30,000m. annually, one of the highest among the western industrialized economies.

Within a corporatist economy, Swiss firms tend to be controlled on a consensus basis by networks of Swiss managers with colleagues sitting on the executive and supervisory boards of each others' companies, the boards being balanced to accurately represent each linguistic and religious group. There are few instances of hostile takeovers and shareholders do not enjoy a great deal of influence. A series of corporate crises in the early 2000s led to the resignation of a number of chief executives and to an opening-up of the Swiss corporate landscape.

Despite Switzerland's wealth, the country has not developed a particularly generous **welfare state**. It is traditionally classified at federal level as a corporatist welfare state, but has strong liberal tendencies. There also exists a strong degree of regional variation in the aspects of the welfare state delivered at cantonal level—social assistance, family policy, social services and education.

Synaspismos – *see* Coalition of the Left of Movements and the Ecology, Greece

T

Telecommunications

The telecommunications sector has changed significantly since the 1980s on account of the growth in demand for global communications and technological innovations such as the internet. To address these new demands, the **European Commission**, business and liberal economies put pressure on **European Union (EU)** member states to deregulate and privatize their telecommunications industries. Traditionally a highly protected and subsidized sector granted special and exclusive rights by national governments, nationalized telecommunications industries provided a public service and were used in national economy policy-making. By the late 1990s telecommunications in the EU had been fully liberalized.

Telecommunications was excluded from the project to complete the **Single European Market**, but the European Commission published a separate Green Paper on the development of a single market for telecommunications services and equipment in 1987. Commission directives in 1988, 1990 and 1993 liberalized, respectively, Customer Premise Equipment (CPE—hardware, computer terminals, telephones), Value-Added Network Services (VANs—fax, data transmission) and voice telephony. While economies such as the United Kingdom were quick to liberalize their telecommunications industries, and in fact sought much deregulation prior to the Commission directives, others, such as France and the southern European states, resisted change. The final directive set 1 January 1998 as the date for full liberalization; Ireland, Greece, Portugal and Spain negotiated an extension until 2003.

In parallel with the liberalization of telecommunications, the Commission issued a directive to ensure that the new competition would be fair and effective. The 1990 Open Network Directive set down the principles of mutual recognition of tests and licences, the setting of minimum **European Community (EC)** requirements and the establishment of voluntary EC-recognized norms and standards. Regulation directives are set at European levels and implemented and checked by independent national regulators.

Terrorism

Terrorism may be defined as the employment of methods of coercive intimidation against non-combatants to further the views of an individual or group. The issue of combating terrorism has been given a particularly high priority in Western Europe since the attacks by the al-Qa'ida terrorist network on the USA on **11 September** 2001, and the bombings in Madrid, Spain, on 11 March 2004, responsibility for which was attributed to that network or organizations linked to it.

Until 2001 there had been little progress in developing common strategies for combating terrorism. At international level several **United Nations** conventions had been adopted to deal with the issue of terrorism, and in 1977 the **Council of Europe** had adopted the Convention on the Suppression of Terrorism, which included a list of terrorist acts. Neither organization had a common or comprehensive definition of terrorism. Similarly, in the **European Union (EU)** no common strategy had been developed before 2001 despite the fact that the legal base for this had been provided for by the **Treaty on European Union** of 1992. Rather, there existed a varied set of definitions of terrorism and at that time six of the 15 EU member states had specific anti-terrorist legislation (France, Germany, Italy, Portugal, Spain and the United Kingdom).

Terrorism in Western Europe in the post-Second World War era had been a phenomenon that arose from predominantly national level territorial conflicts. For example, the Basque terrorist group Euskadi ta Askatasuna (ETA—Basque Homeland and Liberty), which seeks the independence of the **Basque Country** from Spain, has murdered members of the Spanish élite. The Irish Republican Army (IRA), which opposes British rule in **Northern Ireland**, has carried out a number of bombing campaigns in Northern Ireland and Great Britain. In the 1970s left-wing or 'anti-imperialist' terrorism undertaken by the Rote Armee Fraktion (RAF—Red Army Faction) included the kidnapping of leading business figures.

Following the terrorist attacks on the USA on 11 September 2001 the EU developed a Framework Decision on Combating Terrorism. The **Justice and Home Affairs** ministers of the **Council of the European Union** and the **European Council** met on 20 and 21 September 2001 respectively to discuss a common EU strategy. The Framework Decision of 13 June 2002 aims for a common definition of terrorist offences and a uniform legal framework for prosecuting terrorist acts. The EU has developed an agreement on a European-wide arrest warrant, the intensification of co-operation and exchange of information between intelligence services, and measures to combat the funding of terrorist activities.

The EU Framework Decision provides a definition of terrorist groups and terrorist offences to which member states' measures should be approximated. Terrorist offences are defined as those which have the aim of '(a) seriously intimidating a population or; (b) unduly compelling a Government or international organisation to perform or abstain from performing an act; (c) or seriously destabilising or destroying the fundamental political, constitutional, economic or social structures of a country or an international organisation'. Specific terrorist offences are: '(a) attacks upon a person's life which may cause death; (b) attacks on the physical integrity of a person; (c) kidnapping or hostage taking; (d) causing extensive destruction to a Government or public facility, a transport system, an infrastructure facility, including an information system, a fixed platform located on the continental shelf, a public place or private property likely to endanger human life or result in major economic loss; (e) seizure of aircrafts, ships or other means of public goods transport; (f) manufacture, possession, acquisition, transport, supply or use of weapons, explosives or of nuclear, biological or chemical weapons, as well as research into, and development of biological and chemical weapons; (g) release of dangerous substances, or causing fires, explosions or floods the effect of which is to endanger human life; (h) interfering with or disrupting the supply of water, power or any other fundamental natural resource the effect of which is to endanger human life; (i) threatening to commit any of the acts listed in (a) to (h)'.

Thatcher, Margaret

Margaret Thatcher is a **Conservative Party** politician and stateswoman who was Prime Minister of the United Kingdom in 1979–90, and the first woman to hold this post. Her distinct brand of right-wing politics, given the label Thatcherism, promoted free-market economics, a centralization of the state and an independent foreign policy. Thatcherism was more a response to events and a desire to secure re-election than a clear ideological blueprint. Nevertheless, her approach is credited with having halted the United Kingdom's relative economic decline in the post-war period.

Thatcher's economic approach involved cutting income tax, raising value added tax and pursuing a strict monetary policy to keep inflation down. This led to a rapid rise in interest rates, recession and high **unemployment**. Thatcher's policies led over time to a centralization of the state. She removed power from local government, abolishing the Greater London Council in 1986, for example, reformed national institutions and removed many aspects of consensus politics in the United Kingdom. During her three terms in office, she gradually reduced labour rights in industrial relations and privatized state-owned industries. In 1984–85 the miners' union led a year-long strike against pit closures and trade union reforms. Thatcher's governments also aimed to retrench the **welfare state** in order to promote individual initiative. As well as privatizing nationalized industries, Thatcher introduced market forces into institutions such as the National Health Service.

Thatcher fostered Britain's relationship with the USA, especially with President Ronald Reagan, and promoted a strong nationalistic foreign policy. In 1982 she dispatched British troops to fight in the Falkland Islands, which had been invaded by Argentina. She took a strong stance against the project of European integration, supporting instead the sovereignty of nation states. Her attitude towards European integration deeply divided her party, which had traditionally favoured economic integration, and ultimately led to her forced resignation on 28 November 1990. The resignation of her foreign secretary, Geoffrey Howe, over the issue of Thatcher's approach to Europe triggered a leadership challenge by Michael Heseltine. Although she won a majority of votes in the first ballot of this contest, it was insufficient under the electoral rules pertaining, a second ballot became necessary and, knowing that she had lost the confidence of her party, Thatcher stepped down as leader. She remained in the **House of Commons** until 1992 when she was made a member of the **House of Lords** as Baroness Thatcher.

Born on 13 October 1925 in Grantham, Thatcher studied chemistry at Oxford University and later trained as a lawyer. Her political career began at Oxford where she was president of Oxford University's Conservative Association. She first stood for election to the House of Commons in 1950 and 1951 as a Conservative Party candidate for the Dartford constituency and was eventually elected in 1959 for Finchley. Within two years she was appointed parliamentary secretary at the Ministry of Pensions and was then shadow minister during the Conservatives' period in opposition, in 1964–70. When the party returned to office in 1970–74 Thatcher served as Secretary of State in the Department of Education. She was dubbed the 'Milk Snatcher' for her policy to end the distribution of free milk for primary schoolchildren. Thatcher became leader of the Conservative Party in February 1975 when she stood against Edward Heath following his two defeats in general elections. She led the Conservatives to electoral victory in the 1979 election, gaining a majority of 49 seats and the party was re-elected under her leadership in 1983 and 1987.

Margaret Thatcher was married to Dennis, who died in June 2002. They had two children.

Tjänstemännens Centralorganisation – *see* Confederation of Professional Employees, Sweden

Toimihenkilökeskusjärjestö – *see* Finnish Confederation of Salaried Employees

Total

Total is France's largest corporation, and the fourth largest oil and gas producer in the world, operating in more than 130 countries. The business is divided into upstream (oil and gas exploration and production), downstream (refining, marketing and shipping), and chemicals (petrochemicals, fertilizers). Total produced 2.54m. barrels of oil equivalent a day and developed reserves of 11,400m. barrels of oil equivalent in 2003. It has 16,000 service stations world-wide, and is the market leader in Europe.

Total was formed through a series of mergers in 1999. Total, which had existed as a brand since 1954, merged first with the Belgian PetroFina to form TotalFina, and TotalFina then merged with Elf Aquitaine to form TotalFinaElf. This was renamed Total in May 2003. Executives and managers of former Elf Aquitaine, a French state-owned company in 1963–94, came under investigation in 1994 in a large financial corruption scandal. It was alleged that Elf had paid bribes to officials in order to secure contracts, and that Elf company officials and middlemen profited from this system, receiving almost 3,000m. francs (€305m.) in so-called 'kickbacks'. In November 2003 a French court found 30 employees guilty of participating and benefiting from this scheme. These included the company chairman, Loïl Le Floch-Prigent, and the company director, Alfred Sirven. Both were sentenced to terms of imprisonment of five years, and they were fined €375,000 and €1m. respectively. At the trial it was alleged that French politicians and political parties had also benefited from this system of bribery.

Chair. and CEO: Thierry Desmarest
Address: 2 place de la Coupole, La Défense 6, 92400 Courbevoie, France
Tel: (0)1-47-44-63-74
Fax: (0)1-47-44-68-21
E-mail: via www.total.com/en/common/contact/
Internet: www.total.com

Trade Union Confederation of Workers' Commissions

The Trade Union Confederation of Workers' Commissions, or Confederación Sindical de Comisiones Obreras, is a major trade union confederation in Spain. Founded in the late 1950s, it originally represented a broad range of political and ideological views before tending towards communism. It held its first congress in 1978 and today the trade union confederation has 13 affiliated national trade unions. It is itself a member of **ETUC**.

Sec.-Gen.: José María Fidalgo
Address: Calle Fernández de la Hoz 12, 28010 Madrid, Spain
Tel: (0)91 7028000
Fax: (0)91 7028175
E-mail: ccoo@ccoo.es
Internet: www.ccoo.es

Trade Union Congress (TUC)

The Trade Union Congress (TUC) is the central organization of trade unions in the United Kingdom. Founded in 1868, the TUC today has a membership of 70 unions representing more than 6.5m. workers. The TUC campaigns on social and economic issues and lobbies the government to implement policies to benefit working people. The TUC is itself a member of **ETUC**.

Gen. Sec.: Brendan Barber
Address: Congress House, Great Russell Street, London WC1B 3LS, United
          Kingdom

Tel: (0)20 7636 4030
Fax: (0)20 7636 0632
E-mail: info@tuc.org.uk
Internet: www.tuc.org.uk

Treaty of Amsterdam

The Treaty of Amsterdam is a treaty of the **European Union (EU)**. It was agreed and signed in 1997 by the 15 heads of the member states of the EU and came into force on 1 May 1999. The purpose of the Treaty of Amsterdam was to revise the **Treaty on European Union (TEU)** following the intergovernmental conferences on the TEU held in 1996. The treaty sought to clarify the TEU, prepare the EU for future **enlargement** to the east, and address the democratic deficit in the EU between citizens, EU institutions and the national governments of member states. In fact, the treaty made little progress towards preparing the EU for enlargement. No agreement was reached on institutional reforms on issues such as the size of the **European Commission** or the weighting of votes in the **Council of the European Union**. These questions were addressed later by the **Treaty of Nice**. The Treaty of Amsterdam did, however, agree an upper limit (700) on the number of members of the **European Parliament (EU)**. The EP's powers were also increased, most notably through an extension of the co-decision procedure.

The Treaty of Amsterdam developed the EU in the areas of employment, citizens' rights and security and foreign policy issues. The Treaty of Amsterdam introduced new provisions on employment which commit the EU to combating **unemployment**. It also brought fully into the treaty the **Social Chapter** protocol that had been annexed to the TEU on account of the **United Kingdom**'s opt-out. Decision-making by qualified majority voting (QMV) was extended to include employment guide-lines, social exclusion, and equal opportunities and treatment for men and **women**. Since the Treaty of Amsterdam was signed it has been possible to suspend the member states that do not adhere to and respect the basic values which underpin the EU (liberty, democracy, respect for human rights and fundamental freedoms, and the rule of law). The EU does more to protect the rights of individual citizens and can also now take action to combat all forms of discrimination.

With the Treaty of Amsterdam a number of **Justice and Home Affairs** policy areas, such as visas, asylum, **immigration** and refugee persons, were transferred from the third **pillar** into the first pillar of the EU. The third pillar of the EU became **Police and Judicial Co-operation in Criminal Matters**. The **Schengen Agreement** was incorporated into the treaty, although the United Kingdom and Ireland were allowed to opt out. Finally, the Treaty of Amsterdam strengthened the EU's co-operation in **Common Foreign and Security Policy (CFSP)**. The post of high representative for CFSP was established and QMV was introduced in respect of some aspects of CFSP.

Treaty of Nice

The Treaty of Nice is a treaty of the **European Union (EU)**. It was agreed in December 2000, signed in February 2001 and, following a lengthy ratification process, entered into force in February 2003. Its purpose was to prepare the EU institutionally for the **accession** of the states of Central and Eastern Europe, Malta and Cyprus. It also introduced changes in the field of **Common Foreign and Security Policy (CFSP)**.

In order to prepare for an enlarged EU, the Treaty of Nice reweighted member states' votes in the **Council of the European Union**. The treaty extended qualified majority voting in the Council to 27 policy areas and six personnel appointments areas which had previously required unanimity, but the power of veto was retained for the areas of taxation, social security, **immigration**, border controls, culture, broadcasting, health and education. The Treaty of Nice introduced a new distribution of seats in the **European Parliament (EP)**. It raised the maximum number of members of the EP from 700 to 732, achieving this by reducing the number of seats for existing member states. Only Germany and Luxembourg retained the same number. The **European Commission** was limited in size to one European commissioner for each member state. This means that the large countries—Germany, France, the United Kingdom, Italy and Spain—lose their second commissioner. In the Treaty of Nice it was agreed that as soon as the EU has 27 member states, leaders will establish a permanent limit of fewer than 27 commissioners and Commission seats will then be filled by rotation among member states.

The Treaty of Nice also established the possibility of enhanced co-operation among member states in the field of CFSP. By the treaty, the **Rapid Reaction Force (RRF)** that it had been agreed to establish in November 2000, comes under the direct control of EU institutions and the **Western European Union** was formally integrated into the EU.

The implementation of the Treaty of Nice took more than two years. A significant hurdle in the ratification process was that in Ireland the treaty had to be ratified by referendum and then by the **Seanad Éireann** and **Dáil Éireann**. Irish voters rejected the treaty on 7 June 2001 (no 53.87%; turn-out 35%). There were concerns about the impact that further integration would have on Ireland, and whether the new RRF would compromise Ireland's neutral security position. Following a national debate, a second referendum was held on 19 October 2002 and a yes vote was secured (yes 62.89%; turn-out 49.47%).

Treaty of Paris

The Treaty of Paris was the treaty that established the **European Coal and Steel Community (ECSC)**, the first stage in the process of European integration. It is, together with the **Treaty of Rome** and the Euratom Treaty (both concluded in 1957), one of the founding treaties of the **European Union**. Signed in 1951 by the six founding member states of the ECSC (Belgium, France, Germany, Italy,

Luxembourg and the Netherlands), it came into force in July 1952 for a 50-year period, expiring in July 2002.

The Treaty of Paris set up a free-trade area and laid the foundations for a common market in coal, coke, iron ore, steel and scrap. It also established four institutions to govern the ECSC: the High Authority; the Council of Ministers; the Common Assembly and the Court of Justice.

Treaty of Rome

The Treaty of Rome established the **European Economic Community (EEC)**. It is, together with the Euratom Treaty (also signed at Rome) and the **Treaty of Paris**, one of the founding treaties of the **European Union**. Signed on 25 March 1957 by the six founding participants in the project of European integration (Belgium, France, Germany, Italy, Luxembourg and the Netherlands), it came into force in January 1958.

The Treaty of Rome states that the intention of the signatories is 'to promote throughout the Community a harmonious development of economic activities, a continuous and balanced expansion, an increase in stability, an accelerated raising of the standard of living and closer relations between the States belonging to it' by 'establishing a common market and progressively approximating the economic policies of Member States' (Article 2). The common market entailed the removal of all tariff and quantitative restrictions on trade within the EEC. It also set a common external tariff on all goods entering the market. It established rules on competition which prohibit practices that distort free competition and it committed the EEC to the free movement of goods, services, persons and capital.

The EEC Treaty has been revised a number of times by the **Single European Act**, the **Treaty on European Union**, the **Treaty of Amsterdam** and the **Treaty of Nice**.

Treaty on European Union (TEU)

The Treaty on European Union (TEU), or the Maastricht Treaty, was the treaty that founded the **European Union (EU)** and significantly revised the **Treaty of Rome**. Signed in February 1992 by the 12 member states of the **European Community (EC)**, it entered into force on 1 November 1993. The TEU created a structure for the EU that was organized as three **pillars**: the EC; **Common Foreign and Security Policy**; and **Justice and Home Affairs**. The TEU extended the process of European integration into new policy areas.

The purpose of the TEU was to create an 'ever closer union' of member states in which decisions are taken at the level closest to the people. It introduced the principles of subsidiarity and the concept of European **citizenship**. Subsidiarity states that the EC should only take action if the objectives of a particular area cannot be fully met by the member states. The concept of European citizenship meant that every national of an EU member state is given citizenship of the EU; he or she is free to live and work in any member state, and can vote and stand for local and European elections, subject to certain limitations. The TEU introduced a new **European Parliament (EP)** Ombudsman to deal with citizens' complaints about the EU.

A key development of the TEU was that a definition and timetable were given for **Economic and Monetary Union (EMU)**. Both the United Kingdom and Denmark, which opposed EMU, signed separate protocols that allow them to opt out of the final stages of EMU. The TEU also sought to extend integration into social policy and incorporate the social charter into the *acquis communautaire*. The United Kingdom opposed the inclusion of social objectives in the Maastricht Treaty and the **Social Chapter** was annexed to the TEU as a separate protocol so that the United Kingdom could be granted an opt-out.

Other institutional innovations of the TEU included the decision to extend the term of office for the **European Commission** from four to five years. It also made an incoming new Commission subject to the approval of the EP. The TEU introduced the co-decision procedure in decision-making, which allows the EP to veto legislative proposals at a third reading. The TEU gave the **European Court of Justice** the power to impose fines on member states which were in breach of European law and it established the **Committee of the Regions**, made up of representatives of regional and local authorities.

The TEU had to be ratified by 10 national parliaments, and by two referendums, in Ireland and Denmark. In the Danish referendum, held in June 1992, the treaty was rejected (no 52%; turn-out 83%). Further negotiations were held and some concessions were made to Denmark. At a second Danish referendum, held in May 1993, the treaty was accepted (yes 57%; turn-out 86%). France also decided to hold a referendum and both it and Ireland endorsed the treaty. The TEU was reviewed at an intergovernmental conference in 1996 and revised by the **Treaty of Amsterdam** and the **Treaty of Nice**.

Tribunal Constitucional – *see* Constitutional Court, Portugal

Tribunal Constitucional – *see* Constitutional Court, Spain

Trichet, Jean-Claude

Jean-Claude Trichet has been president of the **European Central Bank (ECB)** since November 2003. He was appointed in June 2003 following the announcement by the first ECB president, Wim Duisenberg, shortly after the introduction of **euro** notes and coins in 2002 of his intention to step down. Trichet, who had served two terms as governor of the **Banque de France**, in 1993–2003, had been the favourite to become the first ECB president in 1998. However, Duisenberg was appointed when Germany resisted the appointment of Trichet. At the time it was agreed that Duisenberg would step down after serving four years of his eight-year term. While highly regarded as a central banker, Trichet's appointment to the ECB was nearly jeopardized by an investigation in 2000–03 into the French bank Crédit Lyonnais, which suffered financial difficulties in the 1980s. A treasury official at the time, Trichet was accused of having helped the bank to conceal financial irregularities. Trichet stood trial on that charge in 2002 and was found not guilty in 2003.

Born on 20 December 1942 in Lyons, Trichet graduated from the Institut d'études politiques and the Ecole nationale d'administration. He held various posts in the French Ministry of Finance in 1971–78 and was a government adviser in 1987–91. He joined the French treasury department in 1981 and rose to become its director in 1987. In the same year he became member of the general council of the Banque de France, and deputy governor of the **International Monetary Fund** and the **World Bank**. While governor of the Banque de France in 1993–2003 he also served as governor of the World Bank, as a member of the **European Monetary Institute** and, from 1998, as a member of the governing council of the ECB.

Address: European Central Bank, Kaiserstrasse 29, 60311 Frankfurt-am-Main,
           Germany, or POB 16 03 19, 60066 Frankfurt-am-Main, Germany
Tel: (0)69 13440
Fax: (0)69 13446000
E-mail: info@ecb.int
Internet: www.ecb.int

True Finns Party

The True Finns Party, or Perussuomalaiset, is the nationalist right-wing party of Finland. The successor party of the Finnish Rural Party, it campaigns to protect the basic rights of Finns and on law and order issues. It currently has three members in the **Eduskunta** that was elected on 16 March 2003. That election was contested by the boxer and wrestler Tony Halme as an independent candidate on the True Finns list in Helsinki. He won the fifth highest vote of any single candidate, higher than that obtained by the leader of the large **Centre Party**. Halme's proposals to send rapists, paedophiles and drugs dealers to Russian jails, and to introduce tough policies for immigrants and welfare dependents, were particularly popular among the young, and among the disaffected from poorer parts of Helsinki.

Party Leader: Timo Soini
Address: Mannerheimintie 40 B 56, 00100 Helsinki, Finland
Tel: (0)9 4540411
Fax: (0)9 4540466
E-mail: peruss@perussuomalaiset.fi
Internet: www.perussuomalaiset.fi

Turkey

Turkey is a large country to the south-east of Western Europe and its territory lies in both Europe and Asia. The modern Turkish Republic was founded on 29 October 1923 by the nationalist leader Mustafa Kemal Atatürk. It is a secular state which adopted European laws and the Roman alphabet, and banned the wearing of the fez. Turkey is an important member of the **North Atlantic Treaty Organization (NATO)** and it applied for membership of the **European Union (EU)** in 1987. The EU agreed in December 2004 that **accession** negotiations would begin in October 2005.

Area: 775,000 sq km; *capital:* Ankara; *population:* 66m. (2001).

A parliamentary democracy, legislative power lies with the unicameral 550-seat Grand National Assembly of Turkey (Türkiye Büyük Millet Meclisi). Members are elected by a system of proportional representation for a five-year term and parties must win more than 10% of the vote in order to obtain representation. The most recent elections were held in November 2002. The National Assembly elects the President as head of state for a seven-year term. To be elected, the President must win a two-thirds' majority in the first two ballots or a simple majority in the third. Since 16 May 2000 the President has been Ahmet Necdet Sezer. Executive power lies with the Prime Minister; since 2003 this has been Recep Tayyip Erdoğan of the religiously conservative Justice and Development Party, which won 34.3% of the vote in the election held on 14 March 2003. Governments tend to be coalitions, or short-lived minority administrations.

The Turkish government is advised by a National Security Council which is made up of top military and cabinet officials and is overseen by the President. Turkey's 650,000-strong army (the largest in Europe) occupies an important position in the country. It regards itself as the protector of secular politics and it has intervened three times in domestic political disputes: in 1960, 1971 and 1980. The Turkish army intervened militarily in Cyprus in 1974 to prevent a Greek takeover of the island. Northern Cyprus remains under Turkish Cypriot control. During the 1980s and 1990s the army was engaged in a civil war in south-east Turkey against the Kurdish population (around 17% of the total population) which, led by the Kurdistan Workers' Party, sought to establish an independent Kurdistan.

Turkey occupied a crucial strategic position for Western Europe during the **Cold War**. It joined the **United Nations** in 1945 and became a member of NATO in 1952, providing the second largest army in the military alliance. Turkey has been an associate member of the EU since 1963, and has participated in a full customs union with the EU since January 1996. It applied for membership of the EU on 14 April 1987 and at the EU summit in Copenhagen, Denmark, in 2002 Turkey was informed that negotiations on full membership would begin at the end of 2004. A report by the **European Commission**, published on 6 October 2004, assessed Turkey's suitability for membership, and an EU summit held on 16–17 December 2004 announced that accession negotiations would start in October 2005 if certain conditions were met. International organizations have regularly raised concerns about Turkey's human rights record and restrictive penal code. Greece has also been opposed to Turkey's membership on account of the Cyprus issue. Other states, such as Germany and France, have expressed concern about accepting an Islamic country into the EU.

Economy: The Turkish economy is dynamic and has grown rapidly since the 1980s, but Turkey's standard of living remains significantly below the European average. The economy is dominated by textiles and manufacturing and there is a large rural population engaged in agricultural production; **agriculture** still accounts for 40% of employment.

GNP: US $167,300m. (2001); *GNP per caput:* $2,530 (2001); *GNP at PPP:* $368,000m. (2001); *GNP per caput at PPP:* $5,830 (2001) *GDP:* $147,683m. (2001); *exports:* $50,438m. (2001); *imports:* $25,652m. (2001); *currency:* Turkish lira; *unemployment:* 10.6% (2002).

Turkey has a large public sector; this is a legacy of the statist regime under Atatürk. Turkey created state monopolies in most industries and imposed high tariffs and import bans to protect domestic industry. Trade restrictions were lifted in the 1970s and during the 1980s, under Prime Minister Turgut Özal, the economy abandoned its position of self-sufficiency and support for state industry. A privatization law passed in 1986 did little to take firms out of state ownership as there was a reluctance to sell to foreign buyers. By the end of the 1990s 50% of manufacturing and 60% of the financial sector was still owned by the state.

During the 1980s the economy grew an average rate of 4.6%. However, it suffered from persistent high inflation—60%–90%—and public-sector borrowing rose from 3.7% of the gross domestic product in 1986 to 12.3% in 1993. Turkey suffered recession in 1994, 1999 and 2001. It received financial support from the **International Monetary Fund** and pursued a tight fiscal policy in 2002–03. By 2003 inflation had fallen to 18.4%.

Tweede Kamer

The Tweede Kamer is the lower house of the bicameral parliament, the States General, in the Netherlands. It is made up of 150 members who are elected by a system of proportional representation for a four-year term. The most recent elections took place on 22 January 2003 following the collapse of the first, short-lived, **Balkenende** government.

Nine parties are represented in the Tweede Kamer that was elected in 2003 (number of seats in brackets): **Christian Democratic Appeal** (44); the **Labour Party** (42); **People's Party for Freedom and Democracy** (27); **Green-Left** (8); **List Pim Fortuyn** (8); **Socialist Party** (8); **Democrats 66** (6); **Christian Union** (3) and the **Political Reformed Party** (2). There are two independent deputies. Of the current members of the Tweede Kamer, 55 (36.7%) are **women**.

The Tweede Kamer shares legislative competence with the **Eerste Kamer**. It is the only house of parliament with the right to amend legislation. It controls government, and in conflicts between the government and the Tweede Kamer the latter makes the final decision. It also has the right to approve the national budget.

Address: Plein 2, 2511 CR The Hague, Netherlands, or Postbus 20018, 2500 EA
The Hague, Netherlands
Tel: (0)70 3182211
Fax: (0)70 3182234
E-mail: voorlichting@tweedekamer.nl
Internet: www.tweedekamer.nl

U

Ulster Unionist Party (UUP)

The Ulster Unionist Party (UUP) is traditionally the largest party in **Northern Ireland**. Formally established in 1972, its origins date back to 1905. Its aims are to maintain Northern Ireland as an integral part of the United Kingdom and to safeguard the British **citizenship** of the people of Northern Ireland. It also aims to maintain self-determination for the people of Northern Ireland, and the requirement that any constitutional change should first receive the approval of the majority of the population. It supported the **Good Friday Agreement** and led the unionist camp to the agreement and to a yes vote in the referendum on it held in 1999. Since then the party has become increasingly divided on the issue. In elections to the Northern Ireland Assembly held in December 2003 the UUP increased its share of the vote in percentage terms, but was overtaken in respect of number of seats obtained by the **Democratic Unionist Party**. The UUP won 27 of the 108 seats, compared with 28 in 1998. It won six seats in the UK **House of Commons** that was elected on 7 June 2001.

Party Leader: David Trimble
Address: Cunningham House, 429 Holywood Rd, Belfast BT4 2LN, United
 Kingdom
Tel: (0)28 9076 5500
Fax: (0)28 9076 9419
E-mail: uup@uup.org
Internet: www.uup.org

Unemployment

Unemployment is one of the biggest economic and social problems in Western Europe. It is a cause for concern among economists and politicians because of the strain it places on the public budgets and tax revenues of **welfare states**. Unemployment also affects the region's competitiveness: the rate of unemployment in the **European Union (EU)** is significantly higher than in its main economic competitors, **Japan** and the USA. The rate of unemployment in the EU averaged 7.7% in 2002. In the **euro area** it is 8.4%, and if the 10 **accession** states are included, the rate rises to 8.8%. This compares with overall unemployment levels of 5.4% in Japan and 5.7% in the USA in 2002. The average unemployment rate for the EU, however, conceals wide national differences between countries such as the United Kingdom, Sweden and the Netherlands, where unemployment is lower than in the USA, and Spain, Italy and Germany where it is higher. The EU unemployment rate is particularly high among three groups: the young, the unskilled, and those living in economically depressed areas. There is also significant long-term (one year or longer) unemployment. Unemployment is higher among **women** than among men. The respective rates in 2003 were 9.9% and 8.2%.

The cause of unemployment in Europe is considered to be predominantly structural rather than cyclical. Unemployment has risen steadily in Western Europe since the 1970s and in most European countries it has risen from one recession to the next as the loss of industrial employment during an economic slump has not been compensated by the growth of new employment in, for example, the service sector. In the 20 years to 1997 the EU created only 5m. new jobs, 1m. of which were in the private sector. In the USA the figure was 36m. new jobs, of which 31m. were in the private sector. Economists point to labour market rigidities in EU member states as the key factor explaining high rates of unemployment and the difficulty in creating new jobs. These rigidities include the length and generosity of welfare benefits, employment protection, high payroll taxes, centralized wage-bargaining and mobility problems within and across EU states. From this perspective it is argued that the wholesale deregulation of labour markets would increase the incentive for the unemployed to return to them, and that for employers to create new jobs.

However, the deregulation approach has limited appeal among EU member states. Only the United Kingdom (until 1997) had a US-style deregulated labour market; other governments prioritize income equality, social cohesion and re-election over welfare retrenchment and labour-market liberalization. Research has demonstrated that there is no direct causal link between labour-market regulation and high levels of mass unemployment, and that, therefore, wholesale deregulation is not the most effective way of tackling unemployment. Instead, labour-market regulation affects the structure of unemployment if it favours 'insiders' (core male workers) at the expense of 'outsiders' (the young, the low-skilled, and women). It makes no sense to tackle unemployment with an approach of wholesale deregulation. Rather, measures are required that target unemployment 'hotspots', and that are appropriate to national labour-market institutions.

The Netherlands tackled its unemployment problem in the 1980s (successfully) by negotiating wage restraint with social partners and expanding part-time employment. Sweden and Denmark have (successfully) used active labour-market policies (job search and retraining) to return the unemployed to the labour market. On the other hand, France and Germany have (unsuccessfully) sought to bring down unemployment by reducing the supply of labour (early retirement) and sharing out the work available (e.g. through the introduction of a 35-hour working week and by limiting overtime).

Because of the national contingencies of labour-market institutions and causes of unemployment, it has not been possible for the EU to draw up a single European policy to combat unemployment. Instead the EU, concerned by the level of unemployment, developed a general strategy in 1997, referred to as the **Luxembourg Process**, with the objectives of reducing unemployment, increasing employment and narrowing the gender gap. It aims to do this by co-ordinating the employment policies of EU member states through employment guide-lines, set by the **European Commission**, and National Action Plans, prepared by the member states. This was followed, in 2000, by the **Lisbon Strategy**, which set targets to increase overall employment rates to 70% (from 63%) and the female employment rate to 60% (from 55%) by 2010. A High Level Group, chaired by Wim Kok, reviewed the progress of the member states on meeting the targets of the Lisbon Strategy. Its report in 2004 found that development so far had been slow and that many targets would not be met by 2010. This was attributed to an overloaded agenda, poor co-ordination, conflicting priorities, and a lack of determined political action.

União Geral de Trabalhadores – *see* General Workers' Union, Portugal

UNICE – *see* Union of Industrial and Employers' Confederations of Europe

Union of Centre and Christian Democrats

The Union of Centre and Christian Democrats, or Unione dei Democratici Cristiani e dei Democratici di Centro (UDC), is a conservative political party in Italy that was formed in 2001 following the merger of two existing parties: the Christian Democratic Centre (Centro Cristiano Democratico—CCD) and the United Christian Democrats (Cristiani Democratici Uniti—CDU). The CCD and the CDU had been formed in 1994 and 1995 respectively by breakaway groups that were dissatisfied with the Italian Popular Party (Partito Popolare Italiano—PPI). The PPI was the successor party of the Christian Democrats which dominated post-1945 Italian politics until 1992–93.

In the general elections held on 21 April 1996 the CCD and the CDU campaigned on a joint list in the proportional representation system and, in the election held on 13 May 2001, as the Whiteflower Alliance (Biancofiore), won 40 seats in the 630-member **Camera dei Deputati**. The UDC forms part of the House of Freedoms Coalition (Casa delle Libertà) with **Forza Italia**, the **National Alliance** and the **Northern League**, led by **Silvio Berlusconi**.

Leadership: Pres. Rocco Buttiglione; *Sec.-Gen.* Pietro Cherchi
Address: Via Due Macelli 66, 00187 Rome, Italy
Tel: (0)06 69791001
Fax: (0)06 6791574
E-mail: info@udc-italia.it
Internet: www.udc-italia.it

Union pour la Démocratie Française – *see* Union for French Democracy

Union for French Democracy

The Union for French Democracy, or Union pour la Démocratie Française (UDF), is the non-Gaullist centre-right alliance in France. Originally founded in 1978 by incumbent President **Valéry Giscard d'Estaing** to support his second bid for the presidency in 1981, it was a federation of three pro-European, liberal-right parties— the Parti Républican, the Centre des Démocrates Sociaux (which became the Force Démocrate in 1995) and the Parti Radical—and some social democrats who opposed the **Socialist Party**'s alliance with the **Communist Party of France**.

The UDF lost its purpose in 1981 when Giscard d'Estaing was defeated in the presidential elections by **François Mitterrand** and the alliance remained behind **Jacques Chirac**'s Gaullist **Rally for the Republic** as the second centre-right political grouping. In 1996 Giscard d'Estaing retired as party leader and the alliance of parties in the UDF lost cohesion. Following the 1998 regional elections the federation split because of the component parties' differing attitudes towards electoral co-operation with the far-right **National Front (FN)** in order to keep the left out of office. The neo-liberal Démocratie Libérale, which had collaborated with the FN, left the UDF and the alliance, now dominated by Force Démocrate, was reconstituted as a unified party in 1999.

In the election held in 2002 the UDF refused to merge with other moderate-right parties as the Union for the Presidential Majority, now the **Popular Movement**. The consequence was that the UDF won only 29 seats in the 575-seat **Assemblée Nationale**, compared with 64 in the parliament elected in 1997.

Party Leader: François Bayrou
Address: 133 bis rue de l'Université, 75007 Paris, France
Tel: (0)1-53-59-20-00
Fax: (0)1-53-59-20-59
E-mail: via www.udf.org/contact/index.html
Internet: www.udf.org

Unión General de Trabajadores – *see* General Workers' Union, Spain

Union of Industrial and Employers' Confederations of Europe (UNICE)

The Union of Industrial and Employers' Confederations of Europe (UNICE) is a European-level organization that brings together the main business and employers' organizations in Europe. Founded in 1958, it seeks to promote co-operation between national business confederations, and to promote a competitive, Europe-wide industrial policy. It also lobbies European institutions. Today it brings together 35 members and four observer organizations from **European Union** member states, the **European Economic Area** countries and some **Central and Eastern and European Countries**.

> *Leadership: Pres.* Jürgen Strube; *Sec.-Gen.* Philippe de Buck
> *Address:* ave de Cortenbergh 168, 1000 Brussels, Belgium
> *Tel:* (0)2 237-65-11
> *Fax:* (0)2 231-14-45
> *E-mail:* main@unice.be
> *Internet:* www.unice.org

Union pour un Mouvement Populaire – *see* Popular Movement, France

Union Nationale des Syndicats Autonomes – *see* National Union of Independent Trade Unions, France

Unione dei Democratici Cristiani e dei Democratici di Centro – *see* Union of Centre and Christian Democrats, Italy

United Kingdom

The United Kingdom is a state in the north of Western Europe which comprises England, **Scotland**, **Wales** and **Northern Ireland**. These nations and regions were brought together in stages by Acts of Union: England and Wales were united in 1536; Scotland was added in 1707 to form Great Britain; and Ireland in 1800 to form the United Kingdom of Great Britain and Ireland. The most recent amendment to the Act occurred in 1927 when the United Kingdom of Great Britain and Ireland was altered to the United Kingdom of Great Britain and Northern Ireland following the foundation of the Republic of Ireland in 1922.

> *Area:* 243,000 sq km; *capital:* London; *population:* 59m. (2001).

Until the mid-20th century the United Kingdom had a large empire, but its involvement in the two World Wars (1914–18 and 1939–45) weakened its resources and many states within the empire gained independence (e.g. India in 1947). Some small states in Western Europe remain British dependencies (**Gibraltar**, the **Channel Isles** and the **Isle of Man**). The United Kingdom struggled with its loss of status following the end of empire and tried to maintain its role in the world through bilateral links with the USA and as a member of international organizations, such as the **United Nations**, the **North Atlantic Treaty Organization** and the **Commonwealth**, and regional associations, such as the **European Union (EU)**.

The United Kingdom does not have a codified written constitution, but is governed by a series of laws and conventions. The head of state is Queen Elizabeth II who acceded to the throne in 1952 and was crowned in 1953. She is also head of state of 15 other sovereign states in the Commonwealth Realm. Legislative power formally lies with the **House of Commons** and the **House of Lords**. The first-past-the-post electoral system for elections to the House of Commons—held at least every five years—usually ensures that there are clear parliamentary majorities for one of two main political parties: the **Conservative Party** and the **Labour Party**. The Conservative Party was considered the natural party of government for most of the 20th century. It governed for 57 years of the last century, most recently in 1979–1997 under **Margaret Thatcher** and John Major. The Labour Party won a landslide victory on 1 May 1997, however, and was re-elected at the most recent elections, held on 7 June 2001, with a slightly reduced majority, with **Tony Blair** as Prime Minister.

Despite the distinct national and regional configuration of the United Kingdom, the state is traditionally a unitary state in which power is centralized in the seat of government in Westminster, London. Conservative governments have resisted attempts to loosen the structure of the United Kingdom. Thatcher's governments in 1979–90 reduced the power of local authorities and further centralized the state. Labour governments, however, have supported demands for regional devolution. Referendums were held on the issue in Scotland and Wales in 1979, but a no vote was returned in Wales, and the turn-out in Scotland was too low for the result to be valid. The Labour government elected in 1997 proposed further referendums on devolution and these were held in Scotland and Wales in that year. Following yes votes in both cases, a Scottish Parliament and a Welsh Assembly were first elected in 1999. The successful negotiation and endorsement through referendums of the **Good Friday Agreement** in Northern Ireland led to the establishment of the Northern Ireland Assembly, first elected in 1998. However, direct control from Westminster was re-imposed in Northern Ireland in 2000 as a consequence of a lack of progress in decommissioning weapons. The Labour government also proposed holding referendums on the issue of establishing regional assemblies within England. However, in the first referendum held in the north-east region in November 2004 the electorate overwhelmingly rejected the proposal (no 78%; turn-out 47.7%), and the issue of English devolution has been shelved.

UK politics are divided on the issue of European integration, though this division is not along party lines. The United Kingdom applied for membership of the

European Economic Community (EEC) in 1961 and 1967, but its applications were vetoed by French President **Charles de Gaulle**. It eventually became a member in 1973 under a Conservative Party government. Two years later, in 1975, a Labour Party government held a referendum on the issue in which 67% voted in favour of remaining in the EEC. Conservative governments in 1979–97 were broadly in favour of the process of economic liberalization up to the completion of the **Single European Market**, but opposed further social or political integration which appeared to threaten British sovereignty. The Conservative Party is internally divided on the issue of the United Kingdom's membership of the **single currency**. On election in 1997 the Labour government announced a policy of constructive engagement with the EU. It signed the **Social Chapter** of the **Treaty on European Union** and has promised to hold referendums on membership of the single currency and on the **European Convention**. However, opposition to the EU remains strong and a new political party, the UK Independence Party (UKIP), founded in 1993, has campaigned in national and European elections to withdraw Britain from the EU. The UKIP won 12 seats in the **European Parliament** in elections held in June 2004.

Economy: The UK economy is today the fourth largest in the world (in terms of gross domestic product (GDP) by exchange rate but not by PPP) after the USA, **Japan** and Germany. Since the 1980s its wealth has no longer been based on manufacturing, but, rather, on the service economy. The City of London is classed as a global financial centre, and e-commerce is growing in significance. As part of the legacy of empire, the United Kingdom's economy is open to trade and is characterized by a high rate of foreign direct investment that accounts for some 20% of UK manufacturing. The economy is traditionally a liberal market economy and has a liberal **welfare state**. Following the Second World War, **Labour Party** governments increased the role of the state in managing the economy by nationalizing key industries and expanding the scope of the welfare state. A universal health provision, the National Health Service (NHS), was established in 1947.

GNP: US $1,476,800m. (2001); *GNP per caput:* $25,120 (2001); *GNP at PPP:* $1,431,000m. (2001); *GNP per caput at PPP:* $24,340 (2001); *GDP:* $1,424,094m. (2001); *exports:* $385,830 (2001); *imports:* $418,989m. (2001); *currency:* pound sterling; *unemployment:* 5.1% (2002).

In the first three decades following the Second World War, the United Kingdom experienced a period of relative economic decline—the so-called 'British disease'. The economy grew at an average annual rate of 2.3% in 1960–80, compared with 7.7% in Japan, 4.6% in France, 3.7% in Germany and 3.5% in the USA. The causes of this decline are commonly attributed to key interrelated weaknesses of the UK economy. Productivity in the United Kingdom grew more slowly in the 30 years to 1979 than in other competitor economies, at just two-thirds of the average of 12 other advanced industrial states. The United Kingdom traditionally has a poor level of skills and training of the workforce (13% of school leavers had no qualifications in 1979) and a low rate of capital investment. In 1960–95 the United Kingdom spent

18% of GDP on investment, compared with 22% in France and Germany. UK managers are, on the whole, poorly trained and the UK economy is traditionally characterized by adversarial industrial relations. There has been a tradition of bad macroeconomic management in the United Kingdom: boom and bust cycles and high inflation rates bred a culture of short-termism. Successive governments tended to set interest rates to meet political aims before elections rather than to secure economic stability. The UK economy was severely affected by the oil crises of the 1970s. Inflation reached a peak of 27% in 1975 and the government was obliged to seek a loan from the **International Monetary Fund** in 1976.

Successive **Conservative Party** governments in 1979–97 sought to revolutionize the United Kingdom's economy. The key aims of **Margaret Thatcher**'s policies in 1979–90 were to reduce state intervention in the economy, to encourage the free market, strengthen entrepreneurship, and increase share ownership. These objectives, later labelled Thatcherism, were met with policies to keep inflation low, cut taxation and welfare spending, privatize state-owned industries, deregulate the economy, and reduce the power of trade unions, which Thatcher held responsible for the 'British disease'. Thatcher's trade union reforms introduced a ban on industrial action in firms unrelated to a dispute (secondary picketing) and on closed shops; made parent unions liable for their branches; and required that full ballots of members be conducted before strike action. The Thatcher years were characterized by major battles between employers and trade unions, such as the year-long miners' strike in 1984 and the dispute between News International and print workers' unions in Wapping, London, in 1986.

The economic reforms under Margaret Thatcher and her successor John Major succeeded in some of their aims of reviving the economy and halting relative British decline. The economy grew at an average annual rate of 1.9% in 1979–96, compared with an average rate of 1.5% in 1973–79. Similarly, productivity grew during the 1980s at an average annual rate of 4.7%, compared with an average annual rate of 0.9% in the 1970s. Manufacturing output per worker grew faster than in all comparable countries except Japan in 1979–94. However, during the 1980s there was a significant decline in manufacturing, affecting mostly the industrial regions of the north. Manufacturing's share of GDP declined from 27% in 1979 to 22% in 1989 and to 20% in 1993. One-quarter of manufacturing capacity was lost in two recessions, in 1979–81 and 1990–92. The collapse of manufacturing led to soaring **unemployment**: in the 1980s some 2m. manufacturing jobs were shed (30% of the workforce). The rate of unemployment, which had been 4% in 1979, rose to 8% in 1996. Conservative Party governments' macroeconomic policy continued the boom and bust cycles and there were two massive recessions, in 1979–81 and 1990–92. While inflation rates were kept low, interest rates were high—15% in 1986. As unemployment rose, welfare spending increased from 22% of GDP in 1979 to 26% in 1996, in spite of attempts to restrain it.

The Labour Party government elected in 1997 broadly continued the economic policies of the Conservative Party governments, but placed less emphasis on the orthodoxy of markets and more stress on social fairness. The Labour government introduced a national minimum wage, returned some powers to trade unions and increased spending on the welfare state, targeted in particular on families and children, the National Health Service and education. Labour also sought to improve macroeconomic stability and to end the tradition of boom and bust. As a first move, Chancellor **Gordon Brown** granted operational independence to the **Bank of England**. The government still sets the inflation target, but the Monetary Policy Committee of the Bank of England has responsibility for setting interest rates to meet this target. The average rate of inflation has been 2.4% since 1997. Brown's economic policy also seeks to increase investment; he follows the 'golden rule' that the government will only borrow for investment, and not to fund current spending commitments over the period of an economic cycle.

The structural changes to the economy in the last two decades have halted the process of relative decline. During the 1990s the United Kingdom's annual rate of economic growth averaged 2.3%: this was higher than in Germany (1.3%) and France (1.5%). Unemployment and inflation rates are lower than their respective averages in the **European Union (EU)**. The United Kingdom's economy proved resilient to world economic slowdown following the terrorist attacks on the USA on **11 September** 2001, and economic growth of 3% was recorded in 2002. Since 1992 the United Kingdom has experienced its longest period of sustained economic growth for more than 200 years.

The United Kingdom joined the **European Community** in 1973. During the 1980s it was at the forefront of the process of economic liberalization associated with the completion of the **Single European Market** in 1992, but resisted any attempts at social harmonization: it opted out of the **social chapter** that was annexed to the **Treaty on European Union** in 1992. The United Kingdom joined the **Exchange Rate Mechanism (ERM)** in 1990 in order to improve macroeconomic stability, but it was forced to leave it on 16 September 1992 ('Black Wednesday') when it proved impossible to raise interest rates high enough to defend the pound. This ejection from the ERM was followed by a 15% devaluation of the pound sterling. The Labour government elected in 1997 and re-elected in 2001 has promised a referendum on membership of the single currency 'when the time is right'. In addition to the EU formal **convergence criteria**, Gordon Brown has set further economic tests which the UK economy must pass before a referendum may be called. These are: that the UK economy is compatible with its European partners; that there is sufficient flexibility; and that membership of the **euro area** brings benefits for investment, financial services, and employment, growth and trade. A referendum was promised for Labour's second term of government (2001–05), but has not been held.

United Left

United Left, or Izquierda Unida (IU), is an electoral coalition of socialist and communist parties in Spain, dominated by the Communist Party of Spain. Founded for the 1986 election, it opposes Spain's membership of the **North Atlantic Treaty Organization** and participation in military conflicts. It campaigns against cuts in social benefits and for a 35-hour week without loss of pay. UI won seven seats in the 350-seat **Congreso de los Diputados** when it first contested elections, in 1986. In the most recent elections, held on 14 March 2004, IU won 5.1% of the vote and five parliamentary seats.

Gen. Co-ordinator: Gaspar Llamazares
Address: Olimpo 35, 28043 Madrid, Spain
Tel: (0)91 7227500
Fax: (0)91 3880405
E-mail: org.federal@izquierda-unida.es
Internet: www.izquierda-unida.es

United Nations (UN)

The United Nations (UN) is an international organization that is committed to preserving peace through international co-operation and collective security. The UN was established in 1945 by the UN Charter. This document sets out the organization's key purposes: to maintain international peace and security, to develop friendly relationships between nations, to co-operate in solving international problems and promoting human rights, and to be at the centre of harmonizing the actions of nations. The UN Charter was originally signed by 51 states; the UN now has a membership of 191 states.

The work of the UN is organized in six organs: the General Assembly, the Security Council, the Economic and Social Committee, the Trusteeship Council, the International Court of Justice, and the Secretariat. The General Assembly is described as the parliament of nations. It is a forum that includes all members of the UN, and meets each year, from September until December, in New York, USA. Its decisions are taken by a two-thirds' majority on peace and security issues and regarding new members, and by a simple majority on other matters, such as globalization, HIV/AIDS, the consolidation of democracy and conflict in Africa. The Assembly's decisions are not enforceable, but they do have standing as an indicator of world opinion.

The UN Security Council is responsible for maintaining peace and security, and convenes whenever it is deemed necessary. The membership of the Security Council comprises 15 states. Five of these—China, France, **Russia**, the United Kingdom and the USA—are permanent members and have the power of veto. Ten additional members are elected every two years by the General Assembly and have no power of veto. Decisions in the Security Council require nine votes, and can be vetoed if the permanent members do not vote together. The decisions of the Security Council can be imposed through sanctions, arms embargoes or 'all necessary measures', though solutions to threats to peace are first sought through mediation and by securing cease-fires. Reform of the Security Council is on the agenda of the

General Assembly. Brazil, Germany, India and **Japan** launched a joint campaign in 2004 to become additional permanent members.

The Economic and Social Council co-ordinates the economic and social work of the UN and the UN system of organizations, which includes the **International Monetary Fund**, the **World Bank**, and UN agencies such as the World Health Organization, the International Labour Organization, UN High Commissioner for Refugees (UNHCR) and UN Children's Fund (UNICEF). The 54 members of the Economic and Social Council are elected by the General Assembly for a term of three years. The Trusteeship Council had the role of providing supervision for 11 Trust Territories during their preparations for self-government and independence. This task was completed in 1994 and the Trusteeship Council now meets on an *ad hoc* basis. The International Court of Justice (ICJ), located in The Hague, Netherlands, decides on disputes between countries. Participation in trials is on a voluntary basis, but countries that participate are obliged to comply with decisions. The ICJ comprises 15 judges who are elected by the General Assembly and the Security Council. The administration of the UN organs is carried out by the Secretariat.

The UN is widely respected as an international organization, but is considered to lack power. It experienced a revival as a peace-making body in the late 1980s and early 1990s, and it was hoped that the Security Council would become the key forum for persuading nations to work together. However, in a number of instances it has failed to secure peace (e.g. Somalia, Bosnia and Rwanda), and the US-led war in **Iraq** in 2003 proceeded without the approval of the Security Council.

Sec.-Gen.: Kofi Annan
Address: UN Headquarters, First Avenue at 46th Street, New York, NY 10017, USA
Tel: (0)212-963-4475
Fax: (0)212-963-0071
E-mail: inquiries@un.org
Internet: www.un.org

United States of America (USA)

The United States of America (USA) is one of Western Europe's closest allies. With the **Marshall Plan** the USA supported the economic reconstruction of Western Europe following the Second World War; it provided military support during and after the **Cold War** through the **North Atlantic Treaty Organization**; and it supported the process of European integration. The USA is the **European Union's (EU)** main trading partner (and vice versa) and principal economic competitor. The EU has a larger population and domestic market than the USA, but EU per caput gross domestic product (GDP) is lower and **unemployment** is higher.

GNP: US $9,780,800m. (2001); *GNP per caput:* $34,280 (2001); *GNP at PPP:* $9,781,000m. (2001); *GNP per caput at PPP:* $34,280 (2001); *GDP:*

$10,065,265m. (2001); *exports:* $998,030m. (2001); *imports:* $1,356,320m. (2001); *currency:* US dollar; *unemployment:* 5.8% (2002).

The USA emerged in the second half of the 20th century as the world's largest economy and military power. Its economic strength is founded on the technologically advanced manufacture of computers and electrical machinery, vehicles, military equipment and aircraft, chemical products and food and livestock. It is a liberal economy; there is little state intervention in or regulation of the market, and a residual, under-funded **welfare state**. As a consequence, growing national wealth has been unequally distributed, and this has been evident since the mid-1970s in a persistent growing gap between rich and poor in terms of income and labour-market positions.

Strong and stable economic performance in the mid-to-late 1990s stalled in 2001 around **11 September**, but recovered gradually from 2002. In this period the budget shifted from large surpluses to a deficit that was equivalent to 4.2% of GDP. This can be accounted for by large tax cuts that reduced tax revenues, a growth in government spending on domestic policies, homeland security and military campaigns.

Area: 9,629,000 sq km; *capital:* Washington, DC; *population:* 285m. (2001).

The USA was founded as a federal state by the Constitution drafted in 1787 and effective from 1789. There is a strong separation of power both at federal level and between the federal government and administrations of the 50 states. At federal level legislative powers are vested with the bicameral Congress, which consists of the Senate and the House of Representatives. The Senate is composed of 100 senators who represent their state at federal level. Two members are elected from each state by popular vote to serve six-year terms and one-third of senators are renewed every two years. The House of Representatives is made up of 435 congressmen/women who are directly elected from districts within individual states by popular vote to serve two-year terms. Representation in the House of Representatives is apportioned by population, but each state has at least one representative. Both Houses are currently dominated by the Republican Party.

Executive power lies with the President of the USA who is both head of state and head of government. The President and his Vice-President are elected together for a four-year term by an electoral college made up of electors from the states. In the electoral college, a state has one vote per senator (always two) and per congressman/woman (the number of which varies according to the size of a state's population). There are 538 electors in the college, and a presidential candidate requires 270 votes for victory. At the most recent elections, held on 2 November 2004, the Republican George W. Bush was elected for a second term of office, obtaining 286 college votes (and 51% of the popular vote) compared to 252 (48%) for his Democrat challenger, John Kerry. Bush first became President in 2000 when he won 271 electoral college votes compared to 266 for Al Gore. However, Bush did not win the popular vote, gaining just 47.87% compared with Gore's 48.38%. The winning electoral college votes came from Florida's 25 votes; in that state Bush had won the popular vote by a narrow majority of 537 of 5,950,000 votes cast.

Under President George W. Bush the USA has sought to establish and strengthen its position as a superpower. Following the terrorist attacks of 11 September 2001 the USA staged a series of pre-emptive military strikes on so-called 'rogue states' that were believed to have links with terrorists or to be developing weapons of mass destruction. US-led campaigns brought down the Taliban regime in Afghanistan in 2001 and the regime of Saddam Hussain in **Iraq** in 2003. The growth of the USA in economic and military terms has divided Western Europe between those states that wish to strengthen the transatlantic relationship (the United Kingdom, Spain until 2004) and those that would prefer the EU to pursue a security agenda independent of the USA (France and Germany). The EU-US relationship is none the less fostered by regular (annual) presidential summits, and the New Transatlantic Agenda of 1995, which seeks to strengthen political and economic links and to promote a combined agenda in the global community.

Unity List-The Red-Greens

The Unity List-The Red-Greens, or Enhedslisten-De Rød-Grønne, is a democratic socialist party in Denmark that was founded in 1989 through a merger of three left-wing parties: the Socialist Party, the Communist Party and the Socialist Workers' Party. Unity List aims to combine the politics of social change with a politics of engagement with environmental issues. The party is anti-capitalist and opposes Denmark's membership of the **European Union** on the grounds that it is 'an agent for market forces and the exploitation of Eastern Europe and developing countries'. In elections held on 8 February 2005 the party won six seats in the 179-seat **Folketing**. This was two more than the number it occupied in the parliament elected in 2001.

Party Leader: The party does not have a chairperson, but a collective leadership
of 21 members.
Address: Studiestræde 24, 1, 1455 Copenhagen, Denmark
Tel: (0)33-93-33-24
Fax: (0)33-32-03-72
E-mail: landkontoret@enhedslisten.dk
Internet: www.enhedslisten.dk

V

Vakcentrale voor Middengroepen en Hoger Personeel – *see*
Federation of Managerial and Professional Staff Unions,
Netherlands

Vanhanen, Matti

Matti Vanhanen has been the Finnish Prime Minister for the **Centre Party**-led
coalition since June 2003. He replaced Anneli Jäätteenmaki, Finland's first female
Prime Minister, who resigned after 63 days in office following accusations that she
had lied over how she obtained secret documents which may have helped her win
the March 2003 elections. Vanhanen's political career began in local politics: he
served on the Espoo city council in 1981–84. In 1983–84 he served on the Helsinki
metropolitan area council, and he has served on the Nurmijärvi municipal council
since 1989. He has been a member of the **Eduskunta** for the Centre Party since
1991 and has been vice-chairman of the Centre Party since 2000. A specialist in
European Union (EU) affairs as well as in foreign and security policy, Vanhanen
was Minister of Defence in Anneli Jäätteenmaki's government. He was also Finland's parliamentary representative on the **European Convention** on the future of
the EU in 2002–03.

Born on 4 November 1955 in Jyväskylä, Vanhanen has a master's degree in social
sciences. He worked as a journalist on the local newspaper *Kehäsanomat* in 1985–
88 and was its editor-in-chief in 1988–91. Matti Vanhanen is married to Merja
Hannele and has two children.

Address: Prime Minister's Office, Snellmaninkatu 1A, Helsinki, POB 23, 00023,
    Finland
Tel: (0)9 16001 or (0)9 57811
Fax: (0)9 16022165
E-mail: matti.vanhanen@vnk.fi
Internet: www.valtioneuvosto.fi

Vänsterpartiet – *see* Left Party, Sweden

Vasemmistoliitto – *see* Left Alliance, Finland

Vatican City

The Vatican City, also known as the Holy See, is the world's smallest state: it covers 0.44 sq km and has a population of 921 (2004). Situated in the city of Rome, Italy, the Vatican City is the home of the Pope and the Central Authority of the Roman Catholic Church. The independent state of the Vatican City was established in 1929 by three Lateran Treaties. According to the Fundamental Law of Vatican City, originally signed in 1929 and updated in 2000, the Head of State is the Pope who is elected for life by the College of Cardinals. The current Pope is John Paul II (born Karol Wojtyła), who was elected on 16 October 1978. The state is governed by the Pontifical Commission, which is appointed by the Pope for a five-year term. The head of the commission is the Cardinal Secretary of State, who conducts the secular affairs of the Vatican City. Since 2 December 1990 this has been Angelo Sodano.

The economy of Vatican City is supported by annual contributions from Roman Catholic dioceses throughout the world, and the production and sale of stamps, coins, books and other tourist mementoes. The 2002 budget was the first in eight years to show a deficit (€3.47m.). The Vatican City adopted the **euro** as its currency on 1 January 2002; the state issued its own set of coins displaying the Pope's image.

Venstre – *see* Liberal Party, Denmark

Venstre – *see* Liberals, Norway

Verbond van Belgische Ondernemingen/Fédération des Enterprises de Belgique – *see* Federation of Enterprises, Belgium

Vereniging VNO-NCW – *see* Confederation of Netherlands Industry and Employers

Verfassungsgerichtshof – *see* Constitutional Court, Austria

Verhofstadt, Guy

Guy Verhofstadt is the Prime Minister of Belgium. His first government in 1999 was a coalition between his **Flemish Liberal and Democrat Party (VLD)** party and five other Liberal, Socialist and Green parties. Verhofstadt was the first Liberal Prime Minister of Belgium to be elected for 61 years and he has led the first governments without Christian Democrat participation for 41 years. He was able to form his second liberal-socialist coalition government in 2003, this time without the Greens who had performed badly in the elections held in May of that year. Verhofstadt first entered the **Kamer/Chambre** in 1985 and became Deputy Prime Minister and Minister for the Budget, for Scientific Research and the Plan in the same year. In 1988–99 he led the shadow cabinet for VLD.

Born on 11 April 1953 in Dendermonde, Verhofstadt studied law at the University of Ghent. After graduating in 1975 he became involved in local politics and was elected as a member of Ghent town council in 1976. He became political secretary to the leader of the liberal Party for Freedom and Progress (PVV), Willy De Clercq, in 1977, and chairman of the PVV youth wing in 1979. In 1982 Verhofstadt succeeded De Clercq as leader of the PVV and, in that capacity, oversaw the transformation of the party to the VLD in November 1992 in an attempt to attract more voters and members. **Guy Verhofstadt** is married to Dominique Verkinderen and they have two children.

Address: Chancellery of the Prime Minister, rue de la Loi/Wetstraat 16, 1000 Brussels, Belgium
Tel: (0)2 501-02-11
Fax: (0)2 512-69-53
E-mail: guy.verhofstadt@premier.fed.be
Internet: premier.fgov.be

Les Verts – *see* Greens, France

Vihreä Liitto – *see* Green League, Finland

Vinstrihreyfingin-Grænt Frambod – *see* Left-Green Alliance, Iceland

Vlaams Blok

Flemish Block

Vlaams Blok (Flemish Block) is an extreme right-wing and nationalist party in the Flemish-speaking region of Belgium. Founded in 1977, it campaigns for an independent state of Flanders, to stop **immigration**, reduce crime and repatriate 'illegal' immigrants and 'foreign' criminals. The party was found guilty of breaking anti-racist laws by a Belgian court in Ghent in April 2004, and formally banned in November. However, the leadership stated that it would reconstitute the party under a different name.

Vlaams Blok made significant gains in the regional elections held in 2000. It won slightly less than 10% of the vote in Flanders and became the largest party in Belgium's second city, Antwerp, winning 33% of the vote and 20 seats on the 55-seat council. In the most recent national elections, held on 18 May 2003 Vlaams Blok won 11.6% of the vote and 18 seats in the 150-seat **Kamer**. Despite these successes, Vlaams Blok has no experience of government as other parties, forming a '*cordon sanitaire*', refuse to co-operate with it.

Party Leader: Frank Vanhecke
Address: Madouplein 8 bus 9, 1210 Brussels, Belgium
Tel: (0)2 219-60-09
Fax: (0)2 217-52-75
E-mail: info@vlaamsblok.be
Internet: www.vlaamsblok.be

Vlaamse Liberalen en Democraten – *see* Flemish Liberal and Democrat Party, Belgium

Volkspartij voor Vrijheid en Democratie – *see* People's Party for Freedom and Democracy, Netherlands

Vouli ton Ellinon

Vouli ton Ellinon, or the Hellenic Parliament, is the unicameral parliament in Greece. It is made up of 300 members who are elected by a system of proportional representation for a four-year term. The most recent elections were held on 7 March 2004. In the current parliament there are four parliamentary groups (number of seats in brackets): **New Democracy** (165); the **Panhellenic Socialist Movement** (117); the **Communist Party of Greece** (12); and the **Coalition of the Left of Movements and the Ecology** (6). In the current parliament 42 (14%) of the 300 members are **women**. As well as its legislative role, the Vouli ton Ellinon holds the government to account and is responsible for electing the President of Greece.

Address: Vas. Sophias 2, 100 21 Athens, Greece
Tel: (0)210 3707000
Fax: (0)210 3692170
E-mail: info@parliament.gr
Internet: www.parliament.gr

Wales

Cymru

Wales (Cymru) forms part of the United Kingdom. It was founded as a country in 1536 through the Act of Union, which linked it to England. Wales has traditionally been governed directly from the UK national government in London. The issue of self-government for Wales became part of the political agenda in 1966 when the nationalist party, **Plaid Cymru**, won its first seat in the **House of Commons**. Proponents of Welsh devolution have also sought to promote the Welsh **language** and a series of direct action campaigns since the 1960s have triggered its revival. Teaching in Welsh is encouraged in schools, road signs are bilingual, and a Welsh-language television channel was established in 1982. It is estimated that around 19% of the 2.9m. Welsh population speak the language.

From the 1970s the UK **Labour Party** supported Welsh devolution, but the Welsh Labour Party was divided on the issue. In a referendum held on 1 March 1979, Welsh voters rejected devolution (yes 20.3%; turn-out 58.8%). Following the election of the Labour Party to government on 1 May 1997, Welsh voters were again asked about devolution. In a referendum held on 18 September 1997 the proposal was narrowly supported by 50.3% of voters (turn-out 50.1%). The first elections to a new Welsh Assembly were held in May 1999 and the Assembly was inaugurated in the Welsh capital, Cardiff. The powers of the Welsh Assembly are limited to administering the Welsh budget and passing secondary legislation in such areas as **agriculture**, education, health and local government. The 60-seat Assembly is elected by a system of proportional representation every four years. The Assembly elects a First Minister; since the most recent election, held on 1 May 2003, this has been Rhodri Morgan, who leads a single party Labour executive. The Welsh Assembly elected in 2003 was the first ever legislature in which 50% of the deputies are **women**. Five of Morgan's eight ministers are also women.

The Welsh economy was traditionally dominated by coal and steel production. Since the 1970s, however, the coal mining industry has experienced a significant decline, and most deep mines have been closed. Steel production has increased, both in terms of total output and of Wales' share of the United Kingdom's total steel output. Service industries have been developed and Wales has succeeded in attracting foreign direct investment. The rate of **unemployment** in Wales is higher than the UK average—6.1% 2001—and wages are 20% lower than average (2002).

Welfare state

A welfare state is a socio-economic system in which the state takes responsibility for a large part of the economic and social welfare of its population. The mechanisms used to achieve this include progressive taxation, **unemployment** or sickness benefits, and social services. All Western European countries are welfare states, though they seek to promote the welfare of their citizens in different ways. In Western Europe there are at least three distinct welfare regimes which differ according to the scope and type of welfare provision they offer.

The social-democratic welfare state (e.g. Sweden, Denmark, Finland) aims to achieve social equality. It produces a high level of universal welfare benefits and services, funded through general taxation. The corporatist, or conservative, welfare state (e.g. Germany, Belgium, France) aims to promote social stability. It offers replacement benefits funded by social insurance schemes to which employers and employees contribute and which the social partners manage. The level of provision is linked to contributions to maintain social status, and social services are provided by the family. Liberal welfare states (e.g. the USA and, to some extent, the United Kingdom) seek to promote market efficiency by offering minimal, often means-tested, welfare benefits and services, funded through taxation.

The imperative of competition in the era of globalization led to predictions that Western European welfare states would retrench to the minimal standards of the liberal welfare state. Similarly, concerns have been raised that the market-building exercise of the **Single European Market** programme was neglecting the social side of European integration. Also, member states of the **European Union (EU)** cut welfare budgets in order to meet the **convergence criteria** set for **Economic and Monetary Union (EMU)**. Support for welfare states in Western Europe remains strong and there is little evidence of retrenchment. Government spending is about 45% of gross domestic product in Europe (compared with 30% in the USA), and around two-thirds of this is on welfare. For political and institutional reasons governments have found it difficult to retrench social provision. There is still overwhelming support for welfare states among electorates, and it has been easier to reform welfare states in majoritarian political systems, and in countries where welfare funds are managed by the state rather than social partners.

While the EU has not developed into a comprehensive European-level welfare state, there is an emerging social model which is founded on the consensus that spending on social welfare promotes social cohesion and hence contributes to economic growth. For this reason social policy should correct poverty and social exclusion. The emerging European social model is work-centred. It is premised on the idea that European economies should promote high rates of economic activity and reduce rates of unemployment, and that social legislation should protect the status and rights of workers. The EU is promoting these goals directly through social legislation and the decisions of the **European Court of Justice**; and indirectly through EMU and the benchmarking procedures of the **Luxembourg Process** and the **Lisbon Strategy**.

By encouraging high levels of economic activity for all citizens, welfare states in the EU are transforming rather than retrenching. One theory characterizes the emerging welfare state as an 'adult worker model' in which all citizens—male and female—are expected to work. This transformation particularly affects **women** in many conservative and liberal welfare states who traditionally relied on a male breadwinner for their social rights. It demands of welfare states that they adjust their welfare institutions and provisions to support women in the workplace. As a consequence, welfare policy in recent years has become increasingly family- and child-focused.

Western European Union (WEU)

Western European Union (WEU) is a defence organization which is responsible for undertaking the Petersberg Tasks—crisis management, rescue, peace-keeping and conflict prevention—for the **European Union (EU)**. It also assists the **North Atlantic Treaty Organization (NATO)** in armed conflict.

WEU was originally established in 1954 by Belgium, France, Luxembourg, the Netherlands and the United Kingdom, by the modified Brussels Treaty of 1948. It was established as a response to the Soviet Union's (USSR) growing power in **Central and Eastern European Countries**, and as a way of rearming West Germany, which joined it in 1954. WEU committed signatories to mutual defence if any of its members were the victim of an armed attack. WEU was overshadowed by NATO, founded in 1949, and served mainly as a consultation and co-operation body until its revival in 1984. This was triggered by countries that sought to strengthen Western Europe's voice on defence and security issues, and to strengthen limited military capabilities. There was a further development at the end of the **Cold War**, when the USA began to withdraw troops from Western Europe. WEU's first military operation involved minesweepers in the Persian (Arabian) Gulf in 1987–88.

The **Treaty on European Union** of 1992 developed a commitment to a **Common Foreign and Security Policy (CFSP)**, and made WEU an integral part of the CFSP **pillar** of the EU. The European Council meeting in Cologne, Germany, in 1999 developed **European Defence and Security Policy** and the provision that the **Council of the European Union**'s high commissioner for CFSP is also secretary-general of WEU. The **Treaty of Nice** of 2001 formally integrated most functions of WEU into the EU.

There are four levels of membership of WEU. The organization currently includes 10 full member states, six associate member states, five observer states and one associate partner.

Sec.-Gen.: Javier Solana
Address: rue de l'Association 15, 1000 Brussels, Belgium
Tel: (0)2 500-44-12
Fax: (0)2 500-44-70
E-mail: secretariatgeneral@weu.int
Internet: www.weu.int

Women

Women make up 52.7% (2001) of the population of the **European Union (EU)**. They have a longer life expectancy than men: girls born in 2001 can expect to live for 81.4 years, compared with 75.3 years for men. Western European women are under-represented in political and economic institutions. There are currently two female elected heads of state in Western Europe (in Ireland and Finland), but no female Prime Ministers or finance ministers. The average representation of women in national parliaments in the EU is 25.4%, ranging from 45.3% in Sweden and 36.9% in Denmark to 11.5% in Italy and 9.2% in Malta. At EU level, 30.33% of the members of the **European Parliament** that was elected in 2004 are women, and seven of the 25 European commissioners nominated for the 2004 term are women.

In European economies the employment rates for women and men in 2002 were 55.6% and 78.2% respectively. The rate of **unemployment** in 2003 was higher among women than men—9.9% and 8.2% respectively. The EU has set targets to increase the participation of women in the labour market to 60% by 2010, and to increase the provision of child-care for children between three years of age and school age to 90% by 2010. It has no targets to reduce the gender pay gap, which stands at an average of 16% in the EU, or to increase the proportion of female managers in EU firms—30% in 2004.

World Bank

The World Bank is an international organization—originally founded on 27 December 1945, following the Bretton Woods Agreement of 1944—which provides loans, grants and expertise to developing countries to help those states eradicate poverty. It provided US $20,100m. for 245 projects in 2004. An agency of the **United Nations**, it is committed to the Millennium Development Goals which define specific targets, to be met by 2015, in the areas of poverty, education, child mortality, maternal health, disease, including HIV/AIDS, and access to water. In return, it asks recipient economies to implement political measures to promote democracy and reduce corruption.

The World Bank is made up of the International Bank for Reconstruction and Development (IBRD) and the International Development Association (IDA). Together, these organizations provide loans and credit to developing countries. Loans have to be repaid over a 30–40 year period. The World Bank Group consists of the IBRD, the IDA and three additional organizations: the International Finance

Corporation (IFC), which supports high-risk investment; the Multilateral Investment Guarantee Agency (MIGA), which provides political guarantees to investors and lenders in developing countries; and the International Centre for Settlement of Investment Disputes (ICSID), which settles investment disputes between foreign investors and host states. The number of countries that are members of the organizations in the World Bank Groups is: IBRD—184; IDA—165; IFC—176; MIGA—164; ICSID—140.

The World Bank is run on a day-to-day basis by the boards of executive directors. These are composed of 24 executive directors and the president of the World Bank, all of whom serve a five-year term. It is customary that that president is American and since 1995 it has been James D. Wolfensohn. Five of the directors are nominated by the USA, **Japan**, Germany, France and the United Kingdom; the rest are elected by single states or groups of countries. All member countries are represented in the board of governors by a governor and an alternate governor. This board meets annually.

The World Bank is criticized on a number of grounds: first, for pursuing market-oriented strategies which might not be appropriate in developing countries which are unstable democracies or experiencing conflict; second, for implementing economic strategies which damage the local economy and/or environment; and third, for being closed to public scrutiny.

Pres: James D. Wolfensohn
Address: 1818 H Street, NW, Washington, DC 20433, USA
Tel: (0)202-473-1000
Fax: (0)202-477-6391
E-mail: lnweb18.worldbank.org/institutional/EFeedBk.nsf/MainTopic
Internet: www.worldbank.org

World Trade Organization (WTO)

The World Trade Organization (WTO) is an international organization which manages the rules of trade between nations. Established on 1 January 1995 from the Uruguay Round of the General Agreement of Tariffs and Trade (GATT), it exists to provide a forum for trade negotiations, administer trade agreements and handle trade disputes.

The WTO has a membership of 148 countries which meet at a ministerial conference held at least every two years. Day-to-day decisions are made by the general council, delegates of the member states. Decisions are made by consensus. The four largest members—Canada, the **European Union (EU)**, **Japan** and the USA—are referred to the as the quadrilaterals or 'quad'. Member states of the EU are represented by themselves and the EU. The work of the WTO is supported by the secretariat which is headed by the director-general, currently Supachai Panitchpakdi.

Recent ministerial conferences held in 1999 in Seattle, USA, in 2001 in Doha, Qatar, and in 2003 in Cancún, Mexico, have given rise to much controversy. Anti-globalization protesters disrupted the Seattle meeting and the Cancún meeting ended inconclusively as agreement was blocked by an alliance of southern states.

Dir-Gen.: Supachai Panitchpakdi

Address: Centre William Rappard, rue de Lausanne 154, 1211 Geneva 21, Switzerland

Tel: (0)227395111

Fax: (0)227314206

E-mail: enquiries@wto.org

Internet: www.wto.org

Y

Yrkesorganisasjonenes Sentralforbund – *see* **Confederation of Vocational Unions, Norway**

Z

Zalm, Gerrit

Gerrit Zalm has been Deputy Prime Minister and Minister of Finance in the Netherlands since 2003. A member of the liberal **People's Party for Freedom and Democracy**, he also served as Minister of Finance in 1994–2002.

Born on 6 May 1952 in Enkhuizen, Zalm studied economics at the Free University of Amsterdam, receiving his doctorate in 1975. He worked in the Ministry of Finance in 1975–83, in the Ministry for Economic Affairs in 1983–88 and in the Central Planning Bureau from 1988. He was appointed as Professor of Economics at the Free University of Amsterdam in 1990.

Address: Ministry of Finance, Korte Voorhout 7, POB 20201, 2500 EE
           The Hague, Netherlands
Tel: (0)70 3427540
Fax: (0)70 3427900
E-mail: www.minfin.nl
Internet: www.minfin.nl

Zapatero, José Luis Rodríguez

José Luis Rodríguez Zapatero has been Prime Minister of Spain since 17 April 2004. He was appointed following the general elections of 14 March 2004 when his **Spanish Socialist Party (PSOE)** unexpectedly became the largest party in the **Congreso de los Diputados**. He heads a single party minority government.

The elections of 14 March took place three days after terrorist bomb attacks in Madrid in which at least 200 people died. PSOE's opponents, the governing **Popular Party**, lost support with the electorate by hastily blaming the attacks on the Basque terrorist group, ETA. (The terrorist group al-Qa'ida later claimed that it was responsible for the attacks.) Zapatero strongly condemned the attacks. Prior to the election in 2004, he supported the cause of nationalists in the Spanish regions and opposed Spain's participation in the war in **Iraq** in 2003. On election Zapatero withdrew Spanish troops from Iraq.

Born on 4 August 1960 in Vallodolid, Zapatero studied law at the University of Léon. A member of the PSOE since 1979, he was first elected to the Congreso de los

Diputados in 1986, becoming Spain's youngest member of parliament, and was re-elected in 1989, 1993, 1996, and 2004. He became leader of the PSOE in 2000. José Luis Rodríguez Zapatero is married with two children.

Address: Complejo de la Moncloa, Avda. de Puerta de Hierro s/n, 28071 Madrid, Spain
Tel: (0)91 3353353
Fax: (0)91 3214080
E-mail: portal.presidencia@mpr.es
Internet: www.la-moncloa.es